LEYTE 1944

LEYTE
1944
The Soldiers' Battle

NATHAN N. PREFER

CASEMATE

Philadelphia & Oxford

Published in the United States of America and Great Britain in 2012 by
CASEMATE PUBLISHERS
908 Darby Road, Havertown, PA 19083
and
10 Hythe Bridge Street, Oxford, OX1 2EW

ISBN 978-1-61200-155-5
Digital Edition: ISBN 978-1-61200-156-2

Cataloging-in-publication data is available from the Library of Congress and
the British Library.

10 9 8 7 6 5 4 3 2 1

Printed and bound in the United States of America.

For a complete list of Casemate titles please contact:

CASEMATE PUBLISHERS (US)
Telephone (610) 853-9131, Fax (610) 853-9146
E-mail: casemate@casematepublishing.com

CASEMATE PUBLISHERS (UK)
Telephone (01865) 241249, Fax (01865) 794449
E-mail: casemate-uk@casematepublishing.co.uk

CONTENTS

Maps

All maps created by Mary Craddock Hoffman / STYLOGRAPHIX

To the men and women of all nations who fought, suffered, bled and died on the island of Leyte, and so many other islands and places around the world few had ever heard of before, being thrust into the ongoing battle for freedom.

"The Leyte Operation made inordinate demands upon the troops. It is impossible for me to depict the hardships they had to endure or the desperate resistance they had to overcome. Our troop units included numerous battle-wise veterans, but also many others who received their first baptism of fire on the beaches or in the flooded rice fields or mountain fastnesses of the island. Veterans and recruits alike demonstrated outstanding valor and determination and proved the American Soldier superior to the soldier of Nippon."

General Walter Krueger,
Commanding, Sixth U.S. Army
in *From Down Under to Nippon:
The Story of Sixth Army in World War II*
1963. P. 187

"When [General Walter] Krueger found an infantryman with untreated blisters, athlete's foot, or leaky socks, the soldier's noncoms lost their stripes and his officers got official reprimands. We in the lower echelons sort of loved the crusty old boy, were delighted to learn that he had enlisted as a private and risen through the ranks, and were not surprised when later he turned out to be one of the most distinguished generals in the pacific."

Bill Mauldin, *The Brass Ring* (1971)

"I love the infantry because they are the underdogs. They are the mud-rain-and-wind boys. They have no comforts, and they even learn to live without the necessities. And in the end they are the guys that wars can't be won without."

Ernie Pyle, *New York World Telegram* (May 5, 1943)

"The system was popularly called 'leapfrogging,' and hailed as something new in warfare. But it was actually the adaptation of modern instrumentalities of war to a concept as ancient as war itself. Derived from the classic strategy of envelopment, it was given a new name, imposed by modern conditions. Never before had a field of battle embraced land and water in such relative proportions. Earlier campaigns had been decided on either land or sea. However, the process of transferring troops by sea as well as by land appeared to conceal the fact that the system was merely that of envelopment applied to a new type of battle area. It has always proved the ideal method for success by inferior but faster-moving forces."

Gen. Douglas MacArthur, *Reminiscences* (1964)

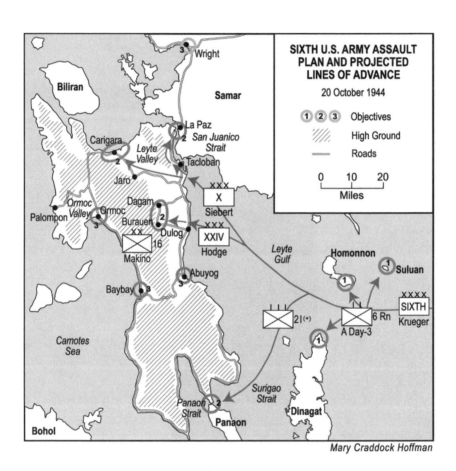

SIXTH U.S. ARMY ASSAULT
PLAN AND PROJECTED
LINES OF ADVANCE

20 October 1944

① ② ③ Objectives

░░ High Ground

—— Roads

0   10   20
Miles

Mary Craddock Hoffman

INTRODUCTION

The story of the U.S. Army's battle for Leyte Island in late 1944–January 1945 numbers among many tales of many battles fought by that army during the global Second World War. But is it just another battle? To military historians who have studied the war in the Pacific, the answer has been lost in the more flamboyant tales of the Battle of Leyte Gulf, which the Battle for Leyte precipitated. In that naval battle, which sealed the fate of Imperial Japan's naval power for the war's duration, the chance for Japan to regain the naval initiative was forever destroyed, as was the fleet Japan sent to contest the American landings on Leyte. With the destruction and retreat of the enemy fleet remnants, the Battle for Leyte was assumed by many to have been won. The decisive battle that Japanese naval leaders had long sought had gone against them, and there now remained only the need to continue moving closer to the home islands of Japan to end the war.

But there was another decisive battle at Leyte, largely overlooked. Although in the years since the war more than a dozen books and monographs have appeared that detail various aspects of the naval Battle of Leyte Gulf, not one non-official work details the army's struggle for Leyte. Again, it appears that the assumption has been that since the naval battle was so clearly successful that the land campaign was simply a pro forma matter, with no unusual or atypical events to make it noticeable and stand out among many similar battles. But was that the case?

It was not. The Leyte Campaign, one of the largest combined operations of the Pacific War, quickly turned into one of the most difficult and deadly ground campaigns of the Southwest Pacific Theater. A full American army, with two corps and more than seven American divisions under it's command in the middle of the campaign, devoted itself for four months to subduing the Japanese defenders of Leyte. If the naval Battle of Leyte Gulf was the decisive naval engagement of the second half of the war, then the land battle for Leyte was the decisive ground forces battle as well. For the Japanese decided to make it so.

The land campaign for Leyte involved more than two hundred thousand American soldiers, far more than the number of sailors and Marines who fought the three-day Battle of Leyte Gulf. These soldiers, many of whom spent the entire four months deep in heavy jungles, fighting in spite of typhoons and the rainy season, basically destroyed the fabric of the planned Japanese defense of the entire Philippines. For the Japanese High Command had decided, albeit late, that rather than fight the decisive battle for the Philippines on Luzon, it would be fought on Leyte. That decision alone made the Leyte Campaign decisive, but when the Japanese poured in their best troops from China, Korea, Japan and other Philippine islands, they also committed their best chance of holding the Philippines and keeping open their essential supply lines to the Southeast Asian natural resources upon which their war effort depended.

Nor did the Leyte Campaign go as planned. Few battles ever did, but the Leyte Campaign was full of surprises. Initially only one Japanese division defended the island, and the four American divisions should have been more than enough to overwhelm the defenders. But the change in Japanese policy changed everything. Before the battle was over another three American divisions had to be committed, another division-sized amphibious landing conducted, and plans and preparations for future assaults changed, delayed, postponed. And the cream of the Imperial Japanese Army died on Leyte. At least two of the reinforcing divisions were rated as among the best in the Imperial Japanese Army in 1944, and the bulk of these divisions were destroyed on Leyte. Japanese air power, husbanded for the defense of the Philippines, was also largely destroyed during the campaign, making the rest of the Philippine battles less deadly then they would otherwise have been. Indeed, the Battle for Luzon, on the main Philippine island, can be said to have been won with the Battle of Leyte, during which Japanese air and naval power was rendered ineffective and the best of the Japanese soldiers destroyed, rather than building stronger defenses on Luzon.

Nor did the Americans hold the upper hand throughout the campaign. The Japanese presence felt by their constantly reinforced garrison, and the Imperial Japanese Navy's continuous presence offshore, combined with the ever present Japanese air power to make the campaign difficult. American troops felt the wrath of Japanese naval bombardments, were hit by the new but already dreaded Kamikaze suicide planes, and were involved in at least two last-stand defenses of positions while surrounded by Japanese forces. As if that were not enough to excite interest in the campaign, a Japanese counterattack late in the campaign was highlighted by the only airborne assault attack against American forces in the Southwest Pacific.

The campaign also featured several leading figures who have otherwise remained hidden from view behind the overpowering figure of General Douglas MacArthur. General Walter Krueger is largely unknown outside the circle of students of the Second World War in the Pacific, yet he led his Sixth Army throughout some of the most difficult campaigns of the war. At times he was fighting a war with his component units as far apart as a thousand miles. Despite these difficulties, the Leyte Campaign was fought successfully due in large part to his skills as a battlefield commander, even with the constant pressure exerted by his own commanding officer, General MacArthur, to rush the campaign so that the island of Luzon, and the Philippine capital of Manila, could be attacked and seized as soon as possible. There was also General Robert Eichelberger whose Eighth Army took over the campaign when General Krueger's men moved on to Luzon. Another competent soldier whose skills were overshadowed by General MacArthur's strict publicity policies, Eichelberger too finished the Leyte Campaign while conducting several other campaigns around the Philippines simultaneously. The corps and division commanders are likewise unknown, but their accomplishments before, during and after the Leyte Campaign remain among the most successful in military history.

There were others, nearly all of whose names are forever lost to history, who deserve recognition. Today they are revered anonymously as "The Greatest Generation," a title most of them ignore or shrug off tired shoulders. Many never lived to hear the accolade, like the twenty-one-year-old sergeant from Chippewa Falls, Wisconsin, who despite being severely wounded, remained fully exposed to enemy fire in a Leyte stream shouting orders to his men, until killed. Or the perennial troublemaker in garrison who turned into a soldier in battle, protecting the beachhead from a battalion-sized attack after all his buddies had been killed or wounded, until he, too, was finally overcome. Or the radio operator who could have remained in the rear but chose to take command of an infantry assault and led it to its objective at the cost of his own life. There were many others, only some of whom are mentioned in this history.

Leyte was also the test of naval and air support for a sustained ground campaign in the Southwest Pacific. Rarely had American naval aircraft been available for support to an ongoing land campaign. Until Leyte, MacArthur's forces usually relied on land based air support, but Leyte was different in that such air support could not be supplied in either sufficient numbers or with sufficient speed. And so the air battle became one of joint army-navy forces, unusual in the Pacific. And finally, the use of sea power to provide continual support for a campaign lasting more than three months was yet another change in the situation, which had earlier faced the Southwest Pacific Theater forces before Leyte.

It was at Leyte that General MacArthur redeemed his famous "I shall return" promise of 1942. And although his return was widely publicized, his interest in the campaign quickly waned in favor of planning his return to Manila. Yet for the three thousand American soldiers who died on Leyte, and the ten thousand who were wounded or injured during the campaign, Leyte was the most important battle of their war. It deserves study as a significant campaign that led directly to the fall of Japan at the end of World War II.

CHAPTER 1

DECISION FOR THE PHILIPPINES

here would have been no battle for the Philippine Island of Leyte had not the United States Joint Chiefs of Staff (J.C.S.) made the determination that the Philippine Islands would be a major objective of the southern advance against Japan.

For some, such as General Douglas MacArthur, there had never been any question that the objective of his Southwest Pacific Theater of Operations was the liberation of the Philippines. He thought of the islands as his personal responsibility, a responsibility made more personal by his defeat in its defense at the hands of the Japanese Army in 1942. Besides his personal commitment to the liberation of the islands, he had a professional one as well, since any other objective would divert forces and resources from his command, making it less important in the overall strategy against Japan.

Although General MacArthur had his reasons for directing his forces on the Philippines, it was not something that had come solely from him. Even before the First World War, plans had been drawn up by the United States War Department for many eventualities. One of these envisioned a war with Japan over the Pacific Ocean. Drawn up in 1906, one such concept, known as the Blue-Orange Plans, expected an early victory by Japan against the holdings of the United States in the Pacific, followed by a steady advance from Hawaii by the American Fleet. The destinations of the fleet were Guam and then the Philippines. From the latter base, once secured, the Fleet would launch a final attack upon Japan itself.[1]

Variations on this plan appeared at irregular intervals for decades afterwards. In one 1926 plan the Philippines had only to sustain themselves against a Japanese attack for sixty days, after which a fleet and invasion force from Hawaii would appear fully prepared to defeat the aggressors. Indeed, for most of the pre-war years the planning was based primarily on either holding or retaking the Philippines and using its magnificent harbor at Manila for the final counterattack on Japan.

Things change. The original plans had been drawn up under certain assumptions and with certain technology. Pre-war fleets needed a base from which to launch attacks, deploy reserves, and store supplies. Air power was in its infancy. There was no such thing as replenishment at sea from specially designed ships bringing supplies to the fighting fleet at the front. Nor was the concept of air power projected by aircraft carriers fully developed. Dependence upon secure land bases within striking range of the next objective was the controlling factor in most pre-war plans for a war in the Pacific.

The situation as it stood in 1944 was far different from that predicted by the earlier planners. The Philippines had fallen, as had Guam. These had been expected, more or less. But the massive conquest of the Pacific by the Japanese and the two-front war in which the United States found itself in 1944 had not been predicted. The early destruction of the main battle fleet at Pearl Harbor was another unpredicted alteration in the scenario. The rise of air power, the improved uses for the submarine, and the developing technology would all change the circumstances under which the pre-war planners had promulgated their predictions.

By the middle of 1943, the United States Joint Chiefs of Staff had developed plans which had only some resemblance to those of the pre-war planners. Further, the plan was self-developing. Changes were being made constantly in direct response to the changing world situation. In the Pacific, for example, planned invasions were cancelled when it became apparent that the need for those bases had diminished or ceased entirely to exist. Such flexible plans did not yet designate a final base for the attack on Japan itself, something which most if not all the planners agreed would be necessary to finalize the Pacific War.

A group of planners favored China as the final base of operations. Aircraft flying from secured bases in China could devastate Japan at will. Since the Chinese coast was largely occupied by Japanese forces, the island of Formosa was selected as a likely base, once seized from Japan. From here a heavy bombardment could be launched by air, naval and undersea forces. If this didn't starve Japan into submission, then the grand final assault would be made from Formosa. Some planners preferred to use mainland China, with more room and greater local populations to assist in the support of the main forces. However, repeated efforts to clear the Chinese coast, and to fly American aircraft from Chinese bases, failed to accomplish the goals set for these operations. It would have to be Formosa or someplace else.

Formosa had much to recommend it. It was located in a strategically important position that impressed most planners and convinced them it would have to be seized, sooner or later. It blocked the water route from the United States directly to China. Its seizure would sever Japanese communications and supplies to the south, from which it got much of its war resources. From bases on Formosa, the U.S. Army Air Forces new Long-Range Bomber, the B-29, could bomb all of Japan with much heavier loads than if they flew from the Philippines or any other projected bases.

Throughout 1942 and 1943, discussions were held which lasted into 1944. Usually the War and Navy Departments disagreed. The Navy Department, under Fleet Admiral Ernest King, adamantly wanted to bypass the Philippines in favor of seizing Formosa. Others, including Admiral Chester Nimitz, King's Pacific commander, favored at least seizing some of the Philippine Islands in order to secure the Allied communications to Formosa. Their biggest concern was that Japanese air power based on Luzon would be able to interdict the Fleet's lines of supply and communication during and after the attack on Formosa.

The War Department and the Army's Chief of Staff, General George C. Marshall, were also ambivalent. Some wanted to bypass both the Philippines and Formosa and simply launch a direct invasion of the main island of Kyushu in southern Japan. Some agreed with Admiral King and wanted to bypass the Philippines but seize Formosa before launching any attack against Japan proper. The Chief of the Army Air Forces, General Henry H. Arnold, also favored bypassing the Philippines and launching his heavy bombers from Formosa. On the other side was Lieutenant General Brehon B. Somervell, commanding the Army Service Forces, who thought that the entire Philippine Archipelago would need to be seized before any assault could be launched against Japan. And of course the senior army commander in the field, General MacArthur, remained adamant that the Archipelago had to be seized before any further major advance was made against Japan. The majority of the senior army leadership of the Pacific agreed with MacArthur.

As a result, in March 1944, the Joint Chiefs of Staff directed General MacArthur to plan to attack the southern Philippines by the end of that year, and Luzon early in 1945. At the same time, they ordered Admiral Nimitz to plan for an assault to seize Formosa at about the same time. These directives were tentative, however. Barely three months after issuing these orders, the J.C.S. again discussed the question of bypassing the Philippines.

This renewed discussion was prompted by developments in the Pacific. Intelligence had reported that the Japanese were increasing the strength of their forces on Formosa. This concerned the planners in that the longer it took to prepare for the Formosa invasion the more opposition it would face. By bypassing the Philippines and moving directly on Formosa before the end of 1944 they hoped to limit as much as possible the cost of seizing a reinforced Formosa. Political intelligence feared an imminent collapse of the allied Chinese government, which would free up even more Japanese strength for other defenses. One suggested solution was to seize Formosa as a way of preventing a Chinese collapse. The success of the invasion of France in the European Theater increased the American level of confidence, so much so that the J.C.S. requested that the field commanders determine if it were sensible to cancel both the Philippine and Formosa operations entirely, pending an assault on Japan itself.

The evaluation was held in June 1944 and both General MacArthur and Admiral Nimitz were unsupportive of eliminating the Philippine-Formosa objectives just yet. The seizure of air bases in the southern or central Philippines was essential, they argued, for any future advance westward in the Pacific. Their replies were studied by the J.C.S. staff and it was agreed that some bases in the Philippines would have to be seized to provide air cover for future operations. Given the Pacific situation as it stood in June 1944, the J.C.S. planners saw no reasonable possibility of an advance directly on Japan from the bases they held at the time.

The following month President Franklin D. Roosevelt, then embroiled in a re-election campaign, called a conference between his Pacific field commanders and himself in Hawaii. During this famous July 1944 Hawaii meeting, both General MacArthur and Admiral Nimitz recommended that, as earlier proposed, air bases in the southern and central Philippines be seized to support future operations in the western Pacific, whatever those operations were finally determined to be. There was disagreement, however, when General MacArthur argued for a following invasion of Luzon while Admiral Nimitz argued that once bases had been established in the Philippines there was no need to take Luzon, and that the forces could better be used in the Formosa operation.

These various discussions, reviews and conferences did not resolve the dichotomy between Luzon and Formosa but they did come to the one conclusion, that the Philippines would not be bypassed. The need for air support, which had become a mainstay of the American attack program, dictated that air bases in the southern or central Philippines were essential. Although the Americans had developed an enormous armada of aircraft carriers, there were not enough to support simultaneously the Central Pacific and Southwest Pacific drives. And so the decision was made that the Philippines would be attacked to provide land air bases from which the Southwest Pacific campaign could launch its future campaigns.

*   *   *

Having decided to establish air bases in the Philippines, the question then became where these were to be established. The southern-most major Philippine island was Mindanao, and plans had been drawn up with that island in mind at least as the initial target within the archipelago. The plan, known as Reno, scheduled an advance to the Vogelkop Peninsula at the western tip of New Guinea and then the seizure of Morotai, before landing in southern Mindanao on October 25, 1944. Once forces had been established on Mindanao, the island of Leyte would be the next target, tentatively scheduled for November 15, 1944. Another plan, submitted to the J.C.S. by General MacArthur, called for the capture of the Talaud Islands as a base for air support prior to the Mindanao and Leyte landings. This new plan called for invasions of Morotai on September 15, the Talauds on October 15, Sarangani on November 15, Bonifacio-Mindanao on December 7 and Leyte on December 20, 1944. The plan went on to schedule invasions on Luzon,[2] as well. This plan was later discarded due to new developments.

Debate revolving around the ongoing Luzon-Formosa controversy continued and caused planning changes and adjustments several times over the next few months. Formosa became less likely when it was found that the shortage of Service of Supply troops necessary for that operation was significant. Yet no decision had been firmly established. While the planners debated, the U.S. Navy and the Fifth U.S. Army Air Force were still preparing the way for the eventual invasion of the Philippines, wherever and whenever that would occur. Over the summer they pounded the Japanese air resources within the Philippines. A particularly heavy air strike by the U.S. Third Fleet under the command of Fleet Admiral William F. Halsey in September prompted that officer to report that air opposition over the Philippines had dwindled to the point where he could recommend that planned operations be accelerated before reinforcements could arrive. Admiral Halsey recommended the cancellation of the impending invasion of the Palau Islands and that its forces be assigned to General MacArthur for an earlier than planned invasion within the Philippines. He also recommended that the preliminary operations at Morotai and Mindanao be cancelled and that a direct strike on Leyte be instituted in their place.

Messages soon flashed across the Pacific and to Washington, D.C. General MacArthur, Admirals Nimitz and Halsey offered their thoughts to the J.C.S., who happened to be meeting in an Allied conference at Quebec. The resulting outcome was that the Palaus operation would go forward, as it was viewed as essential to protecting the flank of the advancing Southwest Pacific Theater of Operations. The invasion of Yap Island in the Carolines was cancelled, and the army units scheduled for its seizure were released to General MacArthur.[3] Finally, the date for the invasion of Leyte was pushed forward two full months to October 20, 1944. The invasion of Leyte was on.

*   *   *

The Philippine Archipelago consists of more than 7,000 islands covering an area of more than half a million square miles. There are three major island groups: in the north the Luzon group, in the center the Visayas Islands which include Cebu, Leyte, Negros, Panay and Samar, and finally Mindanao Island with the Sulu Archipelago, a series of small islands that leads off to Borneo. Individual islands often have differing populations with separate languages and cultures. Relations were often difficult between groups and conflict was common between them.

The island of Leyte is one of two major islands in the Visayan Group, the other of which is Samar. Leyte is a natural gateway to the rest of the Philippine Islands and by seizing it the Americans would have an interior position from which to capture or neutralize the remaining islands. It is the eighth largest island of the Philippines with an area of 2,785 square miles. It is oriented generally from north to south with a length of 115 miles and a width of no more than 45 miles at its widest point. Volcanic in origin, the island has a line of mountains running down its spine from the Biliran Strait in the north to the Cabalian Bay in the south. That mountain range separates the island into the Ormoc and the Leyte Valleys. Southern Leyte, because of its mountainous area, has little military importance, and in the northwest only the port of Palompon would figure militarily in the coming campaign.

The mountain ranges are composed of numerous sharp ridges and spurs with deep ravines and are an effective barrier between the island's eastern and western coastal areas.

Leyte Valley is a wide and fertile plain which runs from Leyte Gulf to Carigara Bay. The mountain range gradually narrows the valley as it moves northwest. The majority of the population in 1944 lived in Leyte Valley. Here, too, were most of the military targets including the principal towns and the Japanese airfields. The valley also contains the island's main road system, along with several streams that irrigate the soil. Using the water from these streams, the islanders cultivated many rice paddies and the water level is rarely more than a few inches below the surface. The existing road network in 1944 was primitive and inadequate, and could not handle heavy traffic, or military traffic.

Across the mountains lay Ormoc Valley, about five miles wide at its widest. This valley extends from Ormoc Bay until a narrow ridge separates it from Carigara Bay. Only one main road existed within the valley in 1944 and like those in Leyte Valley, it was totally inadequate for military purposes. Although partly cultivated, much of Ormoc Valley was covered by large patches of forest, scrub growth and cogon grass, particularly in the north.

The island's largest city, Tacloban, is located at the head of San Pedro Bay. It is the only sizeable port on the island and handled most of the pre-war shipping to and from the island. Near the town of about 31,000 lies Tacloban Airstrip, which is actually on the Cataison Peninsula. The Japanese had built another airfield near the town of Dulag, while three others at respectively, Buri, Bayug and San Pablo, had also been established by them. A final military field lay at Valencia, in the Ormoc Valley north of Ormoc.

There were about 915,000 people on Leyte during the war years, nearly all of them native Visayans. There were a few thousand Chinese, mostly in the retail industry, and small groups of others including Spaniards, Germans, Americans and Japanese. The population was primarily engaged in agriculture and fishing. Rice, sugar cane, corn and copra were the main products on the island. Homes were constructed mostly of bamboo and sheathed with palm leaves on the roof and sides, and rarely numbered more than two rooms. Often livestock were kept underneath the raised homes.

After the surrender of the Philippines in 1942, a number of unsurrendered Americans and many civilians fled into the hills of Leyte, unsure of what to do. Some wanted to continue the fight while others felt they could not live under the terrible conditions of a wartime Japanese administration.

Some felt that this would be an opportunity to settle old grudges or simply to steal for a living, and as time passed, these groups formed themselves into guerrilla bands. With little money or supplies they often raided local farms or villages simply to gather enough food to stay alive. This discredited them in the eyes of the population, but as they grew stronger and acquired better leadership they were formed into semi-military organizations. Oaths of allegiance were required and contacts made with Allied forces, mostly in Australia. Cooperation was slow in coming but gradually the groups came together out of a common purpose and the need to survive. Soon they were allotting food supplies, issuing a currency and punishing criminals.

Soon two leaders emerged. Lieutenant Colonel Ruperto K. Kangleon had been a Philippine Army officer for twenty-seven years and had graduated the Philippine Academy and General Service School. Brigadier General Blas E. Miranda was a former member of the Philippine Constabulary who had an unsurpassed hatred of the Japanese. He was also adamantly opposed to Colonel Kangleon because the colonel at one time had been a prisoner of the Japanese. By early 1943, General MacArthur's headquarters in Australia was reaching out to the various bands of guerrillas in the Philippines. It established military districts for the guerrillas, much the same as the pre-war military districts. Because of a series of confusing orders, both General Miranda and Colonel Kangleon were told that they were in charge of the guerrilla forces on Leyte. This divided command increased the already significant animus between the two chieftains, and disagreements soon caused active operations between the two groups to come to battle. In August 1943 Colonel Kangleon sent a force to attack General Miranda. After several men had been killed[4] General Miranda was forced to withdraw, although several of his men opted to join Colonel Kangleon. With this victory, Colonel Kangleon unified the guerrilla groups on the island into the 92nd Division under his overall command. On October 21, 1943, General MacArthur recognized this organization with Colonel Kangleon as its commander.

One of the results of the guerrilla groups organizing was the additional Japanese attention it brought to Leyte. Initially the Japanese tried to cajole the guerrillas into surrender, and some did so, but overall these methods failed. Beginning in December 1943, increasing numbers of Japanese troops arrived on the island to rout the guerrillas and destroy the bands. The guerrillas withdrew to the mountains and the Japanese soon turned their attention to the civilians who they suspected of supporting the guerrilla movement. In January 1944, Colonel Kangleon issued orders to the guerrillas to fight the

Japanese, which they proceeded to do on a gradually escalating basis. Depending upon whose reports you chose to believe, these battles were won by either the guerrillas or the Japanese.

More important than the fighting on Leyte was the intelligence that was transmitted from the island to General MacArthur's headquarters. Several clandestine radio stations were operated by the guerrillas on Leyte. The first radio provided by General MacArthur's headquarters arrived safely but was soon seized by the Japanese. A new set was sent forward and coast-watcher stations set up to report Japanese naval movements. Japanese troop movements, dispositions, defense fortifications and Japanese defense plans were all transmitted to Australia. These intelligence reports gave General MacArthur's intelligence officers a reasonable picture of Japanese defenses and strength on Leyte as the invasion date approached.

*   *   *

American invasions were not new to the Philippines. When Admiral George Dewey seized Manila, the Philippine capital, on May 1, 1898 during the Spanish-American War, President William McKinley followed up with an invasion force to occupy the former Spanish colony. Reasons for this interest by the Americans in the Philippines range from imperialism, social Darwinism, a quest for Asian markets, the "Yellow Press" and other justifications. For whatever reason you may decide to accept, American troops were dispatched to the Philippines for occupation duty, arriving at Manila on June 30th, 1898. The mix of Regular Army and National Guard regiments, many of whom had no training and had never seen combat, were put to work unloading their transports. As they arrived, the Philippine native leadership proclaimed themselves a republic, free of both Spain and the United States. Negotiations between the two groups continued while the Americans came ashore in and around Manila. As the arguments progressed, however, tensions between the armed Philippine guerrillas and the American leaders increased. Each intended to be the dominant force in the conquest of the Philippines.

The Americans seized Manila from the Spanish while deliberately excluding the Philippine forces, which they then ordered from the conquered city. Predictably, the breach between the two groups widened and was not helped when President McKinley ordered his military commanders in the Philippines to proceed as if the sovereignty of the Philippines had been ceded to the United States. His instructions included the intent to win the confidence, respect and affection of the native population. In his terms it was to be a policy of "benevolent assimilation." No one, however, discussed this with the Filipinos. By February 1899, open hostilities had erupted.

The ensuing war lasted into 1902. While much of the war concentrated on and around Luzon, there was also considerable fighting in the Visayas. A group of revolutionaries on Panay had formed their own government and fighting forces. The Panay Federal State of the Visayas refused to recognize the central Philippine Republic and denied them taxation privileges, military postings, and continued with their own government. But here again internal disputes kept the Federal State of the Visayas in confusion and prevented them from presenting a unified defense strategy. With the war officially in progress in Luzon, Colonel Marcus P. Miller advised the Federal State of the Visayas of his intent to occupy the island, and then sent in a group of Marines and sailors from the nearby U.S. Fleet on February 11, 1899. The first American invasion of the Visayas had begun.

The Marines and sailors were followed by the 18th U.S. Infantry Regiment and the 1st Tennessee Infantry. The battle was haphazard and intermittent but the one that raged between the U.S. Army and the U.S. Navy was far fiercer, since each blamed the other for a premature invasion and the near total destruction of the town of Iloilo, capital of Panay. While they fought a war of words the Americans did establish a military government and began to restore the town and encourage the population to work with them in establishing peace and order. But small-scale resistance continued from outside the American perimeter. Sniper fire was a regular occurrence. Patrols moving through the countryside were constantly ambushed. Finally, on March 16, 1899, a large attack was launched at the American garrison at Jaro. The American counterattack crushed the Filipino rebels and many of the survivors simply went home.

One of the results of this battle and subsequent disarray of the resistance was that the American military government was reorganized and a Visayan Military District was formed, encompassing Leyte, Samar, and Bohol Islands, in addition to Panay. Brigadier General Robert P. Hughes took over this new command and began what was to become one of the more successful pacification campaigns of the Philippine War. General Hughes moved his campaign to Negros and kept his American forces confined to enclaves, letting the rainy season and the lack of crops starve the rebels into submission, while those who rallied to the Americans were fed via a ration system within the protected enclaves. Despite continued instances of rebel outbreaks, murders, kidnapping and the occasional local uprising, the process over time worked.

By March 1899, this policy and a naval blockade of the Philippines had created widespread rice shortages in southeastern Luzon, Samar and Leyte. In some areas starvation allowed the Americans to land unopposed because the population needed the food that came with occupation.

The blockade had other, unforeseen, effects. By blockading the Viasyas the Americans had deprived themselves of hemp, a commodity needed back home. Considered the best in the world, it was valued in the United States, and supplies had dried up since the war. With a Presidential election at home and the farmer's vote in the balance, orders were issued to re-open the hemp markets. In Leyte there was the usual division of loyalties, with no central government to support them. Only a few riflemen "protected" the island, although some guerrilla groups did exist. But these were as likely to attack each other as to defend the island against the Americans. Much of the defenders of Leyte were local militias with few arms and less training. In January 1900, the island of Samar was invaded by the 43rd Infantry Regiment and subsequently, ports on Leyte were opened to trade. After some brief fights around the island a tenuous peace was established.

That peace was soon broken by the Moro Rebellion. Individual garrisons were isolated and attacked at will. The native Filipino guerrilla struck without warning and was a deadly fighter. The Americans still occupied the ports to govern the trade outlets for each island, but food shortages and economic difficulties encouraged resistance. One effort to reduce these guerrilla forces was the formation of two one-hundred-man companies of provincial police. Although intended originally for Samar, they were immediately named the "Leyte Scouts" and sent to other islands.

In May of 1900, General Arthur MacArthur arrived in the Visayan Islands and ordered his troops to hold their enclaves while the main rebellion on Luzon was crushed. The 43rd U.S. Infantry Regiment was assigned to Leyte. The regimental commander[5] disregarded his orders and sent patrols into the interior to pacify the population, which left his garrisons weak and the patrols vulnerable to ambush, a frequent occurrence. Garrison towns were besieged. This state of affairs alarmed American headquarters at Manila and a decision was made to conquer Leyte. Reinforced by companies of the 23rd and 44th U.S. Infantry Regiments, the first American Leyte Campaign began in April 1900. Unlike other areas, the Leyte guerrillas stood and fought rather than fade away into the mountains or jungle. Although defeated in the field, the Filipinos soon found that the Americans occupied each village they seized, leaving behind small and vulnerable garrisons. These they attacked regularly, putting the Americans back in the situation that had begun the campaign in the first place. Finally the Americans abandoned the island's interior and garrisoned only the important export ports.

Here the Americans concentrated on improving the life of the natives. Teachers' pay was increased, schools established, rice imported where necessary, local governments organized and civic improvements made. Patrols still combed the island, however, and combat continued. But by the end of 1900, the 43rd U.S. Infantry controlled all of Leyte's food growing areas and the guerrillas had to hide out in the mountains to survive. Most towns were under civil government and local police began to handle routine duties taken over from the military. With the loss of support of the population, narrow safety zones, and the need to keep constantly on the move, the guerrilla's war in Leyte slowly wound down. More and more guerrillas surrendered. Finally, on April 9th, 1901, the last guerrilla stronghold was located and attacked. The remaining guerrillas were scattered. The first Leyte Campaign was over.

* * *

Militarily, control of Leyte was determined by who controlled the Leyte and Ormoc Valleys and the mountain ranges between them. With control of these and the few ports that supplied egress to and from the island, any force could maintain military control over the island. With this in mind the Americans planned their attack on Leyte. To ensure that there were no unexpected military surprises, as the attack date approached intelligence officers from the Sixth U.S. Army and the Seventh Fleet went ashore clandestinely to personally verify the intelligence reports regarding Japanese coastal fortifications and beach defenses in the planned assault area.

It would have been assumed that since the United States governed the Philippines for decades before 1944, adequate maps would be available, but this was not the case. Mapping of Leyte was poor and efforts during the war to improve it were only partially successful. Many important terrain features were missed altogether, while others were misplaced by as much as a mile or more. However, the results of the guerrilla intelligence reports and the personal visits of American intelligence officers to the island did eventually result in highly accurate maps of the beachhead assault areas.

One concern raised by the guerrilla reports was the increasing strength of the Japanese on Leyte. A June 1944 report placed the Japanese garrison force at 20,000 men, nearly four times what it had been barely a month before. It was determined that these troops were from the Japanese *16th Divi-*

sion, veterans of the Bataan Peninsula conquest in 1942. Additional troops were reported as 4,000 naval troops transferred from the Palau Islands. Further reports described the newly arrived Japanese as building coastal defenses, improving airfield defenses and digging interior garrison defenses.

The fall of the Mariana Islands in June and July to the V Marine Amphibious Corps,[6] and Guam to the III Marine Amphibious Corps,[7] had the additional result of toppling the Japanese military government in Tokyo. Hopes that the new government would be more amenable to ending the war were quickly dashed when new policy merely discussed how the war would be continued and the conquests of the Japanese, including the Philippines, would be defended against all attempts to seize them. As a result of this new determination to defend their conquests, reinforcements were sent to the Philippines, among other areas. The senior Japanese headquarters in the western Pacific was transferred from Singapore to Manila, on Luzon. Individual Japanese brigades within the Philippines were brought up to authorized strength. An estimate of Japanese strength placed about 80,000 on Luzon, 50,000 in the Visayan Islands and 50,000 on Mindanao. This total of 180,000 troops was continually being reinforced throughout late 1944.

The Sixth Army intelligence officers were now concentrating on Leyte, knowing it was their first objective within the Philippines. By September 1944, they had decided that Japanese forces on Leyte consisted of a total of 21,700 troops, mostly of the *16th Division* and supporting troops. It was under the command of the Japanese *35th Army,* headquartered on Cebu. This latter headquarters was charged with the defense of all the Visayan Islands. The Americans also estimated that the *35th Army* was capable of moving one additional infantry division to Leyte once the invasion began, and another soon after. The number of tanks, armored cars and artillery was undetermined, but it was not considered overwhelming. Sixth U.S. Army also believed that there were five operational airfields, three more under construction and seven more in preliminary stages of construction. There was also one seaplane base. The two most important airfields for American purposes were those at Tacloban and Dulag. These were to be put into immediate use by the Fifth U.S. Army Air Force, which would cover the campaign while also covering the rest of the Philippines and protecting the flank of Admiral Nimitz's Central Pacific Theater advance towards Japan. Estimates of the reaction of the *Imperial Japanese Navy* varied but it was believed that opposition to the Leyte landings would come primarily from air and undersea attacks, occasionally supported by cruisers and destroyers. The Americans understood that the limited number of troops available to the Japanese on Leyte would prevent a defense all along the coast. Hence they expected a strong point type of defense, with particular towns and airfields defended strongly. Mobile reserves were expected to be available to strike at American thrusts against these strong points.

*   *   *

Plans for the seizure of Leyte brought together the largest invasion group yet seen in the Pacific War. General Douglas MacArthur commanded the Southwest Pacific Area and was overall commander of the operation. Under his command, Lieutenant General George C. Kenney commanded the Allied Air Forces, which included the Fifth U.S. Army Air Force (Major General Ennis P. Whitehead), the Thirteenth U.S. Army Air Force (Major General St. Clair Streett) and elements of the Royal Australian Air Force (Air Vice Marshal William D. Bostock) with supporting elements.

The naval elements of General MacArthur's invasion force were known as Allied Naval Forces, Southwest Pacific Area and commanded by Vice Admiral Thomas C. Kinkaid, who also commanded the Central Philippine Attack Force (Task Force 77). The Northern Attack Force (Task Force 78) was commanded by Rear Admiral Daniel E. Barbey and the Southern Attack Force (Task Force 79) by Vice Admiral Theodore S. Wilkinson. In support were the Flagship Group (Task Group 77.1), Fire Support Group (Task Group 77.2), Close Covering Group (Task Group 77.3), Escort Carrier Group (Task Group 77.4), Beach Demolition Group (Task Group 77.6), Service Group (Task Group 77.7) and a Minesweeping and Hydrographic Group (Task Group 77.5). Distant coverage of the invasion force was the responsibility of the Third U.S. Fleet under the command of Admiral Halsey.

The ground elements of the invasion force were under the command of Lieutenant General Walter Krueger[8] and his Sixth Army Headquarters. About 174,000 troops were under the command of General Krueger. This force controlled two corps: the X Corps commanded by Major General Franklin C. Sibert and the XXIV Corps under Major General John R. Hodge. Initially these two corps controlled four assault divisions and reinforcing elements. The strength of the X Corps was estimated to be 53,000 soldiers while the XXIV Corps numbered 51,500 men. A reserve force with an additional two divisions totaling 28,500 men was also included in the troop list.

The 1st Cavalry Division, Special, was a unique organization within the United States Army during World War II. It was the only 4-regiment division in the army during the war. As such, it retained the pre-war organization of two cavalry brigades, with two regiments assigned to each cavalry brigade.[9] It also retained its "Cavalry" designation although in all respects it was an infantry division. The balance of the organization was of the standard type common to all infantry divisions in the U.S. Army in World War II. It contained four artillery battalions, an engineer squadron, a medical squadron, reconnaissance squadron, antitank troop, signal troop Ordnance Company and medical support.[10] The division had been assigned to the Sixth Army since July 26, 1943, and had already fought in New Guinea and the Bismarck Archipelago campaigns before shipping out for Leyte. Its commander was Major General Verne D. Mudge.

The 7th Infantry Division was a regular army formation, like the Cavalry Division. Activated in California on July 1, 1940, it had participated in the seizure of Attu in the Aleutian Islands in 1943. After conquering the frozen tundra of Attu, the division trained on Adak Island before landing on Kiska, another Aleutian Island, only to find that the Japanese had evacuated the island before the invasion. The division moved to Hawaii in September 1943, and trained in jungle and amphibious warfare before participating in the seizure of the Marshall Islands in the Central Pacific in January 1944. Returning to Hawaii in February 1944, the division rested and trained for its next assignment, which was the capture of Yap and the Palau Islands, also in the Central Pacific. When these operations were cancelled, the division was redirected to General MacArthur's Theater for the Leyte Operation. Its commander was Major General Archibald V. Arnold.

The 24th Infantry Division was organized from the regular army's Hawaiian division at Schofield Barracks, Hawaii on October 1, 1941. It trained at Rockhampton, Australia before moving to Goodenough Island in February 1944. It conducted an amphibious assault at Tanahmerah Bay, New Guinea on April 22, 1944, and fought in New Guinea before being assigned to the Leyte Operation. As it had in New Guinea, portions of the division were separated for special operations during the Leyte Campaign. The 21st Regimental Combat Team was assigned a landing in the Panaon Strait area of Leyte while the remainder of the division landed in the Palo-Pawing area. The division commander was Major General Frederick A. Irving until November 1944, when he was reassigned, and Major General Roscoe B. Woodruff assumed command.

The 96th Infantry Division had been activated on August 15, 1942, at Camp Adair, Oregon, and after training in Oregon and California the division shipped to Hawaii where it trained for the amphibious assault on Yap Island. It had already moved to Eniwetok Island in the Marshall Islands by September 1944, when that operation was cancelled. As with the 7th Infantry Division, the 96th Infantry Division was redirected to General MacArthur's invasion of Leyte. The division was commanded by Major General James L. Bradley throughout its combat career. It was the only one of the six assault divisions that had no previous combat experience.

A special assignment was reserved for a special unit. The success of five previous Ranger Infantry Battalions in the North African, Sicilian, Italian and Northwest European Campaigns prompted the creation of a similar unit in the Southwest Pacific Theater of Operations. So the 98th Field Artillery Battalion was converted to the 6th Ranger Battalion on September 24, 1944, at Hollandia, New Guinea. Using only volunteers, the battalion was quickly formed and trained for combat operations, the first of which would be at Leyte. Its commander was Lieutenant Colonel Henry A. Mucci.

The Sixth Army also held a reserve force for follow-up operations once the initial amphibious phase of the assault was completed. This consisted of two additional infantry divisions, the first of which was the 32nd Infantry Division. This unit was originally the federalized Michigan and Wisconsin National Guard. It had been inducted into federal service on October 15, 1940, and participated in the Louisiana Maneuvers in 1941. It shipped out from Fort Devens, Massachusetts in March of 1942, and arrived in Australia in May the same year. After training in jungle warfare near Brisbane, the division was moved piecemeal to New Guinea where it fought in the bitter Buna-Sanananda Campaign. After a bloody fight to capture the Buna-Gona beachhead area, the division moved up to the Dobodura area in December 1942. Exhausted and severely under strength, the division was withdrawn from New Guinea between January and February 1943, and returned to Australia for rest and recuperation. It next assaulted Saidor, New Guinea in January 1944, and Aitape, New Guinea in April 1944. Sustained Japanese resistance along the Drinumor River line was overcome by the division which then mopped up in the area and assisted other units in overcoming Japanese resistance on New Guinea, until September 1944, when the division staged at Hollandia, New Guinea for the Leyte Operation. Its commander was Major General William H. Gill.

The 77th Infantry Division was activated at Fort Jackson, South Carolina on March 25, 1942, from elements of the New York State Army Reserve. It trained in the Louisiana Maneuvers before moving to California and participating in Desert Warfare training. It staged for the Pacific at Camp Stoneman, California and left the United States in March, 1944. Arriving in Hawaii at the end of March, the division trained in jungle and amphibious warfare before shipping out to the Central Pacific. Assigned to the III Marine Amphibious Corps, it participated in the assault landings at Guam in July 1944. After overcoming Japanese resistance, the division mopped up on the island until it boarded ship on November 3, 1944, headed for Hawaii. While underway, however, orders where changed and the division's convoy was re-routed to Leyte to be assigned to the Southwest Pacific and the Leyte Operation. The division's commander throughout its combat career was Major General Andrew D. Bruce.

Backing up these combat troops was the essential Sixth Army Service Command (ASCOM), under the command of Major General Hugh J. Casey. This group had a tough assignment as the advance of the invasion schedule had placed the invasion in the middle of the rainy season on Leyte. The engineers had to overcome poor soil, constant rain, poor roads and other obstacles to construct a military base, an air base complex and logistical base in the shortest possible time so as not to delay future planned operations. General MacArthur had directed that within the first thirty days, ASCOM was to have established bases for two fighter plane groups, one night fighter group, one photo squadron, one medium bomber group plus one squadron, three patrol bomber squadrons and one Marine reconnaissance squadron. Additionally, he wanted another base for one photo squadron, one patrol bomber squadron, two troop carrier groups and one combat mapping squadron. All of this was in addition to the normal support and logistical support needed by the ground assault forces, and bases for the naval supporting forces, and topographic and hydrographic surveys. Along with construction of bases, docks, roads and airdromes, ASCOM had to provide for the unloading of all supplies, store those supplies, issue those supplies to the units as needed and cooperate with the Philippine Civil Affairs Units to recruit and direct native labor. It was a daunting task that would become more difficult as the campaign progressed.

*   *   *

American leadership of the coming Leyte Campaign was unique and diverse. A leader among leaders, General Douglas MacArthur was an intense and striking personality whose career was the envy of every military professional. As the son of a Civil War general who had won the Medal of Honor at Missionary Ridge, he grew up in the United States Army. During World War I, he had distinguished himself time and again, earning several medals for personal bravery and promotion to brigadier general for his outstanding leadership. After the war he had become the army chief of staff, its highest position, and served with distinction. An honor graduate of the United States Military Academy at West Point, he was devoted to the army. When his term as chief of staff expired he went to the Philippines, where he had served both with his father and as a young officer himself, and was assigned to develop their military forces for the independence promised by the United States in 1946. Early in the war he had led the defense of the Philippines against the Japanese invasion and suffered what he considered a catastrophic defeat. He had been awarded his own Medal of Honor for his initial defense of the Philippines and his later dangerous withdrawal at presidential order to Australia, where he was to lead the American return to the Philippines.

Glorious as his career had been, there were flaws. He was immune to criticism, considering his detractors motivated by politics or ambition. He controlled the press to his own personal benefit, a trait not unique to General MacArthur but more uniformly practiced by him than most other American leaders of the war. He tended to the dramatic, giving lectures at length to his subordinates, the press, and politicians as if he were the sole source of the correct methods to solve any problem. He was an arrogant man, often emotional, undoubtedly ambitious and charismatic. He had an unquenchable desire for success while exhibiting symptoms of paranoia toward those who dared to disagree with him. He was a difficult man to work for, demanding, unrepentant and refusing to listen to arguments once he had declared a tactic or strategy to be his goal. It was largely MacArthur who accomplished the return to the Philippines, by his determined personal interest in keeping the promise he had made when he left, that of "I shall return."

MacArthur also believed that he was constantly betrayed by both the political and military leadership of the United States during the war. His constant demands for more troops, supplies and equipment were subject to a political policy which set the war against Germany ahead of the war against Japan. General MacArthur did not agree with this strategy, and refused to accept it as a final word, continuing his demand for more throughout the war. After his arrival in Australia he found to his disgust that the "army" he had been evacuated to lead, did not exist. Starting from little, he slowly built up a force to march up the New Guinea coast until he could reach the only important goal for him, the conquest of the Philippines.

Nor was General MacArthur happy with his troops. The few American combat troops he found in Australia were recently called to service and had little training. He would need to train them thoroughly and prepare for a new campaign. And he was less than favorably impressed with his new Allies, the Australians. Their attitude displeased the general and he thought that they lacked the will to defeat the Japanese. Labor strikes, the refusal of the Australian militia to serve in New Guinea, and related obstacles all colored the general's opinion of the Australians. He apparently decided not to use them in the forefront as soon as he could replace them with American troops. And he would not allow them to conduct the major operations which might give them publicity. As this policy developed, he created "Alamo Force," a disguise for an American military force that conducted operations within his area but reported directly to General MacArthur, outside the existing chain of command, which included Australian general officers. It was this force that he used in his major offensives in the New Guinea Campaign.

Now that he had reached the Philippines he took the disguise off Alamo Force—it was in fact now the Sixth Army. Indeed, his repeated demands to Washington had brought additional results, in the form of a second army, the Eighth, which was now available to General MacArthur. With sufficient American troops and headquarters now available to him, General MacArthur planned for his triumphant return to the Philippines at the head of an American army group. His Australian and New Zealand allies were relegated to containing bypassed Japanese garrisons in New Guinea and the South Pacific.

The Sixth Army was one of eleven armies created by the United States during World War II. In the United States Army an "army" was designed to be a command and administrative headquarters, allowing non-independent corps to concentrate on tactical operations and therefore not be burdened by supply and maintenance concerns. It was also responsible for medical evacuation, hospitalization, recovery of damaged equipment and large construction tasks. Lieutenant General Walter Krueger was commanding the Third U.S. Army prior to its deployment to Europe when, on January 12, 1943, he received a radiogram from General MacArthur advising him that he had recommended to the army chief of staff that he, Krueger, and his Third Army Headquarters, be transferred to General MacArthur's Southwest Pacific Theater of Operations. General Krueger was pleasantly surprised by this message. At age sixty-two he had thought himself too old to be permitted to command troops in battle, and had resigned himself to training commands for the rest of the war.

Events moved fast after the first news. By the 13th of January, news that this new assignment had been approved arrived while General Krueger was inspecting troops at Camp Gruber, Oklahoma. He was ordered to Washington the next day to work out the details. There he learned that while he and his staff would in fact go to the Pacific, the Third Army Headquarters would not join him. Instead he was ordered to organize and activate a new army headquarters, to be numbered the Sixth. As he prepared his new command, General Krueger turned over command of Third U.S. Army to Major General Courtney H. Hodges, who had commanded its X Corps.

General Krueger returned to Fort Sam Houston, Texas and began to gather his new command. Sixth Army was activated there on January 21, 1943, with the establishment of headquarters, Sixth Army and Headquarters Special Troops, Sixth Army. Preparations for movement to the Southwest Pacific Theater were begun immediately. Taking a number of his former staff from Third Army, General Krueger set off for the Pacific.

Like his new army, General Walter Krueger was somewhat unique in the U.S. armed forces of World War II. Born 1881 in Flatow, West Prussia[11] his father had been an officer in the Prussian Army, and Krueger appeared destined to join the future German *Wehrmacht* until the sudden death of his father prompted his mother to take her three children to live with her maternal uncle in St. Louis, Missouri. As a result Walter Krueger grew up in Indiana. Trained by his mother in classical music and by his stepfather in mathematics and languages, he was attending Cincinnati Technical School when the Spanish-American War broke out. He enlisted and rose to a top non-commissioned officer rank before being discharged at the end of that war. Having found that he preferred the military life over that of a civil engineer, he re-enlisted in the 12th Infantry to fight in the Philippines. Once again he rose through the ranks to sergeant before receiving a commission as a second lieutenant of infantry in 1901.

Although he never attended West Point, he rose steadily through the ranks over the next fifteen years. He distinguished himself enough to be sent to the Infantry and Cavalry School at Fort Leavenworth, and served a second tour of the Philippines where he led a mapping survey of northern Luzon. He translated a German book on tactics and commanded a regiment of the Pennsylvania National Guard on the Mexican Border in 1916. During World War I, he served in France as a staff officer in an infantry division and with the new Tank Corps. Upon his return he graduated from the Army War College in 1922, and then served at the War Department. Unable to serve with the infantry, he tried the new Air Corps, but his age prevented him from meeting the physical qualifications. Instead, he spent four years on the faculty of the Naval War College. His next assignment was command of the 6th Infantry Regiment, which he turned into one of the finest in the U.S. Army. As his reputation for success grew, his next assignment was to the War Plans Division of the General Staff where he received promotion to brigadier general.

As the army began its slow expansion just prior to World War II, General Krueger commanded in turn a brigade, a division and a corps. The army chief of staff, General George C. Marshall, whose policy was not to promote officers whose age might infringe on their ability to command troops in combat, nevertheless recommended the 61-year-old General Krueger for a promotion to lieutenant general and command of the Third Army. While praising General Krueger for many of his abilities, General Marshall chided him for being especially sensitive to criticism, to suggestion, and to anything he thought might reflect badly upon himself personally. Despite his supposed sensitivity to criticism, General Krueger promised to work on these faults and went off to command the Third U.S. Army. It was there that he received the already-mentioned summons from General MacArthur.

General Krueger earned a reputation as a strict disciplinarian, but also a commander concerned for his troops. One such example was given by Sergeant William Mauldin, the future cartoonist whose characters "Willie and Joe" brightened the troop's day in Italy and Europe while General Patton and others fumed over their remarks. As Sergeant Mauldin remembered, General Krueger suddenly appeared in his company when they were on maneuvers. He ordered them to take off their shoes and socks and show him their feet. Personally inspecting each soldier's feet with "his August nose not six inches away" he then inspected each soldier's socks for holes and shoes for nails. Any deficiencies cost the soldier's non-commissioned officer his stripes and earned the unit's officers an official reprimand. He thus earned the respect and loyalty of his troops. He would bring this concern for troops to U.S. Sixth Army.

* * *

The assault plan called for each of these groups to perform a specific function on a specific schedule. Initially the U.S. Navy was to provide the major portion of the air support from their escort carriers offshore. At a distance, Admiral Halsey's fleet carriers and their support would conduct air strikes against Luzon, Okinawa and Formosa to prevent the Japanese from interfering with the amphibious assault phase, while preventing air reinforcements to the Philippines. Shore-based aircraft from the Palau Islands were to provide support locally around the Visayan Islands. Halsey's Third U.S. Fleet was also to protect and support the various convoys destined for Leyte.

General Kenney's airmen were to make aerial reconnaissance over Leyte and other islands while coordinating with the navy in protecting the amphibious assault phase of the invasion. They were to cover the naval forces as they approached Leyte. They, too, had the task of protecting convoys and providing direct support to the landings. Finally, they were to seek and destroy any and all Japanese shipping found in the area. General Kenney assigned General Whitehead's Fifth U.S. Air Force the task of destroying enemy installations, hostile air and surface forces in the Celebes Sea and other assigned areas within the Philippines. He was also to provide the air defense over existing bases and forces either in transit to Leyte or on the island. Finally, General Whitehead was to be prepared to establish some of his forces on Leyte once a lodgment had been obtained. Major General Street's Thirteenth U.S. Army Air Force was assigned the task of supporting the Fifth U.S. Army Air Force, and the Royal Australian Air Force was tasked with destroying Japanese installations in the Netherlands Indies.

The ground forces had been hastily assembled for the advanced assault date on Leyte. While X Corps had served in the Southwest Pacific Theater for some time, the XXIV Corps had been assigned to Admiral Nimitz's Central Pacific Theater and had been destined for the now cancelled invasion of Yap. Its artillery component, the XXIV Corps Artillery, had participated in the Saipan-Tinian invasions in place of the V Marine Amphibious Corps Artillery, which was sent to the Philippines to replace the army units still engaged in the Mariana Islands. Additionally, the XXIV Corps was slated for future operations in the Central Pacific and was expected to be returned there once the Leyte Operation was concluded. As a result of these issues of time, distance, replacements and supplies, exchanges occurred between the two theaters.

The initial assault was to be made on October 17th by the 6th Ranger Battalion. They were to land under naval protection and seize the small islands that guarded the entrance to Leyte Gulf. Harbor lights on Homonhon Island and Dinagat Island were to be placed to guide the invasion convoy through the relatively narrow waters to the invasion beaches.[12] The Rangers were also tasked with seizing Suluan Island where it was believed charts identifying enemy minefields were kept. The Rangers' assault would signal the start of the invasion. The fire support units would begin the pre-invasion bombardment, and minesweepers would begin clearing channels to the assault beaches; underwater demolition teams would then begin clearing natural and manmade obstacles near the beaches.

A second independent operation was to be conducted by the 21st Regimental Combat Team, drawn from the 24th Infantry Division. This force was designated to land on October 20th in the area of Panaon Strait, located at the extreme southeast tip of Leyte Island. The purpose of this attack was to seize and control the entrance to Sogod Bay.

The main assault was to take place between Tacloban and Dulag with X Corps to the north and XXIV Corps to the south. The mission was to seize a lodgment area and then secure the airdromes and base sites within the designated beachhead area. Once established ashore, the assault forces were to conduct a quick advance through Leyte Valley and occupy the Capoocan-Carigara-Barugo area and then eventually open up the San Juanico and Panaon Straits. The Northern Attack Force (X Corps) was to land with two divisions in the Marasgaras and Palo areas. Fifteen miles south the Southern Attack Force (XXIV Corps) would land in the Dulag area with two divisions, each less one regimental combat team, and establish a beachhead there.

Sixth Army intelligence believed that the strongest enemy positions were located in the north near Tacloban and the airfields. Although these promised to be strongly defended, the eastern beaches were chosen because they were the best available on the island and were the closest to the primary objectives of the campaign. They also provided direct access to Leyte Valley, another major objective. To ease the burden of X Corps, its objectives were initially limited to the capture of Tacloban, Palo and their immediate airfields. Fifteen miles to the south, XXIV Corps was to seize a portion of Highway 1, including the vital bridge near the Marabang River, and the general area of Catmon Hill and Burauen. This would establish a secure beachhead and allow one division to move north should it be required to assist X Corps.

In turn, X Corps assigned the 1st Cavalry Division to land on its north flank with the immediate objective of Tacloban and its airfield. Once accomplished, the cavalrymen were to seize control over the San Juanico Strait. The adjoining 24th Infantry Division, less the 21st Regimental Combat Team, was to seize the Palo Area and then move to the entrance to Leyte Valley. The two divisions were to head for Carigara, the northern end of Leyte Valley on Carigara Bay.

Southern Attack Force was going to land the 96th Infantry Division, less one regiment held in Army Reserve, in the area around Dulag with the assignment of capturing the section of Highway 1 in its zone and Catmon Hill, which overlooked the proposed beachhead. Twenty-Fourth Corps assigned the 7th Infantry Division the bridge over the Marabang River at Dao while its main force attacked along the Dulag-Burauen road to capture the latter town. All airfields in each of the zones were to be captured as soon as possible. The ultimate objective was for X Corps to clear Leyte Valley of Japanese and then join with XXIV Corps in clearing the Ormoc Valley until the surviving Japanese defenders had been driven into the mountains of western Leyte where they could be destroyed at leisure.

Despite the planning and preparation by Sixth Army, there remained concerns. Once a beachhead had been established, the four divisions of Sixth Army were simply not strong enough to cover the whole island sufficiently. A reserve force had been assigned to the army, but the 32nd Infantry Division was at Morotai and Hollandia while the 77th Infantry Division was at Guam slated to return to Hawaii. In either case, neither could arrive before November, fully two weeks or more after the invasion. Shipping resources, or lack thereof, precluded having a floating reserve immediately available for Sixth U.S. Army. As a result, one regiment of the 96th Infantry Division, the 381st Infantry, was designated Sixth Army Reserve on A-Day.[13] That date was now firmly set as October 20, 1944.

*　　*　　*

The fact that the Americans were going to try and retake the Philippines was no surprise to the Japanese. They had expected it for some time. When the outer circle of the Japanese defense circle protecting their new conquests had been breached, and then breached again, the Japanese were well aware that an upcoming target must be the Philippines. By the summer of 1944, *Imperial General Headquarters* was directing the reinforcement of the garrisons. Plans were drawn up that any Allied threat to the Philippines, the Ryukyus or the Kurile Islands would be met with the full remaining forces available to the Japanese military, including sea, air and ground forces. Japanese leaders had long sought the "decisive battle"; while they understood that their strength had dwindled to the point that such a battle was more than likely to go against them, they still sought it out, determined to win or die. The invasion of the Philippines would present them with that long-sought opportunity.

Meanwhile, they prepared. In August 1944, the *Headquarters, 14th Area*

Army, was organized and charged with the defense of the Philippines. This, in turn, was under the command of *Southern Area Army*. The commander of the latter was Field Marshal Count Hisaichi Terauchi. He controlled four area armies which were located in the Netherlands New Guinea, Singapore, Burma and the Philippines. The *14th Area Army* was under the command of Lieutenant General Shigenori Kuroda and had its headquarters in Manila. In addition, *Southern Area Army* had in the Philippines the *4th Air Army*, consisting of two air divisions in the Philippines and one more in New Guinea. Both the *14th Area Army* and the *4th Air Army* reported to Count Terauchi but neither commanded the other. To make the situation more complicated there was another force, the *1st Air Fleet* of the *Imperial Japanese Navy* stationed in the Philippines. This force was under the command of the *Southwest Area Fleet* who, in turn, reported to the *Combined Fleet,* headquartered in Tokyo and under the command of Admiral Soemu Toyoda. Unified command and control were not much in vogue with the Japanese military in the Philippines in 1944.

Field Marshall Hisaichi Terauchi was born in 1879, and was closely related to Japanese Emperor Hirohito. Born in Yamaguchi Prefecture, he was the son of Viscount General Misatake Terauchi who served as governor general of Korea in 1910 and as prime minister of Japan in 1917–1918. Hisaichi Terauchi graduated from the Japanese Military Academy in 1900 and then trained additionally in Germany and Austria. After teaching at the Military Academy he was given command of the *5th Division* before moving to become chief of staff of the *Korea Army*. Later, he commanded the *Formosa Army* and was promoted to full general in 1935. He later served as military councilor and war minister in subsequent Japanese governments. When the Pacific War broke out, General Terauchi was commanding the *Southern Army* with four field armies under control and headquartered in Saigon. He commanded the Japanese conquest of the Southern Resources Area, including Singapore. Promoted to field marshal in June 1943, he moved his headquarters to Manila in May 1944, when Imperial General Headquarters decided to make the Philippines the area of the decisive battle. Nominated to replace Japanese leader General Hideki Tojo upon the fall of that government in June, 1944, he was instead left in command of the Southern Army whose duties included the defense of the Philippines.

The only questions that the Japanese had in 1944 was where and when would the Americans attack. They knew that the Philippines would be attacked, but which island and when?[14] While garrison forces were established on all major Philippine Islands, an attempt was made to retain a mobile reserve which could be rushed to the point of the most danger once the Americans showed their intentions. General Kuroda was left with the choice of where to station his reserves and how to plan for an effective defense. His tenure was short-lived, however. Early in October 1944, General Kuroda had accepted the reality of facts in evidence that his superiors chose to ignore. He advised the chief of army intelligence in the *Imperial General Headquarters* that it would be better for Japan to negotiate a peace now than await the destruction of the nation at the hands of the victorious Allies. He advised a concentration of all available ground forces on Luzon, mentioning in his reasoning that the Americans, with their superiority in air and naval power, could take the Philippines whenever they chose. He detailed the superiority of American air power and remarked that the building of airfields on Leyte was of no benefit to the Japanese since they could not staff or equip those fields. He concluded that in effect, they had been built for the American's to use. Quickly labeled a "defeatist" he was removed from his command and sent back to Japan to await the war's outcome.[15]

His replacement was General Tomoyuki Yamashita. A professional soldier with a distinguished career behind him, General Yamashita also had his disagreements with *Imperial General Headquarters* and had been sidelined earlier in the war. Now he was brought to the front lines to construct a defense of the Philippine Islands.

Tomoyuki (Hobun) Yamashita was born 8 November 1988 in Shikoku, Japan. He was a large man for a Japanese of the period, reaching six feet one inch in height. His father was the village doctor, but since his mother wanted something more for her son, he was sent to the military. Graduating fifth in his class at the Hiroshima Military Academy, he was commissioned in 1906 as a second lieutenant of infantry. He was soon seen as a bright, witty and hard-working officer who knew his business. Unlike many of his contemporaries, he avoided the prevailing military cliques of the era. He graduated sixth in his class at the War College in 1916, and married a general's daughter. He served on the general staff and was sent to Europe to study in Germany and Switzerland, and later served in the War Ministry and taught at the War College. After being promoted to lieutenant colonel he served as military attaché in Vienna and Budapest in 1927. Upon return to Japan he was promoted to colonel and given command of the *3rd Infantry Regiment*.

At some point after his return to Japan, he became involved in the military intrigues which pervaded Japan in the thirties. His involvement in these intrigues made him some powerful enemies and according to some sources, he was removed from the promotion lists for a year. He was then shipped off to Korea to command the *40th Infantry Brigade*. Soon promoted to major general, he commanded the *China Garrison Mixed Brigade* before another promotion, to lieutenant general. He served as chief of staff to the *Northern China Area Army* before commanding the *4th Division* in Manchuria. Upon his return to Tokyo his enemies, led by Japanese Premier General Tojo, got rid of him by sending him to Europe for six months. He was later exiled to the *Kwantung Defense Army* in July 1941.

In September 1941, his fortunes suddenly changed when he was given command of the newly forming *25th Army* and charged with the responsibility for seizing Malaya and Singapore. Operating under another old enemy, Field Marshal Terauchi, he succeeded so brilliantly that he earned the sobriquet "Tiger of Malaya" and captured 100,000 Commonwealth troops along with the critical fortress of Singapore. But his success brought him no relief from his enemies in Tokyo. Denied promotion or promising new assignments, Yamashita was ordered not to return to Tokyo but to take command of the *1st Area Army* in far off Manchuria. There he languished, appeased only by a late promotion to full general in February 1943, until finally a new assignment beckoned.

Coming from Manchuria, General Yamashita arrived in the Philippines on October 9, 1944, barely eleven days before the main attack and only eight days before the preliminary attacks on Leyte were to begin. He had only a partial staff, few of whom were familiar with the Philippine situation. Assuming command of the *14th Area Army* the day he arrived, General Yamashita found conditions "unsatisfactory." In fact, his new chief of staff, Lieutenant General Akira Muto, who came to the Philippines from Sumatra only a few days after his new commander, when told that the Americans had landed on Leyte replied "Very interesting, but where is Leyte?"[16] About the only favorable thing that General Yamashita found in the Philippines was that since it was the central supply hub for much of the southern territory held by Japan, his supply situation was better than he had expected.

Although the Japanese had maintained for years that their defense of their island bastions was to be under the theory of "Defense at the Water's Edge," that theory was, by October 1944, fast losing credence. Although the Americans had suffered heavy casualties at such places as Tarawa and Saipan when the Japanese garrisons had used this technique, it had not prevented the fall of those garrisons and the conquest of the islands they were defending. Even as Saipan was falling in July 1944, *Imperial General Headquarters* was re-thinking its defense policy. Recommendations from staff and from field commanders who had seen firsthand the might of the American amphibious assault forces suggested a change to a defense in depth. In this new theory, the Americans would be allowed to land and then be engaged in an interminable fight for the island's interior which would drag on and hopefully strain American resolve and resources. It would also expose American naval support forces to more attacks by Japanese air and naval forces, hopefully whittling down their massive firepower. As the battle for Leyte approached, this new theory was disseminated to the field forces commanders with a recommendation to put it to use. The Battle of Leyte would be one of the first times it was used.[17]

General Yamashita had found that the defense of Leyte was under the command of Lieutenant General Sosaku Suzuki and his *35th Army*. His corps-sized group was charged with the defense of the entire Visayan Island area as well as Mindanao. General Suzuki had compromised between the two defensive tactics endorsed by the Japanese at this time. He had directed his local commanders that while the main battle line was to be placed away from likely invasion beaches, a defense of those beaches was nevertheless still required. Acknowledging that this would entail early unnecessary losses, he nevertheless insisted to his subordinates that they defend their beaches to a limited degree. Under his control the *16th, 102nd, 30th,* and *100th Infantry Divisions* prepared their defenses accordingly. The *16th Division* was assigned the defense of Leyte, the *100th Division* the defense of the Davao area on Mindanao. General Suzuki held most of the *30th Division* as a mobile reserve to be rushed to wherever the American appeared.

Late in August, General Suzuki received orders to station his troops in specific areas pending an invasion. This changed little on Leyte, where the *16th Division* remained the major garrison force. It did, however, transfer the remaining units of that division that were on Luzon to Leyte. So by August 1944, Lieutenant General Shiro Makino, commanding the *16th Division*, had all of his forces on the island; he had been planning his defenses since April. His first line of defense was completed by October and ran along the east coast in the Dulag area. A second line of defense was between the first and third lines, the latter of which was a line right down the middle of Leyte Valley around Dagami. He had deployed one battalion of his *9th Infantry Regiment* in and around Catmon Hill. The main strength of his *33rd Infantry Regiment* was deployed in the Palo and Tacloban areas. This latter regiment had only arrived on Leyte in mid-September from Luzon and had been living the soft life of garrison troops. Their officers were unfamiliar with Leyte and did not immediately begin preparing defenses, and were soon out of time when, on October 17th, General Makino reported that American warships had been seen entering Leyte Gulf. His report was tempered by another, which he issued on October 18th, indicating he believed that the ships observed were merely seeking shelter within the gulf from an ocean storm. As a result both the *14th Area Army* and its subordinate *35th Army* were unprepared when the storm came to Leyte.[18]

*   *   *

It could be argued that the first shots of the Leyte Campaign were fired in the Formosa Strait by the U.S. Navy. Late in September 1944, the commander in chief of the *Imperial Navy's First Air Fleet* proposed a new tactic for his aviators—suicide by immolation against enemy ships. Interviewed after the war, the operations officer of the *2nd Air Fleet* based on Luzon stated that the air offensive against the attacking Americans at Leyte would have been far more effective had they been able to put more aircraft in the air against them. When asked why they couldn't do that, he replied that there was a shortage of spare parts, thereby grounding many Japanese aircraft that sat idle for lack of these parts, and making them easy targets for marauding American fighter attacks.

One reason that the Japanese had a critical lack of spare parts was the USS *Tang*. This American submarine was commanded by one of the most daring commanders of the war, Commander Richard H. O'Kane, and assigned in September 1944 to interdict the Formosa Straits through which much of the Japanese supplies to Leyte, and the Philippines in general, were routed. The USS *Tang*[19] was a veteran submarine with a veteran skipper and crew. The ship had already been awarded a Presidential Unit Citation for previous patrols.

Departing from Pearl Harbor, Hawaii, on her fifth war patrol, USS *Tang* stopped at Midway for fuel and provisions before sailing September 27th into the deep Pacific. She began her work on October 10th, sinking a large freighter and another the next day. On October 23rd, just as the Leyte invasion was beginning, USS *Tang* encountered a large enemy convoy which she attacked head on, sinking three, probably four, large enemy cargo ships. The next day Commander O'Kane again led an attack on another Japanese convoy, sinking two more large enemy tankers, vital ships to the Japanese at this stage of the war. Later, Commander O'Kane would claim four additional ships. But the luck of the USS *Tang* was running out. As she fired her last torpedo at this second convoy it malfunctioned and made a circular run on the *Tang* itself. With no time to maneuver out of the way, the USS *Tang* was sunk by its own torpedo twenty seconds after it was fired.

The submarine was hit in the after torpedo room and sunk to 180 feet below sea level. Nine men, including Commander O'Kane, had been tossed from the bridge by the explosion into the sea. Many of the rest of the crew were still alive, however, and anxious to escape the sunken submarine. Inside the vessel, the survivors prepared to use the submarine's escape apparatus and reach the surface. As they did so, the Japanese antisubmarine ships attacked. The constant blasts started fires in the electrical system, making escape more urgent. Despite the fire which was burning the paint off the submarine's interior, thirteen men managed to get out by an escape hatch. Eight of these men reached the surface but only five managed to swim until morning, when they were captured by the Japanese. With the four men who survived after being blown from the conning tower, in total nine Americans were captured by the Japanese and interned for the duration of the war. For his gallant conduct in making these attacks and his courage while in Japanese captivity, as well as temporarily blockading the vital Formosa Straits while the Leyte Invasion Force landed, Commander O'Kane received the Medal of Honor,[20] and the crew of the USS *Tang* was awarded a second Presidential Unit Citation. Officially credited with sinking twenty-four ships of 93,824 tons, there is reason to believe that the USS *Tang's* record is understated by half. In any case, those vital spare parts didn't reach the Philippines and significantly hindered the Japanese defense of those islands.

*   *   *

Unknown to General Yamashita or General Suzuki, the storm they thought had driven the American ships into Leyte Gulf had hidden the approach of the first attack force on Leyte. The first ships into Leyte Gulf, perhaps those spotted by the Japanese, were three minesweepers and transports carrying the Rangers of the 6th Ranger Battalion. The USS *Crosby* carried Company D, 6th Rangers, to Suluan Island and waited while the USS *Denver* shelled the island preparatory to the Ranger's assault. When the cruiser finished its bombardment, First Lieutenant Leslie M. Gray led his Rangers ashore at 0805 Hours. The first Americans had returned to the Philippines.

Lieutenant Gray's mission was to locate and seize mine charts believed to be within a lighthouse on the island. After landing unopposed, the Rangers moved inland, locating and destroying four Japanese buildings including a radio station. As they moved past the burning buildings, Japanese fire broke out on the trail ahead of them. Ranger Private First Class Darwin C. Zufall was killed and Private First Class Donald J. Cannon was wounded, the first American ground forces casualties of the Leyte Campaign. When Company D attacked they found that the Japanese had disappeared up the trail. The Rangers moved up the trail unopposed until they reached the lighthouse, which was deserted, as were the surrounding buildings. A search of the buildings and lighthouse failed to reveal the hoped for mine charts. While clearing the rest of the island, the Rangers killed 32 Japanese soldiers. Returning to the beach, the Rangers found that their boats had been too badly battered by the pounding surf to use to regain the transports. They spent the night in a defensive perimeter at the beach.

Shortly after Company D landed on Suluan Island, the rest of the 6th Ranger Battalion, less Companies B and D, landed on Dinagat Island. No Japanese were found on the island and the required navigation lights were installed at Desolation Point. Meanwhile, Company B of the battalion had tried to land on Homonhon Island, but sea and surf conditions prevented that landing. Undeterred, the company tried again the following morning and, led by Captain Arthur D. Simons,[21] secured the island against no resistance and erected the required lights. By midday on October 18th, the necessary navigation lights were shining from both Dinagat and Homonhom Islands with visibility of from ten to twelve miles. The initial phase of the Leyte campaign had been accomplished. The Americans had returned to the Philippines.

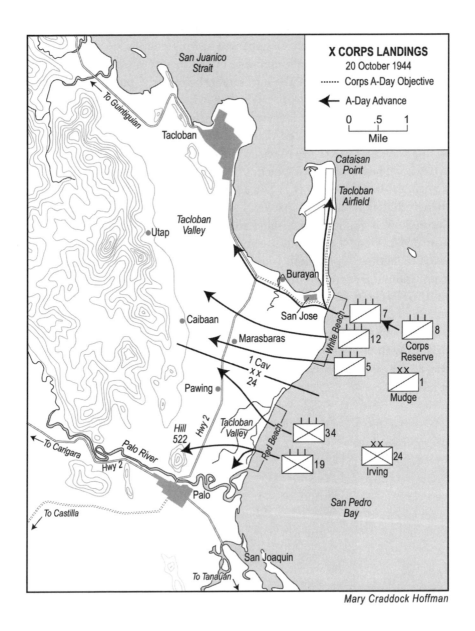

CHAPTER 2

"I HAVE RETURNED"

The American invasion fleet sailed to Leyte as planned but almost immediately those plans had to be altered. The advance force, which included the advance guard of heavy battleships and escorts, plus the Underwater Demolition Teams, ran into the edge of a typhoon. Skirting around the edges they still encountered winds in excess of 100 miles per hour. Fifty-foot waves broke over the ships' bridges, breaking equipment and threatening to tear away the landing craft lashed to the decks. The small minesweepers assigned to clear Leyte Gulf of Japanese mines took a particularly hard pounding. One sank and all of the others were damaged to some extent. Even before the first American soldier landed on Leyte, the schedule was off.

Nevertheless, the program continued. The beach reconnaissance, originally scheduled for the morning of October 18th, was instead launched that afternoon. Covered by the battleship USS *Pennsylvania* and cruisers and destroyers, U.S. Navy Underwater Demolition Teams went into the water off Dulag. As they did so the Japanese opened fire on the landing craft which carried these teams close to the beaches. Rifle and machine gun fire, especially from around Dulag, was heavy and soon joined by mortar shells. Despite this fire the UDT boats came to within two hundred yards of the beach before dropping their swimmers into the water and veering away.

Because the minesweepers had been delayed by the typhoon and the gulf had yet to be swept for mines, the heavy support ships declined to enter Leyte Gulf and instead supported the UDT men from much farther offshore than originally planned. This resulted in some beach areas not being shelled at all, and others received far less than planned. That plan had assumed that the UDT's did not want air support, and by the time they became aware of this oversight it was too late to provide it. Left to their own resources, the swimmers dived and zigzagged in the water to avoid the Japanese fire while they checked the beaches for mines, obstacles and gradients. Commander C. C. Morgan, leading the teams, saw the problem and brought his transport closer to the beaches, using their small but accurate three-inch guns to support his men in the water. Using Dulag as their main target, the transport's guns did decrease Japanese fire.

In the water, the swimmers had other problems. Lieutenant Thomas Crist's Team Three's beach was murky, the result of the recent storm. Visibility was limited to three or four feet. Using touch as much as sight they took soundings and searched for mines and beach obstacles before swimming back out to their waiting boats. Lieutenant Commander William Carberry's Team Four was less fortunate and suffered seven wounded when one of the recovery boats was hit by Japanese fire. Commander Carberry grabbed the wheel of the shattered wooden boat and began to steer out to safety, but clearly the boat was sinking. As the boat began to go under, the wounded radioman continued to call for the reserve boat to come in and rescue the stranded crew. Meanwhile, the wounded were given first aid and placed in life preservers. Before help arrived two more enemy shells hit the boat and it went under. The survivors pulled the wounded men out to sea, and were finally rescued while the Japanese continued to fire on them. Even the UDT transport, which had moved in close to support the swimmers, was hit by enemy fire. A Japanese shell caused 21 casualties while the transport awaited the return of its men.

Since not all the assigned swimmers could be dropped, Ensign John W. Guinnee signaled his eight men to cover the entire beach rather than the originally assigned narrow sector. Two of his swimmers actually reached the beach during their reconnaissance. To the north, Lieutenant Commander Donald E. Young's Team Eight came under mortar fire that almost killed Ensign Donald E. Nourse, gashing his forehead and smashing the swim mask on his face. These stories were repeated all along the beaches. Men were killed, wounded, boats sunk and damaged. But they did the job. The reports indicated that the slope of the beach was steep, permitting tank landing ships to drop their ramps much closer to shore. There were no obstacles or mines. In the ninety minutes it had taken the Underwater Demolition Teams to acquire this information they had lost three men killed and fourteen wounded.[1]

Meanwhile, up in Manila, the staff of the *Fourth Air Army* was still undecided about the recent American landings on Suluan. Because of the absence of a strong American air cover they felt that this was not an invasion, rather a raid or merely a guerrilla aid operation. But soon increased American air activity and radio traffic convinced them that an invasion was indeed imminent. Lieutenant General Kyoji Tominaga,[2] air commander in the Philippines, decided to respond with his forces and make an all-out air strike against the American fleet supporting the landings. Bad weather kept them grounded on the 18th, but they would soon make their presence known.

*   *   *

Compared to the choppy seas that had plagued the Ranger's landings two days earlier, the waters of Leyte Gulf were surprisingly calm on October 20, 1944. At 0600 Hours, the battleships of the support group began their preinvasion bombardment on the Southern Attack Force beaches. An hour later the support ships of the Northern Attack Force did the same. With no specific targets determined, the barrage was area fire, directed at suspected areas of Japanese occupation. Some large explosions and fires indicated hits on enemy supply dumps and beach defenses. In the Southern Attack Force area a pause was called in the barrage at 0850 Hours to allow an air strike on Catmon Hill. Overall some 500 sorties were carried out over the beaches and interior of Leyte on this A-Day morning.

By 0800 Hours, the troops were boarding their landing craft for the run in to the beaches of Leyte. Landing Craft, Vehicle, Personnel (LCVP) were loaded with troops while mortar and rocket ships took their positions off the flanks of the assault waves and prepared to fire the final beach bombardments moments before the assault troops came ashore. These latter boats raced toward shore and delivered their bombardment at 0945, just fifteen minutes before the first assault waves were to land.

In X Corps area, the 1st Cavalry Division was to land on the White Beaches. These were of white coral sand that would only accommodate shallow draft landing vessels. Varying from fifteen- to three-feet in depth and fringed with coconut trees, the beach was about one mile from Highway 1 directly inland from the landing area. The 1st Cavalry Brigade landed on the left or south side while the 2nd Brigade hit the right, north side of the White Beaches. Dazed by the pre-invasion bombardment and the recent rocket strikes, the Japanese defenders of White Beach could offer resistance only in the form of small arms and machine gun fire. One cavalryman remembered:

> As we neared Leyte the navy was all around us. As the first wave formed, I looked at some of my buddies to see if they were as nervous as I was. I was fascinated by the big smoke rings the big guns made as they pounded the beach, and then walked the bombardment inland while we prepared to land. I was amazed at the little resistance we encountered that first day.[3]

Landing abreast, the 7th Cavalry, 12th Cavalry and 5th Cavalry Regiments[4] landed successfully. The 1st Squadron, 7th Cavalry moved immediately to it's right to seize the Cataison Peninsula with its important Tacloban Air Field. To the south the 2nd Squadron, 7th Cavalry targeted the town of San Jose and a bridge across the Burayan River northwest of that town. Against light opposition both squadrons moved successfully to achieve those goals. After knocking out two pillboxes and a squad of Japanese, the 2nd Squadron engaged in a brief house-to-house fight in San Jose before clearing the town. They reached and captured the bridge over the Burayan River which the *33rd Infantry Regiment* had tried and failed to destroy. Similarly, the Tacloban Air Strip was seized against minimal opposition, and the engineers who had landed immediately behind the cavalrymen began to work on the strip before the day was over.

Behind the cavalrymen the tanks of the 44th Tank Battalion[5] came ashore and moved up in support of the advance. They, too, had an easy morning except for one tank that hit an aerial bomb buried as a land mine. The tank was destroyed and the entire crew wounded. But the real problem for the armor was the ground over which they had to move. As the battalion historian later wrote:

> The greatest single factor that hampered employment of tanks in this operation was terrain. In nearly every instance of tank employment, because of impassable terrain on both sides of the road, the tanks were road bound, and their front limited to the width of the road.[6]

The 5th and 12th Cavalry Regiments also landed against light opposition. Delayed more by a difficult swamp and morass area directly in their paths, the regiments reached the highway, making contact with the 24th Infantry Division by midday. Patrols were immediately sent forward to reconnoiter the next day's objective, the foothills west of the highway. Behind them the 8th Cavalry Regiment,[7] held in Corps reserve, came ashore. By 1630 Hours the divisional command post had been established ashore at San Jose. All of the division's artillery battalions were also ashore and prepared to fire on order by darkness. As the division historian later wrote "Then began a battle with an enemy that all through the Leyte Campaign caused more trouble and difficulty than the Japanese ever did. It was mud, mud, mud."[8]

The division command post was established ashore at 1400 Hours near San Ricardo. As night fell in the 1st Cavalry Division's zone, there was no contact with the Japanese except for about seventy-five enemy troops who held Hill 215. But all was not quiet. As Colonel Royce A. Drake was inspecting the front line positions of his 5th Cavalry Regiment, a surprise Japanese counterattack hit the area and Colonel Drake was killed. For his gallant leadership of his regiment from the front, Colonel Drake was awarded a posthumous Silver Star.[9]

The left, or southern portion of X Corps' zone, was the responsibility of the 24th Infantry Division, less its detached regimental combat team. Company Commander Paul Austin, Company F, 34th Infantry remembered "We were awakened about 4:00 A.M., had the usual pre-landing breakfast, steak, and eggs. This was the only time we ever got that kind of food."[10] The beaches were designated Red Beach and although opposition was sparse, the beach conditions prevented even the flat bottomed landing craft from approaching the dry sand of the beach. And so the soldiers had a wet but otherwise safe landing on Leyte. Behind the beach lay another swamp area and a stream bed which General Makino's soldiers had converted into a formidable tank trap. Only after the first five waves had landed did the Japanese open fire on the incoming Americans. Artillery and mortar fire soon fell among the landing craft of the 1st Battalion, 19th Infantry, sinking four of them and causing numerous casualties. The commander of Company C was killed, a squad of demolition engineers wiped out and the Cannon Company severely hurt. The Japanese succeeded in driving off the landing craft carrying the artillery and most of the supporting 603rd Tank Company's tanks.[11] In addition, many casualties were caused among the members of the division's headquarters.

Within the landing parties of the 34th Infantry Regiment were two men whose mission was unique. Private First Class Silas Thomas, of North Carolina, and Corporal Ponciano Dacones, a Filipino, had earlier won a lottery and were now carrying an American and a Philippine flag back to the Leyte beaches. No enemy fire greeted them as they landed, and they raced forward to a line of coconut trees where, side by side, they planted to two flags firmly in Philippine soil.[12]

Nearby, the 3rd Battalion, 34th Infantry landed some 300 yards north of its assigned beach and was immediately hit by heavy machine gun and rifle fire. The regimental commander, Colonel Aubrey S. Newman, immediately saw the danger to his regiment and the invasion. Seeing the bunched-up troops, the skillful crossfire of the Japanese, and the mounting confusion, he took action. He marched up the beach shouting to his men "Get the hell off the beach. Get up and get moving. Follow me." Urged on by their regimental commander, the troops moved off the beach into the wooded area ahead, shielding themselves from the enemy's fire. As it moved, however, Company K ran into five pillboxes defending a stream. These they knocked out with rifles, Browning Automatic Rifles (BAR) and hand grenades. After fighting their way through another swamp that made the advance extremely difficult, the 34th Infantry tied itself in on both sides and established its beachhead perimeter for the evening.

One of the chief reasons for the success of the 34th Infantry's[13] Red Beach landings was Captain Francis B. Wai, an unusual officer. Captain Wai was a Japanese-American officer assigned to the Headquarters Company of the 34th Infantry Regiment. Few Japanese Americans participated in the Pacific War due to American concerns over identification, capture by the enemy and security concerns, but Captain Wai was one of the exceptions. Landing in the fifth wave at Red Beach, he found the first four waves pinned down in a palm grove bounded by submerged rice paddies. Captain Austin and Company F were on the same beach, and he later reported that

> ... rifle fire was coming in pretty heavy. Our Captain Wye [sic] from regimental headquarters was killed a minute after he set foot on the beach. Another company commander from the 1st Battalion was killed very near Colonel 'Red' Newman. I looked back and couldn't see anybody moving forward. Snipers, machine guns, mortars, artillery, had everyone pinned down on the beach sand.[14]

Seeing that the men were leaderless and disorganized, Captain Wai, who had not been killed as Captain Austin believed, immediately assumed command and began to issue orders to organize and move the men inland. As he did so, he repeatedly exposed himself to enemy machine gun and rifle fire. Nevertheless, he began to lead the way inland through the rice paddies, which provided little or no cover to the advance. Inspired by the cool leadership example of Captain Wai, the soldiers followed him inland towards their objective. As he led their advance, Captain Wai continued to expose himself to enemy fire to locate enemy strong points holding up the advance. It was while he led the assault against the last enemy pillbox holding up the advance that Captain Wai was struck down by enemy fire. His inspirational leadership led his landing group off the beaches and allowed them, despite loss of leaders and heavy enemy fire, to achieve their objective. For his gallant leadership on October 20th, Captain Francis B. Wai was awarded a posthumous Medal of Honor.[15]

Technician Harold Rant, a wire man with a battalion headquarters company of the 34th Infantry, remembers Captain Wai:

A hero came forth but we knew he had come to this battle to die. He was a big Hawaiian captain, one of the most popular officers. Before we left Hollandia he had received word his wife just had a baby although he'd been away for twelve months. This shook him and we knew he was going to fight with everything he had even if he got killed in the process. Word passed that he was really ripping and had knocked out three pillboxes. With real luck, he was jumping, running, dodging, and crawling under machine-gun fire to get hand grenades in the fortresses. At about the fifth one they got him, laced him with fire and he was hit ten times through the chest. He was the one who really broke the spell enough for our people to start moving in.[16]

*   *   *

The 3rd Battalion, 34th Infantry's commander, Lieutenant Colonel Edward M. Postlethwait, stopped a light tank that had appeared on Red Beach. Using the tank's exterior telephone, he directed its fire into anything and everything that might possibly hide an enemy soldier or machine gun. After a few rounds, he would direct the tank forward a few yards, repeat the process, and move forward again. He was credited with at least two enemy pillboxes and one building near the beach.

Things were still unsettled within the 19th Infantry's[17] sector, as well. Several landing craft were hit and sunk by Japanese fire and their troops thrown into the water. Here, too, the regiment's Third Battalion hit heavy opposition, and some units landed in the wrong place and/or wrong beach. Confusion was soon cleared up and the advance progressed until Company I, on the left flank, hit a strong point manned by men of the *33rd Infantry Regiment*. Company K was delayed in landing when its command boat broke down, and by the time the company landed they faced heavy fire which killed or wounded all of its officers but one. One of its platoons was completely cut off from the rest of the battalion and could not regain contact until the following day. Company C lost its commanding officer and Cannon Company lost two section leaders, a platoon leader and several members of company headquarters.

Much of this fire came from the strongpoint that Company I faced. This consisted of a tank ditch some five hundred yards inland from the beach. From the ditch, Japanese soldiers of the *33rd Infantry Regiment* pelted them with small arms, machine gun and 75mm artillery fire from prepared positions dug into and around the ditch. Several pillboxes were used to protect the artillery pieces which held up the advance of Company I. Undeterred, Private First Class Frank B. Robinson crawled forward until he reached the rear of one of the pillboxes. There he rose up and dropped three grenades into the position and then reached in and pulled the machine gun out of the box. Grabbing a flamethrower operator, he moved ahead another two hundred yards and attacked another pillbox. When his flamethrower failed to ignite he lighted it by hand with a bunch of discarded Japanese newspapers that he set afire, then threw in front of the pillbox. The flamethrower operator then burned out the second box. To destroy a third pillbox, Pfc. Robinson repeatedly exposed himself to its fire to allow supporting tanks to locate it and subsequently destroy it. For his successful leadership against the enemy defenses at the tank ditch, Pfc. Robinson was awarded a Distinguished Service Cross.[18]

The battles continued, however, and for the next several hours the 3rd Battalion, 19th Infantry fought its way forward in squad- and platoon-sized battles until it reached Highway 1, where it established a defensive perimeter for the evening. Nearby, the 1st Battalion, 19th Infantry also had a rough landing. Several boats were lost and casualties were incurred. Lieutenant Colonel Frederick R. Zierath realized that his men were three hundred yards north of their correct beach and directed them to the correct area before moving inland. As they did so, Company B suffered many casualties from another strongpoint area. Rather than waste time and more casualties, Colonel

Zierath ordered it to bypass the strongpoint and directed his supporting self-propelled guns to move up and knock out the pillboxes. Company C had a similar experience and also bypassed the beach opposition.

Private First Class Arthur Kmiecik of Milwaukee, Wisconsin, had long been kidded about the difficulty in pronouncing his last name, but today the young machine gunner found himself pinned down on the beach with his very serious squad mates. After twenty minutes of that he simply got angry. Together with another volunteer he picked up his machine gun, cradled it in his arms and walked straight toward a Japanese emplacement. Deciding he was finally close enough, he put the gun down and fired it directly into the enemy position until it was silenced. Off Red Beach, Sergeant Ignazio Amato of Brooklyn, New York, lost a buddy. He himself was seriously wounded in the leg by shrapnel. Refusing medical treatment, he led his squad in a charge against the same enemy position that killed his friend. Despite limping along with blood squelching in his boot, forward he goes to knock out the enemy position. And not far off, First Sergeant Russell T. Edbert of Minnesota grew angry when a machine gun pinned down his battalion. Unable to see the gun, First Sergeant Edbert stood up and walked forward under enemy fire until he spotted it. Then he walked back, still under fire, and selected a volunteer to carry a machine gun forward. Getting close enough to fire through the enemy's fire port, he emptied the machine gun into the position. His battalion moved forward again.

Following Colonel Zierath's 1st Battalion ashore was the regiment's 2nd Battalion, which also knocked out a pillbox containing a 75mm gun with a rocket launcher, before overrunning two more such pillboxes that had been abandoned by the Japanese. As Company G prepared to move along the beach to Palo, the extreme flank of the proposed beachhead, they were hit with a counterattack by a platoon of the *33rd Infantry Regiment*. These Japanese soldiers were apparently attempting to recapture the pillboxes the Second Battalion had just captured. The small attack was easily repulsed and the Japanese left behind eleven dead.

Company G resumed its advance until an hour later when they ran into another group of mutually supporting pillboxes near where the beach road meets Highway 1. A battle to overcome these Japanese positions cost the company fifteen casualties, and resulted in a draw when darkness came and the Americans broke off the battle to prepare night defenses.

Meanwhile, Colonel Zierath's battalion had continued to move inland, with its ultimate objective being Hill 522. This hill was the dominant terrain feature blocking American inland progress in the area. Some three months before the Americans arrived, General Makino had ordered it fortified and the entire civilian population of Palo had been impressed to build these defenses under Japanese supervision. When the 19th Infantry landed, there were five pillboxes, well camouflaged and protected by numerous tunnels and communications trenches some seven-feet deep. The American preliminary bombardment had targeted the hill because it was an obvious defensive position, and once the troops moved off the beaches, Battery B of the 13th Field Artillery Battalion[19] and Battery A of the 63rd Field Artillery Battalion[20] landed, set up, and began to bombard the hill.

Indeed, A-Day on Leyte was not a good day for General Makino. He had selected precisely that day to move his headquarters from Tacloban south and inland to Dagami, which was a more central point about nine miles inland on the road from Tanauan. As the Americans landed, General Makino was in the process of making this move, actually on the road between the two locations. Much of his communications and support troops were still around Tacloban, cut off from their division commander. Without communications, it took until noon before General Makino could order any reinforcements forward to strengthen his beach defenses. To make matters worse, the hasty evacuation of Tacloban, in the face of the attacking cavalrymen, caused the abandonment of nearly all of the *16th Infantry Division*'s communications equipment, leaving it out of communication with *35th Army, Fourteenth Area Army* and other higher headquarters. It would be forty-eight hours before communications between the two commands was restored.

Because Japanese resistance continued along the planned route for the 1st Battalion, 19th Infantry's attack on Hill 522, Colonel Zierath sent forward reconnaissance parties to find another route. The scouts reported finding a covered approach on the northern side of the hill and Colonel Zierath sent his companies forward in a column of companies. Leading off, Company A was hit by fire from five enemy pillboxes. Leaving Company A to deal with these, Colonel Zierath led the rest of the Battalion around Company A and attacked Hill 522 directly, with Company C on the right and Captain William J. Herman's Company B on the left. Although tired from a long stressful day, the American soldiers moved up the steep hill. At times the men had to pull themselves up the hill by grasping roots and plants. Supporting fire began to fall too close to their front and a call went back to lift the supporting artillery fire, only to learn that it was not artillery fire, but from American chemical mortars supporting the battalion. That fire was suddenly stopped before the battalion reached the top. Colonel Zierath ordered his companies to "Speed it up."[21]

First Lieutenant Dallas Dick was already exhausted and suffering severely from a shoulder wound. Despite his condition he moved to the front of his Company C, trying to catch up to his lead scouts. When they saw him gaining on them they increased their speed, as did all of Company C and Company B. No lieutenants were going to beat them to the top of this damn hill! It was Company B that reached the first crest of the hill where it came under fire from two enemy bunkers. As the day was fast disappearing, the company decided to halt for the day and dig in. Nearby, the scouts from Company C had reached the highest point of the hill and identified two platoons of Japanese coming up the other side. They shouted for the rest of Company C to hurry to the top to prevent the Japanese from securing the crest. The race was just barely won by the Americans who reached the crest and began a fierce firefight with the attacking Japanese. It continued for several minutes and Company C, with Lieutenant Dick[22] standing upright as a rallying point for his spread-out company, led the fight. He was seriously wounded in the leg and had his carbine shot out of his hands during the battle, but they held the hilltop. Some fifty Japanese were killed before the remainder withdrew. That night saw several attempts to infiltrate the American position, during which the Japanese carried away their dead and wounded from the earlier battle. Fourteen Americans were killed and another ninety-five wounded during the Hill 522 battle.

By the end of A-Day, the 24th Infantry Division had crossed Highway 1 and established physical contact with the 1st Cavalry Division on its right. Hill 522 had been secured, preventing the Japanese from enjoying a view of the beachhead, while giving the Americans a good view of the interior. The town of Palo lay immediately in front of the lines and with that, the entrance to Leyte Valley, a chief objective of the campaign. The X Corps had established a beachhead more than a mile in depth and five miles wide. Tacloban and its important airstrip had been captured as well.

It was at Red Beach, barely secured by the 24th Infantry Division, that General Douglas MacArthur decided to make his formal return to the Philippines, something he had been impatiently awaiting since April 1942. Despite snipers and mortar shells occasionally hitting the beach, he entered a landing craft and ordered it to land. Expecting to land at a pier, the coxswain could find none intact and so headed for Red Beach. A dry landing was expected but fate intervened and the landing craft hit a sandbar fifty yards off the beach. General MacArthur made his return to the Philippines just like his soldiers, through the surf with water in his shoes and his pants wet. But he was there, and soon announcing to the world, "I have returned."

*   *   *

While X Corps established itself to the north, the XXIV Corps was doing the same to the south. The Corps was to land in the Dulag-San Jose area and establish a beachhead in that area. Airstrips were the primary objective in this zone. To the north, the inexperienced 96th Infantry Division would land as assault troops in their first combat experience. Their objectives were to seize a beachhead between the Calabasag River[23] and the village of San Jose. In this zone was the high ground of the beachhead area, known generally as Catmon Hill but actually a long 1,400 foot high ridge which consisted of Labiranan Head, Labir Hill and then Catmon Hill.

Landing on the northernmost Orange Beaches, the 383rd Infantry Regiment[24] would seize Labiranan Head as the initial beachhead line. There would be about ten miles between the northernmost beach of the 96th Infantry Division and the southernmost beach of the 24th Infantry Division in X Corps. The same process of boarding landing craft and the run in to shore supported by the rocket gunships was repeated here. Colonel Edwin T. May and his 383rd Infantry Regiment landed on the Orange Beaches at 1000 Hours. The trip ashore was the usual apprehensive one. "On the way in, one of the guys sitting opposite me in the amtrac was very nervous, as we all were, and fiddling with the safety on his rifle. He had the rifle butt down on the deck with the barrel up alongside his cheek. All of a sudden we heard a loud bang and when we looked at this guy, his eyes were bulging way out with a startled expression on his face. There was a black powder mark up the side of his face and a hole through his helmet. Nobody laughed."[25]

Landing with two battalions abreast, the regiment had landed successfully and moved 1,200 yards inland before any enemy resistance was encountered. At first this consisted of long-range mortar fire from the *9th Infantry Regiment* which was based in the vicinity of Catmon Hill. In a situation identical to that in the northern beachhead, as the two battalions crossed the highway, they fell into an unsuspected swamp. Amphibian tanks bogged down and left the assault troops without armor support for the rest of the day while they struggled to get to firm ground. As they struggled forward the Japanese mortar fire continued and one shell killed the division senior supply officer, Lieutenant Colonel Robert H. Billingsley.[26]

One of the initial problems the Americans faced on Leyte was the climate. "It was 10:00 A.M. when we hit the beach and 98 degrees Fahrenheit. I found one of our guys passed out from heat exhaustion. His canteen was empty. I called a medic over and went inland."[27] The heat and humidity of the Philippine climate would cause many similar casualties throughout the campaign. And here the terrain also limited the tanks of the 763rd Tank Battalion to the roads, with swamps preventing any off-road advances.[28]

The plan was for the 382nd Infantry[29] under Colonel Marcy L. Dill, to sweep inland on the left of the division's zone and protect the beachhead while Colonel May's battalions took Catmon Hill. With the third regiment in Sixth Army reserve, resources were limited and failure not an option. Colonel May planned to send his First Battalion up the southern end of the hill mass while the Second and Third Battalions would attack along the northern axis. A battalion of tanks, under Lieutenant Colonel Harmon L. Edmonson, would support the attack. When the 763rd Tank Battalion[30] became mired in the swamp a key part of the plan was already discarded. There were no roads leading into the interior and not only the tanks, but every other vehicle was stopped cold by the swamps. The infantry had to carry what they needed on their backs through the hip deep swamps to simply approach their first objective. Men had to crawl on hands and knees to avoid being pulled down into the muck of the swamps. Packs and gas masks were thrown away, only the essentials of life remained, weapons, food and water. Days later, when General Bradley showed General MacArthur the area over which his division had advanced, General MacArthur stated "That's impossible. No man can get through those swamps." General Bradley was pleased to respond "Nevertheless they are there."[31] Fortunately for the 96th Infantry Division, the Japanese apparently agreed with General MacArthur, and there were no defenses protecting the approach to Catmon Hill from the direction of the swamps.

Lieutenant Colonel James O. McCray's 2nd Battalion, 383rd Infantry, took the northern route to Catmon Hill. For the next three days they would struggle more with terrain and climate than with the Japanese. Although under sporadic mortar and artillery fire from Catmon Hill, the battalion struggled through the swamps until, three days later, they reached their assault point. Casualties were light but steady in both the Second and Third Battalions.

Back along the beach, the 1st Battalion, 383rd Infantry, occupied the village of San Jose and then moved south to the Labiranan River which it crossed in mid-afternoon. Once across the river, it ran into small-arms fire from the *9th Infantry Regiment*. This continued as the battalion advanced slowly until darkness brought an end to the day and the battle. That night, the 1st Battalion settled in at the base of Labiranan Head and in a good position to launch its assault the following morning.

Alongside, Colonel Dill's 382nd Infantry came ashore on the Blue Beaches. Slowed only by enemy obstacles on the beach, the regiment moved steadily inland to a distance of about 700 yards by midday. As it crossed Highway 1 it encountered the first enemy opposition by elements of the *9th Infantry Regiment*, which defended a series of trenches paralleling the beach. Having moved inland about 2,500 yards the regiment settled down for the first night ashore on Leyte.

The regiment's Third Battalion was directed on Hill 120. This height was some 600 yards inland and dominated the local beach area. Third Battalion was ordered to seize this hill as its A-Day objective. When it approached, the battalion was quickly pinned down by enemy fire coming from Hill 120. Calling for mortar and naval gunfire support, the resulting barrage cleared the way for 3rd Battalion, 382nd Infantry to advance and capture Hill 120 when the Japanese evacuated it under the heavy fire. Once established atop the hill, the 3rd Battalion was the target of enemy fire from a nearby swamp, but this fire did not dislodge the Americans. But combined with the swamp immediately to the front of the hill it did halt any further advance for the day. At the end of the day, the 382nd Infantry had moved from 1,300 to 2,500 yards inland and seized the initial objectives for A-Day. Indeed, for its first day in combat the 96th Infantry Division had acquitted itself well. It had seized its assigned beachhead, captured San Jose, both sides of the Labiranan River, Hill 120 and moved well inland. Although not all A-Day objectives had been taken, much of that could be attributed to the deep swamps which had been unexpectedly found in the division's path. By 1800 Hours on A-Day, General Bradley had established division headquarters within the beachhead, and most of the division artillery was ashore.

The first night ashore was unpleasant, to say the least. "Of course, no one slept that first night. Off our left flank we heard a lot of shooting and noise. We heard that Japs had made a banzai charge in the 7th Division area. One of our guys, whom I knew very well, got out of his foxhole and crawled toward the company CP. Someone shot him in the head. We had been told over and over not to get out of our foxholes at night."[32] Even the shelters were miserable. "We dug foxholes by nightfall but because of the water table, they filled up with water. Because we could not leave the foxholes, we remained in water up to our necks all night. In the morning, our entire bodies, hands, etc, were wrinkled from being soaked."[33]

*   *   *

The 7th Infantry Division landed on the left of the 96th Infantry Division. It was to establish a beachhead between the Calabasag and Daguitan Rivers, capture Dulag and the airfield, secure the bridge over the Daguitan River at the village of Dao and another crossing over the Talisay River. It was to land with two regiments abreast. Colonel Marc J. Logie's 32nd Infantry Regiment[34] was to land on the northern beaches, known as Violet Beach, while Colonel Curtis D. O'Sullivan's 184th Infantry Regiment[35] hit the Yellow Beaches. Colonel O'Sullivan's objectives were the airfield and town of Dulag and the crossings over the Daguitan River.

Here again, the procedure was the same as on all the other assault beaches. The troops loaded into their landing craft and were accompanied to the beaches by rocket ships and amphibian tanks. Escorted by the 776th Amphibian Tank Battalion[36] the assault waves moved ashore as the amphibian tanks knocked out hostile mortar and small-arms fire coming from a tank barrier ashore. Once ashore, the battalion moved inland some 200 yards to provide protection for the infantry landing behind them. For these troops, carried ashore by the 718th Amphibian Tractor Battalion,[37] the landing proved unexpectedly easy. Apart from a few mortar shells falling amongst the first waves and a machine gun or two, enemy fire was largely absent. The infantry dropped from their tractors and in squads and platoons fanned out to cover the beach and advance inland. On the extreme left, the Japanese had established some beach obstacles which caused the amphibian tractors to veer off course. And on the extreme right, Japanese positions including a 70mm gun position, poured fire on the 2nd Battalion, 32nd Infantry, killing four men and wounding another twelve of Company E. Indeed, all opposition seemed to be in front of the 32nd Infantry. As other companies landed, they found themselves faced by Japanese soldiers hidden in tall grass and among the tombstones of a cemetery. Crawling forward, the American infantry forced the Japanese to retire inland. Within ninety minutes, the 2nd Battalion, 32nd Infantry, had reached Highway 1. Just as they did so, however, another enemy defensive position revealed itself and Company F suffered the loss of six killed, including First Lieutenant John R. Ening, leader of its 2nd platoon. Tanks were called up and the position destroyed. Lieutenant

Colonel Glen A. Nelson reported his battalion was crossing the highway at 1400 Hours.

The tanks were from the attached 767th Tank Battalion[38] which had come ashore about 1015 Hours. They immediately found themselves involved in the action when within five hundred yards of the beach, Company A's 2nd platoon was fired upon by an enemy antitank gun. Tank number 18 was knocked out and several of its crew injured, and tank number 17 took three hits including one which locked the 75mm main gun in place. Cooperating with Company F of the 32nd Infantry, the tanks eliminated the enemy position.

As they did so, a patrol was detached from E Company to seize the bridge at the Calabasag River. This they did only to find that the bridge was down. The patrol did manage to cross the river, however, and by 1610 reported that they had made physical contact with elements of the 96th Infantry Division, thereby tying in the XXIV Corps beachhead. Meanwhile, the rest of the Second Battalion crossed the highway to find themselves in swamps much like those further north. By 1540 Hours, Colonel Nelson withdrew his men to firmer ground and prepared night defensive positions.

To the left, the 3rd Battalion, 32nd Infantry, had what was probably the toughest fight of the day. Major Charles A. Whitcomb's battalion had landed and moved inland with Company K on the right and Company L on the left. As they moved through heavy grass just before noon, they came out in a small clearing with a hedge fence which ran perpendicular to their line of advance. Behind this lay a Japanese defensive position unseen by the advancing Americans. As they entered the clearing, both companies were caught in a heavy barrage of machine gun fire and immediately lost eight men killed and nineteen wounded. Both companies were pinned to the ground by the enemy fire.

The Japanese had built three log pillboxes which protected a 70mm mountain howitzer and several machine guns hidden behind the hedge. A system of radiating trenches and spider holes[39] filled with enemy riflemen protected the pillboxes. Just as the Americans looked about for a way to overcome this position, a few American tanks, which had recently landed, rolled up on the scene. Major Whitcomb sent tanks to both companies to support them while reducing the enemy defenses. As the leading tank moved into the open to attack the hedge position, the 70mm mountain howitzer opened fire and knocked out the tank with one round.[40] The two following tanks veered desperately to the left to get out of the line of fire, but in doing so,

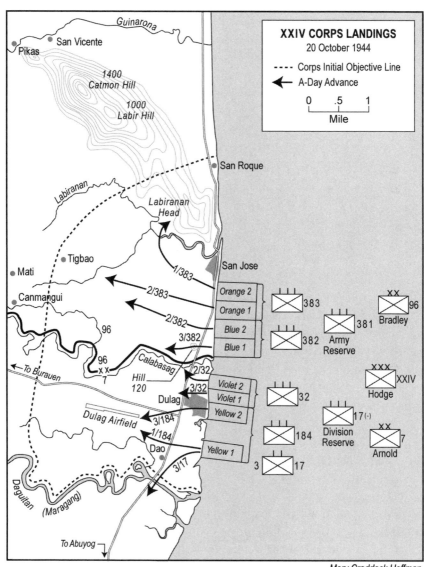

XXIV CORPS LANDINGS
20 October 1944

- - - Corps Initial Objective Line
← A-Day Advance

0   .5   1
Mile

Guinarona

San Vicente
Pikas

1400
Catmon Hill

1000
Labir Hill

San Roque

Labiranan

Labiranan
Head

Tigbao
Mati
Canmangui

San Jose

1/383

2/383

2/382

96

3/382

96
96
XX
7

Calabasag

Hill
120

To Burauen

Dulag

Dulag Airfield

Dao

Daguitan   (Maragang)

To Abuyog

Orange 2
Orange 1
Blue 2
Blue 1

Violet 2
Violet 1
Yellow 2

Yellow 1

2/32

3/32

3/184

1/184

3/17

383

382

381

Army
Reserve

32

184

3   17

XX
96
Bradley

XXX
XXIV
Hodge

17 (-)
Division
Reserve

XX
7
Arnold

Mary Craddock Hoffman

lost communications with the infantry. The two tanks that had been assigned to K Company next came forward and both were quickly knocked out by the enemy gun.

With the loss of its tank support 3rd Battalion, 32nd Infantry, was now without means to destroy the enemy defenses. Undeterred, First Lieutenant Alfred E. Grantham, commanding Company L, crawled through enemy fire to a nearby ditch, and then crawled along the ditch to a point near the two tanks which had lost contact with the infantry. From there he sprinted under enemy fire to the rear of one of the tanks, and using its exterior phone directed the crews toward the enemy. Finally, at about 1400 Hours, a joint tank-infantry attack destroyed the enemy strongpoint. With that destroyed, the battalion crossed Highway 1 and moved west to Dulag, which it bypassed. Just past Dulag, another hedge position was encountered and Lieutenant Grantham treated it the same as the first. A hundred yards further on was another, which suffered the same fate. This time the cost was high, with another eight men wounded and one of the two remaining tanks knocked out. As the fight for this last hedge continued, Major Whitcomb received orders to detach his Company I to make physical contact with the 184th Infantry. The resistance and need to reorganize his battalion caused Major Whitcomb to call a halt for the day.

Behind the assault waves of the 32nd and 184th Infantry, the 3rd Battalion, 17th Infantry,[41] was to land and seize the bridgehead over the Daguitan River. Coming ashore at about 1500 Hours on the southern Yellow Beach, the battalion pushed west and south through light opposition until they reached the Daguitan River at Dao. Within a few moments they had established a bridgehead over the river and made contact with the 184th Infantry on their right.

The 184th Infantry landed over the Yellow Beaches and encountered minimal resistance. By 1300 Hours, the 1st Battalion had pushed nine hundred yards inland without serious opposition. Twenty minutes later, the 3rd Battalion reached Highway 1 after searching through the ruins of Dulag. Soon the regiment was rummaging amongst the ruins left at Dulag Airfield. By 1700, Hours Colonel O'Sullivan could report his regiment well established ashore and moving against no opposition. However, behind the lines, General Arnold was growing more concerned with an increasing gap between the two assault regiments. To close this mile-wide gap, General Arnold ordered the two regiments to consolidate towards the center. This was the cause for Major Whitcomb's halt to detach Company I and also forced

Colonel O'Sullivan to halt his advance for the day. Contact between the two regiments was established just before dark. While the infantry consolidated its gains, light tanks of Company D, 767th Tank Battalion rolled ahead and captured the town of San Roque, some two miles north of Dulag.

Seventy miles to the south of the 7th Infantry Division's beaches, the 21st Infantry,[42] detached from the 24th Infantry Division, had landed in the area of the Panaon Strait at 0930 Hours and found no Japanese opposition. It prepared for the defense of the area and awaited events.

*　　*　　*

At the end of A-Day on Leyte, Sixth Army had established itself ashore on two beachheads. Four infantry divisions had landed with their armor, artillery, medical and support units ashore or on the way. Casualties had been relatively light[43] and enemy resistance less than expected. Although not all A-Day objectives had been taken, this was no cause for concern since the reasons were more natural than enemy-caused. The gap of ten miles between X Corps and XXIV Corps had been planned. Major objectives such as the Tacloban Airfield and the one at Dulag had been captured easily. Hill 522, which potentially both threatened the beachhead and provided access to Leyte Valley, had also been captured, although the 1st Battalion, 19th Infantry, would remain surrounded on the hill for the next two days.

Behind the assault troops major headquarters were preparing to establish themselves on the island. By the next day, the Sixth Army, X Corps and XXIV Corps would have their headquarters established on the island. Cargo vessels were being unloaded as fast as possible to keep the assault troops supplied as they advanced. Some problems were encountered here when it was discovered that not all ships had been combat loaded.[44] As a result, supplies were unloaded in random fashion which delayed unloading, reduced the efficiency of moving it forward, and delayed delivery of critically needed supplies to the front line troops. In the X Corps area, the 2nd Engineer Special Brigade[45] supervised the unloading and delivery of supplies. In XXIV Corps area, this assignment was the responsibility of the 1122nd and 1140th Engineer Combat Groups.[46]

*　　*　　*

As mentioned, one of the Sixth Army's support units at Leyte was the 2nd Engineer Special Brigade. This was one of six such units developed by the U.S. Army during the war to aid the amphibious assault landings that were going to be executed in the war effort. The point at which the Navy landed the army on the beaches and the support still needed by Navy water-borne craft had yet to be determined, but it was obvious that the ground troops, when first landing on an enemy-held beach, would need continuous support. How long and how detailed this support needed to be would vary with each assault landing. To address this need, the army developed within its Engineer Corps, the Engineer Special Brigade. These units were essentially seaborne army engineers whose tasks included landing army units on opposed beach-heads, preparing the beaches to receive the heavy equipment needed by the troops ashore, to unload heavy artillery, tanks and other large pieces of equipment and generally support the ground troops as they expanded the beach-head. The unit consisted of boat engineers, boat maintenance engineers, shore engineers and miscellaneous special troops, including communications personnel.

When the Leyte invasion was planned, the 2nd Engineer Special Brigade had already had much experience in New Guinea. Its boats were badly used, some damaged, others mechanically unreliable. To get its 400 small boats ready, the unit exchanged the less seaworthy ones with its sister Brigades[47] in New Guinea, and then loaded them aboard Navy ships for the passage to Leyte. This would be the first time that the engineers made a sea landing, all others in New Guinea having been shore-to-shore assaults.

After an uneventful trip to Leyte Gulf the landing craft were lowered, filled with troops, and the run to the beaches began. Enemy fire hit four of the Brigade's Landing Ships, Medium, some of them six times in a row. These guns were, however, in fixed positions and could not follow the landing craft once they landed on the beaches. Once ashore, the engineers found that the White Beaches were best suited for landing equipment and supplies. At Red Beach a bulldozer attempted to land to prepare the beach for incoming supplies, but as it rolled off the boat, it drowned in eight feet of water. The brigade had expected this, and also the grounding of the damaged LSTs who blocked access to the best beaches. They quickly went to work to clear the beaches. Causeways had been built to facilitate landing supplies and equipment and were installed that evening. The swamps behind the beaches presented obstacles to the engineers as did the antitank ditches the Japanese had built. Nevertheless, all the LSTs which landed on either Red or White Beaches were unloaded quickly and able to withdraw safely before dark. By A plus 1 the causeways were in place, making unloading easier and faster. Tide conditions also hampered the engineers who had to extend the causeway when the tide was low. They also had to implement repairs when one LST hit a causeway at full speed, damaging several sections.

As the invasion progressed, air raids became a problem, interrupting work each time the Japanese flew over. Beach parties from the assault troops and from the Naval transport vessels offshore were added to the beach engineers to expedite unloading, and this succeeded enough so that in some cases vessels were unloaded a day ahead of schedule. By A plus 2 they were handling an average of 100 tons per hour across the assault beaches. Meanwhile, a smaller detachment worked on the beaches of the detached infantry regiment to the south. There, small boats provided transportation for 72 patrols which explored the southern portion of Leyte without meeting opposition. Supplies were delivered to guerrillas and various contacts made throughout the area. When the typhoons hit the island, the army boatmen had to struggle to keep their boats afloat and most did so. The resulting deterioration of the Leyte road system placed an even heavier burden on the small craft, who now had to make up much of the transportation fleet whenever they could reach the troops in need. On return trips, they carried the sick and wounded. On many trips they had to fight off attacking Japanese aircraft. When elements of the 1st Cavalry Division landed on Samar, they were transported and defended by elements of the 2nd Engineer Special Brigade.

*   *   *

The landing beaches presented additional problems for the support troops. While XXIV Corps' beaches were relatively good for storing and moving supplies, those of X Corps were less satisfactory. The Red Beaches, where the 24th Infantry Division had come ashore, had poor beach exits and limited space for dispersal areas or storing supplies. Initially Landing Ships, Tank (LSTs) bringing supplies to the Red Beaches came under enemy fire and four of them received direct hits. Because of the beach gradients most LSTs had to land between 100 to 200 yards offshore. This further hindered swift unloading and sometimes cost valuable equipment. Because of unexpected delays the shore parties whose duties were to keep the beach clear and the supplies moving arrived late in X Corps sector and, therefore, started their job already well behind, with supplies dropped haphazardly all over the beach area. To reduce this backlog, additional units were assigned to assist the shore parties. To alleviate the congestion on the Red Beaches, many craft were diverted to the 1st Cavalry Division's White beaches where they could unload in under three feet of water. While this sped the unloading process it delayed the delivery process as the move from the White Beaches to the 24th Infantry Division now became much lengthier. Soon, however, the engineers built a two-lane road from the beach and Military Police were assigned to control traffic, making distribution easier. The swamps encountered by the assault troops also blocked the progress of the support troops. They limited the area in which supplies could be stored and forced considerable detours when delivering those same supplies to the combat troops. The more experienced 7th Infantry Division used a system in which the delivery vehicles, in their case DUKWs,[48] not only brought the supplies ashore but also delivered them to the assault troops as close to the front as possible. With this system it was not unusual for critical supplies to arrive within an hour of the original request.

Engineers began work at once, as soon as the beaches had been cleared by the assault troops. Obstacles were cleared and roads begun. Supply dump sites were chosen and built. Working in six hour shifts around the clock the engineers slowly but surely began to develop a base area behind the advancing infantry. So efficient were these engineer battalions that within seven hours, after landing 107,450 tons of supplies and equipment were landed and while some congestion remained, the flow of supplies was improving hourly.

*   *   *

The Japanese had begun the Battle of Leyte confidently. In part this was because they believed the stories told by their aviators about their great successes in the naval battle off Formosa. From these tales most Japanese leaders regarded the United States Navy as a severely damaged force incapable of major offensive action. Even those leaders who recognized the inflated claims of the Japanese fliers believed that serious damage had been done to the American fleet. This improved outlook changed the way *Imperial General Headquarters* decided to conduct the Battle for Leyte.

Originally, the decisive battle was to be fought on Luzon, the largest of the Philippine Islands and the location of its capital city, Manila. Hence, the major Japanese forces within the Philippines were stationed on, or destined for, Luzon. Only delaying actions, such as the defense of Leyte by the *16th Division*, would take place elsewhere to delay and damage the Americans further before the decisive battle took place. There was not complete agreement, however, and several senior Japanese leaders believed that Luzon could not be defended if other major islands in the Philippines were conquered by the Americans. These leaders believed that the decisive battle would be fought wherever and whenever the Americans landed in the Philippines.

To the Japanese, the naval battle off Formosa changed things. With a "damaged" American fleet now a reduced threat, *Imperial General Headquarters* decided that the Americans would not be attacked as they approached the Philippines. Only when they were close and committed to an attack on the islands would they be struck by the full might of the *Imperial Japanese Navy* and the *Imperial Japanese Army*. This was to be a knockout blow which would forever restore Japanese military power and lead to the war's negotiated conclusion.

The American Ranger landings had not, as the Americans first believed, gone unnoticed by the Japanese. When American forces were identified as standing off Suluan Island the *4th Air Army* ordered the *2nd Air Division* to launch full scale attacks against the Americans off Leyte. As of October 17th, the main strength of Japanese air defenses in the Philippines was to be concentrated against the central and southern Philippines. In accordance with these orders, the *2nd Air Division* began a move from Clark Field on Luzon to Bacolod on Negros Island. Only bad weather prevented a timely move and also prevented the Japanese air power from striking the Americans as they entered Leyte Gulf. By the time the weather broke it was realized that the American objective was, in fact, Leyte and new orders were issued directing the full weight of Japanese air power in the Philippines against the Americans at Leyte. In addition to the *2nd Air Division*, the *7th Air Division* and *30th Fighter Group* were directed to Leyte on October 21st. A coordinated aerial attack was to begin on October 23rd, and continued on the following day.

The *Imperial Japanese Navy* had established operational plans for the next major American offensive as early as July 1944. These plans called for a full-scale effort by the *Combined Fleet*, the majority of the capital ships left to Japan, to strike when and where the Americans revealed their intentions. Known as the Shō (Victory) Operation, it called for an all-or-nothing effort to smash the American Fleet and then smother any beachhead which had been established. Weak in aircraft carriers, and with little in the way of naval aviation resources, the Japanese planned to use the surface gunfire of their battleships, cruisers and destroyers to accomplish this goal. Their aircraft carriers would be used to decoy the main strength of the American Fleet, which was its large Fleet Carriers, away so that the Japanese surface fleet could get in close to the American fleet covering the amphibious landing. Like the air forces, the *Imperial Japanese Navy* issued orders to implement the Shō Operation on October 18th with Leyte Gulf as the area for the decisive battle.

The Japanese were determined to make Leyte the decisive battle that they had long been seeking. The air forces would strike the Leyte assault forces on October 23rd and 24th while the *Combined Fleet* expected to strike the same forces on October 25th, after they had been weakened by the Japanese air strikes. With the destruction of the Leyte invasion forces, the tide of war would have turned in favor of the Japanese or at the very least have prolonged the war giving Japan a more favorable bargaining position should a negotiated peace become possible. In the meantime, the battle on Leyte continued.

*   *   *

Private Harold H. Moon, Jr., was not your typical soldier. Indeed, he seemed to fit more the Hollywood character-type than the recruiting poster-type of soldier. As a member of Company G, 34th Infantry Regiment, Private Moon had some difficulties while in garrison. He had led several card playing games with his buddies on the way to Leyte and had won an estimated $1,200. While on the transport, he had sometimes slipped into Navy uniforms to get ice water or other luxuries not available to soldiers aboard ship. He had even worn a First Lieutenant's insignia on his army fatigues for reasons never explained. Landing in the third wave at Red Beach, he had fought his way forward with Company G until nightfall. As the battalion settled in for the night, several outposts were set out to warn of enemy attack. Private Moon manned one of these outposts.

The Japanese did indeed intend to counterattack. Three companies of infantry from the *33rd Infantry Regiment* gathered in front of Lieutenant Colonel James F. Pearsall, Jr.'s 2nd Battalion, 34th Infantry. They came at about 0100 Hours on the morning of October 21st with rifle and machine gun fire. Mortar shells began falling among the Americans on the front lines. Private Moon called in from his outpost and warned the rest of Company G that an attack was coming. They were all around the outposts with several floating down the rice paddies with mortars and machine guns. Armed with a Thompson sub-machine gun, Private Moon began to fight back. As others in nearby positions were killed or wounded, the soldier from Gardena, California, covered their positions with fire from his own. He, too, was soon wounded by the attacking Japanese.

Still firing back, Private Moon became the focus of the enemy attack. Machine gun, mortar and rifle fire pounded his foxhole. Refusing to be driven out, he maintained his defense while shouting encouragement to those who still survived around him. Repeatedly he exposed himself to direct fire at the attacking enemy troops. A Japanese officer, covered by machine gun and mortar fire, attempted to destroy Private Moon with grenades. The two called each other names in English while each tried to kill the other. Each time the enemy officer tossed a grenade, Private Moon would yell back, "missed." Likewise, when the American tried to shoot the Japanese as he tossed his grenades, the Japanese officer would yell across the same reply. Eventually, however, Private Moon sat up on the edge of his foxhole and dared the enemy officer to toss another grenade. When he did, Private Moon cut him down.

The Japanese then moved a machine gun to within twenty yards of Moon's foxhole, pinning down the entire platoon. Private Moon stood up to locate the gun's exact position and called back the coordinates to the mortar squad, all the while still exposed to enemy fire. The mortars knocked out the weapon and Private Moon directed his fire on more attacking Japanese. Two Japanese attacked an American aid man, but Private Moon cut them down before they could reach the man and his wounded patient. As dawn approached, he was surrounded by Japanese, all of his companions having been killed or wounded. His isolated position alone prevented the Japanese from achieving a breakthrough to the beach with its supply installations, hospitals, and other rear echelon services.

The Japanese now directed their full attention at Private Moon, allowing the rest of Company G to better prepare themselves for a continued attack. Japanese soldiers shouted insults in English. Private Moon, not to be outdone, yelled back, "Come and get me! If you want me, come and get me!"[49] To overrun this stubborn American, an entire Japanese platoon charged him directly. Private Moon stood his ground, and unleashed his automatic weapon on the charging Japanese. As the Japanese retreated, Private Moon stood up yet again to toss a grenade into a nearby enemy machine gun. He was hit and instantly killed. When dawn finally came, some 200 Japanese dead were found around his position and there had been no breakthrough. For his courage and devotion to duty, Private Harold H. Moon, Jr., was awarded a posthumous Medal of Honor.[50]

The time gained by Private Moon had permitted Company G to organize a counterattack during which a bayonet charge drove off the surviving Japanese. But before they withdrew, Private First Class Samuel Jerma, another member of Company G, held a machine gun position with two buddies in the forefront of the Japanese attack. After repulsing one attack, a second struck supported by mortars and machine guns. A grenade fell into the foxhole and wounded one of his assistants. Private First Class Jerma moved the wounded man to the rear for treatment and then returned to his gun. Firing again as the Japanese came on, he saw his other buddy killed. By this time the machine gun position was surrounded and Private First Class Jerma, although wounded himself by this time, moved the gun to a new location alone. He remained there firing his gun until its ammunition was exhausted. As dawn broke, Private First Class Jerma took his wounded buddy further back to safety, then returned to lead his squad as Company G launched their own attack.

Not far from Private First Class Jerma, Private First Class John W. Ray, of Company C, 34th Infantry, had fought off four suicide attacks by the Japanese at his forward position. He, too, soon found himself surrounded as the Japanese penetrated between his position and others of men killed or wounded. The few men left around Private First Class Ray began to withdraw just as dawn broke over the battlefield. Private First Class Ray decided to cover their withdrawal with his rifle. Although already seriously wounded by this time, he placed a deadly fire upon the advancing Japanese to allow his buddies to safely withdraw from their exposed positions. Finally, he followed the last man out of the position, all the while providing covering fire as he withdrew, protecting his friends. When he noticed a wounded man lying on the ground, he enlisted the aid of another soldier and pulled the man fifty yards to the rear, despite direct Japanese fire. Spotting an enemy machine gun and a sniper up a nearby tree, Private First Class Ray opened fire on both, killing them before they could injure his companions. While guarded by his comrades, Private First Class Ray administered first aid to the other wounded Americans and hid in the high grass those too critically injured to be moved. Still suffering from his own untreated wounds, he again covered his buddies as they withdrew further to the rear. Despite suffering from fatigue, shock and blood loss, he volunteered to lead a platoon back to the front line to rescue the wounded men he had hidden.

As Company G mopped up, they found some 600 dead Japanese in the general area of the company's defense. Although some of these were credited to air support, the majority had been the result of the defense led by Private Moon and Privates First Class Jerma and Ray. Company G lost fourteen men killed and twelve wounded.[51]

The nearby 3rd Battalion, 34th Infantry, had also been hit by a counterattack that night. After probing the perimeter of Company L for several hours, Japanese machine guns opened a covering fire while a platoon of infantry attacked, supported by mortar fire. Company L counterattacked the

Japanese and after several hours of fighting, repelled the Japanese, who left approximately one hundred dead in front of the American lines.

In the 19th Infantry's zone, the surrounded 1st Battalion was also attacked. With yells and grenades coming in out of the dark night, the Japanese struck Hill 522. Coming up the Palo-Tacloban Highway, the Japanese hit the battalion with a fierce attack aimed at pushing them off the vital hill. An American machine gun section under Sergeant Karl Geis of the Bronx, New York, stood guard near the highway. Enemy mortar and machine gun fire came out of the darkness, but no enemy was seen. Scouts could see no enemy troops on the road. And then suddenly the Japanese came out of the bushes, trees and brush along the highway and charged the guns. Covered by mortars, machine guns, grenades and rifle fire, the Japanese came after Sergeant Geis' two machine guns. The gunners fired without resting or cooling their barrels. Several were wounded but others quickly took their place. Those not firing or feeding ammunition to the two guns, fired their rifles and carbines as fast as they could. Finally dawn came, and the guns remained in place. In front of them lay one hundred-sixty dead Japanese soldiers.

On the right flank of the battalion was another machine gun section under Sergeant Eric Erickson of Blairstown, New Jersey. They, too, were hit with a strong enemy counterattack. At one point, the Japanese managed to place one of their own machine guns behind a mound of rubble and fire into the flank of Sergeant Erickson's position. This fire forced his gunners to seek cover, and slowed his fire at the oncoming Japanese. Sergeant Erickson knew he had to do something. He belly crawled through grass and mud until he outflanked the enemy gun. Getting close enough to see its muzzle blast, Sergeant Erickson tossed three grenades into the position. No more fire came from the enemy gun and Sergeant Erickson's gunners returned to their work of breaking up the attacking enemy.

With dawn, the Americans counterattacked. Supported by the 63rd Field Artillery Battalion and navy aircraft from the Seventh U.S. Fleet, Colonel Pearsall's advance soon broke the back of the enemy counterattack effort. Japanese were observed scattering into the rice paddies in an effort to avoid American fire during their retreat. In this, many were unsuccessful, and the 2nd Battalion, 34th Infantry counted several hundred more enemy dead during their advance that morning.

*　　*　　*

Now that the American invasion of Leyte had changed the plans of the

Japanese with regard as to how to defend the Philippines, General Yamashita reluctantly directed that the main effort be made on that island. On October 21st, he advised the *35th Army* that it should concentrate all of its forces on Leyte for the decisive battle in cooperation with the *Imperial Japanese Navy* and air force units. General Suzuki was ordered to transfer the *1st* and *26th Infantry Divisions* as well as the *68th Independent Mixed Brigade* to Leyte where they would engage in that decisive battle for the Philippines. Artillery units of the *14th Area Army* were also being sent to Leyte in support. He was further advised that Japanese naval and air forces would cooperate in this final battle. This news was welcomed by the *35th Army* who until now had believed that they were to be sacrificed in a delaying battle. Now they were to lead the main defense of the Philippines on Leyte.

Their morale was helped by the fact that their intelligence remained incomplete. At this time, General Suzuki believed that only two American divisions had landed on Leyte and that with his full *35th Army*, which also included the *30th* and *102nd Infantry Divisions,* he could readily crush the invaders, winning the decisive victory. He immediately ordered the *30th Infantry Division* from Mindanao to Leyte, leaving behind three infantry battalions as garrison. Battalions from the *102nd Infantry Division* and the *55th* and *57th Independent Mixed Brigades* were also ordered to Leyte. Knowing that the Americans would need some time to consolidate their two beachheads and that the seizure of Catmon Hill and Tacloban would take additional time, he believed that his *16th Infantry Division* could delay them until these reinforcements arrived to begin the final battle for Leyte. With Japanese naval and air forces about to shatter the enemy fleet offshore, the Americans would be hard pressed to maintain even their existing beachheads, much less move inland. Most of his orders for the next few weeks were based upon these faulty assumptions.

Accordingly, General Suzuki ordered that the reinforcements from Mindanao and other islands were to be concentrated in the Carigara vicinity. While the reinforcements arrived and concentrated for the final counterattack, the *16th Infantry Division* would defend the area around Burauen and Dagami while elements would occupy Catmon Hill and the plateau west of Tacloban. This would protect the concentration of his reserves while slowing the American advance to a crawl. Behind the *16th Infantry Division,* the *102nd Infantry Division* would occupy Jaro to protect the concentration of the *1st* and *26th Infantry Divisions.* The *30th Infantry Division* would land at Ormoc Bay and then move forward to Burauen to support the *16th*

Infantry Division's defense of that area. Reinforcements would be landed as early as possible at both Ormoc Bay and Carigara Bay. One phase of the plan originally called for the *68th Independent Mixed Brigade* to land near Catmon Hill if the situation permitted, which of course it never did. Once the bulk of the *35th Army* had assembled it was to move from Carigara down Leyte Valley, annihilating the Americans as they marched.

Catmon Hill was a key feature of General Suzuki's defense. A series of smaller hills and ridges rather than one single hill mass, the hill starts at the Labiranan River near San Jose and runs generally northwest towards San Vincente where it drops to meet the coastal plain. Although few trees were in evidence it was covered by thick and tall cogon grass which provided sufficient concealment for its defenders. Its height and position overlooking the coast gave it critical tactical importance.

The Japanese defenders were two battalions of the *9th Infantry Regiment* supported by elements of the *22nd Field Artillery Regiment*. Using caves for shelters, artillery positions and supply dumps, they constructed coconut log pillboxes of considerable strength and easy concealment. Spider holes protected the pillboxes and caves. American naval and field artillery had pounded the hill since prior to the invasion and these had caused some casualties and seriously disrupted communications. Several guns of the *22nd Field Artillery Regiment* had been knocked out by this fire. To further disturb the Japanese defenders the guns of the 361st Field Artillery Battalion[52] shelled the hill throughout the night of 20-21 October.

October 21st opened with an air strike against Labiranan Head, followed by three hours of naval and field artillery gunfire. The 96th Infantry Division was to move inland, seizing Catmon Hill while maintaining contact with the 7th Infantry Division on its flank. General Bradley had assigned the task of seizing Catmon Hill to the 383rd Infantry while the 382nd Infantry maintained contact with the neighboring division. In turn, Colonel May had ordered Lieutenant Colonel Edwin O. List to attack the hill with his 1st Battalion, while the other battalions tried to outflank the hill from the northwest.

The assault force was a composite company under the command of Captain Hugh D. Young[53] His force consisted of a rifle platoon each from Companies A, B and C along with a weapons platoon from Company C. They started out well, moving up the hill and knocking out two machine guns within ten minutes of starting the climb. The Japanese quickly abandoned the hill under the cover of mortar fire. Rather than continue in the face of enemy fire, Captain Young's group was ordered off the hill to allow for a further naval bombardment of the hill mass. They worked their way down to the Labiranan River and swam across to rejoin their battalion.

While Captain Young's force had been attacking, a platoon under Second Lieutenant Maurice Stein from Company C had been manning a roadblock along the coastal highway across the river from the objective. When Captain Young attacked, Lieutenant Stein and his men moved up the slopes of Liberanan Head in an attempt to hit the flank of the Japanese defenders. When they got to within twenty yards from the Japanese, they were hit with fire from three sides. After knocking out another machine gun, the platoon withdrew.

The following day after hours of artillery bombardment the battalion attacked again. Under continual artillery support from the 921st, 362nd and 361st Field Artillery Battalions,[54] Companies A and C worked their way steadily through the enemy defenses, knocking out pillboxes and entrenchments as they went. A strong Japanese counterattack was launched against the battalion but pre-registered fires from the supporting artillery battalions stopped the attack before any progress could be made. Not to be outdone, Lieutenant Stein's platoon picked up some tanks from the 763rd Tank Battalion and additional support from the Regimental Cannon and Antitank Companies to push through the enemy defenses along the road and occupy San Roque along the coast. A few days later, a group from Cannon Company pushed along the coast as far as Tanauan, where they made the first physical contact with a patrol of Alamo Scouts[55] that the 24th Infantry Division had sent out from the X Corps perimeter.

For the next several days the 383rd Infantry Regiment held what they had gained. This was easier said than done. All supplies, including food, water, ammunition and medical needs had to be hand-carried up the hill by soldiers. These carrying parties usually consisted of cooks led by the company mess sergeants and were constantly under sniper fire and the occasional long-range mortar or artillery fire. On the 27th of October, Colonel List led a combat patrol from Company B, reinforced with machine guns from Company D, against Labir Hill. As they reached the crest of the hill, enemy mortar and machine gun fire hit them hard. Captain Richard C. Ufford, the commander of Company D and Captain Walter J. Guthridge, the battalion operations officer, were killed along with seven enlisted men. Colonel List and thirty-two others were wounded. Sergeant Alonza Self, a B Company mortar man, volunteered to be the rear guard as the patrol withdrew. He covered the withdrawal with his BAR until five enemy soldiers attacked him. Although he killed his attackers, he himself was mortally wounded. He received a posthumous Silver Star. Major Byron F. King took command of the battalion.

* * *

While the First Battalion went after Catmon Hill directly, the regiment's other two battalions tried to outflank it. For three days these two battalions struggled through the swamps which General MacArthur believed were impassable. Fighting the swamps was bad enough but enemy artillery fire took a steady toll in casualties among the Americans as they worked their way forward. There were Japanese casualties, too, as the Americans occasionally encountered small groups of Japanese in the swamps or night-time infiltrators, who were quickly eliminated.

On October 23rd, Company G, leading Lieutenant Colonel James O. McCray's 2nd Battalion, 383rd Infantry, reached the Guinarona River near the town of Pikas. Apparently the defending Japanese, like General MacArthur, did not expect Americans to cross the swamp. A group was surprised while swimming in the river. Opening fire immediately, Company G and Company F crossed the river and had a brief firefight with about fifty Japanese who were killed. Followed by Lieutenant Colonel Edward W. Stare's 3rd Battalion, the Americans dug in for the night in a perimeter defense. Soon after dark, the Japanese launched an attack against the perimeter held by Company F. Under the cover of machine guns and mortars, the Japanese charged. Private First Class Clyde O. Franklin of Company F, was firing his BAR when it was shot out of his hands. Instead of reporting to the aid station, he grabbed another weapon and continued to defend the perimeter. He was awarded a Silver Star. Company F's mess sergeant, Staff Sergeant Barney Hewitt led a patrol back to the rear for supplies as the battle raged. Knowing that anyone moving around at night was subject to fire from both sides, he nevertheless led his patrol there and back successfully and without casualties. Soon after the patrol returned, the Japanese withdrew.

Reports from Philippine Guerrillas indicated that there was a large enemy troop concentration around the town of Tabontabon, which lay beyond Catmon Hill. Company K sent a patrol to investigate. The patrol found extensive enemy fortifications, but no troops. Knowing that possession of Tabontabon would cut off enemy communications to Catmon Hill, Company K, reinforced with a platoon of machine guns from Company M, set out to seize Tabontabon.

As the leading Americans entered the town they were hit by enemy fire.

In the time it took for Company K to reach the town, some two hundred enemy troops had occupied it. A fierce firefight developed. Two scouts, Privates First Class Samuel Mendoza and Warren L. Gullickson, crawled into town ahead of the leading platoon. Private First Class Mendoza killed two Japanese in spider holes but was wounded in the process. Despite his wounds, he continued forward and was joined by Private First Class Gullickson. Together they knocked out an enemy machine gun but both men were hit again. By this time, Private First Class Mendoza had three wounds. Still they moved forward, knocking out a second machine gun with grenades. Finally, with their wounds still untreated, they crawled back to their company. Private First Class Mendoza received the Distinguished Service Cross[56] and Private First Class Gullickson, the Silver Star. Having lost seven men killed and ten wounded, and with one officer dying of his wounds, the company withdrew.

San Vincente Hill lay at the inland end of Catmon Hill, between that hill and Tabontabon Village. Capture of the hill would serve the same purpose in cutting Japanese communications to Catmon Hill and perhaps force a withdrawal of the garrison. Company E was given the assignment of seizing San Vincente Hill. Captain Jesse Thomas led his men forward after a ten-minute artillery barrage by the 155mm guns of the 363rd Field Artillery Battalion. Observing the fire, Captain Thomas remarked, "The artillery fire came down but was not quite far enough down the hill and in my opinion was ineffective in that we were unable to get it just where we wanted it on the hill."[57] Nevertheless, the attack went in against rifle and grenade-launcher fire from the *9th Infantry Regiment*. Using his supporting mortars to silence some of the enemy fire, Captain Thomas worked his company forward. As he did so, Colonel McCray joined Captain Thomas in his command post. Several wounded lay in front and Colonel McCray crawled out to assist in bringing them to safety. Soon snipers were firing into the command post from the rear. With enemy fire from front and rear, Captain Thomas still worked his company toward their objective. As he did so, he suddenly passed out from heat exhaustion. The Executive Officer, First Lieutenant Owen R. O'Neill, took over and came forward.

Using smoke to conceal the recovery of his wounded, Lieutenant O'Neill directed a withdrawal from San Vincente Hill. Four hours under enemy fire, the heat and humidity of a Philippine day had depleted the company significantly. Lieutenant O'Neill later said, "The wounded could be heard groaning and crying for help. Japs could be heard yelling. Then the men who had been groaning would cry out in pain and then cease moaning. The Japs had bayoneted them."[58] Volunteers from other companies came forward to help with the evacuation of the wounded. Captain Thomas revived and resumed command. Colonel McCray continued to help with the wounded. Litters with wounded soldiers had to be dragged along the ground until they were away from the battlefield, to avoid enemy fire. As the evacuation progressed, searches were conducted to ensure that no wounded men were left behind. Captain Thomas was one of the searchers. "We started searching the area for wounded in order to evacuate them. I found the body of Colonel McCray. From the position his body was lying in, it seemed that he was coming back from dragging the wounded out of the field. Three of us tried to bring his body back with us, but this caused so many casualties that we had to leave him and move the wounded instead."[59] The fight cost the battalion sixty-five casualties.

For the next two days, the two battalions probed San Vincente Hill, trying to locate the main enemy defenses. Meanwhile, Colonel Michael E. Halloran's 381st Infantry Regiment[60] had been released from Sixth Army Reserve to General Bradley. He decided immediately to add them to the ongoing battle for Catmon Hill. They were to pass through the 1st Battalion, 383rd Infantry, and attack. Advancing after a heavy barrage of division artillery and the massed fire of 4.2-inch mortars of the 88th Chemical Mortar Battalion,[61] Lieutenant Colonel Russell Graybill's 2nd Battalion, 381st Infantry, soon reached the top of Labir Hill against minimal opposition. Once on top they captured some 3,000 rounds of Japanese artillery ammunition. On the opposite side of the hill, Lieutenant Colonel John G. Cassidy led his 1st Battalion, 381st Infantry, up from the seaward side but heavy enemy fire soon turned them back. The next morning, the 780th Amphibian Tank Battalion[62] massed some forty-five tanks which fired directly into the enemy positions while Colonel Cassidy's men forced their way up the hill. There they joined the Second Battalion on top and mopped up the area for the next two days. The Americans cleared fifty-three pillboxes, seventeen caves and numerous smaller entrenched positions.

Clearing the final beachhead zone remained dangerous and deadly, however. On 28 October, Technical Sergeant John C. Rea was leading his platoon of the Company I, 381st Infantry, 96th Infantry Division near Kiling, when it came under enemy fire. Technical Sergeant Rea, commanding the right flank platoon, ordered his men to seek cover along a nearby road while he arranged for cover fire. Once covering fire had been established, Technical Sergeant Rea led his men across 150 yards of open area to a new location where he reorganized them in preparation for a further advance. The soldier from Salem, Oregon, then moved his platoon to the edge of another clearing where they were pinned down by enemy fire. Sergeant Rea jumped to his feet and armed only with his M-1 Rifle advanced walking slowly towards the enemy. Firing from the hip, he killed several Japanese who attacked him with small arms and grenades. When his ammunition was exhausted, Sergeant Rea fixed his bayonet and continued his attack, despite the heavy Japanese fire still sweeping the clearing. Observing their platoon leader's advance and additional Japanese falling to the gallant sergeant's bayonet, the rest of the platoon rallied and charged across the clearing into the Japanese position, clearing it and releasing Company I and others from the accurate enemy fire which had earlier pinned them to the ground. For his courage and leadership that day Technical Sergeant John C. Rea was awarded a Distinguished Service Cross.[63]

The Japanese had apparently decided that the Catmon Hill positions could no longer be held after suffering heavy casualties from the earlier attacks of the 383rd Infantry at San Vincente and Labir Hill. The remaining enemy evacuated the hill mass sometime between those attacks and the advance of the 381st Infantry. Survivors assembled near Dagami where they rejoined the rest of the *16th Infantry Division*. Catmon Hill was secure, as was the American XXIV Corps beachhead.

*   *   *

While the ground forces had been struggling to secure their beachheads, the Japanese had been struggling to destroy them. On October 24th, a heavy Japanese air attack struck the area when an estimated 200 enemy aircraft flew to northern Leyte. American air claimed sixty-six shot down and others damaged. Americans flying from the now operational Tacloban airfields, flew air cover over the fleet and the beaches. Meanwhile the *Imperial Japanese Navy* launched its attempt at the decisive battle off Leyte. The naval Battle of Leyte Gulf, well covered by other histories on World War II, was the largest naval battle of the Pacific War, but in the end it availed the Japanese nothing. Despite sinking one light carrier, two escort carriers, two destroyers and one destroyer escort and crippling several other ships, the beachheads were never endangered and the essential transports untouched.

The enemy air activity did not cease with the defeat of the *Imperial Japanese Navy*. Japanese aircraft continued to fly over Leyte. On October 27th, several enemy planes bombed Tacloban with 100-pound bombs but were unable to damage the airfield. Daylight raids were becoming common, and night raids were expected each night. Often the entire night was filled with air raids. The airfields and shipping offshore were the main targets. The *2nd Air Division* kept up a full schedule of air attacks from October 24th through October 28th. The *4th Air Army* was occupied covering the reinforcement convoys which were transporting troops and supplies to the *35th Army*.

American air power attacked repeatedly the airfields from which the Japanese were believed to be launching their air attacks. They also directed much of their air power against the Japanese planes escorting the reinforcement convoys to Leyte. These combined attacks soon began to tell on the *4th Air Army*. Their losses, which were difficult to replace, began to increase alarmingly. The battle slowly began to go against the Japanese until by November 1st, after a failed aerial counterattack, the *4th Air Army* received orders to withdraw its remaining assets to protect the Leyte reinforcement convoys forming in and around Manila. By this time, the well-equipped and well-manned Japanese air forces were so reduced that the new concept of the suicide pilot, or *Kamikaze*, seemed their only hope of a successful intervention in the battle for Leyte. That, and the still creditable hope of defeating the American army on Leyte, was all that remained of the decisive battle upon which Japan had placed its last hope of a successful conclusion to the Pacific War it had started barely three years earlier.

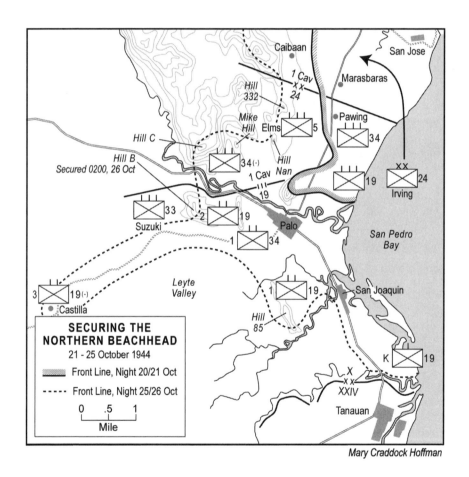

Caibaan
San Jose
1 Cav
XX
24
Hill
332
Marasbaras
Mike
Hill   Elms
Pawing
Hill C
5
34
Hill B
Secured 0200, 26 Oct
34(-)
Hill
Nan
1 Cav
19
19   24
Irving
33
19
Suzuki
2
19
1   34
Palo
San Pedro
Bay
Leyte
Valley
1   19
San Joaquin
3   19(-)
Castilla
Hill
85
K   19

SECURING THE
NORTHERN BEACHHEAD
21 - 25 October 1944

▨ Front Line, Night 20/21 Oct

- - - Front Line, Night 25/26 Oct

0   .5   1
Mile

X
X X
XXIV

Tanauan

Mary Craddock Hoffman

CHAPTER 3

INTO THE VALLEYS

D espite the loss of Catmon Hill and their other beach defenses, the Japanese remained confident that they would defeat the American invasion of the Philippines at Leyte. There were 432,000 Japanese soldiers in the Philippines, who were well supplied, and who believed that their naval and air forces were strong enough to support their counterattacks. One of the *14th Area Army's* staff officers was quoted as saying, when he learned of the Leyte invasion, "Good, they have picked the place where our finest troops are located."[1] Japanese troops and supplies were already in the process of being transported to Ormoc and Carigara Bays on Leyte. So quickly did this transfer begin that by October 25th, less than a week after the invasion, a battalion of the *55th Independent Mixed Brigade* and another from the *57th Independent Mixed Brigade* had already arrived on Leyte as did two battalions from the *30th Infantry Division*. These reinforcements made up for Japanese losses at the beachheads. Japanese commanders still believed that the American forces were much weaker than they actually were and that the Americans were already having a hard time consolidating their beachheads. As the *35th Army's* Chief of Staff, Major General Yoshiharu Tomochika later put it to American interrogators, "We were determined to take offensive after offensive and clean up American forces on Leyte Island . . . We seriously discussed demanding the surrender of the entire American army after seizing General MacArthur."[2]

Things looked differently from the "other side of the hill." General Krueger was ashore on October 22nd visiting X Corps in the Dulag and Palo areas. The visit "satisfied me that everything was going well."[3] Due to congestion on the beaches, Sixth Army Headquarters remained aboard ship for the first few days until a suitable location was found ashore. Finally, a spot near San José, south of the Tacloban Airfield, was selected and the army staff settled in. Information soon began to come in that the Japanese were sending reinforcements to the Leyte garrison through Ormoc Bay.[4] Information from guerrillas soon identified the *41st Infantry Regiment* of the *30th Infantry Division* among the reinforcements. Within a week the *169th* and *171st Independent Infantry Battalions,* as well as two battalions from the *102nd Infantry Division,* had also been identified by Sixth Army intelligence. The *20th Antitank Battalion* and other elements of the *30th Infantry Division* were soon added to the growing list. As if the rapid enemy reinforcements weren't enough of a problem, three successive typhoons with torrential rains and winds hit the east coast of Leyte. Trees were uprooted, terrain flooded and all movement halted until repairs could be made. "But in spite of all these difficulties and the stubborn resistance of the enemy, we were making satisfactory progress and I (Krueger) so informed General MacArthur when he visited my headquarters early on the 28th."[5]

*   *   *

North of XXIV Corps, the X Corps had also moved ahead. The 1st Cavalry Division was to secure Tacloban, pushing the *33rd Infantry Regiment* away from one of the cornerstones of General Suzuki's delaying line. Anxious to push into Leyte Valley and secure critical road junctions, roads and airfields, General Krueger ordered the advance to continue without pause. Capture of Tacloban would allow the Americans to control San Juanico Strait which, coincidentally, put an end to the Japanese plan to land the *68th Mixed Brigade* near Catmon Hill. It would also secure Tacloban Airfield and open a route into Leyte Valley.

General Mudge gave the 7th Cavalry the assignment. Colonel Walter Finnegan's regiment brought its two squadrons to bear and attacked through swampy terrain which slowed but did not stop the attack. As the Cavalrymen approached, resistance was minimal, and while they conducted a house-to-house search for hidden Japanese, the local Filipinos gave them a riotous welcome, waving American flags and showering them with gifts of eggs and fruit in general celebration. On the flank, however, the 2nd Squadron, 7th Cavalry, was stopped by 200 Japanese entrenched in pillboxes and foxholes on 1,500-foot Hill 215 and hidden in thick vegetation. Colonel Finnegan sent the regimental Antitank Platoon and Weapons Troop to assist. Private First Class Kenneth W. Grove, an ammunition carrier from Racine, Wisconsin, volunteered to knock out a bunker which had pinned down his platoon. Working his way forward under fire through the underbrush to the rear of the bunker, he then charged across a remaining open area and killed the enemy gun crew. For his courage, Private First Class Grove received the Silver Star.

It took the rest of the day and into the next to clear Hill 215, but the 7th Cavalry secured the area and found 335 dead enemy troops in and around the hill. With the fall of the hill, Tacloban was in American hands. As General Mudge inspected the town from a tank, he ordered it to clear an overturned truck which the Japanese had left as a road block. As he did so, forty Formosan laborers happily gave themselves up to the commanding general. Elements of the 8th Cavalry Regiment established themselves along the beach at Anibong Point to control San Juanico Strait. The 1st Cavalry Brigade moved forward apace protecting the division's flank. As they did so, the 12th Cavalry captured a large Japanese supply dump with food, vehicles and equipment. Nearby the 5th Cavalry encountered a group of Japanese who indicated they wished to surrender. An experienced unit, the 5th Cavalry set up machine guns before allowing the Japanese to approach their positions. As they did so the Japanese opened fire on the Americans who returned the fire effectively. Five Americans were wounded in the encounter. For the next few days most skirmishes were like this, small groups of Japanese eliminated or pushed back by the advancing Cavalrymen.

In order to fully secure San Juanico Strait, elements of the 8th and 7th Cavalry made a number of waterborne movements to establish bases along the Leyte shoreline. Occasional Japanese resistance was soon overcome and the strait secured. Other elements landed on the adjacent island of Samar and established bases there as well. By the end of October 24th, the 8th Cavalry was firmly established, with tank and artillery support, on Samar.

To the south, the 24th Infantry Division had established its firm beachhead near Palo. They had seized Hill 522 and overlooked the critical village of Palo, which became the next objective. Using a road which led northwest through Leyte Valley towards Carigara, the 34th Infantry Regiment placed two battalions on either side of the road prepared to advance. Covered by the 19th Infantry on Hill 522, the advance began after the Japanese counterattack at 0100 Hours the morning of October 21.[6] After the attack was defeated the Americans instituted heavy artillery, air and mortar barrages on suspected

Japanese positions to their front. This delayed the advance until about 1400 Hours when Companies E and F were ordered forward to seize a hill. Company E encountered no opposition but Company F, under Captain Austin, faced a steep hill covered by cogon grass. Visibility was limited and access restricted to a trail leading to the top. Moving in a column of platoons, F Company reached the foot of the hill without difficulty. While the 2nd Platoon continued up the trail the other platoons turned to advance directly to the top. Just as the 1st Platoon reached the hill's crest, about 200 Japanese from the *33rd Infantry Regiment* opened fire. With the 1st Platoon pinned down the Japanese began to toss grenades onto the 2nd Platoon still struggling up the hill. This defense stopped the attack. Soon both platoons were forced off the hill entirely.

The following morning, an air strike by Navy planes was requested, but did not arrive until afternoon. After ten minutes of close air support the Japanese fire seemed to weaken considerably and Captain Austin, this time accompanied by the regimental commander, Colonel Newman, led Company F back to the hill. The Americans swept over the hill, suffered no casualties and secured the area by mid-afternoon.

Nearby the 19th Infantry finished mopping up around Hill 522 and eliminated the last of the *33rd Infantry Regiment*'s survivors in the area. In the rear the 3rd Battalion, 19th Infantry prepared to seize a bend in the beach road near Palo, to secure that area. Naval gunfire was used to clear a path toward the objective, which was known to be defended by mutually supporting and well-built pillboxes of logs and earth, with trenches and spider holes throughout the area. After bombarding the area all night with naval gunfire, mortars and artillery, the 3rd Battalion attacked on the afternoon of October 22nd. The advance of the leading units, Company I and the Antitank Company, was halted at the bend in the road some 200 yards short of the town. The following morning, reinforced with the 1st Battalion, 34th Infantry, the attack was renewed. Corporal Irving Duane of Sacramento, California rolled his big tank destroyer through the dense thickets until reaching a clearing. There he knocked out one enemy position after another as they opened fire on him. Enemy fire eventually knocked out his vehicle's periscope, but after pulling back and replacing it, Corporal Duane returned to the fight until he ran out of targets. The two battalions pushed the *33rd Infantry Regiment* out of its defenses, leaving two hundred and seventy-six dead behind, while to the north the 2nd Battalion, 19th Infantry attacked Palo directly.

Moving through machine gun and rifle fire, the soldiers bypassed enemy defenses and reached the junction of the beach road and Highway One before noon. Still under enemy artillery and automatic weapons fire, the battalion scattered small groups of Japanese who resisted their advance until they reached the critical steel bridge over the Palo River. Here incoming artillery fire increased in intensity but the Americans speeded their advance and crossed the bridge into Palo by mid-afternoon. Once again the Americans were welcomed with an exuberant group of Filipinos who had to be ordered to seek shelter while the Americans cleared the town. After booby traps and field entrenchments were found and destroyed, but no Japanese were seen, they set up a defensive perimeter for the night.

Just before dark the 2nd Battalion, 19th Infantry was joined by the 13th Field Artillery Battalion.[7] The artillerymen immediately opened up on the Japanese surrounding Palo. Incoming fire exploded a Japanese ammunition dump in one of the houses and the fire burned, illuminating the night, for three hours. Shortly before dawn, the *33rd Infantry Regiment* launched a counterattack, coming down Highway Two. Outposts managed to deflect the attack, which then hit Company F and Company G. The battalion mortars soon exhausted all their ammunition in supporting the defense. So Battery B of the 13th Field Artillery moved closer to the lines—for artillery it was point-blank range—and opened fire on the attacking Japanese. Despite this fierce defense the Japanese continued with their attack. One platoon attempted to reach the steel bridge which was the American lifeline into Palo but were unsuccessful. Lieutenant Colonel Robert B. Spragins directed the defense from the window of a Philippine house in Palo, looking over the battlefield. Wounded in the forehead by shrapnel, he was bandaged and back at his window seat within minutes. After losses of 16 men killed and 44 wounded, the 19th Infantry had repulsed the Japanese, who left behind 91 killed. In daylight the battalion requested an emergency re-supply of ammunition and evacuation of wounded, both of which were accomplished despite the Japanese mining the supply route. That afternoon the 3rd Battalion moved into Palo, as did 19th Infantry Regimental headquarters. Palo was now secure. Contact with XXIV Corps to the south was made on October 25th by patrols.

The Japanese were not finished with Palo, however. Colonel Tatsunosuke Suzuki, commanding the *33rd Infantry Regiment*, organized a raiding party armed with rifles, swords, grenades and mines. He led this group into Palo on the night of October 23rd. Using civilian Filipinos as shields to screen them from the Americans, they fooled guards at the outposts into believing them to be guerrillas and letting them pass. Some of the captured Filipinos, at the risk of their lives, alerted the guards to the oncoming Japanese. But the enemy quickly captured two American machine guns and a 37mm anti-tank gun. Charging through the town they tossed grenades into houses, vehicles and a tank. Some entered a hospital where they killed helpless wounded. They were only prevented from burning down the hospital by Sergeant George Nieman and Corporal Eugene Holdeness, both wounded, who opened fire on the Japanese and distracted them. Others moved toward the steel bridge where they mounted the captured machine guns and opened fire. However, the bridge guards were not unprepared and responded with such accurate fire that the Japanese were forced to abandon the guns and retreat. Private First Class Frank Wisnieuski took over a machine gun when the gunner was wounded. Alone, he faced a large attacking force. Three of them threw grenades into his hole. He jumped clear, waited for the explosions, and then jumped back in the hole. He had no idea if the gun would still fire, but he was determined to make a stand. As two Japanese charged him with fixed bayonets, he grabbed the gun's trigger and squeezed. The charging Japanese went down, and by dawn, there were twenty more enemy dead counted in front of Private Wisnieuski's position. African-American Quartermaster troops in the town joined in the defense. Colonel Chapman, the regimental commander, whose headquarters had just moved into the town, organized his headquarters clerks, linemen and messengers into a fortress defense. The next morning, some fifty dead Japanese were counted around the bridge alone. Colonel Suzuki did not survive the raid. Another 14 Americans were killed and 20 wounded during this night of terror.

*　　*　　*

Clearing the beachhead area began to develop into a pattern. When the 24th Infantry Division tried to clear the remainder of its area, it found that due to the detachment of one of its regiments and combat casualties, it could not accomplish all of its objectives with the forces at hand. Accordingly, elements of the 1st Cavalry Division, which had encountered significantly less opposition than expected, were used to relieve battalions of the 24th Infantry Division so that they could be freed to complete their other assignments. This usually involved seizing a hill which blocked the American advance or overlooked a critical American objective. The pattern was that the Americans would advance until fired upon. They would attempt to clear the opposition but if they were unable to do so they withdrew while artillery and air pounded the hill, usually for much of a day. Then the infantry battalion would attack again. More often than not, the opposition had departed or been killed. The process would then be repeated at the next objective. The 34th and 19th Infantry Regiments encountered this pattern repeatedly over the next few days as they cleared Hills B and C and other final Japanese defenses around the beachhead area.

Sometimes the Americans got lucky, as when Lieutenant Colonel Spragins' 2nd Battalion, 19th Infantry attacked Hill B near Palo. Companies E and G attacked as usual and Company E was soon forced back. But Company G managed to hold its position on the hill. Moving the rest of the battalion to reinforce Company G, Colonel Spragins lost his way in the dark.[8] Just at midnight, they came upon an enemy observation post which was empty. Apparently the Japanese had gotten into the habit of spending their nights in nearby local villages. They left no guard in their positions. The night movement of the 2nd Battalion caught them completely by surprise. The 19th Infantry now owned Hill B. With both the 1st Cavalry Division and the 24th Infantry Division now poised to strike directly into northern Leyte Valley, X Corps was ready for the next phase of the Leyte operation.

*   *   *

To the south, XXIV Corps was about to implement a rarity of the Pacific War, an armored thrust against enemy positions. Usually the Japanese were too well entrenched to make an armored thrust successful, but occasionally there were opportunities.[9] Now an opportunity was seen in the sector of the 7th Infantry Division. Its objective was to move into Leyte Valley along the Dulag-Burauen Highway. Previously Company C, 767th Tank Battalion, had crushed an enemy antitank position protecting the road in this sector. This had instigated a fierce firefight in which Company G, 32nd Infantry was hit by concealed enemy machine guns. Three men were killed and nine wounded. One of the wounded was Technician 4th Class Boyd J. Davis, a company aid man. Despite leg wounds, Sergeant Davis crawled to the other injured men and treated their wounds, while shouting to the others how to treat their own wounds while they waited for him. Every time he moved or yelled aloud, the Japanese would concentrate their fire on him. Two of the wounded were hit a second time, and as Sergeant Davis treated one man, the sulfa powder packet was shot out of his hands by enemy fire. He then saw one wounded man fall into a small creek. At the risk of his life, he raced to the wounded man and pulled him to a position of temporary safety. After all of the wounded had been ministered to, he remained in the fire zone to assist the litter bearers in evacuating them. Only when the last of the men left the field did Sergeant Davis allow his own wounds to be treated. He received the Distinguished Service Cross.[10]

General Arnold now decided to make a thrust down the road led by tanks, with infantry following. Led by five tanks from the battalion Headquarters Company moving straight down the road, Companies A and B would flank the road in support of the leading tanks. Company C was to follow while Company D, the light tanks, followed in reserve protecting the supply and maintenance vehicles.

Leading off on October 23rd, the "flying wedge" of tanks pushed forward. They soon overran three enemy machine gun posts in the town of Julita. Soon, however, two leading tanks of Company A bogged down in the usual swampy terrain. The company commander simply ordered another platoon to take the lead, leaving the stalled tanks behind. Moving well past Julita, Headquarters Company lost its lead tank to mines on the road. A small group of Japanese then appeared from the brush and tried to place a satchel charge on the rear deck of the tank. The effort was made futile when the following tank shot the demolition charge off the tank with its machine gun. The Japanese were killed by tank fire and the disabled tank abandoned. Meanwhile the "flying wedge" moved forward again.

It continued for another ninety minutes when once again, Company A ran into swamps. This time there was no way around and Company A moved onto the road behind Company C. The advance continued, and another Headquarters Company tank was knocked out by a mine. Once again the disabled tank was abandoned and the advance pushed ahead. Ten minutes later a Japanese assault group rushed the leading tanks with satchel charges. Tank number 17 was hit and caught fire, the crew escaping unharmed. Again the advance pushed on. Soon the armor reached the village of San Pablo. Quickly the tankers took possession of the village. Company B moved to San Pablo Airfield, one of the key American objectives of the campaign, and took control. Behind them Company D's light tanks escorted the supply and maintenance vehicles into the circled American perimeter.

That afternoon the column moved on. Company B again went off by itself and seized Bayug Airfield, another key objective. By late afternoon the column had seized Burauen against light opposition. However, the armor had far outdistanced its infantry support, and without it could not risk staying overnight in the advanced positions they had carried during the day. The

767th Tank Battalion withdrew to San Pablo where they met the advancing infantry and settled in for the night. The following day they did it again. This time Company D followed immediately behind Headquarters Company as they led the column and reached San Pablo and its airfield before lunch. Company C took Bayug Airfield, again, and a group of Japanese was spotted along the road to Burauen. The tanks moved toward them, and they scattered. But the leading tank hit a mine as it reached the area where the Japanese had been seen. Soon a second tank was knocked out by a mine. It was now clear that the Japanese had been mining the road. Undeterred, the American tankers moved off the road and continued on to Burauen. Company B circled the town and captured its northern end and the road leading to Dagami. The tanks of Company D entered the town but lost two vehicles to mines. Again the road was blocked. Using side streets, First Lieutenant Frances M. McGuin continued to lead his men into the town. As he directed the tanks forward from behind the two disabled tanks, he was killed by a Japanese sniper. As Company A's commander, Captain Bruce B. Scott, was trying to organize his tanks for a push into the town, he, too, became the victim of a sniper. Soon after, the 17th Infantry Regiment of the 7th Infantry Division arrived and began clearing the enemy snipers out of the town.

Meanwhile, Company C captured both Bayug and Buri Airfields but were under heavy fire from north of the field. Swamps prevented them from outflanking the enemy. Under increasing artillery fire and with one tank disabled, the company could not hold its conquests without infantry support, and withdrew to Burauen. Later when the 7th Infantry Division arrived, they too, were hit by this fire and waited for the next day to move on the two airfields. An attempt by Companies B and D to advance on Dagami was halted by strong Japanese resistance and a heavily mined roadway. That night the Japanese seized one of the abandoned tanks and turned its guns on the 17th Infantry. Fortunately, they were shooting high, and nobody was hurt.[11]

* * *

The 7th Infantry Division had been advancing steadily from its invasion beaches, limited more by terrain than enemy resistance. In one case, the swamps were so deep and wide that the 32nd Infantry had to leave its 2nd Battalion behind because it could not cross or bypass the swamp. The route of advance also brought problems to the advancing infantry. The same 2nd Battalion which had become stalled in front of a swamp had to cross the Calbasag River twelve times in one day during its advance. It was also this battalion which encountered the only serious enemy resistance when Captain Roy F. Dixon's Company G was pinned down for the day by a strong enemy defensive position. The remainder of the battalion moved around the enemy resistance, and after darkness, Captain Dixon led his company after the rest of the battalion.

A brief enemy attack against Company G, 184th Infantry by the *7th Independent Tank Company*[12] at the junction between the 32nd and 184th Infantry Regiments was stopped by the Americans. Three enemy tanks rolled down the road and sprayed the area with machine gun fire, but no Americans were injured.[13] The Americans fired back with rifles, bazookas and mortars but also caused no damage. A return an hour later resulted in one Japanese tank knocked out with its crew killed. Soon after, an enemy scout car met the same fate.

General Arnold wanted to keep the pressure on the retreating Japanese in order to prevent them from establishing new defenses in front of his division. He had determined to push ahead to capture the airfields in his zone as soon as possible, allowing the Japanese no time to set up defenses and to allow American air power to use the fields to provide support. It was this intent which resulted in the formation of the strike force made up of the 17th Infantry Regiment and the 767th Tank Battalion, resulting in the "flying wedge" previously described.[14] Supported by the 48th Field Artillery Battalion,[15] the attack led off with the 767th Tank Battalion's "flying wedge." Behind it came the 1st and 2nd Battalions, 17th Infantry Regiment under the command of Lt. Colonel Francis T. Pachler. Alongside, the 184th Infantry Regiment was to mop up any opposition that might develop along the Daguitan River south of Burauen. The 32nd Infantry was occupied with the seizure of the San Pablo Airfield Number 1 and the Buri Airstrip. Both regiments were to try to keep abreast of the advancing 17th Infantry's attack. It was known, however, that the terrain was more than likely to hinder their advance.

Moving from its reserve position near the beaches, the 17th Infantry Regiment moved to Dulag Airfield on October 22nd and the following morning moved to a line of departure, passing through its two sister regiments. The 767th Tank Battalion had already set off and the 17th Infantry moved behind the advancing tanks until they returned from Burauen, when both units settled in for the night. Intense heat and moving through thick vegetation had slowed the infantry advance during the day. Men passed out in the high cogon grass and the number of heat exhaustion casualties soared.

Swamps and rice paddies were everywhere and had to be crossed. Nevertheless, by mid-afternoon they had reached San Pablo Airfield Number 1 and secured one end as a part of their night defensive perimeter.

The next day, October 24th, the riflemen were able to stay closer to the tanks, which advanced more slowly. Early in the morning the 2nd Battalion, 17th Infantry secured San Pablo Airfield Number 2 against no opposition. By mid-morning the first infantry scouts had arrived at Burauen. Again, no enemy opposition appeared. Within Burauen, however, as we have seen, there were several enemy snipers and antitank teams from the *20th Infantry Regiment* which the infantry cleaned out over the next two hours. The heat and closeness of the village caused several more heat exhaustion cases. Colonel Pachler ordered his battalion commanders to pause, allowing the men to rest and rehydrate.

Up ahead, the patrol of the 767th Tank Battalion had hit the newly laid enemy minefield on the Burauen-Dagami Highway. Engineers of Company A, 13th Engineer Combat Battalion, went forward and cleared the road of the Japanese mines under the cover of the infantrymen. By mid-afternoon the mines had been removed and the infantry moved forward along the road. Some two hundred yards further the leading infantry came under rifle and machine gun fire. Scouts trying to locate the main enemy position suffered four killed and four wounded. Colonel Pachler called it a day and ordered his task force to set up night defensive positions. On the left flank was another swamp which came to within a hundred yards of the road while on the right lay a fifty-foot ridge that was within 250 yards of the road and defensive positions. Although no fire had been received from the ridge, Colonel Pachler was concerned since it dominated the entire road in his sector. He ordered Lieutenant Colonel Delbert Bjork, commanding the attached 2nd Battalion, 184th Infantry, to secure a line near the hill as a part of the night defensive position. Although not ordered to seize the ridge, Second Lieutenant Thomas Humfreville decided to take his platoon of Company F to the ridge. Other platoons had been stopped and only Lieutenant Humfreville's platoon advanced. Very quickly they ran into several mutually supporting enemy machine gun positions. The first burst of Japanese fire wounded eleven men, including Lieutenant Humbreville, who despite his wounds knocked out the enemy gun. He then moved to the front to lead the advance squad in resuming the assault. He and several men were wounded in this new attack. He called his platoon sergeant to him to issue orders for the continued assault, when an enemy counterattack struck. Despite his already serious wounds, Lieutenant Humfreville stood erect and drew the enemy's attention on himself to allow his men to prepare to meet the attack. As he diverted the enemy's attention long enough to allow his platoon to defeat their attack, he was bayoneted and killed by the attacking Japanese. His Distinguished Service Cross was posthumously awarded.[16]

Staff Sergeant Charles D. McRunnels took command and moved the wounded back while trying to find a way to knock out the enemy positions. Even while he did so, he soon realized that he was still being attacked by large numbers of Japanese. Some came close enough to bayonet wounded Americans. Automatic weapons fire drove off the Japanese and the surviving platoon members took cover. Calling his company commander, Captain James B. Hewette, Staff Sergeant McRunnels was told that the rest of Company F was coming forward. The added firepower of the infantry company allowed the trapped platoon to withdraw to the defensive perimeter.

Now alerted to the Japanese presence on his flank, Colonel Pachler expected an attack. It began after dark with mortar fire falling among the foxholes of his men, along with coordinated machine gun fire from the ridge. This was the point when the Japanese seized the abandoned tank of the 767th Tank Battalion and used its guns on the Americans. Japanese patrols of twenty to thirty men began moving on the outposts. Using only grenades to not give away their positions, the combat-experienced Americans responded. Captain George E. Adams, commanding Company F, 17th Infantry, against whom the main attack developed, called in artillery fire so close to his own lines that the Japanese were forced back. After two hours the Japanese withdrew.

The Japanese were not quite through, however. After midnight a company of enemy infantry attempted to rush Captain Adams' F Company. Machine guns and antitank weapons slowed the attack, and when they reached the barbed wire in front of the American perimeter, every weapon in Company F and their supporting arms opened fire. It was the heaviest concentration of fire that the 17th Infantry, a veteran of two previous campaigns, remembered seeing to that point. Realizing that the attack was defeated, Captain Adams tried to order a cease fire, but the din was so great that messengers had to be sent to each platoon to stop the firing. The rest of the night was unusually quiet.

The following morning, however, provided evidence that the Japanese were still present. A platoon from Company C, 17th Infantry was moving forward when it was struck by machine gun fire from a nearby hill. As the platoon sought cover, Private First Class Edward F. Jeffers, an automatic rifle-man with the flanking squad, noticed several Japanese soldiers moving to get behind them. He immediately leaped to his feet and opened fire on the enemy squad, neutralizing them. Then he noticed another group of Japanese in a nearby trench firing on his platoon. He raced forward under Japanese fire to the lip of the trench and opened fire, killing several and forcing the rest to withdraw. Then he saw that one of the platoon's wounded lay fully exposed to enemy fire and could not be reached by litter bearers. He ran to the wounded man and set up to protect him until the fight was over, at the same time administering first aid. Private First Class Jeffers survived to receive a promotion to sergeant and the Distinguished Service Cross.[17]

*   *   *

The advance of the Americans off their invasion beaches caused General Makino, commanding the *16th Infantry Division*, to reconsider his plans for the defense of Leyte. His division had been divided into the *Northern* and *Southern Leyte Defense Forces*. The *Northern Defense Force*, which defended the Catmon Hill area and faced the 96th Infantry Division consisted of the *9th Infantry Regiment* and the *22nd Field Artillery Regiment*. The *Southern Defense Force* faced the 7th Infantry Division and included the *20th Infantry Regiment* less one battalion, the *2nd Battalion, 33rd Infantry Regiment,* the *7th Independent Tank Company* and two platoons of the *16th Engineer Regiment*. This latter force was to concentrate around the area of San Pablo and the Calbasag River where they would defend against an American advance while making night raids against American positions, all in order to delay the American advance. Some 600 men of the *98th Airfield Battalion* and the *54th Airfield Company* were to defend the high ground around Burauen and at Buri Airfield. A small naval force was defending a supply dump east of Dagami, where the headquarters of the *16th Infantry Division* was now located.

These dispositions were in place when the 7th Infantry Division attacked. While the 17th Infantry Regiment fought for the airfields, Burauen and Dagami, the 32nd Infantry, under Colonel Marc J. Logie, would guard the right flank, protecting and supporting that advance while maintaining contact with the 96th Infantry Division. Moving alongside, but somewhat behind, the 17th Infantry, the 1st Battalion, 32nd Infantry, also experienced the terrible heat, stifling vegetation and difficult terrain. Julita and San Pablo were quickly secured, as was San Pablo Airfield. The regiment settled down for the night protecting the division's right flank. Later it was learned that the commanding officer of the *20th Infantry Regiment* had been killed during the day's advance.

The following day, October 24th, the 32nd Infantry moved on Buri Airstrip. That morning Colonel Logie was transferred to Division Headquarters.[18] Lieutenant Colonel John M. Finn, now commanding the 32nd Infantry, ordered the 1st Battalion to advance on Buri Airstrip. Here the Japanese had constructed pillboxes hidden in the tall grass and brush. Machine guns with interlocking fire covered the approach routes. Extensive trench systems and field fortifications also protected approaches to the field. Manning these impressive fortifications were members of the *20th Infantry Regiment, 98th Airfield Battalion* and *54th Airfield Company*. One hundred-pound aerial bombs had been buried as land mines along the runways and dispersal areas. Some could be electrically detonated from a safe distance by the defenders.

The 1st Battalion, 32nd Infantry encountered no opposition on their approach to Buri Airfield. Shortly after midday they ran into the enemy defenses at the airstrip. Attacking with Company A on the right and Company C on the left, they opened with rifle, machine gun and mortar fire on the Japanese positions, which slowly were overcome. Company C encountered the main opposition, which held it up for a while. Major Leigh H. Mathias, the battalion commander, soon lost contact with Company A, which had moved ahead while Company C fought to reduce the main enemy defenses. As he searched for Company A, he was wounded by enemy fire. Major Robert C. Foulston, Jr., the battalion executive officer, took command.

Captain Rollin T. Jones, commanding Company A, had his own problems. When the attack signal was given, half the company moved forward while the other half were occupied with a group of Japanese who were digging additional defensive positions. Since these were in front of Company C, not Company A, Captain Jones ordered his men forward. Soon they were 500 yards ahead of any of the other units in the battalion. Unknown to the Americans, the Japanese commander was organizing a counterattack while the Americans remained divided and confused. As he sought to locate his battalion commander for instructions, Captain Jones was killed in action. The situation deteriorated further when Captain Robert J. Kretzer, a veteran of two previous campaigns and commanding Company C, saw that his men needed to reorganize. Pulling his platoons back, his orders failed to reach all the men of the company. Men were already fighting hand-to-hand in some places. Others had no idea of where they were or who was nearby. Five men, included one wounded, went the wrong way and wound up nearly a mile behind Japanese lines before they realized their mistake. Most of the company pulled back in good order. Technical Sergeant Johnny H. Bosworth found a trench which he used as a defensive line to cover the withdrawal, gathering men as they passed him. This group was instrumental in delaying and turning the oncoming Japanese counterattack.

On Company C's flank, Major Mathias had placed one platoon of Company B as flank security. This platoon did not get the withdrawal order. First Lieutenant Marshall J. Hamilton only learned of the withdrawal when First Lieutenant Marvin Watkins and some of his Company C men joined the Company B platoon. They held their positions and helped repel the Japanese counterattack. When Company C reunited after the fight, they counted twenty-two men killed and another thirty wounded. Colonel Finn ordered his 3rd Battalion to move to the 1st Battalion's left in support, but swamps and dense undergrowth slowed this movement until the best the 3rd Battalion could achieve before dark was to get within 600 yards of its sister battalion. Colonel Finn came forward and observed the situation, determining that the 1st Battalion should withdraw to San Pablo Airstrip covered by the 3rd Battalion. There, joined by the 2nd Battalion released from division reserve, the regiment formed a night perimeter.

About the only bright spot for the 32nd Infantry on October 24th was information from a prisoner captured by the 2nd Battalion who reported that he was a member of the *7th Independent Tank Company*. He reported that eight of the tanks had been destroyed at Julita and the remaining three were out of action due to mechanical failures. In any case, the tanks were obsolete and had been used to help level the runways of the various airfields.

*   *   *

The 32nd Infantry returned to the attack the next day, October 25th. Offshore on this day, Admiral Halsey's Third Fleet was heading north to engage forces of the *Imperial Japanese Navy,* Admiral Thomas C. Kinkaid was heading south with his Seventh Fleet for the same purpose, leaving Leyte Gulf only protected by small forces of escort carriers and destroyers. At the airfield, the 49th Field Artillery Battalion[19] fired a half-hour bombardment to the front of the 32nd Infantry. Moving off with the fresh 2nd Battalion in the lead, Colonel Finn had the 3rd Battalion on their right. Again, there was no opposition on the approach, but once the field was reached scouts were hit by strong fire from enemy bunkers on the edge of the airfield. Company F tried to determine an approach to the enemy defenses but the bunkers were invulnerable to anything but a tank, which because of the terrain could not reach the field. An antitank gun was dragged forward but had no effect on the strong enemy bunkers. After four men had been killed and fourteen wounded, Colonel Nelson pulled his battalion back for the night. Without heavier supporting weapons the Japanese positions could not be overcome.

However, the 3rd Battalion continued ahead. Not having hit the main enemy defenses, Lieutenant Colonel Charles A. Whitcomb's battalion was ordered to continue its attack to seize the airfield. As they came to the corner of the field, machine gun fire stopped the advance. Although anxious to press the attack, Colonel Whitcomb knew night was now approaching and the terrain was unfavorable for defense. With four men killed and eleven wounded, the battalion set up a night perimeter just east of the airstrip. As they did so, a company of Japanese came yelling and shouting at them from across the airfield. Aiming for a gap between the two assault battalions, they focused on Company K. Having ample warning from the enemy's shouts and calls, Company K immediately deployed and opened fire. When it was all over, seventy-five Japanese lay dead on the field against not a single casualty in Company K.

Colonel Finn was determined that the field would fall to his regiment on October 26th. He managed to get a platoon of medium tanks attached to each battalion and further attached a platoon to each from the regimental Cannon Company.[20] All three battalions would attack together, each targeted on a different portion of the objective. The 1st Battalion replaced the 3rd Battalion and attacked, despite the fact that the long roundabout route delayed the tanks which did not join up in time. The attack moved slowly against strong resistance until Company A found itself out of the jungle and at the airstrip itself. To the right was the end of the Japanese trenches facing the rest of the battalion. They immediately opened fire on the enemy within the trench and eliminated them. Return fire from unseen enemy positions pinned the company down.

Company B, under Captain Rudolph Hagen, ran into one of the main pillboxes protected by at least three machine guns. The platoon, under First Lieutenant Salvatore A. Toste, tried to flank the pillbox but two men were killed immediately. Lieutenant Toste took a squad around the other flank but one of the machine guns opened fire, killing the lieutenant and three of his men while wounding ten others. Company B was effectively pinned down.

Captain Hagen now called for the tanks, which had been further delayed when appropriated by the 2nd Battalion. Using the time to evacuate his wounded, he had them all off the field when the tanks came up. One tank quickly knocked out the pillboxes one by one. Protected by a rifle platoon each, the tanks ran over each pillbox and each trench. Within half an hour the enemy defenses had been reduced and forty-seven dead were counted. The destruction of these positions also freed up Company A, who had been pinned down by their fire. By late afternoon, both Companies A and B were positioned four hundred yards down the airstrip. Finding no enemy opposition, they remained for the night. Buri Airfield was now secured.[21]

*   *   *

Along the highway, the 17th Infantry still faced the ridge from which the Japanese had launched the counterattack on the night of October 24th. Colonel Pachler and General Arnold had conferred that evening and determined that a large enemy force held the hill and could not be left along a main supply route. In addition, the enemy force was between the 17th Infantry and 32nd Infantry Regiments, presenting another threat. Briefly considering bypassing the enemy on the ridge, General Arnold and Colonel Pachler quickly agreed that it had to be destroyed before the advance on Dagami continued.

The mission was given to Colonel Bjork's 2nd Battalion, 17th Infantry. Companies E and F moved out in a skirmish line opposed initially only by scattered rifle fire. By early afternoon, the ridge had been secured. Either the enemy had been wiped out by his own counterattacks and the American artillery, or he had withdrawn. To ensure the enemy's absence, a patrol from the 1st Battalion was sent towards Buri Airfield. First Lieutenant Daniel E. Blue led his 3rd Platoon of Company C and five Medium tanks of the 767th Tank Battalion toward the field along a road that had little clearance on either side. Coming to a destroyed bridge, the Japanese sprung an ambush on the American column. Heavy fire broke out and individual Japanese soldiers ran towards the tanks with satchel charges, mines and cans of gasoline. The tanks, in attempting to maneuver had become bogged down in swampy ground and stalled. Protected by the infantry, the tanks pulled each other out of the bog in turn. It took most of the day, and by late afternoon the tanks were free, but five of Lieutenant Blue's men, including the lieutenant, had been wounded. Deciding that the enemy was too strong to continue, Lieutenant Blue ordered a withdrawal. He reported in to Colonel Pachler shortly before darkness.

Colonel Pachler now ordered a resumption of his advance on Dagami. Because the terrain prevented a broad-front advance, he ordered an advance in column of battalions with two companies on either side of the road to a depth of one hundred yards. Companies A and C would lead the regimental advance, and they moved out on October 26th. During the day, the 2nd Battalion, 17th Infantry reverted to its parent regiment and relieved the 2nd Battalion, 184th Infantry, which went into division reserve. Because of the difficult terrain, the tank support was restricted to a platoon of tanks while the rest waited in reserve.

The infantry led the way forward. Passing the village of Buri, which was unoccupied, they cautiously searched every building, high grass spot, and any potential obstacle. As two scouts of Company C were searching a patch of high grass, they suddenly found themselves in the middle of an extensive enemy trench system. The defenders were taken completely by surprise and eliminated by the attacking Americans. Encounters with enemy groups continued without hindering the advance. By late afternoon the advance had reached some high ground where Colonel Pachler ordered a night defensive position to be established.

After a quiet night, Colonel Pachler sent the 3rd Battalion in the lead and continued towards Dagami. Lieutenant Colonel Lew Wallace placed Captain Charles T. Frazee's Company K in the lead with troops covering both sides of the road. Coming to the village of Guinarona, a cluster of twenty to thirty native shacks along a stream, they were hit by heavy enemy fire as they attempted to cross the stream. Two machine guns supported by a platoon of infantry were hiding in the village. Captain Frazee ordered a three-minute artillery, mortar and machine-gun barrage which destroyed the machine guns and scattered the infantry. On the flank, the 3rd platoon came under fire from two additional machine guns. Private First Class Clive McPeek placed his first bazooka shell directly into the schoolhouse where one of the guns was located. The second gun was knocked out by a direct hit from an 81mm mortar. First Lieutenant Lester O. Lingren brought up two of his self-propelled guns from the Regimental Cannon Company and eliminated the remaining Japanese infantry.

The battalion moved on and for the rest of the day no serious opposition was encountered. By nightfall, Colonel Wallace settled his battalion in for the night less than two miles south of Dagami. Just north of the position was a destroyed stone bridge in a causeway over which the main road crossed a wide swamp. Enemy machine-gun fire came out of the swamp as Company

K settled in for the night and Captain Frazee had his 60mm mortars respond. Enemy fire soon ceased, with only some enemy air activity seen that night. Overall it was quiet. On the next day Lt. Colonel William B. Moore's 2nd Battalion would take the lead into Dagami.

*   *   *

The road ahead of the 2nd Battalion led into a swamp at least 100 yards wide. The road crossed the swamp on a causeway with the destroyed stone bridge in the middle of that causeway. On the north was a huge coconut grove which ran 100 yards east of the road in a long arc which ran west and south, forming in effect a semicircle. West of the grove the marsh resumed. Prisoners captured during the advance had revealed that Lieutenant Colonel Kakuda, commander of the *Central Area Unit* of the *20th Infantry Regiment,* had ordered that the regiment take a position west of Dagami and annihilate the Americans before they reached the town. Besides elements of his own regiment, Colonel Kakuda had under his command the *2nd Battalion, 33rd Infantry Regiment,* and elements of the *16th Engineer Regiment* and *9th Infantry Regiment.* All were considerably understrength, but nevertheless this was a formidable defensive force. Estimates gave Colonel Kakuda between 1,500 and 2,500 troops under command outside of Dagami.

Colonel Pachler decided to attack in column of battalions, in the order 2nd, 1st and 3rd. The tanks and other supporting arms[22] were attached to the 2nd Battalion. As Colonel Moore's battalion moved forward early the next morning, with Company F on the left and Company G on the right, it was hit with intense rifle, machine gun and mortar fire from Japanese hidden in the grove and swamp. Wading through waist-deep swamp water, the footing became so difficult that it was soon realized that the battalion could not continue. Colonel Moore recalled his leading companies and sent them forward along the causeway, normally not a proper military course of action. Instead of being cut to pieces, however, the leading companies crossed the causeway against limited opposition. Apparently the Japanese wanted to let them move into a bottleneck from which they could not escape. Engineers of the 13th Engineer Combat Battalion followed closely and began to fill the gap at the stone bridge with debris. This allowed three 767th Tank Battalion tanks to cross as well, something the Japanese had not planned. Unfortunately, the three tanks moved swiftly forward and lost contact with the infantry for the rest of the morning.[23]

Once across the causeway, Captain Adams moved Company F forward.

It was now that the Japanese revealed the full extent of their defenses. Small-arms fire pinned the leading platoon to the ground. Although initially well hidden, the Japanese soon began to move about, revealing their positions. Private First Class Decidero Codena, wielding a Browning Automatic Rifle, spotted one Japanese and rose up after him. The enemy replied with a grenade which severely wounded Codena, but his action had lifted his platoon from the ground. Staff Sergeant Herman Judd grabbed the BAR and killed the enemy soldier. He then moved to an enemy trench where he dispatched fifteen more enemy troops before running out of ammunition. First Lieutenant Jerrel F. Wilson brought up the rest of the platoon and led them in attacking the remaining enemy positions. Company F's other platoon faced a series of bunkers and fortified positions. Following the 3rd Platoon into the swamp, they charged the enemy defenses. Led by Private First Class Leonard C. Brostram, the leading scout, the platoon engaged the enemy in hand-to-hand combat. Hit early in the fight by three enemy bullets, the native of Preston, Idaho continued to lead the platoon into the enemy positions. Realizing that a key enemy pillbox in the center of the strong point would have to be knocked out if his platoon was to survive and advance, Private First Class Brostrom decided on his own to attack the pillbox. Already wounded, he charged forward with grenades. As he did so, he was the prime target for every Japanese weapon in sight. He miraculously reached the rear of the pillbox and tossed his grenades into the position. Six enemy soldiers rose from a nearby trench and charged the Idaho soldier with bayonets. Private First Class Brostrom killed one and drove off the others with rifle fire. He then threw more grenades at other enemy defenses from a completely exposed position. Suffering intense pain from his wounds and weakening from blood loss, he continued to toss grenades at the enemy pillboxes. Finally, he collapsed. Just as he did so, however, the Japanese broke and ran, many being killed by members of Company F as they fled. Medics carried Private First Class Brostrom from the field but he died while being carried to safety. For his self-sacrifice on October 28, 1944, Private First Class Leonard C. Brostrom was awarded a posthumous Medal of Honor.[24]

Staff Sergeant Paul Doty now came up and finished off the remaining enemy within the pillbox. Assisted by Privates First Class Howard J. Evans and Eldridge V. Sorenson, they proceeded to move into the center of the enemy defenses, which consisted of dozens of trenches and spider holes. While Private First Class Evans knocked the covers off the holes, Private First Class Sorenson provided cover. Meanwhile, Private First Class William

Schmid took a bullet in the arm but knocked off another nearby pillbox. Behind them Captain Adams had requested more support. Tanks were unavailable due to the terrain, but Lieutenant Colonel Edward Smith, the 17th Regiment's Executive Officer, gave Colonel Moore Company C of the 1st Battalion. Moving across the causeway in mid-morning, they moved to secure the left flank of Company F. Immediately taking enemy fire, Company C also plunged into the swamp. Soon both Companies F and C were deeply involved in their individual firefights with different groups of the enemy.

Shortly after Company C entered the swamp, the three light tanks that had disappeared up the road at the beginning of the fight suddenly reappeared. Sergeant Leland A. Larson ran out under fire and grabbed the exterior phone on one of the tanks and halted them on the road. Captain Adams stopped another by risking his life climbing on top of the tank and blocking its vision with a hand over its periscope. The third tank, never seeing the infantry, continued down the road and disappeared. With two tanks now under his control, Captain Adams organized a new attack against the main enemy positions. A squad under Sergeant Everett C. Mann would advance protecting the tanks, while 1st Platoon under Technical Sergeant James M. Madison followed mopping up behind the advance. Reaching the northern edge of the swamp and having cleared his area, Captain Adams turned the tanks over to G Company. Then Captain Adams lined up his company shoulder to shoulder and covered his area again, determined not to bypass any enemy soldiers.

The tanks and Company C knocked out fourteen enemy strongpoints while clearing their zone. The west side of the Dagami-Burauen highway was now cleared. Company B attempted to clear a strong position at the bend in the coconut grove but they were turned back by strong enemy fire and barbed wire strung within the swamp through which they had to wade to reach the enemy. Meanwhile, on the east side of the highway, First Lieutenant William J. Schade's Company G faced the same kind of opposition that Company F had met. Just deploying off the highway had cost the company four men killed and seven wounded. Lieutenant Schade ordered his men to continue forward, but after an advance of about thirty yards they stalled. Supporting fires were impossible because the trees would cause premature bursts and might injure Americans. Colonel Moore, keeping in touch, decided to send Company E around the swamp to the right, hoping to outflank the enemy. This took time, but soon began to have an effect. More and more enemy troops abandoned their positions as Company E closed in from their rear and flank. Finally, medium tanks reported to Lieutenant Schade who now launched a frontal and flanking attack.

The flanking attack was the platoon under First Lieutenant George B. Rodman, which moved through Company E and hit the enemy's flank. They soon came up against a heavily fortified enemy position consisting of pillboxes and trenches. A BAR man from Armstrong, Iowa led the attack. Private First Class John F. Thorson volunteered to take the lead and entered an enemy trench, killing its occupants despite intense fire directed at him. As he cleared the trench, he was wounded and fell barely six yards from the enemy. His platoon immediately came up to assist him, and as the remaining twenty men arrived an enemy grenade landed in their midst. Shouting a warning and making a final effort, Private First Class Thorson rolled over onto the grenade, absorbing the blast with his body. Killed instantly, he had saved the lives of his fellow platoon members. For his leadership and self-sacrifice, Private First Class Thorson was awarded a posthumous Medal of Honor.[25]

The action of Lieutenant Rodman's platoon ended the battle except for the remaining enemy pocket in front of Company B. Colonel Pachler now attached a platoon of Cannon Company self-propelled guns to Captain Davis and ordered him to eliminate this last opposition to the advance on Dagami. Moving out the next morning, the combined force passed through the areas cleared by C, F and G Companies into the remaining enemy defenses. The Cannon Company guns knocked out six pillboxes while the infantry cleared out dozens of spider holes and trenches. Company B spent the day thoroughly combing the area to ensure that no Japanese remained to oppose their advance. Estimates later stated that two companies of Japanese had been defending these positions. Few escaped to Dagami.

*　　*　　*

The 17th Infantry finished clearing the swamp around the stone bridge and then moved further along the road to Dagami for some 300 yards before establishing a night defensive perimeter. Enemy machine gun and mortar fire harassed the perimeter all night, and several stray Japanese soldiers stumbled into the protecting barbed wire, where they were eliminated by grenades during the night.

Since the 2nd Battalion, 17th Infantry had carried the burden the day before, the other two battalions would lead the attack on October 29th. Company B, with support from a platoon of Cannon Company self-propelled guns, would clean out the remaining pocket of enemy at the edge of the swamp which flanked the regimental line of advance. Platoons under Staff Sergeant Tim E. Lopez and Technical Sergeant Frank J. Gonzales fought from pillbox to pillbox by attacking from the flanks and rear of each enemy position until it was overrun. The self-propelled howitzers used time-burst fire to keep the Japanese pinned down while the infantry moved in with rifles, machine guns and grenades. By 1600 Hours, Company B had cleared the area and was firing at several Japanese who had thrown down their arms as they attempted to escape towards Dagami. More than 120 enemy dead were counted in this area after the battle.

Meanwhile, the 3rd Battalion led off on the right and the 1st Battalion on the left against no serious opposition. By 1400 Hours, they were both on the outskirts of Dagami. Warned that upwards of 400 enemy troops were expected to garrison the town, they advanced cautiously. As the 3rd Battalion approached a cemetery overgrown with weeds, one company entered the grounds while the others bypassed it. The leading platoons of Company L climbed over the stone wall surrounding the cemetery and moved through it without a shot being fired. As the 1st Platoon, in reserve, entered the cemetery, a headstone tilted back, and from the open grave Japanese opened fire using a captured Browning Automatic Rifle. The platoon leader, First Lieutenant Aldo J. Freppoli, and two men were killed, three others wounded. One American scout who watched the whole process was too surprised to fire a shot, as was most of the platoon. After firing off one magazine, the Japanese pulled the headstone back into place and disappeared into the grave.

Because Colonel Pachler wanted to secure Dagami immediately, Company L was ordered to continue forward while the reserve company, Company K under Captain Frazee, was ordered to clear the cemetery. Small-arms fire had no effect on this position, and a flamethrower was brought forward. But it swiftly became clear the Japanese had fortified the cemetery by emptying the graves and drilling holes through the stones, converting the crypts into individual foxholes. Because other Americans were on all sides of the cemetery, Company K had difficulty employing support weapons. As they regrouped, a Japanese captain jumped out of one of the graves and charged Staff Sergeant Jack T. Lewis, firing his pistol. A nearby BAR man, Private First Class Harold R. Peckman, tried to shoot Staff Sergeant Lewis' attacker, but his weapon jammed. Hearing the click of the BAR, the Japanese captain turned his attention to Private Peckman, wounding him. He turned back to Sergeant Lewis, but this time the Japanese weapon jammed. The captain pulled his sword and charged Sergeant Lewis, cutting him severely across the arm. Private First Class Harry Trahan, hearing the noise, raced to the scene and killed the attacking officer. The cemetery was cleared after this incident by men like Private First Class Odell Clark, who with his flamethrower and a squad of riflemen, moved cautiously from grave to grave and burned the Japanese out of their holes. When asked if his company was being counterattacked, Captain Frazee replied, "Hell no, we're just fighting for a bivouac area."[26]

The clearance of the cemetery and the entrance of the 17th Infantry into Dagami on October 30th accomplished a major objective for the 7th Infantry Division. Patrols soon made contact with the 24th Infantry Division of X Corps north of Dagami and with the 382nd Infantry of the 96th Infantry Division to the east. The main limits of the final beachhead line had been reached and secured. To protect the new main line of resistance, the 7th Reconnaissance Troop and the 2nd Battalion, 32nd Infantry moved down the road to Abuyog, a potential route for Japanese reinforcements. No resistance was encountered, and on November 2nd a patrol from Company G seized the village of Baybay, across the island from Abuyog. Further south, the detached 21st Infantry Regiment had been protecting the Panaon Strait area. Orders soon sent the 2nd Battalion, 32nd Infantry to relieve the 21st Infantry, which in turn left to rejoin its parent unit, the 24th Infantry Division.

By November 2nd, General Hodge's XXIV Corps had accomplished its initial missions on Leyte. The southern part of the Leyte Valley had been securely captured along with its airfields, roads and base sites. The Corps had pushed across to the west coast and stood ready on army orders to advance towards Ormoc, which was the next phase of the Sixth Army plan. Up north, the X Corps had been busy securing the northern entrance to Leyte Valley.

*   *   *

Tenth Corps had already secured the Tacloban area, Hill 522, Palo and the San Juanico Strait, all of which allowed the Americans access to the northern entrance of Leyte Valley. The final objective was to secure Carigara Bay, halting the increasing Japanese amphibious reinforcement of the Leyte garrison. This would also put X Corps in a position to continue south through Ormoc Valley and secure the other vital port at Ormoc. In order to achieve these goals, the Corps directed a two-pronged attack into Leyte Valley, each led by one of its divisions.

General Krueger had expected the Japanese to strongly defend Tacloban, with its airfields, and therefore expected the 1st Cavalry Division to face the bulk of the resistance.[27] However, the Japanese had not acted as expected, and the 24th Infantry Division faced the most severe resistance upon landing on Leyte. As a result, General Krueger moved some of the Cavalry battalions to the 24th Infantry's sector to aid them in clearing their zone. After the capture of Palo and Hills B and C, the 24th Infantry Division was to attack west while the 1st Cavalry Division protected its northern flank. Because the 24th Infantry Division had not received its third regiment back from the Panaon Strait assignment, the 1st Cavalry Brigade was to relieve all of its combat troops assigned to rear area or security duties to allow the full weight of the 24th Infantry to be available for the renewed drive west. The attack would be made along Highway 2, a one-lane all-weather road, which was twelve feet wide and made of crushed rock and gravel.

Lieutenant General Sosaku Suzuki, commanding the *35th Army*, had originally planned that once the Americans had reached the entrances to Leyte Valley, he would withdraw his troops, along with sufficient supplies for six months, to the hills overlooking the valley. But the swift advance of the Americans had made this plan impossible to carry out. Instead, he directed his troops to assemble in the vicinity of Jaro at the southern edge of Leyte Valley. Here, he ordered the *41st Infantry Regiment* of the *30th Infantry Division* and the *169th Independent Infantry Battalion* from the *102nd Infantry Division* to prepare to stop the advancing Americans. Soon after, the *17th Independent Infantry Battalion*, also of the *102nd Infantry Division*, was ordered to join them. These units were all new to Leyte, having arrived through Carigara Bay by sea since the Americans landed on the island. For when the Japanese had changed their plans to make Leyte the decisive land battle, they had moved swiftly.

Within days of the American landings, the commander of the *Southwest Area Fleet*, Vice Admiral Gunichi Mikawa, ordered reinforcements to Leyte. Two nights later, October 25th, the first 2,550 Japanese reinforcements of the *41st Infantry Regiment* landed at Ormoc, transported on high-speed naval transports from Mindanao. On their return, American naval planes flying off escort carriers protecting the Leyte beachheads, sank two escorting warships and one of the transports, which delayed two more regiments awaiting transport. Nevertheless, over the next four days, four more infantry battalions arrived at Ormoc, sent by the *35th Army*. Initially these moves confused the American commanders, with some believing that the Japanese were withdrawing from Leyte instead of reinforcing it. Radio intelligence and guerrilla reports soon cleared up the confusion as they reported additional reinforcements landing, not departing.

Still believing the claims of the *Imperial Japanese Navy* that the American fleet was severely damaged, the Japanese viewed the Sixth Army as trapped on Leyte, and a vital target waiting to be destroyed. All they had to do was to assemble sufficient ground troops to accomplish it. As a result, the *1st* and *26th Infantry Divisions* were ordered to Leyte. The *68th Independent Infantry Brigade* was next. The *Imperial Japanese Navy's Southwest Area Fleet* was strengthened to both protect and implement the passage of these reinforcements. Under the code name *"TA"* (many), the operation was also to be protected by significant additional air resources allocated to the Philippines from as far away as the Japanese Home Islands. Initially, this effort went better than expected. The *1st Infantry Division*, an experienced and highly respected unit, was transferred all the way from Manchuria through Shanghai to Ormoc Bay without the Americans being aware of it. Neither the code breakers nor aerial reconnaissance spotted its convoy at any point during its long passage. The Japanese helped by creating a deception. The *1st Combined Signals Unit,* based in Manila, sent out plain-language messages, supposedly from an American B-24 Reconnaissance aircraft, reporting a Japanese fleet steaming westerly towards Leyte. This report, which grew to include enemy battleships, cruisers and destroyers, attracted the attention of General Kenney's sir forces to the extent that they completely missed the reinforcement convoys. Included in the real convoy were the *35th Army's* commander, General Suzuki, and his staff. It was not until the following morning that American planes discovered the Japanese shipping in Ormoc Bay and attacked it, but the damage had been done. General Krueger would later comment in his memoirs that "this unit, more than any other hostile unit on Leyte, was responsible for the extension of the Leyte Operation."[28]

Radio intercepts soon revealed the presence of General Suzuki on Leyte, which also resolved the question of whether the Japanese were reinforcing or retreating. With an army commander arriving on Leyte, the answer became obvious. Philippine guerrillas soon provided an identification of the *30th Infantry Division* from ID tags taken from their most recent victims around Ormoc. Finally, reports that the *1st Infantry Division* had reached Leyte also reached Sixth Army Headquarters.[29] It was now, on November 2nd, clear to both General MacArthur and General Krueger that the Japanese intended to make a major fight for the island.

* * *

The flow of intelligence information on the Japanese reinforcements was valuable to Sixth Army, but caused significant concerns as well. The Sixth Army now feared being outnumbered, with dwindling air support due to miserable weather conditions, and without a strong fleet immediately behind it. The weather ruined the roads, impeding supplies headed for the front. The army soon realized that it was short several thousand riflemen, replacements for casualties, which would not be made up. And Japanese intentions were still unclear. An enemy landing behind Sixth Army's lines, at Carigara Bay, was considered a possibility. With limited air and naval resources, such an attempt had a good chance of success. This landing could result in the Japanese outflanking American troops via Ormoc Valley, splitting the Sixth Army in two. These concerns, as we shall see, influenced General Krueger's conduct of the battle.

Meanwhile, the fighting continued. Tenth Corps now began its fight for the northern Leyte Valley with the 24th Infantry Division leading down Highway 2. Colonel Pearsall led his 34th Infantry forward on October 26th, the same date the first Japanese reinforcements landed, against slight resistance. Supported by the 3rd Engineer Combat Battalion, the 34th Infantry progressed smoothly over several streams. By dinner time the entire regiment was in Sante Fe. The next day, Lt. Colonel Thomas E. Clifford, Jr., the 1st Battalion commander, had established his unit along the Mudburon River.

As daylight broke in Leyte on October 28th, Colonel Clifford ordered his battalion to move in a column of companies along Highway 2 to the town of Alangalang, a little over a mile to the northwest. The advance went as planned and continued on another mile to the Mainit River. Here the remnants of the *33rd Infantry Regiment* made a brief stand at a bridge over the river but was easily pushed aside. As they retreated, however, units of the newly arrived *41st Infantry Regiment* took over the defense of the area and halted the Americans. The 34th Infantry then sent both the 1st and 2nd Battalions against the defenses in a pouring rain. Supported by tanks and the 63rd Field Artillery Battalion, the advance, despite significant opposition, went through the enemy defenses. These consisted of covered emplacements six feet deep and connected by tunnels. The Japanese used periscopes to watch the Americans while not revealing themselves. Yet, so quick was the American advance that the Japanese had no chance to blow up the steel bridge which brought Highway 2 over the river, even though they had previously prepared it for demolition.

One of the reasons this advance near Alangalang went so well was the actions of Private First Class Teddy Szymanski of Company F, 34th Infantry. A runner for his company commander, Szymanski was instrumental in keeping the company commander in communication with the assault platoons as they advanced over an open area some 500 yards wide. But he went further than simply passing on orders. He pointed out to the assault platoons enemy spider holes and aided in their destruction. When the left flank assault platoon was stopped by enemy fire, Szymanski rushed forward in the face of heavy small-arms fire and single-handedly destroyed three enemy emplacements dug deeply into the ground, using a sub-machine gun and grenades. Spotting an enemy mortar firing on his company, the Indiana soldier again ran forward alone under rifle and automatic weapons fire and destroyed the enemy position. For his single-handed efforts to advance his company, Private First Class Teddy Szymanski received a Distinguished Service Cross.[30]

To the south, the 19th Infantry Regiment sent Major Elmer C. Howard's 3rd Battalion towards Castilla. Arriving there, Howard learned from local Filipinos that there were no Japanese between Castilla and Pastrana, the next objective. He requested permission of Lt. Colonel George H. Chapman, Jr., to advance and seize Pastrana. After some adjustments in orders, Major Howard was authorized to seize Pastrana. Proceeding over a trail so narrow it could not accommodate vehicles, Company I soon reached the edge of the town. Here they came under heavy enemy fire. Major Howard pulled Company I back and organized an attack with Companies I and K, which soon ran into a star-shaped fort that halted the advance. Protected by pillboxes and trenches, the fort defeated two attempts by the 19th Infantry to destroy it. Colonel Chapman, seeing his casualties increase dramatically, ordered a halt to operations for the day.

Battery C, 11th Field Artillery Battalion, took the position under fire, but after forty-two rounds reported that its guns were out of action because they were sinking into the mud. Battery A of the 14th Field Artillery Battalion, and the 13th Field Artillery Battalion took over the mission. This bombardment went on all night, and the next morning was reinforced by 4.2-inch chemical mortars and 81mm mortars. When, on the morning of October 27, Company K resumed its attack, the Japanese had gone, pushed out by the heavy weight of the American bombardment. The 19th Infantry moved in and secured the area.

With the 24th Infantry Division moving on Carigara, the 19th Infantry advance was next directed on Jaro, the town designated for the assembly of the *35th Army*. Intelligence had reported this to Sixth Army, and General Krueger wanted to capture the area to upset Japanese plans. The advance went well with Japanese resistance at a minimum. On October 30th, Company C, 19th Infantry, encountered a strong force near Rizal, but after a strong artillery barrage, the enemy retreated, opening the way for the Americans to advance on Jaro. But the Japanese had another defense line at the Mainit River. As the Americans approached the river, passing quiet, abandoned villages and moving unopposed along the road, they were suddenly ambushed by a prepared Japanese defense. Several men in the leading column fell dead or wounded on the road, under direct enemy fire. The enemy's position on the other side of the river could not be seen.

Those Japanese were well dug in with earthen pillboxes covered with grass, and narrow firing ports invisible from just a few feet away. But soon the very cleverness of their defenses gave them away. As the Japanese guns continued to fire, they set the dry grass around their pillboxes afire, revealing them to the Americans. Two assault companies attacked on either side of the Mainit River Bridge. They reached the river bank but were soon pinned down by enemy machine-gun fire. To cross the open water was certain death. A withdrawal was ordered but the leading elements could not move. They could neither go forward nor backward. Tanks were brought up and these opened fire on the now revealed enemy positions. But some machine guns, now joined by snipers, maintained their fire and kept the American infantry pinned to the ground. A Cannon Company platoon came up and expended its ammunition, knocking out more, but not all, of the Japanese guns.

Meanwhile, scouts had continued along the river bank, seeking a ford. To the rear, Corporal Albert Nichols of Oklahoma was waiting for the order to move up, and in the meantime searching for souvenirs. As he did so, he noticed figures crouching in the underbrush. At first thinking they were natives, he wondered why they were trying to conceal themselves. Then he realized they were Japanese soldiers, a raiding party which was about to attack a field artillery battery supporting the attack at the Mainit River Bridge. He opened fire, and despite return grenade and rifle fire, he dispersed the raiders, protecting the vital artillery. In the interim the scouts had found a ford.

The ford required a trek through thick jungle to the river, a twenty-foot drop down the bank, a river crossing and then an attack on the flank of the Japanese Mainit River Line. Colonel Newman led a battalion over the river and hit the vulnerable Japanese flank by mid-afternoon. While the flank attack was getting into position, the assault battalion facing the line kept up the pressure, preventing the Japanese from learning too soon that they were about to be flanked. By the time the Japanese realized that they were being attacked from behind, it was too late. Led by Captain Austin's Company F, with fixed bayonets, the 2nd Battalion, 34th Infantry charged the enemy defenders, clearing the river line.

Even then, the battle remained fierce. Sergeant Ernest Reckman, from Valley Stream, New York, was leading his squad forward. As his men passed some brush, he noticed that there were concealed spider holes in the area. He called his squad back and led them in a charge on the holes. Further along he discovered an enemy mortar, well-concealed, firing on his men. He charged the position singlehandedly and knocked it out with a grenade. Private First Class William Thomas of Fort Wayne, Indiana, was right behind his squad leader when he was cut down by machine-gun fire. Private First Class Edward R. Thomas dragged the wounded man to safety and then alone charged the machine gun position and knocked it out. Private First Class Thomas of Trappist, Kentucky, was then fired on by an enemy machine gun as he crossed the river. After climbing the high bank he attacked and knocked out the enemy gun. Discovering three other machine guns firing on his buddies, he took them under rifle fire and kept them pinned down until help arrived and the guns were destroyed.

Both regiments crossed the Mainit River and moved on Jaro, supported by the tanks of the 603rd Tank Company. Company L, 34th Infantry, leading the advance, moved unopposed until reaching the village of Galotan, where a small force of Japanese dug into the shacks and had to be rooted out with rifles, mortars, grenades and bayonets. By 1700 Hours on October 29th Jaro had been secured. To the east, the 19th Infantry had maintained contact and secured the eastern flank.

One column of this advance was accompanied by the assistant division commander, Brigadier General Kenneth F. Cramer of Wethersfield, Connecticut.[31] As he consulted maps with the leading platoon commander, an enemy sniper opened fire. This happened several times; each time the general removed his helmet to wipe his bald head in the hot, humid climate. Finally, the lieutenant realized what was happening. "By God, Sir," he said, "your pate is the target." From that moment, General Cramer kept his helmet on, and the sniper was soon firing at other, less obvious, targets.[32]

General Sibert, commanding X Corps, remained anxious about Carigara Bay. He wanted to secure that area to prevent enemy reinforcements from using it to arrive and also to prevent a concentration of Japanese forces there for any counterattack. He ordered the 1st Cavalry Division to take over the zone of responsibility of the 24th Infantry Division. The latter unit was then to continue the attack as fast as possible and secure Carigara Bay. General Suzuki, on the other side of the battle lines, had been caught unprepared for the rapid American advance. Much of his earlier planning had now been negated. The town of Jaro could no longer be used to assemble his *35th Army* for a counterattack. Instead, he now ordered his troops to Carigara as an assembly point for future operations. Even as he did so, Colonel Newman was ordering his troops forward.

The 1st Cavalry Division was following closely behind the 24th Infantry Division, protecting the flanks and rear of the advance. General Hoffman had also ordered his troopers to advance, sending the 2nd Cavalry Brigade towards Carigara. Both the 7th and 8th Cavalry Regiments moved forward, sending patrols in advance. One of these patrols, led by First Lieutenant Tower W. Greenbowe of Troop C, 7th Cavalry, actually reached the outskirts of Carigara, only to be pushed away by strong enemy resistance. General Sibert, estimating some 5,000 enemy troops defending Carigara, ordered a two-division assault. The 24th Infantry Division would attack from Jaro while the 2nd Cavalry Brigade would advance from Barugo.

General Suzuki's planning took another blow when on October 29th, just as the Americans were advancing on Carigara, he learned that the great naval victory at Leyte Gulf had been won not by the Japanese, but by the American navy. This put further difficulties in the way of accomplishing his plans for Leyte. Indeed, the only good news came from *14th Area Army Head-quarters,* which relieved him of responsibility for the island of Samar so he could concentrate on the defense of Leyte. Undeterred, General Suzuki ordered his *102nd Infantry Division* to Leyte from Panay. The *1st Infantry* and *26th Infantry Divisions* were already under orders for Leyte from Manila. With the enemy too close to Carigara for comfort, these additional reinforcements would use Ormoc Bay as their arrival point. Once there, they would march up Highway 2 through Ormoc Valley to Carigara Bay. From that point General Suzuki would launch his grand counterattack to sweep the Americans off Leyte Island. Only the *68th Brigade* was still destined to land at Carigara Bay, since General Suzuki was unaware of Colonel Newman's coming advance.

By October 28th General Suzuki had the *41st Infantry Regiment,* the *169th Independent Infantry Battalion*[33] and a battalion from the *57th Independent Mixed Brigade*[34] under control on Leyte. These units, except for elements of the *41st Infantry Regiment*, which had inadvertently run into the 24th Infantry Division near Jaro, moved into the hills above Carigara to prepare defenses and assemble for the grand counterattack. The Americans were, for the moment, ignoring these mountain defenses. The reason was that General Krueger, well informed on Japanese reinforcements, was concerned about an enemy buildup at Carigara. As he later recorded, "As it appeared that the Japanese would probably put up a determined defense at Carigara, General Sibert [CG, X Corps], who had assumed command on the 21st of his troops on shore, held up any further advance of his cavalry units until the 24th Division was up and he could launch a coordinated attack."[35]

Colonel Newman launched his attack on October 30th with the 3rd Battalion, 34th Infantry in the lead. Using tanks and artillery to clear a path, the battalion advanced down the Jaro-Carigara highway. But the Japanese resisted fiercely and attacked the tanks with antitank assault teams who struck at the tank treads, periscopes and observation ports. Mines were placed under the tanks as they moved slowly up the road. "Molotov cocktails" were tossed at and on them as well.[36] Others jumped on the tank and tried to find openings through which they would throw grenades. Smoke grenades blinded the tanks, making them more vulnerable to attack. Suicide attackers strapped mines to their bodies and lay down on tanks, then set off the mine. Only close infantry protection kept the tanks able to continue with the attack. While the tanks needed the infantry to protect them, the infantry needed the tanks to make any forward progress.

Many wounded lay exposed and without medical treatment along the road and in the brush nearby. These men had to be evacuated and treated for their wounds. But enemy fire prevented any vehicles from approaching the area. Undeterred, Sergeant Robert Bowman of Massachusetts, and Sergeant Louis H. Hansel of Mount Vernon, Kentucky, brought forward their self-propelled howitzers. Remaining outside the vehicles to guard them from Japanese antitank teams, they guided them forward, knocking out Japanese positions as they went. When it came time to withdraw, they moved slowly back, picking up the wounded as they went. Both men survived but Sergeant Hansel was later killed in action.

When Company L was stopped by hidden Japanese who could not be rooted out by tanks or artillery, Colonel Newman came forward and asked, "What's the holdup here?" Told the reason was heavy enemy fire, and advised by the leading platoon's lieutenant to take cover, Newman declared, "I'll get the men going okay." With the regimental commander leading them, the infantrymen moved forward into increasing enemy artillery and mortars. An enemy shell fell on the road and Colonel Newman fell with wounds to his stomach. Badly wounded, he remained calm, and as the aid man worked quickly over his wounds, he continued to issue orders for the advance. He ordered that he be left while the infantry placed mortar fire on the now disclosed enemy positions. Colonel Newman was later dragged to safety by his orderly and awarded the Distinguished Service Cross.[37]

With Colonel Newman out of action, Lt. Colonel Chester A. Dahlen, the Regimental Executive Officer, assumed command. He ordered a renewal of the attack after the leading elements had withdrawn. Lt. Colonel Postlethwait's 3rd Battalion attacked again into heavy artillery, machine gun and mortar fire. Supported by the 2nd Battalion's flanking attack, they were still unable to progress. That night the 11th, 52nd, and 63rd Field Artillery Battalions pounded the front, supported by Corps Artillery. Colonel Dahlen launched another attack the next day, October 31st, which resulted in a day-long battle moving from one hill to the next. Using tanks, self-propelled guns and flanking maneuvers, the 34th Infantry fought to overcome the *41st Infantry Regiment*. When night came the battle still raged, but under cover of darkness, the Japanese withdrew.

The division commander, General Irving, ordered a resumption of the attack the next day, November 1st. As he and a staff officer, Colonel William J. Verbeck, were reviewing a map just behind the lines, a Japanese soldier suddenly came out of the brush brandishing a grenade and a dagger, and charged the two American officers. All General Irving had was a pair of dividers he was using on the map. Colonel Verbeck pulled his automatic .45 caliber pistol and fired. He missed, and then proceeded to miss with the next six rounds, with the Japanese soldier getting closer each second. Finally, with his last bullet, Colonel Verbeck hit his target and the threat vanished.[38]

With the 19th Infantry covering flanks and rear, the 34th Infantry went forward again. This time the advance moved rapidly, the *41st Infantry Regiment* having withdrawn into the mountains. By nightfall, the 1st Battalion, 34th Infantry established a perimeter well along the road to Carigara. Guerrilla reports estimated the enemy defenders there as numbering between 2,000 to 5,000 troops, well armed and well equipped. Unknown to the Americans, however, was that General Suzuki that very same night had ordered a withdrawal from Carigara to an assembly point in the nearby mountains. The Japanese would not fight for Carigara as feared by the Americans.

American artillery fire bombarded the area of Carigara throughout the

night of November 1. General Sibert now had his units in position for the
two-pronged assault on the town as planned. Leading was the 34th Infantry,
which reached the outskirts of Carigara at 0900 Hours on the morning of
November 2nd. Patrols reported no enemy contact within the town. Contact
was made with Troop E, 5th Cavalry, at 1100 Hours and the cavalrymen
entered the town shortly thereafter. The 1st Battalion, 34th Infantry, then
continued on to Capoocan. After crossing the Carigara River, the battalion
was halted by enemy fire near Balud. Behind them, the rest of the regiment
set up defensive positions protecting Carigara. The advance had cost the 24th
Infantry Division 210 killed, 859 wounded and 6 missing in action. An estimated 2,970 Japanese had been killed, along with 13 prisoners taken during
the advance on Carigara.

General Krueger had now completed the second phase of his operation.
Panaon and San Juanico Straits had been secured, Sixth Army had reached
the west coast of the island, and the entire force was in place for a drive on
the Ormoc Valley, which was believed to be the last Japanese stronghold. All
the airfields had been seized, as well as most of the ports and Leyte Valley.
Things were looking good for U.S. Sixth Army. But in fact, the Japanese were
just beginning their battle for Leyte.

CHAPTER 4

INTO THE MOUNTAINS—
BREAKNECK RIDGE

With the capture of Carigara on November 2nd, the 24th Infantry Division had completed another phase of General Krueger's plan to seize Leyte. Panaon and San Juanico Straits, each at opposite ends of the island, had been secured. The Sixth Army had forces on the west coast at Baybay on the shores of Ormoc Bay. Strong forces were now at Carigara at the northern entrance to Ormoc Valley These two forces were now to be coordinated in a drive into Ormoc Valley, believed to be the last enemy stronghold on Leyte. All tactical objectives either had been seized or were within view of the assault forces.

Concerns remained, however. The flow of enemy reinforcements to Leyte continued unabated, and exactly when and where these additional troops would be encountered remained a mystery. Their numbers and strength remained another mystery. General Krueger had other concerns as well. Although the main reason for seizing Leyte had been the establishment of airfields and logistics bases on the island to support future landings in the Philippines, that aspect of the invasion was not progressing as planned. Soil and weather conditions on Leyte made most of the airfields useless, and the miserable road conditions hampered the engineers who were trying to improve them. Even before they could work on the fields, the engineers had to build or repair their access roads. Three typhoons in quick succession hit the island, making things even more difficult. Rain was nearly constant, with both combat troops and engineers being slowed, often halted, by the torrential downpours. Many engineer units had to be redirected to work on the roads leading to the front lines, in order to supply the combat troops, before they could work on their logistic problems. Even the highly regarded Highway 1 along the beach fell apart in the heavy rains of October 25th, making movement of troops, supplies and vehicles all but impossible. While X Corps suffered most from these poor conditions, they affected all of Sixth Army. When the rains didn't destroy the roads, the heavy military traffic tore them up. In order to deal with this issue, traffic was restricted to the most essential military vehicles, and civilian traffic was severely curtailed. Even transporting soldiers to and from the front had to be restricted to the lightest type of transport available to the unit that was moving.

It continued to get worse. In November 1944, some 23.5 inches of rain fell on Leyte. Mud was everywhere all of the time. Equipment, including tanks, self-propelled guns and other essential support weapons were often mired in the ever present muck, making progress on the front lines, as well as in the rear, excruciatingly slow. Civilian pick-and-shovel crews were added to the roadwork crews to replace or add to the work done by the engineers, but throughout the campaign transportation remained a major concern, and often dictated the progress of the battle.

Early in the campaign, engineer units dedicated to building and restoring airfields had determined that, despite earlier predictions, all of the airfields on Leyte, except those at Tacloban, were unsuitable for use during the rainy season. Even Tacloban was found to be too short for Allied planes and in dire need of resurfacing just to make it useable. In effect, the engineers had to construct an entirely new airfield based upon the old Japanese field. Here again, poor roads and slow resupply limited the progress of the construction program. As they worked, the Army Air Corps engineers realized that they were building an airfield surrounded by a swamp. To add insult to injury, the Japanese made nightly raids over the field, disturbing the work crews and sending them running for cover in the midst of the construction. Despite these difficulties, by October 30th the field was operational, although not completed. Because of this, only limited air support was to be available to the combat troops securing the rest of Leyte.

In the end, the San Pablo and Buri Airfields were abandoned as unusable. The Fifth Air Force, charged with protecting the Sixth Army and preparing Luzon for the next major invasion, insisted upon using Bayug Airfield, although it was never fully developed. A new airfield near Tanauan, between Dulag and Tacloban[1] was built from scratch and was operational by December 16th. Nevertheless, the Fifth Air Force was never able to fully deploy forward to Leyte, and as a result was unable to prevent the constant reinforcement attempts by the Japanese which increased their garrison significantly and made the campaign so much more difficult.

General Krueger was seriously concerned about the lack of sufficient hospital facilities on Leyte, also far beyond schedule due to lack of suitable space and delayed construction. Despite giving hospital construction a priority immediately behind the repair of the airfields and roads, insufficient facilities had been completed. Although General Krueger, known as a commander who cared for his men, made every effort to increase the number of hospitals available to Sixth Army, the overwhelmed engineers simply could not comply. In response, Krueger employed several hospital ships and specially equipped LSTs.[2] These, operating under Navy control and with Navy staff, adequately filled the gap created by lack of field hospitals ashore.[3]

Supply was another concern. The nearest main supply base was at Hollandia, New Guinea, more than 1,500 miles from Leyte. Supplies had to be transported over this distance and in the face of increasingly accurate Japanese air attacks on American shipping. The damage to several LSTs on A-Day caused a dumping of supplies in disorder and at locations difficult to access. The supply situation deteriorated from that point. Several entire units had their food and equipment on ships which could not unload even after their troops went ashore. This affected only the support troops destined to repair the airfields and roads, but the delays further increased the difficulty of keeping to the schedule. It was not until November that supplies began to flow as intended. To alleviate the situation, General Krueger set up a committee to determine priorities on unloading. The decision was to unload food, ammunition, airfield landing mats and aviation gas as priorities. Once ashore, the problem became getting them to the troops who needed them. Again, the terrain, roads and weather all factored in, usually in a negative manner. When roads deteriorated, water transportation was used whenever possible. Naval vessels and amphibian vehicles carried supplies as close as they dared to the front-line troops who were at or near the coastal areas. Motor vehicles, men and mules carried supplies to the units which were inland or up in the mountains, a back-breaking task.

Finally, the Sixth Army had to deal with the local civilians. Many volunteered to work for the Americans and were paid accordingly. Others, too weak, young, old or otherwise unable to work, had to be fed. This was handled by the Civil Affairs section, which as early as October 24th, less than a week after the landing, was feeding more than 45,000 civilians. These people were fed the normal U.S. Army C and K Rations until an adequate supply of civilian staples could be acquired and distributed.[4]

*   *   *

General MacArthur's Advance Headquarters established itself on Leyte soon after the invasion, while a significant rear headquarters detachment remained at Hollandia. Throughout the war, as early as the first offensive at Buna, New Guinea, in late 1942, General MacArthur's Headquarters displayed a penchant for announcing victories well before they had actually been achieved. This happened repeatedly during the Southwest Pacific Theater's campaigns, and Leyte was to be no exception. As early as November 3rd, headquarters was announcing that merely enemy "remnants" or "final remnants" were left on Leyte and that they were being swiftly mopped up. Comments such as "The end of the Leyte-Samar Campaign is in sight" were made even as the Japanese were pouring more and more troops into the battle. In fact, by November 3rd, only Leyte Valley had been secured, Ormoc Valley lay completely in Japanese hands, and the Japanese were still sending fresh troops into the battle nearly every night.

General Krueger had his hands full. In addition to the many problems of the front lines, he had to deal with the inability of the engineers to establish the required airfields, the supply difficulty, the lack of sufficient medical facilities, the civilian population, and now the demands from his commanding officer to end the campaign quickly so that General MacArthur could get on with his real concern, the conquest of Luzon and Manila. Yet, throughout these difficulties, Krueger kept his attention on the job at hand. His concern with the continuing Japanese reinforcements made him alter the plan of the campaign so as to direct the full resources of X Corps on Carigara, one of the major ports used by the incoming Japanese. This delayed the move toward Ormoc Valley and its mountainous barriers. For this change he would be criticized later, but at the time and given the information available to him, it was a sound decision.

It was during the drive on Carigara, near Glagsam, that the 34th Infantry hit more serious opposition. On October 31, a squad of the regiment's Anti-tank Company was protecting the point of Company E, when it was hit by heavy Japanese artillery, mortar and small-arms fire. Enemy automatic weapons and snipers joined in the battle. Company E was immediately pinned down and suffered several casualties. Private First Class Walter F.

Lauie, a member of the Antitank Company, was leaning against a jeep when the firing broke out, and he immediately mounted the vehicle and turned its heavy machine gun against the Japanese. He swept the nearby tree line to eliminate the snipers and then turned his powerful weapon against the hidden Japanese positions. The enemy turned the bulk of their fire on to Private First Class Lauie, but he remained at his exposed position atop the jeep and continued firing. Using his actions as a cover, the infantrymen evacuated their many wounded and then under this same cover fire, renewed their advance, routing the Japanese. Private First Class Lauie continued to provide cover fire for Company E until he was killed by an artillery burst. For protecting the wounded and providing cover fire for the infantry at the cost of his own life, Private First Class Lauie was awarded a posthumous Distinguished Service Cross.[5]

Now, however, with Carigara in American hands, the battle turned toward Ormoc. As noted, two drives would be launched: one south through the valley by X Corps and the other north from Baybay by XXIV Corps. The intent was to force the Japanese into the mountains west of Ormoc where they could be dealt with at leisure by the Americans. The XXIV Corps was to move west to reinforce the troops on the shores of Ormoc Bay and mop up within Leyte Valley while X Corps secured Carigara Bay between Carigara and Pinamopoan. With this done they would then be in a position to drive south down Highway 2 through the mountains to reach the plains of Ormoc Valley.

General Sibert set his X Corps off by ordering the 1st Cavalry Division to relieve the units of the 24th Infantry Division around Carigara. Once assembled, the 24th Infantry Division would lead the X Corps attack south. This was why the 7th Infantry Division had been ordered to send a battalion to relieve the 21st Infantry Regiment at Panaon Strait, so that the "Victory Division"[6] would have all of its major components available for the new advance. In turn, General Irving ordered his 34th Infantry Regiment to continue its attack on Capoocan, followed closely by the 19th Infantry Regiment.

Colonel Clifford led off with his 1st Battalion, 34th Infantry, which reached and secured Capoocan on November 3rd without difficulty. As they moved further south to Pinamopoan, they were stopped by a strong enemy force. When artillery and mortar fire failed to move the Japanese out of their positions, a platoon of Company B moved on a ridge paralleling the road, only to run into more Japanese. Colonel Clifford sent up Company A, which accidentally stumbled directly into the main Japanese positions and had to withdraw. Colonel Clifford reinforced Company A with Company C and sent them against the ridge once more. As they advanced, the leader of the advance squad of Company A was killed and Sergeant Charles E. Mower took command. A nineteen-year-old native of Chippewa Falls, Wisconsin, he faced a strong enemy position along both sides of a stream within a wooded gulch. The Japanese had excellent concealment and good lanes of fire to stop any American attack with heavy casualties. Nevertheless, Sergeant Mower began to lead his squad across the stream to approach the enemy positions. Even before he entered the stream, the water was churning with machine gun and rifle fire, but he pressed ahead. He was about halfway across the stream when he was severely wounded by enemy fire. Sergeant Mower ordered his men to halt and looked around, realizing that his exposed position was the best location to direct American fire against the Japanese. Lying half-submerged and gravely wounded, he refused to seek shelter or accept the risk of someone coming to apply medical aid to his injuries. Instead, he began to shout commands to his men, directing them in the elimination of two enemy machine guns and several riflemen who had held up the advance. Eventually, the Japanese discovered that the man in the water was the source of their troubles and directed a tremendous volume of fire upon Sergeant Mower. While still directing his men in the attack, Mower was killed. He was awarded a posthumous Medal of Honor.[7]

Despite Sergeant Mower's gallantry, Colonel Clifford withdrew Company A to allow the 63rd Field Artillery Battalion to pound the ridge. Once they had done so, Company B attacked while Company C flanked the enemy positions. Together, the two companies eliminated the enemy position and destroyed the Japanese. The battalion settled down into a night defensive perimeter.

That same afternoon, Company K of the Third Battalion had made an amphibious reconnaissance to a point just west of Pinamopoan with the mission of cutting off the Japanese defending the road and forcing them to retreat. Carried on seven amphibious tractors that sprayed the landing beach with machine-gun fire, the troops landed as planned and moved up steep, grassy slopes against a strong enemy force. They encountered heavy enemy fire from antitank guns, field cannon and heavy machine guns. This fire was returned by the company's mortars, machine guns and rifles, but as the fight went on, an observation plane's pilot reported a strong enemy convoy moving toward the scene. Only long-range artillery fire, firing at five-mile range and dropping 155mm howitzer shells upon the Japanese, kept Company K intact.

A retreat was ordered and Company K loaded aboard the amphibious tractors, which had stood by offshore, and returned to Capoocan. The observation plane was shot down by enemy fighters as the company withdrew. During the night, both the 11th and 63rd Field Artillery Battalions harassed the Japanese with long-range fire.

The 1st Battalion, 34th Infantry renewed the attack the next morning, but the Japanese had gone. After reaching Colasian, Colonel Clifford set up defenses while the other two battalions passed through and continued the advance. The 2nd Battalion, 34th Infantry soon entered Pinamopoan without opposition, counting over 200 Japanese dead from the previous day's battle. The 3rd Battalion moved another 1,700 yards down the highway where it set up a defensive position in front of a ridge of hills. The Japanese retreat had been disorganized, leaving behind three 75mm guns, one 40mm gun, and five 37mm guns. Much signal equipment, documents and supplies had also been abandoned by the retreating enemy. The coastal corridor was now secured by the 24th Infantry Division. The next move was to the ridge of hills to their front, which would soon be known to history as Breakneck Ridge.

*　　*　　*

While the Americans were securing Carigara and moving south, the Japanese had continued to bring in reinforcements. With the *1st Infantry Division* and considerable elements of both the *26th Infantry Division* and *102nd Infantry Division* now at hand, General Suzuki planned his move north along Highway 2, through Ormoc Valley, to capture the Carigara-Jaro Road. In effect, he was attacking north in the face of the American attack south. After he had defeated the Americans in his path, the *35th Army* would turn east and overrun the American airfields and rear areas, destroying the Sixth Army. Once Carigara had been reached, the *68th Independent Mixed Brigade* was to land in the north and become the *35th Army Reserve*. The *30th Infantry Division* would, in the meantime, land at Albuera on Ormoc Bay and then advance on Burauen to neutralize American bases in the Dulag area.[8]

The American capture of Carigara altered General Suzuki's plans, much like it had those of General Krueger. Realizing that he could not fight through to San Pedro Bay with American forces on his left flank, he instead directed the *1st Infantry Division* on Carigara to destroy the American garrison there before implementing the rest of his planned counterattack. Major elements of the *102nd Infantry Division* were attached to the *1st Infantry*

Division to ensure the success of this mission. The *26th Infantry Division* was to continue with the attack on Jaro. As the Japanese attempted to put this plan into operation they ran afoul of the U.S. Fifth Air Force. The *1st Infantry Division* was moving north in Ormoc Valley on November 3rd, in a ten-mile long convoy of trucks, tanks, and artillery pieces, when the airmen struck. They left some thirty trucks, two tanks and untold numbers of Japanese troops disabled. Two American planes were shot down by the Japanese. The somewhat shaken *1st Infantry Division* continued its march north.

Not all of the Japanese reinforcements arrived safely or intact. Many were attacked during their passage and suffered from American interdiction efforts. Elements of the *362nd Independent Infantry Battalion* were sent from Luzon on a small wooden schooner. On Wednesday, October 25, it was attacked and sunk by an American submarine.[9] The survivors struggled to reach the northwest coast of Leyte where they found their battalion commander dead, their company commander wounded, and many missing. Only a few weapons had been saved, and no food. Deciding that they had to locate other Japanese units, the group sent out a patrol to find friends. The patrol did not return, so the rest of the shattered battalion set off toward Ormoc. Without maps or compasses, they had little idea of the way to go. Most of the wounded died, and others were killed by American air raids. After three weeks on Leyte they were still wandering around, their strength dwindling with each day. Finally, they reached Ormoc as stragglers, and not as the *362nd Independent Infantry Battalion*.[10]

The more successful Japanese landings still worried General Krueger. He was especially concerned that Japanese landings along Carigara Bay would isolate X Corps forces in that area. With the U.S. Seventh Fleet weakened by the recent Battle of Leyte Gulf and the Fifth Air Force limited in the amount of aircraft it could base on Leyte, his support to prevent such a landing was less than adequate. The Third Fleet under Admiral Halsey was too far away to give immediate assistance should a counter-landing occur. Consultations with U.S. Navy officers indicated that the Navy discounted the possibility of a counter-landing. They claimed that the Japanese never had made an opposed amphibious landing,[11] that they were known to be short of amphibious shipping to sustain such a landing, and X Corps artillery would decimate any such landing attempt. Nevertheless, General Krueger decided to order General Sibert to ensure the security of the Carigara Bay area with defenses directed seaward before any major move to the south. He further directed that patrols be sent south to learn as much as possible about the enemy defenses and to locate a site for a battalion of 155mm guns within range of Ormoc. General Sibert immediately ordered General Irving to halt the advance of the 24th Infantry Division and had both General Sibert and General Mudge establish defenses against an amphibious counter-landing throughout the Carigara area. Both division commanders immediately repositioned their infantry and artillery units to ensure a strong defense of the beaches along Carigara Bay. While this was going on, the 21st Infantry rejoined the 24th Infantry Division, and relieved the 34th Infantry at Pinamopoan.

On November 6th, General Krueger was satisfied that his X Corps was prepared to repel any seaborne attack. Repeated assurances from the U.S. Navy that such an attack was highly unlikely had also reassured the general. He ordered the attack south to be resumed. Later he would be again criticized for these few days delay which, according to some, allowed the Japanese to dig in along Breakneck Ridge in complete safety.

General Sibert was now to continue to attack south with the main effort while strong elements of X Corps were to secure the mountain passes between the Ormoc and Leyte Valleys. Once they had secured these locales, long-range artillery would be able to fire directly upon Ormoc and harass any further Japanese attempts at reinforcements. The XXIV Corps was to guard the mountain passes in southern Leyte to prevent any Japanese attempts to enter it from that direction while cutting the island in two at its narrowest point, then striking north to attack the Japanese from the south.

*   *   *

The 24th Infantry Division's attack began on November 7th with a reconnaissance by the newly arrived 21st Infantry against Breakneck Ridge. Lt. Colonel Frederick R. Weber, the regimental commander, led one of these patrols which progressed for over 7,200 yards along Highway 2. Shoulder-high cogon grass and forested areas provided excellent defensive cover for enemy positions. The ridge itself was a hill mass with spurs running off from the crest toward Carigara and Leyte Valley. These hills were heavily forested and had steep sides, making progress difficult. Formed by volcanic upheavals long ago, they had never been thoroughly explored, nor mapped. The map would show one huge hill mass when actually there were five such ridges. Hills were often miles from where they were indicated on American maps. Knobs rose on these ridges, making them ideal defensive locations. Thickly wooded ground pockets were all over the area, adding defensive strength. With the road from Pinamopoan running upward and twisting through these ridges, crossing streams and ravines, it was as if the enemy had designed the terrain for defense. It reminded many veterans of the terrain on Guadalcanal.

The Japanese had used this terrain to the best advantage with trenches, spider holes and pillboxes located in tactically significant places. Many were below the reverse crest lines and immune from direct fire. Fire lanes had been cut through the cogon grass. The continuing rain made climbing these hills slippery and treacherous. The rain also provided cover for enemy movements. To the Japanese, these positions were known as the "Yamashita Line."

Before the new attack even started, fighting had begun along Breakneck Ridge. An observation post of the 34th Infantry and 52nd Field Artillery Battalion had been attacked on a knoll later called OP Hill. Colonel Weber had sent his 3rd Battalion, 21st Infantry to assist the forward observers. Company K moved up the right side of the highway and rescued the observation party. Captain Thomas Suber of South Carolina led Company K in a wild screaming countercharge against the Japanese surrounding the observation group. Company I moved along the left side and ran into stiff resistance at a hill which came to be known as Corkscrew Ridge. This hill formed the southern spur of Breakneck Ridge. Both companies soon ran out of ammunition, and resupply parties were ambushed by hidden Japanese along the supply route. After vehicles had their tires shot out, infantrymen carried resupply up to the two companies. Company I cleared out the enemy along the supply route, but mortar fire continued to harass the groups.

Both companies were far in advance of the main American force. This became more apparent when the pressure from the *57th Infantry, 1st Infantry Division* began to increase. Supplying the two companies became more and more difficult but the companies held their positions and repulsed several counterattacks during the night. The next morning, the Japanese added mortar and artillery fire to the troubles of the Americans on Breakneck Ridge. This finally forced the withdrawal of both companies back to the main American line of resistance.

The difficulty faced by the attackers is clarified by the experience of one scout. Private Charles Feeback of Carlisle, Kentucky, was a lead scout in the 21st Infantry. Leading an advance, he pushed through head-high kunai grass, using his Thompson sub-machine gun to push the grass out of his face. As he pushed one clump of grass aside, he suddenly saw a Japanese soldier in a spider hole not four feet away. The enemy's rifle was cocked and pointed in his direction. Private Feeback was quicker on the trigger, however, and killed the enemy soldier. Waving his arm over his head, he continued forward. Then he heard a click off to his right. The experienced soldier knew this sound to be the noise Japanese grenades make when primed. The grenade landed at his feet and the scout dived sideways into the thick grass. The blast did not injure him, but he lay quiet in the grass, waiting. His patience paid off when the enemy soldier poked his head up to see the results of his grenade. Private Feeback shot him.

The 1st Battalion, 21st Infantry had tried all day to secure a position from which it could support the two advance companies, but without success. The Japanese were well dug in using spider holes, tunnels and prepared fire lanes to blunt any attack against their positions. By the end of November 6th the *57th Infantry* again owned Breakneck Ridge undisputed. To emphasize their ownership, a strong counterattack hit the 2nd Battalion, 21st Infantry that night. Using mortars and grenades, the *57th Infantry* tried, but failed, to penetrate the American perimeter. Reinforced by the 3rd Battalion, 19th Infantry, Colonel Weber ordered his regiment to renew the attack the following morning.

Supported by the 52nd Field Artillery Battalion, the 44th Tank Battalion, the 632nd Tank Destroyer Battalion and the 85th Chemical Mortar Battalion, the 2nd Battalion of the 21st Infantry led off the attack on Breakneck Ridge on November 7th. That same morning, General Suzuki was bombed out of his headquarters by the 308th Bombardment Wing, and Ormoc came under fire from long-range 155mm guns based at Jaro. Meanwhile, Companies E and G ran into the *3rd Battalion, 57th Infantry*, on the forward slope of the ridge. Colonel Weber brought forward the self-propelled guns of the tank destroyer battalion which fired directly into the enemy positions, eliminating the enemy battalion commander but not pushing the Japanese out of their defenses. Colonel Weber next called two tanks forward, but as they moved up, a Japanese soldier disabled one of them with a magnetic mine. The other tank withdrew.

Enemy troops infiltrated around the American positions. When a group of Company M men brought up a resupply of ammunition in a truck along the road, they were hit with sniper fire, then mortar fire directed by the Japanese from somewhere behind American lines. Machine guns peppered the truck and finally a mortar shell landed immediately in front of it, disabling it. Japanese troops attacked the group, determined to capture or destroy the ammunition within. The Company M group, under Sergeant Paul Carfield of Cato, New York, defended their truck. From alongside and underneath the ammunition-loaded truck, they fought off the attacking Japanese. One by one the defenders were killed until only Private Melvin Taylor of Alton, Illinois, remained. He continued the defense alone. Finally an American patrol, drawn by the firing, arrived and drove off the remaining Japanese. The ammunition was safely delivered.

Dissatisfied with Colonel Weber's progress, General Sibert took his intelligence officer, Colonel William J. Verbeck along for a visit to Weber and an evaluation of the situation.[12] Not pleased with what he learned, General Sibert relieved Colonel Weber and replaced him with Colonel Verbeck. Weber remained as the regimental executive officer. Additional efforts to secure a foothold on Breakneck Ridge this day proved unsuccessful and the battalion established a night perimeter at the foot of the ridge. Indeed, things did not go well at any point during this attack. Company G, 19th Infantry got lost and reported itself nearly a mile from its actual position. Support from artillery was impossible due to lack of observation. Nothing seemed to go right.

November 8th began with Colonel Verbeck ordering an artillery barrage before the morning attack. The 1st Battalion was directed on Hill 1525, where Company G had gotten lost the day before, and the 2nd Battalion would try and envelope the flank of the *1st Infantry Division.* But before anything could begin, a huge typhoon swept over the island. Floods were pervasive; trees bent almost horizontally, palm fronds were flying, and trees crashed down. Supplies stopped coming. Planes were grounded. Trails disappeared in the rain and flood. The sky blackened. Artillery barrages directed on Breakneck Ridge sounded dim in the deluge. But the attack went in. The 2nd Battalion used flamethrowers to eliminate the enemy pocket which had held them up the day before. Shelled by mortar and artillery fire, the battalion kept advancing despite fierce opposition from the *57th Infantry.* Enemy riflemen fired on the advancing Americans from every angle. Supply parties, medical-aid men and communications patrols were constantly fired upon. Small enemy detachments infiltrated the American lines and harassed rear areas. When Lieutenant Colonel Robert B. Spragins, commanding 2nd Battalion, 19th Infantry, finally joined up with Company G on the hill, the Japanese had been driven off that spur. Much in the way of abandoned equipment was found, most of it new and in good order. In one case, an order from the *1st Infantry Division* was captured, letting the Americans know for certain who they were fighting.

As always, leadership was critical to success in combat. Sergeant Dominic Castro of Los Angeles led a squad of infantry on one of these hills. One of his men lay exhausted, a victim of battle fatigue. As he looked ahead, Sergeant Castro saw the enemy attacking, and yelled out to his squad to get ready. In the dark of night the Japanese came on with rifles, bayonets and grenades. Yelling threats in Japanese and English they tossed grenades and then moved in for the kill. The Americans dropped to the ground to avoid the grenade blasts, and then opened fire. Sergeant Castro was wounded by a grenade, after which an enemy soldier drove a bayonet into his body. He killed the bayonet wielder and fired until his weapon was empty, then reversed it and used it as a club, beating back his attackers. He stayed leading his squad until the fight was over. His squad survived.

Colonel Spragins soon learned that like Company G the night before, he was lost. His battalion was not on Hill 1525, but some distance east of it. Even his Filipino guides were unsure of their location. His battalion could observe Leyte Valley, but not Ormoc Valley. He had to move west. This he managed to do with Company E leading the way to another ridge some thousand yards to the west.

That night the rain continued falling. By dawn on November 9th, the two leading battalions were soaked through and tired. Facing enemy positions armed with machine guns and mortars, with a bridge knocked out to prevent American tanks from supporting them, the 21st Infantry moved out. It moved fairly well, supported by artillery and mortars. Using their grenades, rifles and flamethrowers, the Americans moved up the ridge. By mid-morning, the 21st Infantry had reached the crest of the intermediate ridge east of the road which ran right through the center of Breakneck Ridge. Company E moved out to attack the rear of the Japanese covering the site at the downed bridge.

Progress remained slow but steady in the face of continued enemy fire. Just before noon, Company L managed to reach the top of the ridge. Company E also reached its objective. Both battalions settled in for the night, with each rifle company reinforced with a platoon of heavy machine guns. The following morning Colonel Verbeck's Regiment was ordered to move east and relieve the 1st Battalion, 21st Infantry on Hill 1525. The latter battalion was to establish positions which overlooked Highway 2 and others, which cut the Ormoc Road, in order to prevent the escape of the Japanese then defending Breakneck Ridge. The move was quickly halted by strong enemy fire. A renewed attack made some progress but in the meantime, an attack on Company A holding Hill 1525 almost succeeded. Despite fourteen tons of mortar shells fired by the guns of Company A, the Japanese still came on. A pillbox on "Bloody Knob" was finally overrun by the Company, and some seventy-five dead Japanese were found inside.

Colonel Verbeck ordered the 1st Battalion, 21st Infantry back to Hill 1525 to reinforce Company A. One group moved up the slopes of "Suicide Hill" only to be attacked from the rear. Outnumbered and outgunned, they withdrew. In another instance, Captain Robert Kilgo was surprised when one of his own machine guns began firing on his company. Going forward to investigate, he found that the enemy had captured his gun. Returning to his command, he grabbed a heavy machine gun from a portion of his perimeter not under attack and, followed by the gun crew, he raced back under Japanese and friendly fire to plug the hole in his defensive line. The battalion returned to Hill 1525 just in time to face a renewed Japanese attack by an estimated battalion from the *57th Infantry Regiment*. The depleted and tired Americans—Company B lost two out of every three men who started the attack—could not hold, and left Hill 1525 to the Japanese.

Behind the lines, outposts at the beaches of Pinamopoan noticed a group of armed men coming towards them along the road. It was dark and the men could not be identified, but they spoke English and were approaching in a casual manner. Nevertheless, following the rule that anyone moving after dark was an enemy, the outposts opened fire. They heard more shouts, in English, to cease fire or calling for medical-aid men. Fire directions were also shouted. But the outposts were not fooled and in the morning, they counted fifteen dead Japanese along the beach.

Meanwhile the 2nd Battalion, 19th Infantry, had learned that Hill 1525 was under attack and tried to reinforce the garrison. Colonel Spragins pushed ahead with two of his companies trying to reach the 1st Battalion in time. But the steep slippery slopes stopped his efforts before they could take any effect. Blocked by mud, the steepness and downed trees, the Spragins battalion never even got close enough to hear the battle for Hill 1525, much less participate in it. Finally the battalion reached what it believed to be Hill 1525, but found no sign of friend or foe. It was now that the Americans began to understand that their maps were wrong, and that Hill 1525 was not one hill but a long ridge of many knolls and hills. Breakneck Ridge still belonged to the Japanese.

*   *   *

Behind Japanese lines, the newly arrived *26th Infantry Division* had assembled at Ormoc and was moving up Ormoc Valley. Equipment and ammunition had been left behind to avoid more attacks on the convoy's staging area by aircraft of the U.S. Fifth Air Force. Other ships of the convoy had been sunk along the way. Nevertheless, General Suzuki now had another well-organized force to add to his attack. This planned attack, and much of its details, was known to General Krueger. The attack order had been taken from the body of a Japanese officer on November 8th, and rushed to Sixth Army Headquarters. General Krueger immediately saw the significance of the captured order and disposed his forces to meet the threat. General Sibert and his X Corps would continue his attack down Highway 2 but was at the same time to send forces into the central mountain range to block the routes which ran from Ormoc Valley into Leyte Valley. General Hodge's XXIV Corps was to send a reinforced regiment into the hills northwest of Dagami to do the same, blocking access into Leyte Valley. General Hodge was to allocate forces which could assist the X Corps in its missions while sending another reinforced regiment into Sixth Army Reserve. Finally the 112th Cavalry Regimental Combat Team,[13] expected to arrive on Leyte on November 14, would relieve those units of the 1st Cavalry Regiment guarding the beaches in the Carigara-Barugo area. Once relieved, the 1st Cavalry was to move south and join the 24th Infantry Division in its attack south.

General Hodge moved to comply by ordering his 96th Infantry Division to seize the high ground between Jaro and Dagami. This would block all routes between the two critical valleys and put his patrols on the west coast of Leyte. His 7th Infantry Division, which had reached Baybay on the shores of Ormoc Bay, was ordered to send patrols towards Ormoc to learn as much as possible about the terrain and enemy defenses for a future attack on Ormoc in strength. General Krueger also considered that if the Japanese attention could be concentrated on the X Corps attack in the north and northeast, it might be possible for XXIV Corps to push a strong force south over the mountains using the Abuyog-Baybay road to reach the east shore of Ormoc Bay, reinforcing elements of the 7th Infantry Division already there. He also considered an amphibious landing, perhaps as large as a division, at a point near Ormoc, to cut off the flow of Japanese reinforcements and in effect, surround the *35th Army* in Ormoc Valley. But for this plan to proceed, the Japanese main forces, the *1st* and *26th Infantry Divisions,* had to be kept in the north of Ormoc Valley.

General Irving launched his 24th Infantry Division against the *1st Infantry Division* on Breakneck Ridge again on November 10th. The plan placed the 21st Infantry in the lead with the 2nd Battalion, 19th Infantry establishing a roadblock on Highway 2 some 2,000 yards south of Limon, behind the ridge. Meanwhile the 1st Battalion, 34th Infantry was to set off on a wide flanking move around the west flank of the *57th Infantry Regiment* to seize a position to their rear, later known as Kilay Ridge, about 700 yards from Highway 2 and west of the proposed roadblock. These units set off in continuing rain and winds, through thick, slippery mud. After a brief artillery barrage, the 1st Battalion, 21st Infantry pushed into the hills. The Second Battalion followed. The attack saw some early successes as when Company G, pulling tank destroyer guns behind them, seized OP Hill, and Company I took the site of the destroyed bridge, 300 yards to the southeast. Colonel Verbeck then sent the First Battalion against another ridge by outflanking maneuvers on either side of the ridge. This tactic failed, however, and the battalion returned to its start point.

So short of infantrymen was the 21st Infantry at this point that rear echelon men were drafted to the front lines, men such as Sergeant James Nesbitt of Arkansas. The mess sergeant led a patrol to root out enemy snipers. When his men became separated in the tall grass, Nesbitt began a circular search for them. As he did so, he stumbled upon a sniper whom he killed. Almost immediately, however, another sniper opened fire on him. Then a grenade landed nearby. The mess sergeant lay quiet for a few moments, shaking off the concussion blast, and then hunted for the second sniper, whom he also killed. Private Francis Anderson of North Dakota was normally a messenger. But when the crew of an antitank gun in Company E was knocked out, leaving a hole in the defense, Private Anderson moved into the breach with only his rifle and held it closed until the Japanese retired. Despite such efforts, all attempts to advance beyond OP Hill failed. The Japanese resisted stoutly and denied any further movement forward by the 21st Infantry.

While this frontal attack continued, the 1st Battalion, 34th Infantry and the 2nd Battalion, 19th Infantry each made their advances to Kilay Ridge and Limon, respectively. The Japanese, too, moved up new forces and the *2nd Battalion, 1st Artillery Regiment, 1st Infantry Division,* moved to a position east of Limon where they were able to support the *57th Infantry Regiment.*

While the rest of the regiment fought its battles, Company F of the 21st Infantry spent eleven days fighting for possession of Arson Hill, one of the many deadly knobs along Breakneck Ridge. In jungle grass seven feet high and with visibility limited to a yard at a time, the company fought for possession of the hilltop. Rarely were the opposing forces more than ten yards apart. Soldiers fired by sound and feel rather than by sighting any enemy.

Blind volleys were used to clear the advance, hoping that they would eliminate any enemy in their front. Spraying bullets into the fog was common, but not usually successful. In eight days, the company fought off sixteen Japanese counterattacks. One in three of its men fell to enemy fire. When the typhoon came over the area, the wind blew in the faces of Company F, and the Japanese set fire to the grass, hoping to burn the Americans out. Wounded men were burned to death when they could not escape the blaze. The wind and rain, now mixed with heavy smoke, eliminated all visibility. From the heights around them, Company F was additionally subjected to enemy machine gun fire. A messenger, Private First Class William Phipps of Idaho, was ducking enemy fire when he saw the crew of a machine gun fall under Japanese fire. The gun was a critical part of the company's flank defense, and he quickly ran to the gun and took over. As he fired, a lone Japanese soldier tossed a grenade into the hole. Blasted aside by the explosion, Private Phipps shook off the concussion effects, regained his balance, and resumed firing.

Men ran from the blazing fire while others dug deeper holes and let the fire burn over and past them. First Lieutenant Benjamin Rosenblatt of Chicago, found his platoon isolated. His men were exhausted but he needed to move them to a safer position. Many, even though unwounded, could not walk. Others lay in the mud, glassy-eyed and beyond all caring. Rosenblatt, himself wounded and bleeding, moved up and down the ridge exhorting his men to move to a safer location. He encouraged them to withdraw, carrying their wounded with them. As they did, Lieutenant Rosenblatt was himself cut down. But Company F remained on Arson Hill. And when the fire finally cleared, there were far less problems with visibility.

November 11th began auspiciously when the 1st Battalion, 21st Infantry moved to within 300 yards of the crest of Breakneck Ridge against minimal opposition. However, once they reached this point, Japanese resistance stopped them in their tracks. The battalion then moved west to a position where their supporting tanks from the 44th Tank Battalion could attack. These tanks, from 2nd Platoon, Company A moved down Highway 2 knocking out an estimated twenty-five enemy automatic weapons positions. The depth of the ravine in which the Japanese had established themselves prevented the tanks from using their cannon or machine guns, which could not be lowered enough to hit the enemy. Instead, the tanks fired over the heads of the Japanese while the tank commanders stood exposed in their turrets and threw grenades and fired sub-machine guns at the fortified enemy. The tankers themselves modestly claimed only fifteen enemy positions destroyed, along with an estimated seventy-five Japanese troops. One tank was stuck when it ran off the edge of the road during the withdrawal, but the crew was rescued by another tank which then destroyed the stalled vehicle. The tank company commander, Captain Julian Van Winkle, was wounded in the hand and side while trying to rescue the stalled vehicle.[14]

The tanks had enabled the 1st Battalion, 21st Infantry to achieve its objective for the day. This was a ridge some 300 yards southwest of OP Hill. That night the battalion consolidated its position and directed harassing fire on the Japanese from the 226th and 465th Field Artillery Battalions.[15] The 2nd Battalion was not as fortunate, and made no discernable progress during the day toward Corkscrew Ridge. That night, when an enemy counterattack struck a rear area battalion command post, Private First Class Woodrow W. Haskett, a cook from Wyoming, was the first to see them coming. He raced to a machine gun and opened fire. Despite close quarters fire and incoming grenades from the attacking Japanese, Haskett stood his ground. When the attackers retired, the Wyoming soldier lay dead at his gun.

*   *   *

The twelfth of November was an even better day for the 21st Infantry. On this morning, the 3rd Battalion used six tanks and a platoon of tank destroyers from the 632nd Tank Destroyer Battalion to move along the road edging around Breakneck Ridge. By noon, the battalion had passed over the crest of the ridge and was moving down the reverse slope. This success allowed the 1st Battalion to renew its attack of the day before and attempt to envelop the Japanese north flank. Little enemy fire was encountered and the 1st Battalion, too, crossed Breakneck Ridge. Once on the crest, however, heavy artillery fire from the *2nd Field Artillery Battalion, 1st Infantry Division* halted the attack for the day.

The next day, the 1st and 2nd Battalions attacked in unison, supported by machine gun fire from OP Hill. Resistance from the *57th Infantry Regiment* seemed markedly reduced and the advance made some ground. By the following day, General Irving had decided that the enemy resistance on Breakneck Ridge had been broken, although several of the notorious spurs were still owned by the Japanese, including Corkscrew Ridge. The battle would continue, but with the arrival of the 128th Infantry Regiment[16] of the 32nd Infantry Division,[17] the Battle of Breakneck Ridge was about over for the 24th Infantry Division. It had lost 630 men killed, wounded or missing while another 135 men had been lost to other causes, including illness, injury, trench foot and disease. Counted Japanese casualties came to 1,779.

*   *   *

By the last days of October, General Hodge's XXIV Corps had secured the southern portion of Leyte Valley, the vital road net and all of the airfields in that area. His next objectives were to liberate the southern portion of Leyte while assisting X Corps' drive in the north. As already noted, General Krueger had ordered XXIV Corps to close the passes between the Ormoc and Leyte Valleys to frustrate General Suzuki's plans for a counterattack. To implement his orders, General Hodge sent the 96th Infantry Division to make an attack east of the mountains while the 7th Infantry Division moved from Baybay towards Ormoc Bay. The former division would relieve the latter's units garrisoning the Tanauan-Dgami-Burauen-Dulag area.

The men of the "Hourglass" Division[18] had not been idle while the rest of Sixth Army had been fighting in the north. They had been constantly pushing forward, moving to the south to find a good road across the island, while clearing enemy opposition as they went. When, on 30 October, a squad of Company L, 184th Infantry, was attacking one of these small enemy enclaves near San Victor, Private First Class Samuel B. Kite, an automatic rifleman, was knocked down by enemy fire. Wounded severely in both legs, he continued to fire at the enemy. When the squad was forced to withdraw to organize for a second attack, Kite moved to an exposed position and opened a covering fire on the Japanese. When told the squad was retreating, Kite refused to go, telling them "I can't make it, go back yourself, and I'll cover you." He continued to hold his advanced position, covering his squad, until he was killed by the enemy. For saving the lives of his squadmates at the cost of his own, Private First Class Kite was awarded a posthumous Distinguished Service Cross.[19]

General Bradley sent his 382nd Infantry Regiment to relieve the 17th Infantry Regiment in the Dagami area. Unknown to the Americans, this placed the 382nd Infantry in exactly the area that General Suzuki deemed had the best access into Leyte Valley for his counterattack. The village of Dagami was at the center of a road net which led to all parts of Leyte Valley and the airfields which were the Japanese objectives. Located in the area were all the major elements of the *16th Infantry Division*. Although weakened by casualties and hunger—they had run out of food and been forced to live off the land—the *16th Infantry Division* was still a strong viable force, estimated at some 6,000 men. These units were dug in on a small hill on the road west of Dagami.[20] A waist-deep swamp lay immediately in front of the hill, forming in effect a moat between the Japanese and Americans.

On November 2nd, the 382nd Infantry relieved the 17th Infantry. The 1st Battalion, 382nd Infantry attacked into the swamp under enemy fire but could not reach the hills prior to darkness, so it settled in for the night. The following day, another attack faced strong enemy fire while the soldiers were still struggling through the rice paddies in front of Dagami Heights. Mortar, artillery and automatic weapons fire hit the Americans as they cleared the swamps and came out in the open directly under the Japanese guns. Supporting tanks were driven off by accurate enemy artillery. The battalion spent the day under fire without being able to make progress in any direction.

Finally, late in the day, the battalion withdrew under cover of smoke screens provided by the artillery. It was a terrible withdrawal. "Men threw away their packs, machine guns, radios and even rifles. Their sole aim was to crawl back through the muck and get on solid ground once more. Some of the wounded gave up the struggle to keep their heads above the water and drowned in the grasping swamp."[21] Every officer in B and C Companies had become casualties. First Sergeant Francis H. Thompson of Company C saw the crisis and, despite his own serious wounds, immediately took command and organized the withdrawal. When an enemy machine gun threatened the withdrawing Americans, Thompson attacked and knocked it out with grenades taken from his wounded comrades. Seeing wounded unable to withdraw, he helped them to the rear. For his leadership in successfully withdrawing the two companies, First Sergeant Thompson was awarded the Distinguished Service Cross.[22] As if adding insult to injury, as the battalion finally reached safety, it was strafed by five Japanese planes. The regiment's 2nd Battalion came forward to assist the 1st.

The day's effort had cost the 382nd Infantry fifteen men killed, 44 wounded and 18 missing. One of the missing was Private First Class John W. Turner, a Company D machine gunner who had been wounded and crawled into a nearby shack. He spent the night there playing dead when Japanese soldiers came by and kicked and searched him. He survived the night to be rescued the following morning.

The Japanese sensed their success and launched a strong counterattack on the night of November 3-4, against the 1st Battalion, 382nd Infantry. Two companies of the *16th Infantry Division* hit the perimeter of the battalion but strong artillery and mortar fires repulsed the assault. Once the Japanese had been turned back, the artillery concentrated its fire on Dagami Heights for the rest of the night. In the morning, both the 1st and 2nd Battalions, 382nd Infantry attacked. Led by Lieutenant Colonel Cyril D. Sterner of the 2nd Battalion, the advance met only light resistance and moved past the site of the previous day's repulse. In mid-afternoon, Lieutenant Colonel John G. Cassidy's 1st Battalion took fire from a new enemy position. Colonel Dill immediately ordered Colonel Sterner to bypass the block by the left flank, but darkness prevented a coordinated attack.

Brigadier General Claudis M. Easley, the assistant division commander, had been with the 96th Infantry Division since it was organized back at Camp Adair, Oregon in August 1942. He had seen it through all of its training and testing at the various maneuvers over the years, and was determined to remain with his soldiers throughout their battles. In battle barely two weeks, he had already earned a reputation as a "fighting general" for his constant presence at the front lines, leading, encouraging and advising his troops. During this attack, he was once again in the front lines of the 382nd Infantry and suddenly found himself nearly stepping on a Japanese soldier in a spider hole at his feet. Pulling his pistol, General Easley fired two shots before his pistol jammed. The Japanese fired back and wounded General Easley in the arm and side. The general's aide, First Lieutenant Leslie A. Parish, Jr., opened fire with his M-1 carbine and killed the enemy soldier. General Easley was back with his troops before the month ended.[23]

The Japanese allowed the Americans no rest and attacked again the night of November 4–5. Another heavy attack supported by harassing fire from automatic weapons and mortars hit the 2nd Battalion shortly before midnight. Once again, American artillery and mortars stopped the attack, leaving 254 Japanese casualties on the field. American artillery fired on the known Japanese positions throughout the night. Again, the Americans attacked in the morning, this time with two companies of the 3rd Battalion joining the attack. An advance of 1,000 yards went well until another pocket of enemy resistance was encountered.

Private First Class Donald O. Dencker was with the mortar section of Company L, 3rd Battalion, 382nd Infantry, which joined the attack November 5th. He recalled that the road forward "was a mass of mud and potholes" and that even before the company attacked, they had lost a man to enemy fire. As they advanced, they came under 75mm fire from Japanese who "had been waiting for us." Supported by light tanks from Company D, 763rd Tank Battalion, the infantry advanced with the tank flamethrowers in the lead.

Artillery observers in light planes overhead spotted and directed artillery fire on the enemy guns, which were soon knocked out. At a cost of one man killed and four wounded, Company L achieved its objective.[24]

The 1st Battalion had more trouble. It came up against what the Americans described as a "Headquarters Fort." A concrete fortification, it defied all of the weapons the infantry could bring against it. Rockets and grenades did nothing but bounce off the concrete sides. Finally Privates First Class Frank Hartzer and Charles A. Greenback[25] crawled up to the emplacement and destroyed it by pouring gasoline into the air vents and setting it afire. A score of enemy soldiers ran from the blazing fort and were cut down by American fire. By nightfall, assisted by more tanks from Company A, 763rd Tank Battalion, the regiment had reduced all enemy positions to their front and settled down for the night.

Just before dark, a patrol set out to reconnoiter enemy pillbox positions further along the road. This was an unusual patrol in that although it was led by the 2nd Battalion's Intelligence Officer, First Lieutenant Lester Mack, it included Captain (Chaplain) Leonard F. Todd. The patrol was spotted by the Japanese who opened fire. Lieutenant Mack was killed and Captain Todd brought the survivors back to American lines. On the next day fighting continued as the enemy was reduced individual position by individual position. The Japanese did not withdraw—in accordance with General Suzuki's orders they were to protect the flank of the coming counterattack—but fought back fiercely, defending every position to the death. By November 6th, all of the battalion commanders, most of the company commanders, and half of the artillery battery commanders had been killed. Losses among enlisted personnel were equally heavy. Finally, on the night of November 6th, the *16th Infantry Division* pulled back, but only a few thousand yards to a new position in the Dagami area.

The 382nd Infantry followed up the Japanese withdrawal. On November 7th, led by tanks, they pushed the enemy rear guards back. A Japanese foray tried to destroy the tanks but failed due to close infantry protection. In an action typical of the fierce fighting, Company L came up against a pillbox. Private First Class Harvey Glaess was the scout who first approached it. He was killed instantly. Private First Class Joseph Winters was wounded trying to reach Glaess. Technical Sergeant Philip A. Martorelli brought up a machine gun, only to be wounded. He grabbed an M-1 rifle and fired on the enemy until he was killed. Privates First Class Victor Kuczynski and Loren Read tried to reach the wounded, only to be killed themselves. Technical Sergeant Truman Frost was moving up when he was killed by a mortar fragment. The advance continued, but it remained costly as ever.

Using flamethrowers, tanks, machine guns and rifles, the 382nd Infantry pushed so hard the Japanese became disorganized and fled in some disorder. An estimated 474 enemy dead were found in the area. Tired but determined, the soldiers pushed ahead until they located a strong enemy position about 2,600 yards west of the village of Patok. Another heavy rain delayed the attack by a day, and when the battalions attacked on November 10th, they found no resistance. Swamps again slowed the attack, but the Japanese were gone. By noon, the regiment occupied the ridge which had been the next main enemy defense line. All organized enemy resistance in the Dagami area was considered over.

*   *   *

While the 382nd Infantry was clearing Dagami Heights, the 381st Infantry had been extensively patrolling the southern flanks to ensure that no organized enemy forces threatened the division's flank. Captain Robert B. O'Neill led the 96th Cavalry Reconnaissance Troop on a wide-ranging foot patrol through miserable terrain to ensure the flanks were covered. On November 10th, as the patrol was moving out from a night position, Staff Sergeant John M. McHenry, Jr., slipped and fell in the mud. Badly injuring his ankle, he was sent to the rear escorted by men from his section. As they moved back to the division, they came across a Japanese aviator whose plane had been shot down. The Japanese officer was surprised by the patrol but pulled his pistol and attempted to shoot himself. Corporal Charles J. Kubitz and Private Rudolph N. Pizio would not let that happen to such a potentially valuable prisoner and physically restrained him, so much so that Private Pizio broke his wrist in the act. The Japanese aviator was safely escorted to division intelligence officers.

Having secured the Dagami area the 96th Infantry Division now drew new orders. It was to relieve the 7th Infantry Division and move north to the Jaro-Palo road area and secure the mountain passes in that sector. One regiment was to be held in reserve while another was to prepare for a landing on Mindanao.[26] Meanwhile the 7th Infantry Division would take over the Dagami area.

*   *   *

When Company G, 32nd Infantry Regiment, 7th Infantry Division reached

Baybay on the west coast at the tip of Ormoc Bay, it had found it unoccupied. Colonel Finn reacted immediately to the good fortune which had laid this tactical opportunity in his hands. He ordered the rest of the 2nd Battalion, 32nd Infantry over the long winding road which led across the island from Abuyog to Baybay. He brought his regimental command post there the next day, and then called for his 3rd Battalion to join him. Realizing that the road back to Abuyog was his lifeline, Colonel Finn ordered the 3rd Battalion to guard the cross-island road from a headquarters location along the road.

Meanwhile, Company G had been patrolling up to five miles north from Baybay. No Japanese were found. Before more could be done, the three days of typhoon stymied any action Colonel Finn contemplated. At Division Headquarters, General Arnold had been receiving disturbing intelligence about strong Japanese reinforcements arriving at Ormoc. Up to ten thousand Japanese were reported to have landed on the night of November 3–4.[27] Guerrillas reported that the Japanese were building a road across the mountains directed on Burauen over which the reinforcements would move to seize the American airfields. Uncertain of his information, General Arnold sent the division's 7th Reconnaissance Troop north in the middle of the typhoon. The troopers moved nearly to Albuera, across the island from Dulag, without meeting the enemy. But again, guerrilla intelligence informed them that the Japanese were strong and that they were moving forward. The reports clearly stated that they were also headed south, towards Baybay and the 7th Infantry Division.

The Japanese could use the reported road they were building or they could come south to Baybay, to use the same road the 32nd Infantry had used to cross the mountains, then swing north and attack U.S. Sixth Army's flank. General Arnold ordered the 2nd Battalion, 32nd Infantry forward to Caridad as a blocking position if the Japanese came south. The next day, November 11th, Captain O'Neill and his 96th Reconnaissance Troop completed their long patrol and arrived at Damulaan. Captain O'Neill reported that he had come over the mountain passes from Burauen and had seen no sign that the Japanese were building any roads over the mountains.

The next day, guerrilla reports had small Japanese forces making amphibious landings between Albuera and the Palanas River. When General Hodge at XXIV Corps learned of this, he ordered Arnold to push any and all Japanese forces north of Albuera. The order specified that no major engagement was to be brought on, since XXIV Corps had no troops to spare to reinforce Colonel Finn's regiment at the moment. Supplies and reinforcements were being rushed to Baybay but it would take time, and no major battle was desired until the Americans were ready.

Once again Company G drew the assignment. On November 12th, the company moved north towards Damulaan under orders to reach Albuera the following day. As they prepared to move out on November 13th, the company had the unique experience of being the object of a Japanese landing from barges. Half the enemy force of fifty was killed and the rest fled back to their barges. First Lieutenant Thomas Hindaman led a combined force of Company G and Filipino guerrillas to Balogo and then to the Tabgas River where they were stopped by enemy machine gun and rifle fire. The patrol spent the night in Balogo where they were attacked by a company of Japanese. The patrol successfully defended itself, forcing the Japanese back north. But Lt. Colonel Glenn A. Nelson was now concerned and ordered them back to the south side of the Palanas River. He was bringing up the rest of his 2nd Battalion, 32nd Infantry.

General Arnold now understood that the Japanese were moving south to cross Leyte on the same road that his division had used. Without sufficient forces at Baybay to attack, his only immediate option was to establish a blocking position to prevent the Japanese from reaching the Baybay-Abuyog Road. To this end he ordered his 2nd Battalion, 32nd Infantry to Damulaan to establish defensive positions. He recalled his 3rd Battalion, 32nd Infantry from guarding the Baybay-Abuyog Road and assembled them in Baybay, as his only reserve force. Additional support was being brought up in the form of Battery B, 11th 155mm Howitzer Battalion, USMC. Two battalions of the 184th Infantry Regiment were put on alert to join the 32nd Infantry at Baybay.

*   *   *

The Japanese that Company G had encountered at Albuera were from the *364th Independent Infantry Battalion*. When Company G had first arrived at Baybay, General Suzuki had learned, apparently from an American broadcast, that American troops were on the west coast to his south. He believed this force to be a small one of American and Philippine troops. In order to protect his rear areas, he dispatched a company of the *364th Independent Infantry Battalion* to Albuera to protect the terminus of the mountain trail that the Japanese had tried, and failed, to turn into a road over the mountains into Leyte Valley.

Meanwhile at Ormoc, the *26th Infantry Division* landed after a most difficult journey from Manila. The convoy had been repeatedly attacked, many ships being sunk with men and supplies aboard. Several of the smaller landing craft were so damaged that they had to run themselves aground at Ormoc in order to deliver their cargoes. Others departed before daylight, with only a part of their cargoes delivered, in order to avoid the American aircraft. This didn't work, as all ships of this convoy were sunk either on the way to Leyte or on the way back to Luzon. As a result, the *26th Infantry Division* was badly hurt even before it landed on Leyte. Only the *Headquarters Battalion,* a battalion of the *11th Independent Infantry Regiment* and the *13th Independent Infantry Regiment* landed, as did the *2nd Battalion, 12th Infantry Regiment.* Most of the heavy weapons of these units were lost. Some retained their machine guns and mortars, but ammunition was in short supply. Casualties were already severe in certain units.

Once again General Suzuki was forced to change his plans. With American forces on his southern flank at Baybay, he needed to protect that flank. He then received orders from Manila that the *26th Infantry Division* was to be used in the counterattack at the Burauen airfields. Since this meant that the division would have to move south to reach its assigned attack area, he now had a unit to address the threat to his southern flank. Accordingly, General Suzuki sent the main force of the division to Albuera. Leading off was the *13th Independent Infantry Regiment* under Colonel Jiro Saito, soon to be followed by the rest of the division.

General Krueger also had to adjust his planning. Sixth Army Field Order Number 23, September 23, 1944, had directed the approach to the west coast of Leyte via the Abuyog-Baybay Road which General Krueger soon "found personally to be an extremely rough, wide trail, was certain to be difficult."[28] He now was aware of General Suzuki's coming attack, although it "did not disturb" him. General Krueger was determined to retain the initiative by pressing his attacks in both the north and the south. He still harbored the idea of an amphibious landing behind the Japanese landings at or near Ormoc. Indeed, by this time, he was tending to think that whatever General Suzuki planned with regard to a counterattack, he was far too busy fending off American attacks, and losing troops too fast, to actually prepare for such an attack. The loss of the area around Breakneck Ridge and Limon had deprived him of a start line for such an attack.

But there were other problems. Before the campaign he had requested, from General MacArthur, 18,800 replacements, with the first 10,000 to be received by A+10. Two-thirds of these were infantry replacements, where the most casualties would obviously occur. But these did not arrive as planned. It was now the third week of the campaign and Sixth Army was short 1,050 officers and 11,754 enlisted men from its Table of Organization strength. Some seventy-nine per cent of these losses were in the infantry.[29]

But there was an answer. General MacArthur, already well along in his plans to liberate Luzon and then the rest of the Philippines, had been forwarding troops to Leyte in preparation for these future operations. The 32nd Infantry and 77th Infantry Divisions had been designated as a strategic reserve for Sixth Army, and these either were on Leyte or soon to arrive. In addition, the 11th Airborne Division[30] and 112th Cavalry Regimental Combat Team were already coming to Leyte, where they would stage for future operations in the Philippines. As mentioned earlier, the 112th Cavalry Regimental Combat Team had already been assigned to X Corps to protect its seaward flank, and would soon join the 1st Cavalry Division in a drive south. The 32nd Infantry Division was now in the process of relieving the exhausted 24th Infantry Division. Both the 11th Airborne and 77th Infantry Divisions[31] were due on Leyte shortly. With these, General Krueger believed he could successfully complete the Leyte Campaign.

*   *   *

While the 21st Infantry had been breaking its collective neck at Breakneck Ridge, another of the division's battalions, Colonel Spragins 2nd Battalion, 19th Infantry was fighting an epic all its own. Known as "Doughboy White" from its radio call sign,[32] the battalion had been ordered from Hill 1525 to establish a roadblock 3,000 yards south of the town of Limon and 4,000 yards in the rear of the Yamashita Line. Although his battalion had been without food for more than a day and was significantly under authorized strength, Colonel Spragins led his men into the jungle, asking only for guides and rations. Both arrived shortly before the battalion moved off on November 10th.

Led by a platoon under First Lieutenant George Whitney of San Francisco, the battalion struggled for two days over a route blocked by fallen trees and cliff-like inclines. In one skirmish, Lieutenant Whitney killed a Japanese captain who was carrying a dispatch case filled with vital intelligence material. These were sent back to division headquarters for evaluation. With no trails to follow and under orders to avoid open areas where they could be seen or opposed by the enemy, the battalion followed a circuitous route which tested the endurance of the already tired and hungry men while adding miles to their trek. The first night the men spent along the route, they opened the single ration per man that had been delivered to the battalion before departure. Ordered to make it last two days instead of one, pleas for additional food were left unanswered.

As the battalion advanced, their patrols discovered strong groups of Japanese to their front. The patrols also found a wooded streambed which offered cover and concealment as the battalion bypassed these enemy groups. Under strict noise discipline, the battalion advanced as stealthily as possible, often covered by the sounds of battle nearby or the usual noises of the jungle. Only once did they have to open fire, when they came upon a squad of Japanese getting water at the stream the battalion was using to move forward. These men, including two officers, were killed before the battalion continued its march.

On November 12th, now nearly two days into the march, Colonel Spragins decided to follow a compass bearing to his objective. The native guides would find a trail to match the bearing the colonel determined to be best. That morning, the battalion forded the Leyte River and moved up a deep gorge before following a trail over the next ridge. Alerted by the guides that the trail they were now following was probably a Japanese trail, the battalion remained on high alert. As the Filipino scouts moved up the trail, one of them spotted an enemy soldier and opened fire before he could be stopped. The element of surprise was now lost. A few moments later a Japanese patrol appeared, apparently investigating the earlier firing. These men were killed, but soon thereafter, the battalion came under attack. They had been discovered.

Fortunately, the Japanese were unsure of exactly where the battalion was, and how strong it was. So they were firing blindly into the general area they suspected held the Spragins Battalion. Captain William R. Hanks led his Company G up the next defended hill and attacked the defenders from the flank. A strong force of Japanese counterattacked, and soon the fighting was hand-to-hand. As Captain Hanks led the charge, he heard a scream behind him. Turning, he saw a yelling Japanese soldier charging him with fixed bayonet. Captain Hanks fired twice and killed his assailant. Sergeant Peter R. Slavinsky of Pennsylvania was on a trail when a Japanese grenade landed at his feet. Knowing he had seconds to save his life, he scooped up the grenade and threw it back at his attacker. Still the battalion attacked, pushing onto and over the hill. Suddenly a shout from the forward elements came back, indicating that the scouts had reached the hard-surfaced Ormoc Valley Road.

Colonel Spragins had reached his objective. The main Japanese supply line providing the enemy on the Breakneck Ridge-Yamashita Line with food, ammunition and reinforcements had been cut.

Captain Hanks rushed forward to confirm his company's find. Heavy firing continued from a ridge on the far side of the road. A frontal attack was suicidal, as the ridge was steep and the enemy fire intense. Colonel Spragins called for a thorough reconnaissance before any attack was launched, hoping to find a weak spot in the enemy defenses. Time was short, however, with only two hours before darkness set in and ceased operations. The battalion set up night defenses at the head of a ravine and waited for the Japanese to react to their presence, a reaction most dreaded. Artillery fire from friendly guns was called on and sited on the likely approaches of any counterattack.

The Japanese were unprepared for the sudden appearance of the Spragins' Battalion in their rear. Usually it was the Japanese who infiltrated their enemy's rear areas, spreading confusion and cutting supply lines. Now "Doughboy White" had turned the tables on them and they were unprepared for a quick reaction. Combined with the heavy defensive fires of the American artillery, the confusion prevented any counterattacks that first night. But during the night the ominous sounds of Japanese vehicles moving along the Ormoc Valley Road kept the battalion officers awake.

The fighting flared up again at daylight. Enemy mortars fell on the battalion, and patrols encountered groups of Japanese trying to feel out the American position. These groups were killed or dispersed. Near noon, the fighting had calmed down. Now Colonel Spragins looked for resupply. His men were without food, and ammunition was a concern. Medical supplies were also low, and if his battalion was to fight to cut the road, casualties were inevitable. Air resupply was requested.

Company F counterattacked, in early afternoon, a group of Japanese which had come too close to the battalion perimeter. No supporting fire accompanied the attack because Colonel Spragins wanted to preserve what was left of his mortar ammunition in case a major enemy counterattack developed. Company F hit a strong force of Japanese machine guns, mortars and infantry and was recalled. By afternoon it was apparent that the Japanese had dug in across the battalion's front and across its route of withdrawal to the coast. Clearly, they were now surrounded. The requested airdrop for November 13th failed to materialize.

Colonel Spragins dug his battalion into the ground. The men, without food for more than a day and a night, ate palm hearts for food. Packs were stripped from the enemy dead and searched, mostly for food. Cooking fires, which would bring down enemy mortar or artillery fire, were prohibited. Once again the battalion passed the night without a counterattack, although the heavy rains caused almost as much discomfort.

Patrols moved out of the perimeter again on November 14th and discovered additional enemy dead. This time there was some food in the packs and this was returned to the battalion. Inside the defenses, Captain (Chaplain) Lamar Clark of Texas conducted funeral services for two men who had been killed the day before. The patrols reported well-armed Japanese groups moving around the American defensive lines. Several communication wires had been found and cut by the patrols. Observers along the road identified groups of Japanese moving both up and down the road. Finally one patrol leader reported that he had found some high ground to the west on which a dip in the height, or a saddle, offered a good defensive position and observation of the Ormoc Valley Road.

That afternoon came the first airdrop of supplies. The hungry, exhausted men of the Spragins Battalion watched as the desperately needed supplies floated down on parachutes directly into the Japanese positions. Radios operating on dying batteries immediately contacted the planes and corrected the drop zone. The second drop landed between the Americans and the Japanese. Unable to observe anything in the thick jungle below them, the pilots were helpless to correct their drops without some identifying signal. The Japanese realized this and held their fire so that no flashes could reveal to the pilots overhead where the opposing lines lay. Americans shouted directions to the unhearing pilots in desperation, but the third drop of food and supplies went to the Japanese. A fourth drop again landed between the opposing forces. The planes turned for home, their bellies empty of supplies for that run.

Captain Hanks sent out patrols to bring in as many supplies as they could. He specifically told them to find and return with the radio batteries. Without radio communication, "Doughboy White" was doomed as it controlled not only their artillery support but also their resupply drops. When the American patrols advanced, the Japanese opened fire. Skirmishes broke out as the Americans tried to recover their supplies and the Japanese tried to prevent them. Sergeant Wesley Greer was detaching a parachute from a supply bundle when a Japanese soldier came from behind a tree and attacked. Sergeant Greer killed him and hauled away his one hundred pound prize. Private John Miller of the Bronx found a box of radio batteries but had to fight his way back to the perimeter, which he did. The inventory taken after the "battle for the rations" showed a few radio batteries, some medical supplies, sixty-four mortar shells and six cases of rations had been recovered. There were now two hundred meals for seven hundred starving men. Later that same day, patrols reported many groups of Japanese combing the hills, recovering the misdropped American supplies. That night four men were killed within the perimeter by friendly artillery fire.

Colonel Spragins decided that he would move his battalion to the saddle which had been discovered by his patrols. On November 15th, he put his plan into effect. Anxious not to let the Japanese know the strength of his battalion, thus making them more cautious in their reactions, he refused artillery support for his move. Led by patrols the battalion moved by protected routes to "Saddle Hill." Only one enemy patrol was encountered and its members were all killed by "Doughboy White" sharpshooters. By 0800 Hours, the battalion was attacking up "Saddle Hill," using only Company G in the attack, again hiding its actual strength from the enemy. Reinforced with machine guns and attachments from Companies F and H, Company G attacked, led by Colonel Spragins. The rest of the battalion remained hidden under the command of the executive officer, Major Charles Isackson of South Dakota.

As Company G attacked to the front of the battalion, the rear came under fire from a group of Japanese who were trying to outflank the Americans. During the attack, Major Isackson controlled the defense from behind a tree in full view of the enemy. Nearby, a Sergeant from Texas, Edward Gauthler, noticed a bush moving and shouted to the major "Look Out"! The major ducked just in time to avoid a bullet, which hit the tree about where his head would have been had not Sergeant Gauthler shouted his warning.

Meanwhile, Company G avoided trails and struggled through the jungle to reach "Saddle Hill." They reached the east side of the Ormoc Valley Road and paused while Captain Hanks decided where to cross the road. A nearby pillbox was knocked out with rifles and grenades. Captain Hanks then sent his command across the road and prepared to assault the hill from its base. Enemy fire came at them from the hilltop. With a platoon covering the road to protect the advance, the company, in a skirmish line formation, began to climb the hill. Camouflaged strong points stopped the advance with machine gun fire. Captain Hanks called for mortar fire to support his attack.

While support was being arranged, Colonel Spragins sent Company E on a different track to "Saddle Hill." This group also crossed the road to the north and charged up the hill while the Japanese were busy fighting off Captain Hanks. They reached the top and began eliminating Japanese opposition.

Captain Hanks immediately disengaged his Company G and moved around to support Company E. By late afternoon, both companies were dug in atop "Saddle Hill." From where they rested, they directly overlooked the Ormoc Valley Road. At one point on the new defensive perimeter, the advance elements of Colonel Spragin's battalion were only ten yards from the edge of the road.

Colonel Spragins now ordered Major Isackson to take the rest of the battalion, which had not crossed the road, and establish a secret perimeter on the east side. Colonel Spragins' position was now known as the West Perimeter while Major Isackson's was the East Perimeter. So far, the Japanese were unaware of the East Perimeter's existence. Communication was established with another isolated American battalion, the 2nd Battalion, 34th Infantry, on Kilay Ridge, about which more will be heard later.

The Japanese did not quickly get the word that their main supply route (MSR) was cut. About midnight on November 14, a truck convoy rolled down the highway, but because of the pitch darkness nothing could be seen from the West Perimeter. Estimating the range by the sound of the truck wheels, American machine guns opened fire on the road. A considerable amount of noise and shouting resulted, indicating that the trucks were carrying troop reinforcements for the Yamashita Line. The remnants of the convoy quickly backed down the road, out of hearing. Colonel Spragins then had his men cease fire. He had issued orders that they were to fire only when they had targets and to stop immediately once the targets disappeared. This would serve to continue to deceive the Japanese as to the strength of the American force within the West Perimeter as well as conserve ammunition. And the enemy was still were unaware of the East Perimeter.

A few hours later, a column of troops was heard marching up the road. Once again, the Americans opened fire. Once the commotion on the road stopped, the Americans ceased fire and listened as the Japanese medical-aid men hauled away the dead and wounded. Later that morning, two enemy field guns opened fire on the West Perimeter. These were soon countered by American artillery firing counter-battery directed by observers within the West Perimeter. The constant barrage tightened the already strained nerves of the men of Spragins' Battalion. They had not eaten in twenty-seven hours and were exhausted from marching and fighting all through that time. Many were so weak that they could not stand or walk. Their declining alertness was of great concern to Colonel Spragins, who feared that they could be overrun. Patrols sent out to contact the other battalion on Kilay Ridge in the hope of getting supplies through them and evacuating the wounded, found that the hills and jungle between the two battalions was thick with Japanese soldiers. There was no way a line of communications could be opened between them.

The two perimeters of 2nd Battalion, 19th Infantry were also separated from each other. Three attempts to pass between them resulted in firefights with Japanese. With the battalion aid station in the East Perimeter, those wounded within the West Perimeter went without medical aid beyond that which could be provided by the company aid men. The wounded lay in water-filled foxholes, exposed to enemy fire and the constant rain. Although they didn't complain, their suffering was clear to all and lowered morale as a result. Reminiscent of the Battle of the Little Big Horn seventy years earlier, even drinking water, in the midst of constant rain, had to be brought in by combat patrols which ventured to the bottom of a nearby hill where a supply had been discovered. Water was carried in helmets to avoid the clanking noise emitted by American canteens.

That afternoon, a carrying party from the regimental Cannon Company arrived from the rear with chocolate bars and cigarettes. Then an airdrop was conducted from which a portion of the supplies were recovered by the garrison. Both of these operations were heavily opposed by Japanese fire. One of the incoming mortar rounds landed near Colonel Spragins, who had been wounded twice earlier in the campaign, and covered him with mud and earth. But as a result of the arrival of the Cannon Company party, the men had their first meal in forty-eight hours. And there were enough chocolate bars to issue ten to each man. That night was again quiet except for the rain and the deaths of several seriously wounded men.

The next day, November 17th, the Japanese tried a different tactic. Instead of boldly moving large groups of men and material down the now blocked road, they began to send small groups alongside the road, trying to filter past the roadblock. The Americans spotted these groups and opened fire as they tried to pass. Up on the West Perimeter, Japanese patrols constantly probed the American defenses, trying to locate a weak spot for an assault. And that afternoon, another airdrop landed eighty-three cases of rations within the East Perimeter. The Cannon Company detachment was used to bring the West Perimeter's share across the road. Some men fainted while eating. Colonel Spragins and other officers gave their rations to the wounded. But no radio batteries were recovered and the sole generator radio had rusted out.

Toward darkness, two Japanese tanks loaded with supplies ran the roadblock. So surprised were the Americans that the antitank gunners could not fire in time. Later, these two tanks ran the roadblock in the opposite direction. This time the Americans were ready and one tank was damaged. Again, Japanese artillery opened fire on the West Perimeter but counter-battery fire knocked it out. That day saw the last of the Japanese attempts to move troops or supplies past the "Doughboy White" roadblock.

November 18th brought word that the 32nd Infantry Division was now attacking at Breakneck Ridge and that a battalion of the 34th Infantry was trying to break through to Colonel Spragins' battalion with food and supplies. If successful, they would also evacuate the wounded. The relief force came in early that morning. And that afternoon, another airdrop was made but most of it landed on or near the Japanese positions. Patrols from both sides tried to recover as much of the haul as they could, and some skirmishing broke out. Americans and Japanese were soon battling over food. That night, three Japanese tanks made the run down the road three times. The bazooka men fired their remaining ammunition at them in the dark and scored some hits, but none were apparently disabled.

Dawn of November 19th saw preparations being made for the wounded to be evacuated. Rations for two days per man had been recovered and distributed. By midday, the carrying party departed with 23 wounded men on litters and another 27 walking wounded. The carrying party disappeared into the jungle. On the road, four Japanese tanks ran the roadblock again, this time firing at the West Perimeter as they passed. After they had returned north, a group of Japanese soldiers came from the direction of Breakneck Ridge. They seemed unaware of the Americans and were caught by their fire on the road. The columns dispersed and then tried to reform, but were shattered again by the American mortars and machine guns.

The morning of November 20th brought orders to Spragins' battalion to withdraw back to Hill 1525, from which they had started their odyssey. As Colonel Spragins digested this news a group of Japanese assaulted his perimeter. The firefight lasted for an hour, but Colonel Spragins grew suspicious and reinforced other sectors of the line. After he did so, a large enemy group attacked the East Perimeter in a banzai-type attack. American return fire halted it within a few yards of a breakthrough, and the Japanese left behind more than a hundred dead. Three more attacks met the same fate. Some of the men of "Doughboy White" began to think that the Japanese knew of the withdrawal order and were trying to kill them before they could get away.

But they didn't. In mid-morning the battalion crossed the Ormoc Valley Road once again, each man one at a time running, avoiding enemy fire. Company G covered the withdrawal and soon the two groups were reunited within the East Perimeter. The battalion moved back to the Leyte River, which they found in flood. No ford was found so they used bamboo vines tied together to cross the raging stream. Colonel Spragins crossed the river twice, once to lead the battalion across and a second time to assist with the wounded men. The crossing took time but by mid-afternoon was completed. Not one weapon had been lost or abandoned. They moved to some nearby high ground and settled in for another rainy night.

The following day the march continued, and Colonel Spragins received some welcome news from local natives. They reported that a day earlier another group of Americans, carrying the battalion's wounded, had safely passed the same way. The battalion continued toward Hill 1525 and, when within some 600 yards of it, heard firing. The signs were that the carrying party had been ambushed by the Japanese. Ordering the two groups to join forces, Colonel Spragins waited until Major Carl E. Mann brought his carrying party safely back into the battalion's lines. Major Mann had lost seven men killed and added sixteen wounded to his carrying load during his four-day march to the rear.

November 22nd was spent getting the wounded to the crest of Hill 1525. Many of the men of "Doughboy White" were exhausted, having—again—been without food for forty eight hours. The litter party still carrying the wounded men were equally spent. Many had lost their shoes to the rain and the mud and walked barefooted. Their boots had simply fallen apart. Some wore shoes taken from Japanese casualties. Additionally, 113 men suffered from jungle rot, foot ulcers, dysentery and various fevers.

Having successfully reached Hill 1525, the battalion was now ordered into reserve near Pinamopoan. Japanese forces were reported between Hill 1525 and the rest area. Patrols preceded the battalion as it made its painful way to reserve. Protected by three rifle companies, the litter column followed close behind. Each litter had a carry party and an assigned group of protecting riflemen. Enemy fire occasionally struck the column, but no attack developed and a change in route brought it safely to the coast. The litter party was less fortunate, and incoming mortar fire killed two men and wounded three others.[33] Snipers killed another of the walking-wounded and a soldier accompanying him.

The depleted column passed through Pinamopoan on November 24th.

Even after their arrival in the reserve area, the exhausted men were forced to walk another mile to Pinamopoal Point because enemy machine gun fire prevented landing craft from picking them up any closer to the front. Wounded men were immediately evacuated, including two hundred and forty-one officers and men who had made the return march unaided. Those remaining were treated to their first cooked meal in fourteen days: peas, carrots, bully beef and coffee. It was Thanksgiving Day. For his courageous leadership of the 2nd Battalion, 19th Infantry during those fourteen days Lieutenant Colonel Robert B. Spragins was awarded the Distinguished Service Cross.[34]

The battalion had killed hundreds of Japanese but the exact number could never be established since the nature of the battle precluded a count. The Japanese removed their dead whenever possible and the several nights of firing on the road had been unobserved. Uncaring, the battalion returned to Tanauan to rejoin its regiment and prepare for its next assignment.

CHAPTER 5

INTO THE MOUNTAINS—KILAY RIDGE

W hen the 2nd Battalion, 32nd Infantry, 7th Infantry Division established itself at Baybay, on November 2nd, the island of Leyte was cut in half at its narrowest point. The bulk of the Japanese forces on Leyte were now surrounded along the west coast between Baybay to the south and Carigara in the north. To the east was the X Corps, blocking the path into Leyte Valley. To the west lay the Camotes Sea, with little chance of escape. Patrols of the 96th Reconnaissance Troop and 7th Cavalry Reconnaissance Troop indicated that only stragglers were south of the Abuyog-Baybay Road. Another phase of General Krueger's plan had been completed.

This was not yet apparent to the Japanese command, however. General Suzuki believed that only small reconnaissance forces, aided by Philippine guerrilla forces, had actually reached Baybay. His intention to push the *26th Infantry Division* over the same road to encircle the U.S. Sixth Army would easily deal with these once they reached Baybay, on their way to attack the American rear areas around Dulag. In the meantime, he would hold off the American attack at Breakneck Ridge while his army prepared for its counterattack.

That battle had exhausted the 24th Infantry Division's resources for the moment. But as the 19th and 21st Infantry Regiments struggled against Corkscrew Ridge, the Sixth Army's reserves were beginning to arrive on Leyte. The first of these, the 112th Cavalry Regimental Combat Team, had already been assigned to relieve elements of the 1st Cavalry Division. Next to arrive was the 32nd Infantry Division, an experienced combat unit which had first seen combat against the Japanese in New Guinea in 1942. Originally destined to sweep Samar for any enemy troops on that adjacent island, events on Leyte had altered its destination. Major General William H. Gill's division was instead to land on Leyte and join in the continuing battle. Ordered to relieve the 24th Infantry Division, General Sibert attached the leading battalions of the 19th and 34th Infantry, who had achieved the heights overlooking Highway 2 south of Limon, to the 32nd Infantry Division. As noted, the 128th Infantry, 32nd Infantry Division was to replace the 21st Infantry on Breakneck Ridge itself. Behind them the 1st Cavalry Division was to drive to the southwest after relief by the 112th Cavalry Regimental Combat Team. The artillery of the 24th Infantry Division would remain in place, attached to the 32nd Infantry Division.

The 32nd Infantry Division had to fulfill other missions while en route to Leyte. As General Gill later recalled, "The 31st Division was on Morotai, an island to the west, and the 32nd was directed by the army commander to reinforce them with the 126th Regimental Combat Team, plus the 120th Field Artillery and other supply units. Therefore, they were not available to the army commander as part of the reserves. Likewise, the 32nd was instructed to furnish the 41st Division, which had the job of reducing the island of Biak, with the 121st Field Artillery Battalion. They did a splendid job supporting the 41st until they later rejoined the 32nd at Hollandia. So while the 32nd was waiting to get off to Leyte, it was short a good many combat units because of these various reinforcement missions."[1]

With its flanks protected by the 2nd Battalion, 19th Infantry's roadblock on Highway 2 south of Limon and 1st Battalion, 34th Infantry on Kilay Ridge, west of that roadblock, General Gill sent Colonel John A. Hettinger's[2] 128th Infantry Regiment forward to relieve the 21st Infantry Regiment. It was to conduct the relief and then attack south along Highway 2, push past Breakneck Ridge and then capture the town of Limon further south. This operation began November 16th, when the 3rd Battalion, 128th Infantry under Lieutenant Colonel William A. Duncan moved south on the west side of Highway 2 and the 1st Battalion, under Lieutenant Colonel James P. Burns did the same on the east side.[3]

Colonel Burns' battalion drew the mission of Corkscrew Ridge. A key point on Breakneck Ridge, it had never been taken during the earlier battles and had resisted repeated attacks by the 24th Infantry Division. In accordance with its history, it halted the initial attack of the 1st Battalion, 128th Infantry.

Mortar, machine gun and rifle fire pinned down the lead elements of Company A, and Company B proceeded barely 150 yards when it, too, was driven to ground. Alongside, but across the road, 3rd Battalion met no opposition but delayed its advance to keep abreast of its sister battalion in front of Corkscrew Ridge.

The following morning, the 1st Battalion reached the base of Corkscrew Ridge where it dug in. Again, the 3rd Battalion kept pace against no opposition. Its Company L was stopped by elements of the *57th Infantry* but managed to get a platoon around an open flank and knock out the pocket of resistance, advancing 1,000 yards along the road and reaching the ridge. By the end of the day the battalion was within 500 yards of Limon. Noting that the enemy was strong only on Corkscrew Ridge, Colonel Hettinger brought forward his 2nd Battalion under Lieutenant Colonel Herbert A. Smith. After one more day of vainly attempting to seize Corkscrew Ridge, Colonel Hettinger ordered his 1st Battalion to contain the Japanese on that strong point while his other two battalions bypassed it and proceeded on to Limon, a key objective.

That night the 128th Field Artillery Battalion[4] pounded the area between Corkscrew Ridge and Limon. In the morning the two battalions attacked. Once again the 3rd Battalion met little opposition but the 2nd Battalion hit strong elements of the *57th Infantry* which yielded no ground until killed or driven off. Nevertheless, the Americans pushed into and beyond Limon, reaching a hill which overlooked the town and a bridge over a branch of the Leyte River. Company K crossed the bridge, where it was hit by a strong counterattack from the *57th Infantry*. Behind Company K, the constant rains suddenly flooded the stream they had just crossed, leaving Company K isolated on the wrong side of the water. The Americans moved off to a hill which Company I had seized and together the 2nd Battalion settled into a night defensive perimeter. Over the next three days the 128th Infantry straightened its lines, organized its units and used patrols to clear up bypassed areas and reconnoiter a hill some 1,000 yards ahead which was heavily defended by the *1st Infantry Division*. Although some of these bypassed pockets of resistance held out into December, the battle for Breakneck Ridge was considered over. It had cost the 24th Infantry and 32nd Infantry Divisions some 1,500 casualties. The Japanese were estimated to have lost 5,252 men with 8 captured. More importantly, Highway 2 was now open to the Americans for a drive into Ormoc Valley. The Japanese had failed to hold open, for their own planned attack, a critical pathway into Leyte Valley, and had left themselves vulnerable to an American attack in the opposite direction.

One of the reasons for this success was the actions of First Lieutenant Leo F. Reinartz, Jr. An infantry officer, he commanded a tank platoon near Limon in November 1944, and was instrumental in knocking out some of the most stubborn defenses. Taking on a deeply dug-in position consisting of automatic weapons and 77mm howitzers, he led his tanks over a mined road into the enemy lines, his infantry protection unable to follow due to the mines and intense enemy fire. Keeping his head exposed outside the protection of the lead tank to better observe the enemy and direct his tank's fire, he directed the destruction of many of the Japanese emplacements. When it came time to return to American lines, he noticed one tank stuck in the mud and not responding to radio calls. Disregarding the risk, he left the protection of his tank and went to the aid of the disabled tank, successfully withdrawing it with the rest of his platoon. A few days later, now a tank company commander, Lieutenant Reinartz led his tanks forward along a narrow trail on foot under direct Japanese fire, so that they could reach the front lines and assist the embattled infantry. He also led a group of combat engineers to remove the mines blocking the trail. On 27 November, when one of his platoons was advancing, he noticed a heavy Japanese barrage falling ahead of them and tried to contact the platoon to warn them of the danger. When they did not respond, he again went forward alone, on foot, to contact the endangered platoon. The enemy, firing heavy 150mm guns, pounded the area into which the platoon was advancing, and shortly after he reached the platoon and warned them to seek protection, Reinartz was killed by enemy shrapnel. For his courageous leadership of his tanks during the month of November 1944, First Lieutenant Leo F. Reinartz, Jr. received a posthumous Distinguished Service Cross.[5]

As previously related, the American success was due in no small measure to the roadblock which the 2nd Battalion, 19th Infantry had established on Highway 2 and held against all attacks for eleven days, from November 12th to November 23rd. The description of their battle cannot be described better than it was in the 24th Infantry Division Operations Report for Leyte[6] which stated of the battalion, "These bearded, mud caked soldiers came out of the mountains exhausted and hungry. Their feet were heavy, cheeks hollow, bodies emaciated, and eyes glazed. They had seen thirty-one comrades mortally wounded, watched fifty-five others lie suffering in muddy foxholes without adequate medical attention. Yet their morale had not changed. It was high when they went in and high when they came out. They were proud that they had rendered invaluable aid to the main forces fighting in Ormoc Corridor, by disrupting the Japanese supply lines and preventing strong reinforcements from passing up the Ormoc Road. They were proud that they had outfought the Emperors toughest troops, troops that had been battle trained in Manchuria. They were certain they had killed at least 606 of the enemy and felt that their fire had accounted for many more. And they were proud that this had all been accomplished despite conditions of extreme hardship. Two hundred and forty-one of the battalion's officers and enlisted men were hospitalized for skin disorders, foot ulcers, battle fatigue, and sheer exhaustion." For its stand on Highway 2, the battalion was awarded a Presidential Unit Citation.[7]

$$* \quad * \quad *$$

The stand of the 2nd Battalion, 19th Infantry was matched by that of another battalion from the 24th Infantry Division, Colonel Clifford's 1st Battalion, 34th Infantry, on Kilay Ridge. Little credited at the time, it has since become the stuff of local legend and a proud moment in the history of the 34th Infantry Regiment.

When General Sibert ordered the 24th Infantry Division to push down Highway 2 towards Ormoc, General Irving, the division commander, had wanted to prevent enemy reinforcements from making the already formidable enemy defenses even stronger. He ordered the 34th Infantry Regiment to send one of its battalions around the Japanese flank to harass the Japanese rear and to relieve the pressure against the 21st Infantry, then attacking Breakneck Ridge. General Irving was also concerned that the Japanese had planned a defense in depth and that the ridge on which he directed this battalion was a backup position for the Japanese. His staff had selected the target ridge from aerial photographs as the most likely next line of defense on the Yamashita Line.

Lieutenant Colonel Dahlen, commanding the 34th Infantry, selected his 1st Battalion for the task. The battalion had been in continuous combat since landing twenty-one days earlier and had been reduced to an effective strength of 560 officers and men, from the normal 870 total strength of an American infantry battalion of the period. Given an observers party from the 63rd Field Artillery Battalion, the force was to move from Capoocan in eighteen LVTs[8] some seven miles up the shore of Carigara Bay, where they were to land and then march overland to seize Kilay Ridge, which lay west of the Ormoc Road some 3,000 yards behind Japanese lines.

Colonel Clifford stripped his battalion to its most effective status. Only the barest minimum of cooks and drivers were left behind to guard the battalion's vehicles and heavy weapons. Because they would have no vehicles, the antitank guns were also left behind. So were most of the heavy machine guns and 81mm mortars, although one section of each with a minimum of ammunition was hand-carried forward. Dragging themselves and their equipment up and down the hills would be difficult enough without having to haul the heavy weapons as well. The men of the battalion heavy weapons company, Company D, instead carried additional ammunition and supplies. The battalion departed Capoocan early on November 10, and as earlier related, landed without opposition. They managed to proceed to their intermediate objective without serious interference from the Japanese who were fully occupied with the ongoing battle at Breakneck Ridge.

Once in the hills, Colonel Clifford, like other American battalion commanders, soon realized that his maps were inaccurate. Joined by Filipino guides, he relied on them to lead his battalion towards its final objective. Throughout the coming battle these Filipino guerrillas would render invaluable services to Colonel Clifford and his battalion. One of these came in and asked to speak to the commanding officer. Colonel Clifford asked him what he wanted and the reply was, "I want to help. My name is Kilay." "Kilay?" queried Colonel Clifford. The native replied, "I am the owner of Kilay Ridge. I know it as I know the lines of my hand. The Japanese have set a price on my head. Now I shall go back with you." Colonel Clifford quickly agreed. "Fine" he said.

Having departed in haste and with a minimum of supplies, Colonel Dahlen had arranged for supply drops from transport aircraft for the battalion. The first of these was scheduled for mid-afternoon on November 11th, but failed to materialize when the transport aircraft could not identify the drop zone in the thick jungle and misty rain. Colonel Dahlen then ordered Colonel Clifford to proceed to Agahang where supplies were reportedly waiting.

Once again the promised supplies failed to appear. Local Filipinos provided the battalion with bananas, cooked rice, boiled potatoes and some chickens to alleviate the men's growing hunger. It was not until the morning of the next day, 12 November, that the promised drop of rations actually arrived. As they were collecting the airdrops, the commander of the 1st Battalion, 96th Philippine Infantry made contact with Colonel Clifford. This guerrilla band had been operating in the area for many months and provided

Colonel Clifford with important details of the terrain and enemy defenses. They would remain with the Americans, providing valuable intelligence and protecting their rear areas, throughout the coming battle.

At noon on November 12th, the 1st Battalion moved to the town of Consuegra where Colonel Clifford briefed his officers on plans for the next two days. That afternoon the battalion would advance to Cabiranan where they would spend the night. On the morning of November 13th, it would split into two columns and make rapid advances upon Kilay Ridge where it would organize its defenses. During the briefing, a group of LVTs arrived bearing more rations for the troops. They had found a water route from Carigara Bay through Biliran Strait and then down Leyte Bay and up the Naga River. The river brought them to the vicinity of Consuegra where they dropped their cargos for the 1st Battalion. These, in turn, were hand-carried to the battalion by Filipino men, women and children. And that day also saw the first successful airdrop of supplies when the drop zone was marked by red and yellow smoke from chemical grenades. Colonel Clifford established a supply base on the shores of the Naga River at Consuegra.

November 12th also saw the first skirmish of the operation. Sergeant Donald P. Mason of West Virginia was leading his platoon of Company A up a hill. So far the battalion had not seen any enemy troops and they did not expect to encounter any on the hill. But suddenly enemy machine guns, mortars and riflemen fired on the platoon's right flank. Sergeant Mason quickly realized his situation and ordered his platoon to stay on the ground and return fire. He turned back three enemy attacks on his understrength platoon. Then he took two squads and counterattacked up the hill. His attack was met with superior force, but only after he had reached the top of the hill. Here, the fighting became hand-to-hand. Sergeant Mason organized a defense. "Keep the bums off this hill," he ordered. Three more times the Japanese attacked, and three more times Sergeant Mason's platoon turned them back with bayonets and grenades.[9] But the Japanese now knew that Colonel Clifford's battalion was behind their lines, although in what strength and what he intended remained a mystery.

Colonel Clifford's plan brought his battalion to Kilay Ridge without any more enemy opposition. Once on the ridge the Americans found prepared trenches, gun positions and spider holes throughout the area. Clearly the *1st Infantry Division* had prepared the area as a secondary line of defense should Breakneck Ridge fall to the 24th Infantry Division. General Irving had been correct. They also found themselves on a narrow ridge, which at its widest was only 400 yards across. The ridge itself was about three miles long. It was 900 feet in height and ran generally southeast to northwest. The top of the ridge was a series of high knolls from which the Americans could see the entire Limon area as well as some part of the Ormoc Road. The Ormoc Road lay 1,000 yards to the east and was easily visible in clear weather. Ormoc Valley lay open to the artillery observers' binoculars for about fifteen miles of its length. They were about 3,900 yards to the southwest of Breakneck Ridge and equally as far behind Japanese lines. Looking around, Colonel Clifford understood that he held a critical position that gave a strong advantage to whichever side held the ridge.

November 14th opened with Colonel Clifford ordering his battalion to dig in and prepare to defend the ridge. Each company and platoon was assigned a section, and positions were chosen with the best tactical advantage. A series of strongpoints was established and observation points set up for the forward artillery observers of the 63rd Field Artillery Battalion. Trails into the area were blocked. Reconnaissance patrols were sent out to find the nearest enemy positions. The Filipinos who had joined the battalion acted as guides and supply carriers. A trail at the north end of the ridge could be used for this latter purpose and to reach the supply dump that had been established at Consuegra. More rations and radio batteries were quickly brought up the hill. Scouts went out to try and contact Colonel Spragins' 2nd Battalion, 19th Infantry at the Ormoc Valley roadblock.

The first Japanese reaction came shortly before noon. Enemy artillery shells fell on the southern edge of the ridge. The men of "Dragon Red"[10] battalion jumped into their water-filled foxholes and waited. This fire later shifted to Limon. No physical contact could be made with the 2nd Battalion, 19th Infantry, east of the road—the Japanese were between the two battalions—but radio contact was soon established and maintained. The balance of the day remained quiet, with patrols still searching out the enemy. That night they heard shouting and other noises which seemed to come from the area of the American roadblock on the Ormoc Valley Road. They also heard sounds of digging from much closer, on a ridge which ran between the battalion on Kilay Ridge and the Ormoc Valley Road. Colonel Clifford referred to the diggers as "Moles, little yellow moles," and assumed the Japanese were digging in on that ridge.

On the morning of November 15th, Company A sent a patrol to what they referred to as Ridge Number 2, or "Mole Hill," about 600 yards east of the battalion's main perimeter and with a view of Ormoc Road. This patrol soon found that Ridge Number 2 also had been prepared for defense by the Japanese. They ran into a group of about fifty enemy troops who opened fire with mortars. The patrol responded with rifle fire, killing five Japanese in an outpost, and then withdrew to the battalion perimeter. Captured documents from the slain revealed that the enemy troops on "Mole Hill" were from the *1st Infantry Division.*

After Company A returned, the 24th Cavalry Reconnaissance Troop reported to Colonel Clifford for assignment. He ordered them to patrol the area west of the battalion to ensure his position was not being outflanked by the Japanese. Battalion patrols did better this day, crossing the highway south of Limon, bypassing "Mole Hill," but were still unable to physically contact the 19th Infantry. Heavy rains kept the main forces of both sides in their water-filled holes all day. The next day was a repeat of this day, with many patrols but no contact with friendly forces.

One patrol, under a battalion cook, Mess Sergeant Jose Carrasquillo of Long Island City, New York, led a patrol which managed to gain the top of "Mole Hill." Perhaps due to the heavy rain, the top of the hill was empty. Looking around, Sergeant Carrasquillo saw another ridge to the east on which Japanese were busy building defenses. This ridge overlooked the Ormoc Valley Road. Deciding to call it "Busyman's Ridge," Carrasquillo returned to report to Colonel Clifford who, upon hearing the news, sent a force to occupy "Mole Hill."

On November 17th a platoon from Company B tried to force its way beyond Ridge Number 2 and got into a running fight with a Japanese force. It kept up the fight and succeeded in crossing the Ormoc Road, making physical contact with the 2nd Battalion, 19th Infantry at its roadblock. No permanent line of communications could be established because of the large Japanese forces between the two isolated American battalions. American casualties were one killed and seven wounded.

Meanwhile, Companies B and D moved some six hundred yards east of the battalion perimeter to Ridge Number 3, "Busyman's Ridge," where they became involved in a firefight with about 200 enemy soldiers. Mortars, machine guns and riflemen were well dug in on Ridge Number 3 and the Americans could make no headway. After losing one wounded and two men missing, a patrol was sent to outflank the position. The patrol was ambushed and had to scatter to survive. Only three of its members returned, including one who was critically wounded. Hearing the sound of an intense fight, Colonel Clifford came up to Company B to investigate. While he was observing the fight, six casualties were incurred by Company B. Each would require four men to carry him back to the aid station, and the company commander was hesitant about losing too many men from his firing line. One of the men had been shot through the thigh and was unable to walk. The narrow trails and thick underbrush made it impossible for litter bearers to carry him to safety so Colonel Clifford, a former All-American football player at West Point, carried the wounded man on his back for a mile under sniper fire to his command post, where first aid could be administered. For his leadership of Dragon Red and his role in evacuating a wounded man under fire in such difficult terrain, Colonel Clifford would receive the Distinguished Service Cross.[11]

Colonel Clifford decided to replace Company B with Company C. The former spent the night isolated from the battalion in front of Ridge Number 3, and in the morning Colonel Clifford brought up his few heavy machine guns and placed fire on that ridge. The opening burst caught a group of twenty-five Japanese who had come into the open to cook their breakfast. When this fire pinned down the Japanese, a Philippine carrying party brought rations and medical supplies to Company B. They were followed by Company C, who was to replace Company B at Ridge Number 3. The relief was carried out under severe enemy fire and more casualties were incurred, including a Filipino soldier and guide, Henry ("Joe") Kilay, whose services had been indispensable to the battalion.[12]

Meanwhile, other patrols had been seeking out enemy artillery observers who had been directing harassing fire onto the ridge. One of these, led by Sergeant Frank Huber of Milwaukee, Wisconsin, crossed two streams before coming upon a trail. This led uphill to a ridge about 1,500 yards from the American perimeter. One of his scouts pointed, bringing Sergeant Huber's attention to a wire that was hidden in the undergrowth alongside the trail. Seeing that the wire was rust colored, Sergeant Huber immediately identified it as Japanese. He led his men along the wire into a small clearing. An enemy soldier was squatting in the clearing armed with a machine gun. The lead scout shot the enemy soldier. Sergeant Huber ordered his men to remain in place, quietly, thinking there might be more Japanese troops in the area. When nothing occurred, Sergeant Huber's eyes followed the wire and noticed it disappeared into the base of a large tree. Then he saw the canvas at the tree base. Moving up, covered by his squad, the Wisconsin Sergeant pulled off the canvas to reveal four spider holes, each with two Japanese inside. Two of them wore officer's insignia and all appeared to be dead. One of the Americans threw some earth on one of the soldiers in the hole and noticed him twitch. Immediately the Americans opened fire and eliminated the Japanese forward observer party.

On the morning of November 18th, all of the battalion machine guns were moved to support an attack on "Busyman's Ridge." Captain Edger W. Rapin of Bensenville, Illinois, commanding D Company, led a patrol which ambushed another twenty-five enemy soldiers intent on cooking their breakfast. Seventeen were killed and the others scattered into the nearby jungle. But as the patrol pushed on, it was ambushed by Japanese with machine guns dug under the large roots of trees. The first scout was killed and the other was hit and lay under enemy fire. Captain Rapin crawled forward to rescue his wounded man. Just as he reached the scout's side, he was himself wounded. As he was dragging the man to a nearby shallow dip in the ground, the scout was hit again and killed. Captain Rapin took cover.

A Texan, Corporal Arlton Brower, took command of the patrol and maneuvered it so as to provide cover fire, while Captain Rapin was pulled to safety. Two attempts were then made to recover the bodies of the two dead scouts, but each time Japanese fire drove the men back. Finally, the patrol returned to the perimeter.

During the struggle in front of Ridge Number 3, the battalion had been attached to the 32nd Infantry Division. That night, November 19th, Japanese heavy machine guns opened a steady fire on Ridge Number 2, into the American defensive perimeter. Heavy fire was also directed at Company B, which had moved to the south flank of the ridge. Believing the enemy force to be a reinforced company, Colonel Clifford noted that they had destroyed two of his few heavy machine guns and were trying to flank the southern outpost of Company B. Clearly, this was a major effort to drive the Americans off Kilay Ridge. He ordered the artillery observers forward to Company B. They immediately brought fire upon the encroaching Japanese, but the enemy came on anyway. Company B was on the verge of being surrounded and its ammunition was running low. The battle raged for seven hours. Personally reconnoitering Company B's position, Colonel Clifford ordered them to withdraw 100 yards and set up a new strongpoint with Company A. He planned to have Company A attack the next morning, to retake the Company B position.

With ammunition reaching critical levels, two Dragon Red men volunteered to go back for more. Privates Fred Finke of Nebraska, and Richard Batkies of Virginia crept out of the perimeter during the attack and managed to slip past the Japanese, alternately crawling and rushing from cover to cover.

Often they had to lie motionless while Japanese troops moved past their hide-outs. Finally they reached the knoll where Company A was dug in, only to be greeted by friendly fire. After shouting back and forth, and finally convincing the defenders that they were Americans, they were allowed into Company A's perimeter. They loaded up one hundred pounds of ammunition each and made the harrowing return journey. Arriving just as the Japanese renewed their attack, the two privates began distributing the ammunition. As they were doing so, Private Finke was killed by enemy fire. All day during the attack, First Lieutenant Russell Pyle of Newark, Ohio had been alternately yelling instructions to his men and firing his carbine. Then one of his BAR men tried to change firing positions only to be cut down by a Japanese machine gun. Lying wounded in the open the gunner cried out for help. Lieutenant Pyle saw the man and also saw enemy bullets striking the ground between his position and the wounded man. Undeterred, Lieutenant Pyle crawled out of his foxhole and managed to drag the wounded man back with him. In the water-filled hole under enemy fire, he dressed the man's wound and covered him with a poncho, which was about all that could be done under the circumstances. Lieutenant Pyle then picked up the BAR and took the gunner's place, alternately firing and directing the defense of his sector.

With his ammunition running low, casualties increasing, and in the face of strengthening Japanese resistance, Colonel Clifford decided to consolidate his battalion. He withdrew Company C from Ridge Number 2. Colonel Clifford knew his battalion was tired. Indeed, it had been tired before the battle began. The continuing rain made every movement difficult, turning the ground into a slick mass of mud and slime. Rations were inadequate, sleep was a luxury, and many men, who otherwise were unwounded, went down with varying degrees of sickness, suffering from fevers, dysentery or foot ulcers from the ever-present dampness. Constant enemy harassing fire only added to the misery. Nevertheless, Company C managed to slip away from the Japanese on Ridge Number 2 ("Mole Hill") without alerting the enemy. So quiet was their withdrawal that the Japanese actually launched a company-strength attack on their vacated positions barely half an hour after the company slipped away. Instead of running into Company C, they were hit by an artillery barrage that Colonel Clifford had planned for just this event.

Colonel Clifford now had a tightened battalion perimeter. Still the Japanese came on. About noon on November 20th, they again struck at Company B, which held the southern perimeter. Artillery fire was directed on them, but so heavy was the rain that the artillery forward observers could not see the fall of shot, and had to adjust their fires by sound. Company B launched a counterattack in an attempt to retake the knoll from which the enemy had launched their attack, but heavy enemy fire drove them back. Lieutenant Pyle directed the withdrawal, personally walking the perimeter to make sure that no wounded man, weapon or supplies were left behind. This attack had lowered the battalion ammunition supply to critical levels. Colonel Clifford made his rounds of the battalion perimeter, to ensure that all avenues of approach had been covered.

That afternoon Company B attacked the abandoned hill in order to drive the Japanese off the tip of Kilay Ridge. Company A, now with only sixty men left, launched a similar attack to the rear of the hill. Heavy enemy fire from machine guns, rifles and huge 90mm mortars drove the Americans back. As they pulled off the hill, the Japanese counterattacked. Sergeant Donald Watson, of Iowa had already been badly wounded but refused to go to the rear, remaining with his platoon until the Japanese counterattack was repulsed. Similarly, Private Nelson Coder of Kansas had been wounded twice this day, but remained at the front blazing away with his Thompson sub-machine gun until he was ordered to the rear for medical attention. Medical aid men like Leo McDonnell of South Dakota made repeated trips through enemy fire zones to treat and rescue wounded. By day's end, the situation remained essentially unchanged.

The rain continued for the rest of the day and all night long. Japanese machine guns had identified the Company B perimeter and fired throughout the night, keeping the infantrymen in their water-filled foxholes. Many of the men had yet to dig new holes and were fully exposed to this enemy fire. Sergeant James McFarland of Kentucky was determined to put a stop to the harassment. He crawled forward to a knoll in the rainy darkness to direct mortar fire on the enemy guns. Unable to see anything in the inky blackness, he stood up to see better and soon spotted the gun barrel flashes. Using these, he directed the mortar fire until it ceased sufficiently for the company to dig new holes. Calls for Sergeant McFarland to return to safety went unanswered, for he had been killed while saving his friends.

Patrols were sent out to find a way to outflank the Japanese, but were unsuccessful. They did, however, manage to locate several enemy positions on which the forward observers then directed artillery fire. Late in the afternoon of November 21st, Colonel Clifford received word from guerrillas that two strong enemy forces were marching toward his position. He immediately moved a platoon of Company C to cover the supply route to Consuegra and had a carrying party from that base bring up rations. Toward dark, the battalion received an airdrop of blankets, ammunition and litters.

The weather was almost as much of an enemy as the Japanese. It rained almost constantly, and the terrain and climate caused as many casualties as did battle. The ridge was a slick mass of mud and slime. Rarely were the soldiers dry. They were exhausted before the battle began, and then they had marched for days, carrying everything they needed to survive on their backs. Food was barely sustainable, sleep rare. They spent their days under sniper and artillery fire. These circumstances prevented them from taking proper care of themselves. As previously noted, the usual diseases and physical ailments weakened the troops. Colonel Clifford, who had begun the battle short-handed, ordered that only the most severe cases be evacuated. Those who could still walk and handle a weapon remained on the perimeter.

There were other enemies, too. First Lieutenant James A. Waechter of St Louis was an artillery observer with Dragon Red. Leading a small observation party into the jungle, they stopped for the night along the banks of the Naga River. Digging shallow foxholes, the men tried to sleep in the wet ground. Lieutenant Waechter couldn't sleep, even wrapped in his poncho. He looked at his watch and waited while the long hours crept away. It was just before 0400 Hours that he heard a shrill cry pierce the night. Tossing aside his poncho he pointed his carbine in the direction of the sound. There were no shots, no more outcries. Other strange sounds came, unidentifiable in the quiet darkness. Lieutenant Waechter moved out of his hole and began checking his men. He found one hole empty, the man missing. He and the others searched the area but could find no sign of the man. When daylight came they renewed the search. The missing man's rifle was found at the edge of the river. A guerrilla scout accompanying the group studied the tracks around the discarded rifle. "Crocodile," he said. "Crocodile come to foxhole, drag boy into river."[13]

It was still raining on November 22nd while patrols continued to try and find the enemy flanks. That morning another airdrop brought ammunition, medical supplies, dry blankets and ponchos to the exhausted soldiers of the 34th Infantry. The day remained quiet until mid-afternoon, when heavy fire pinned down Company B, and Company A was subjected to a heavy ground assault. The intensity of the Japanese attacks grew until in some cases the fighting became hand-to-hand. Technical Sergeant Donald T. Mason, a platoon commander in Company A, remained at his post despite the loss of his hand, directing his men in repulsing the assault. Another Company A Sergeant, Forest Clark of Kentucky, ran through enemy fire to lead reinforcements into the company's perimeter. Although wounded, he continued with his mission, running head on into a Japanese patrol in the jungle. An experienced veteran, Sergeant Clark knew that in this kind of fighting the one who reacts first usually wins the fight. Although he fired first, he was outnumbered and killed before he could aid his platoon. Soon both companies were all but surrounded. By dark, Company B was completely cut off from the rest of the battalion.

Technical Sergeant Michael Szymko of Company A soon found that his men were running out of grenades, essential weapons in the close-quarter type of fighting now being conducted atop Kilay Ridge. Twice he ran back to the command post for new supplies of grenades, each time fully exposed to Japanese fire. When he returned the second time, he found that his platoon leader had been wounded and evacuated. He assumed command of the platoon, now numbering little more than a dozen men, and found that due to lack of numbers it was necessary to consolidate their position. Technical Sergeant Szymko crawled from position to position, always under Japanese fire, to reposition his platoon to better defend itself. As darkness approached on 22 November, the Japanese launched a renewed attack with grenades and mortar fire. An infantry charge followed the barrage. Despite being wounded in the head, Sergeant Szytmko killed three of the advancing enemy soldiers and deflected the attack. Then a Japanese officer, leading the attack, charged directly at the sergeant brandishing his saber. The Brooklyn-born non-commissioned officer, nearly blinded by the blood from his head wound, fought off the saber blows furiously, parrying each blow until he was finally able to wrest the samurai sword from the Japanese officer and kill him with his own blade. This action so demoralized the rest of the Japanese attackers that the attack was immediately over and they withdrew. For his incredible display of leadership and intrepid courage, Technical Sergeant Szymko was awarded the Distinguished Service Cross.[14]

Colonel Clifford ordered Company B to return to the battalion perimeter through the Company A area. Using artillery and machine gun fire to cover the movement, the company conducted the withdrawal. Although largely successful, one convoy of wounded men on litters was attacked and some of the men killed. The success of this withdrawal was in large part due to First Lieutenant Thomas Rhem of Memphis, Tennessee, who led his platoon in a bayonet charge against the blocking Japanese to cover the withdrawal of the rest of the company. Each man threw three grenades at the enemy and then stormed forward with fixed bayonets, yelling at the top of their lungs. The blocking enemy force melted away, leaving twenty-five dead behind. Five enemy machine guns were captured by Lieutenant Rhem's men, who returned to the company without having anyone killed or wounded.

Upon returning to the battalion command post, Company B was ordered to move 750 yards beyond and set up a new defensive position. Here Colonel Clifford moved his headquarters, including all communications, within Company B's new perimeter. The mortars from Company D were also moved here and continued to cover the outlying units. All reserves of ammunition and supplies were centralized within Company B's base. So close did the Japanese come that night that the Company D mortars were laying their barrage within yards of Company A's front line.

Concerned about a breakthrough, Colonel Clifford made plans to withdraw. Advising General Gill of his plans, he was ordered not to pull back but to hold his position on Kilay Ridge. Any withdrawal would have exposed the flanks of the 32nd Infantry Division units then entering Limon. Colonel Clifford settled down for another Japanese onslaught.

The night was long and difficult. As the evacuation of wounded continued a Japanese machine gun suddenly opened fire, blocking the trail used to move the wounded men to safety. Sergeant Oliver A. Young was a former University of Arkansas athlete. Now he used his skills to crawl down the trail in the direction of the machine gun in the pitch dark. Following the gun flashes he found the gun dug in under a huge tree. Sergeant Young crawled around to the other side of the tree, within feet of the Japanese. Keeping the tree between himself and the enemy he primed a grenade, counted off the seconds, waiting until he was sure the Japanese could not throw the grenade back. Reaching around the tree he dropped the grenade into the enemy hole. Even before it landed it exploded, killing the crew and destroying the gun. Sergeant Young himself was so close that he was wounded in the arm by his own grenade. Not far away, First Lieutenant Thomas McCorlew of Texas was searching in the dark night for Company A's position when he ran into another man. Putting his hand on the man's shoulder he inquired as to the location of A Company. A startled Japanese soldier turned and ran off into the dark.

*   *   *

The Japanese didn't come on the morning of November 23rd. For this Colonel Clifford was especially grateful. His battalion had been severely handled in the preceding days, and any break was welcome. Although strong harassing fire continued against the Americans all that next rainy day, November 23rd, no ground attacks developed. A small enemy attack the next day was turned back by friendly artillery fire. One of the battalion's platoons even managed to pass through enemy lines and report conditions to General Gill at 32nd Infantry Division Headquarters. The platoon managed to return safely, after a ten-hour trip during which, more than once, they had to dodge enemy troops, with renewed orders to hold Kilay Ridge. An airdrop that afternoon replenished supplies while enemy fire tried, but failed, to discourage the gathering of the parcels. That same afternoon, enemy reinforcements were observed digging in east of the battalion's perimeter.

The next two days were relatively quiet on Kilay Ridge. Other than patrol actions and the ever-present Japanese harassing fire, no significant actions developed. General Gill sent a message of encouragement to Colonel Clifford citing how important his battalion's stand was to the battle at Breakneck Ridge. On Thanksgiving Day, the battalion was even treated to a brief glimpse of the sun. That night things changed suddenly. As darkness settled over Kilay Ridge on November 25th, a strong Japanese force hit Company A with artillery, mortars and automatic weapons fire. After suffering several casualties, Company A repulsed the attack, thanks in large measure to Lieutenant Waechter, who rushed to an exposed knoll to direct American artillery fire on the attackers. His assistant was killed by an enemy shell that blew the lieutenant down the hill. Finding himself still in one piece, Waechter climbed back up the hill and continued directing fire on the Japanese. The next morning Colonel Clifford had Company C exchange places with Company A. He also learned from his regimental commander, Colonel Dahlen, that the 32nd Infantry Division was fully committed to the battle for Breakneck Ridge and could provide him with no immediate help. He was out there on his own. Colonel Dahlen advised him to rely on the artillery and hang on until the situation improved.

On November 27th the Japanese finally discovered the Americans' supply line and placed a blocking platoon directly on the vital trail to Consuegra. A platoon from Company B attacked and pushed the Japanese away, killing several. Colonel Clifford now deduced that the *1st Infantry Regiment* had one reinforced company to his south, two more were on the ridge to the east, and a strong force was facing him to the west. This latter force was the most dangerous, for if it pushed ahead and cut his supply line to Consuegra he would quickly run out of food and ammunition. As he contemplated his difficulties, he was cheered when a patrol from the 128th Infantry appeared within his perimeter to report that reinforcements were on their way.

His good humor didn't last long, however. Early the next morning, November 28th, a strong Japanese effort to overcome the Americans on Kilay Ridge struck. Using 90mm mortar fire and heavy automatic weapons firing from nearby ridges, the Japanese directed their main effort at Company C at the southern end of the ridge. Company D's mortars began to fire a protective barrage but the Japanese charged with fixed bayonets, throwing grenades. The fighting soon came to close quarters and individual Japanese began to infiltrate past Company C into the battalion perimeter. For much of the day the battle continued to rage, with Japanese infiltrating while their mortars pinned the Americans down. One reason the Japanese didn't overrun Dragon Red was Sergeant Irving Greenberg from New York City. Under enemy fire, he crawled down the ridge to a position from which he could observe the enemy's progress, and then signaled it back to the Company D mortars who adjusted their fire every time the Japanese moved.

The final attack came after dark. Heavily supported by their big 90mm mortars the Japanese made the ridge shake and tremble. Men were killed, wounded or buried in their foxholes by the huge blasts. Machine-gun fire hit the ridge from the east and west. It continued to increase in intensity as enemy assault teams forced their way up a gully leading to the western end of the ridge. Meanwhile, another attack hit Company C from the south. Telephone lines were cut between platoons and to Colonel Clifford. The Americans fought with mortars and artillery, and by 2030 Hours, the battle had become hand-to-hand. The attached Company D machine gunners fired without pause, burning out barrels and repairing their guns under fire. By 2200 Hours that night, Company C was again surrounded.

As dawn rose on November 29th, Kilay Ridge was in joint custody. Both the Americans of the 34th Infantry and the Japanese of the *1st Infantry Regiment* held adjacent portions of the high ground. The Japanese renewed their attack with automatic weapons and soon had the entire battalion under direct fire. Company C was somewhat separated from the rest of the battalion so a platoon from Company B broke through to them, in the process knocking out two machine guns and killing six enemy soldiers. Company D had nearly exhausted its ammunition and Colonel Clifford sent a carrying party forward with resupply. The Japanese were ready for that and had covered the trail. The carrying party was stopped and pinned down before reaching Company D. Ironically, a carrying party with ammunition and food, including the battalion's Thanksgiving dinner of roast turkey and fresh eggs, entered the perimeter from Consuegra as the battle raged.

During the fighting around Company C on 29 November, Private First Class Melchor L. Cotelo found himself the target of a large infantry force attacking up the ridge. Waiting until there was a lull in the incoming fire, Cotelo stood up and opened fire, being better able to see his targets from a standing position. The Japanese replied with a barrage of grenades directed at Cotelo, who without hesitation picked them up and threw them back. Then he noticed a wounded buddy nearby and went to his aid. As he did so, however, another grenade came at the pair. This Private Cotelo caught in the air, but before he could throw it back, it exploded in his hand, destroying his right hand at the wrist. Despite the extreme pain and heavy blood loss, he pulled the pin from one of his own grenades, using his teeth, and with his left hand threw it into an enemy machine gun pit, destroying both gun and crew. When daylight came, there were at least sixteen Japanese dead around the wounded Monterey, California native, and the Japanese attack in his area had been defeated. For his vital part in the defense of Kilay Ridge by Company C, 34th Infantry, Private First Class Melchor L. Cotelo received the Distinguished Service Cross.[15]

Colonel Clifford knew that his battalion was on the verge of being over-run. He contacted General Gill and requested immediate reinforcements. General Gill agreed and ordered the 2nd Battalion, 128th Infantry to proceed to Kilay Ridge immediately and come under Colonel Clifford's command. Soon lookouts on the ridge spotted friendly troops advancing toward the ridge. Using Company C, Colonel Clifford opened the supply trail to his forward companies and sent food and ammunition to them. Soon after, Company G, 128th Infantry Regiment, arrived in the perimeter. Colonel Clifford immediately sent them forward to reinforce his depleted Company C in the forward positions. The rest of the 2nd Battalion, 128th Infantry arrived that afternoon.

*   *   *

Reinforced and resupplied, Colonel Clifford went back on the attack. His mission was still to hold Kilay Ridge, and he held only a part of that terrain. The Japanese held about 800 yards of the hilltop. On December 1st, he sent a patrol from Company B to a draw west of the ridge, in the hope of finding a way to flank the strong Japanese positions on the south of it. Supported by a heavy concentration of artillery and mortars from both battalions, and the newly arrived heavy machine guns of the 128th Infantry, Company E of the 128th Infantry launched a direct attack on the Japanese-held knolls. The first knoll fell quickly but a second held up the attack with heavy fire. A bazooka team dispatched from Company A, 34th Infantry, tried to knock out the position, but failed. Another effort using grenades collected from Company C also failed to dislodge the Japanese. Meanwhile, the patrol reported that they had been able to reach the rear of the enemy position via the draw and had seen no enemy activity.

No further progress could be made on December 1st. That afternoon, General Gill ordered Colonel Clifford to gather up the remnants of his 1st Battalion, 34th Infantry and withdraw. The rest of Kilay Ridge was now a problem for the 128th Infantry. Even then, things did not go easy for Colonel Clifford's battalion. As he gathered his men for a withdrawal off Kilay Ridge, Companies E and F of the 128th Infantry launched new attacks on the stubborn Japanese knoll. Company E seized its objective but Company F was stopped fifty yards short of the knoll top. As Colonel Clifford gathered his men, the regimental commander of the 128th Infantry ordered him to halt in place in the event his men were needed for the ongoing attack. Fortunately, the exhausted men were spared another attack when Company F, 128th Infantry, pushed ahead and seized the enemy position.

The next day, December 3rd, the two battalions searched Kilay Ridge and took stock of what had happened there over the past three weeks. Some 900 men of the *1st Infantry Regiment* were counted or estimated dead on the ridge. Japanese equipment found abandoned or destroyed included three 70mm mountain guns, four heavy machine guns, seventeen light machine guns, one 90mm mortar, and uncounted rifles, swords, pistols and field glasses. Against this, the 1st Battalion, 34th Infantry, lost 26 men killed, 2 men missing and 101 wounded. It had also contributed materially to the battle to crack the Japanese defense line at Breakneck Ridge, prevented reinforcements from reaching Limon and thus blocking further American advances into Ormoc Valley. It had protected the flank of the 32nd Infantry Division. Finally, on December 4th, the battalion was allowed to withdraw for rest and recuperation. It arrived at Calubian only to be greeted with the news that another Japanese landing on the Leyte Peninsula near San Isidro, five miles to the west, had just occurred. After a meal of fresh eggs, the battalion mounted up again and moved to meet this new threat. The 1st Battalion, 34th Infantry would receive the Presidential Unit Citation for its stand at Kilay Ridge.[16]

*   *   *

While the men of the 24th Infantry Division were fighting and dying on Breakneck Ridge, their general was relieved of his division command. It has never been made clear why General Irving was relieved of his command of the 24th Infantry Division on November 18th, 1944. Neither the official history nor the division's own history explain it. Indeed, General Krueger merely states matter-of-factly that, "On the 17th Major General Roscoe B. Woodruff took over command of the 24th Division and its former commander (Major General Frederick A. Irving) assumed command of Leyte Garrison Force, which would hold the island upon completion of the operation."[17]

General Woodruff had been brought along almost as an afterthought, after the planned invasion of Yap in the Central Pacific had been cancelled and the XXIV Corps assigned to General MacArthur for Leyte. As a part of the Yap assault, an army garrison force had been assigned to that corps to garrison the island after its conquest, and General Woodruff had been assigned as its commander. When the XXIV Corps was moved to the Southwest Pacific Theater, General Woodruff and his Yap Garrison Force came along. Garrison forces such as these, used in the Central Pacific, had not been used to date in the Southwest Pacific Theater of Operations. As a result, General Krueger had little for General Woodruff and his men to do.

Before his assignment to command the Yap Garrison Force, General Woodruff had commanded combat troops while in training, including positions as the assistant division commander of the 2nd Infantry Division, commanding general of the 77th Infantry Division, and commanding general of the VII Corps. When the VII Corps was sent to the European Theater, General Dwight D. Eisenhower, commanding there, preferred his own choice for corps commander[18] and, in effect, General Woodruff was cast adrift, winding up as commander of the Yap Garrison Force.

General Irving, on the other hand, had commanded the 24th Infantry Division since August of 1942, and led it through its first campaigns in New Guinea with no known difficulties. Although he had never commanded a corps in training or in combat, he had served with his division for more than two years when he was relieved. He had essentially the same background as General Woodruff, both men graduating West Point, two years apart. Both men graduated from the prestigious Command and General Staff School. General Woodruff had also graduated from the Army War College, while General Irving did not. And finally, shortly before the end of the Pacific War, General Irving was given command of another infantry division[19] which he led until the end of the war. After the war he was made a deputy commander of the Sixth Army and Superintendent at West Point, positions not given to men who had earlier failed in their assignments. General Woodruff held two corps commands after the war until he retired.[20] Clearly, there was little evidence that either man had failed or that either one outshone the other.

So what then was the reason for General Irving's relief? This is another mystery of the Leyte Campaign. It could possibly have been that after two years of combat he was tired and in need of a rest, a not unusual event in such a long war. Or it could have been army politics, with the mysterious "higher authority" desirous of giving General Woodruff a combat command to enhance his career resume. Any number of possibilities can be discussed, but the answer remains shrouded in secrecy.[21] For the infantrymen on Leyte, it made little difference who commanded them as long as he knew his business and did not abuse their lives in combat.

*   *   *

Behind the 24th and 32nd Infantry Divisions fighting at Breakneck Ridge, the 1st Cavalry Division was given the job of securing the Central Mountain Range that divided the Leyte and Ormoc Valleys. Here again the objective was to prevent any Japanese counterattack toward the American rear areas. While General Suzuki had sent the *57th Infantry Regiment* to hold the Limon area, he had dispatched the other two regiments of the *1st Infantry Division* to the same Central Mountain Range to secure access to Leyte Valley for his repeatedly delayed counterattack. These two regiments, the *1st Infantry* and *49th Infantry Regiments*, were to hold the passes while seeking opportunities to open up a way into Leyte Valley for the Japanese. They were reinforced beginning about November 8th by elements of the newly arrived *102nd Infantry Division.*

Fully expecting General Suzuki to occupy the Central Mountain Range, General Krueger had sent elements of both of his corps to clear the area. The first to move was X Corps' 1st Cavalry Division on November 10th. The Cavalrymen moved into the high, rugged and steep-sided hills covered with thick forests and wooded clearings, which provided ideal natural fortresses for the Japanese defenders. Trails were few and barely large enough for small animals to travel. Maps were poor and usually wrong. The constant rain on Leyte which had so hampered the other operations did not spare the 1st Cavalry Division. The lack of roads and the constant rain hampered supply and reinforcement efforts.

Nevertheless, the 1st Cavalry Division sent its patrols into the mountains. Using motor transport, LVTs, tractors and trailers whenever possible, they came to also rely on native carriers and air drops in order to keep troops supplied. The LVTs of the 826th Amphibian Tractor Battalion[22] were especially useful in crossing the ever-present rice paddies that dotted the area. From their drop-off point, the supplies were then manhandled into wheeled cargo carriers which were towed by the tractors of the artillery battalions into the foothills as far as possible. Mud made these journeys more difficult, as did the constant rain. Finally, the supplies were brought up to the front lines by Filipino carriers.

The 12th Cavalry Regiment established itself at the high passes through the mountains. Here they had to develop a native camp for the carriers, a hospital and a rest camp, since it was simply too far to send those who needed these resources back to the rear areas, miles and many hills to the rear. Guerrillas protected the Filipino carriers as they did their essential work of bringing up supplies and bringing down wounded or sick American soldiers. Since the trek was simply so arduous, relay stations of carriers had to be established along the way to relieve the weary men carrying tons of supplies, food and ammunition. Even so, the men averaged a speed of three miles every five hours. Due more to terrain than anything else, it was an epic unto itself.

Supported by the 271st Field Artillery Battalion, the 12th Cavalry attacked to clear the Japanese from their positions in the Central Mountain Range. In one engagement, F Troop, 12th Cavalry, pushed a small Japanese force back. As they did so, the flank squad was suddenly counterattacked. The squad's machine gunner and his assistant were killed and the gun left unmanned. As the Japanese came on, Private First Class Ben Quintana, an ammunition carrier from Cochita Pueblo, New Mexico, raced forward and took over the gun. He inflicted heavy casualties on the attacking Japanese but was mortally wounded in the process. Despite his wounds, he remained at the gun until the attack was repulsed, allowing F Troop to overcome the enemy resistance in this area. For his gallantry, Private First Class Quintana was awarded a posthumous Silver Star.[23]

The attached 112th Cavalry Regimental Combat Team was also soon involved in the fight in the Central Mountain Range. Relieved from its initial chore of watching for a Japanese counter-landing in Caragara Bay, it was ordered into the mountains by General Mudge on November 23th, and headed southwest from Mt. Minoro towards Highway 2. Advancing against light enemy resistance, the combat team came to a ridge about 2,500 yards east of Highway 2, perhaps some 5,000 yards south of Limon. Here a strong enemy force stopped all attempts of the 112th Cavalry to advance. Facing foxholes, prone shelters, communication trenches and palm-log bunkers, the Cavalrymen could see little of the enemy. Rain, mist and heavy foliage screened the enemy defenses.

The 112th Cavalry stopped for the night. As they settled in, the Japanese launched heavy artillery attacks against the two squadrons. Enemy patrols probed the perimeter. Yet, no major attack developed and the patrols were beaten off. For the next two days the regiment tried to dislodge the Japanese from their strong defenses. When ordered to move and join elements of the 32nd Infantry Division near the Leyte River, the regiment was still facing the Japanese. Troop A was sent off to make the contact while the rest of the regiment tried to push the Japanese on their entrenched ridge back. The approach to the enemy position was limited by terrain to a 100-yard front up a very steep and slippery slope. Troop G launched an attack on December 3rd, during which they could not fire their weapons while climbing the steep sides of the ridge. Japanese rolled grenades down on the climbing Americans and finally the troop withdrew. Another artillery bombardment was called for, after which Troop G again went up the ridge. Little had changed and once again Troop G retired to the bottom of the ridge. Artillery once more pounded the ridge while patrols sought another way to the top of the enemy position.

Meanwhile, Troop A reached Highway 2 and made contact with the 32nd Infantry Division's 126th Infantry Regiment.[24] The 1st Squadron, 112th Cavalry was ordered to join Troop A while the 2nd Squadron dealt with the Japanese on the fortified ridge. For the next several days, repeated attacks were made on the ridge without success. Patrols could not find a flank or a weak spot in the enemy's defenses. On December 8th and 9th, the 1st Squadron tried to find and cut the enemy supply lines, but they were equally unsuccessful. Finally the 2nd Squadron, 112th Cavalry was relieved in front of the ridge by the 2nd Squadron, 7th Cavalry and sent into Sixth Army reserve.

Supported by the guns of the 82nd and 99th Field Artillery Battalions,[25] and acting on the reports of patrols sent out to reconnoiter the enemy defenses, the 2nd Squadron, 7th Cavalry found that the enemy positions were "just as bad" as reported by the 112th Cavalry. Aerial observers reported that the approach from the rear of the enemy position was as bad as the frontal approach. The patrols were ambushed after they passed over the hidden

Japanese. The Cavalrymen resorted to an old World War I tactic, the rolling barrage. With artillery falling only twenty-five yards ahead of them, the platoons attacked from the front and the sides. They achieved little and were soon pinned to the ground. The cavalrymen stopped for the night and dug in. Although they had not taken the ridge, the troopers had managed to reach positions so close to the camouflaged Japanese that they could now identify their locations for the supporting artillery. Some fifteen bunkers were identified and fired upon by American guns. That night patrols were sent to knock out those that had escaped the artillery. Two machine guns were definitely destroyed and several Japanese casualties caused by these patrols.

The attack the next morning faced two machine guns dug into a cliff. The only approach was a ridge ten feet wide with a sixty degree slope, making a charge impossible. Again, the troopers were pinned down. An attempt by F Troop to outflank the position failed. The squadron returned to its previous positions for the night.

Once more, the artillery pounded the Japanese before Troop G jumped off in another attack on the ridge. Troop F again moved off on an angle to try and outflank the enemy defenses. Using flamethrowers, Troop G managed to knock out four more enemy bunkers and several machine guns while penetrating some fifty yards beyond the main enemy line of resistance. A good part of the success was attributed to Private First Class Henry Steinbach of Staten Island, New York, who fearlessly exposed himself to enemy fire, firing his BAR to protect the advancing flamethrowers. By the end of December 14th the Japanese had been forced off the high ground. Equipment captured included 12 light and 3 heavy machine guns, 9 grenade launchers, 73 rifles and large amounts of ammunition, grenades and other supplies. Over 5,000 rounds of American artillery had pounded the ridge during the assault. For its achievement between December 12–18, Troop G, 7th Cavalry, was awarded a Presidential Unit citation.[26]

Not to be outdone, the 32nd Infantry Division continued its struggle in the mountains. The battle continued to be as vicious and determined as had those before it. On December 10th, Company E, 126th Infantry Regiment, was attacking yet another Japanese-held ridge and moved to within twenty yards of the main defenses when a heavy barrage of hand grenades, mortar and automatic weapons fire struck the company. Sergeant Raymond W. Baser was carrying an automatic rifle and leading his squad when he was seriously wounded by a grenade. Refusing evacuation, he moved ahead of the attacking line, firing furiously with his BAR. He drove several Japanese from their defenses only to see them reorganize on a nearby hill. Here they attacked Sergeant Baser's platoon with automatic weapons and grenades. Once more, Sergeant Baser went forward alone, automatic rifle blazing away, and killed five of the foremost Japanese. As he did so, however, he again encountered enemy grenades, taking a serious wound in the leg. Despite the seriousness of his wounds, he continued to move forward, firing as he went, loading and firing until he was struck down, this time by rifle fire. Only then, after three serious wounds, did he consent to stop for medical treatment. For his material contribution to the success of this attack at the risk of his own life, Sergeant Baser also received the Distinguished Service Cross.[27]

*　　*　　*

While the infantry battled on Leyte, the U.S. Navy was still fighting to protect the rear of the Sixth Army. Ships of the Third and Seventh Fleets were constantly on patrol offshore to prevent enemy air or naval interference in the ground battle. While generally successful in keeping the *Imperial Japanese Navy* away from the beachhead, they had less success with the *Japanese Air Force*. On November 29th, the destroyers USS *Aulick* and USS *Saufley* were conducting an anti-submarine patrol between Homonhon and Dinagat Islands at the entrance to Leyte Gulf. At dinnertime, the *Aulick* (Commander J. D. Andrew) made radar contact with an incoming flight of enemy aircraft. Six planes were identified, one of which immediately dived on *Aulick* and passed so close aboard that it took off the ship's radar antenna before crashing into the sea not twenty yards off the port bow. A second plane came roaring in and hit the ship's mast before crashing into the windshield of the bridge. Both the plane and its bomb exploded just above the main deck, killing thirty-two of the ship's crew. Another sixty-four were seriously wounded and holes were punched all over the ship's superstructure.

Nearby, the USS *Saufley* was also under attack. She shot down the first two planes to make a run on her, and her captain, Commander D. E. Cochran, kept the ship in such agile maneuvers that the other planes had difficulty in lining up an attack. One suicide plane, for they were now identified as such, hit so close aboard that the side of the ship was scorched by the blast. About a minute after this close call another plane glanced off the port bow. Yet another plane, apparently not a kamikaze, made a bomb run and dropped two bombs astern of the racing destroyer. These blasts sent waves of green water over the ship and wounded several of the crew. As the plane attempted its escape, the *Saufley* gunners shot it into the sea. That ended the day's attack and *Saufley* took its twenty-one wounded into San Pedro Bay for medical treatment. The *Aulick* stayed on patrol until the USS *Pringle* arrived to relieve her, after which she, too, limped into San Pedro Bay for medical treatment and repairs.

*   *   *

In the XXIV Corps area, the 96th Infantry Division was still fighting around Dagami, to prevent General Suzuki from achieving his goal of acquiring the road net toward the American rear areas. On November 8th, the 2nd Battalion, 381st Infantry ran into stiff resistance around Malgnon ridge, about a mile west of Buri. Companies F and G started up the ridge and before they had moved very far enemy fire cut down Technical Sergeant Marvin A. Dawson. Private First Class Morris H. Barstein tried to aid Dawson, only to be killed himself. Both companies pulled back to assess the situation. That night the typhoon hit, soaking the men in their foxholes and flooding them. They had unwittingly stopped for the night in an old Japanese bivouac area, and some of the former residents returned during the night unaware that their unit had left. One of these lost Japanese soldiers walked past Captain Willard Bollinger's command post and was yelled at by the Captain to "Get the hell into a hole or you'll get shot."[28]

Not all of the wandering Japanese were so fortunate. Private First Class Andrew B. Query shot four of them within feet of his hole during the night. The next day, patrols tried unsuccessfully to find a way around the enemy hill. And so on November 11th, Companies F and G launched another attack across a steep, jungle-covered gorge. This time they reached the top of the hill with little difficulty. That didn't last, and when Second Lieutenant Frederick H. Dilg's platoon of Company G moved up the hill, a hidden machine gun opened fire. Fifteen casualties were suffered by the platoon before they realized what had happened. Another platoon rushed to help and Technical Sergeant James J. Ruth, Staff Sergeant Halan E. Stretch and Private First Class Joel M. Gross fired into the enemy nest until the gun was knocked out. Captain Louis Reuter, Jr., formerly the regimental quartermaster, came forward to take command of Company G, as Lieutenant Dilg was the only officer still remaining in the company.

A bombardment by the 361st Field Artillery, followed by another assault by Companies G and E the next morning, found the hill empty. Moving to join up with the 382nd Infantry, the battalion pushed on to the next ridge where sniper fire was encountered. Patrols went after the snipers, and mortar fire was called on for cover fire. But the wires to the mortars had been cut. Under enemy fire, Private First Class Earl J. Fouts took forward a new wire. When he returned, he was told that the new wire was cut, too. Undismayed, Private First Class Fouts took a second wire forward, again risking getting shot, and this time the wire lasted.

Private First Class LeRoy R. Crandall, Jr. made six trips forward carrying litters until he was killed. Private First Class Gerald S. Abrego brought up his BAR to cover the evacuation of the wounded and did so successfully until he, too, was struck down. The company aid man, Technician Fifth Class William B. Webber, discarded his helmet as too bothersome while he ran from casualty to casualty, disregarding the continuing enemy fire.[29] First Lieutenant Jack D. Blair, III, developed a system. He directed mortar fire on the Japanese machine guns which had by now opened fire on his company. When the Japanese ceased fire to duck the incoming American fire, Lieutenant Blair would race out of his hole and pull a wounded man to safety. Then he would repeat the process.[30] In between, he shot four enemy soldiers.

Company F was in reserve but sent forward its' BAR men to aid Company E. Staff Sergeant Harold Lowe fired so fast and so long that he burned out three BARs. Staff Sergeant Lloyd E. Dodd helped Lieutenant Blair direct the mortar fire until he became the personal target of an enemy sniper. He noticed that one of the enemy shots had pierced a leaf near him, so sighting through the leaf, he was able to see where the sniper was and kill him with a return shot. The battalion surgeon, Captain Samuel H. Brown, moved his aid station up to the front lines while Captain (Chaplain) Sigmund Rovinski went from wounded man to wounded man providing any aid and comfort that he could. Before the battle could be resolved, orders arrived to withdraw. The regiment was being relieved by the 17th Infantry Regiment, 7th Infantry Division, and was needed elsewhere.

Meanwhile just to the north, the regiment's 1st Battalion ran into opposition along an outpost line. Using the heavy weapons of the Marines' 155mm guns at the beachhead, Company A went completely through the line and another 1,000 yards beyond. This was the day after the typhoon, and while the Japanese were not a serious problem yet, the water and mud certainly were. Amphibious vehicles bringing up supplies actually used their waterborne propulsion rather than their tracks to make progress in several of the flooded areas. Company A pushed on to find a trail across the Central Mountain Range. As the country became more difficult and the jungle grew much thicker the trip became slower. As Captain Myron L. Stillman, the respected commander of Company A, led his command forward in this heavy jungle, an enemy machine gun cut him down. Even as his men deployed to destroy the enemy gunners, the company was recalled for another assignment.

The other assignment proved to be a position as the Sixth Army reserve. While they were there they spent time mopping up bypassed pockets of enemy resistance and guarding rear areas. During this period, the 96th Cavalry Reconnaissance Troop made its epic patrol all the way across the island to within shouting distance of Ormoc. During one period they were forced to ford the same river eighteen times. Pack horses and Filipino guides led the way, but the terrain and rains soon made even the passage of horses impossible. The horses were released and the heavy weapons and ammunition they carried buried. The men still pushed forward carrying rifles and rations. As earlier related, the patrol reached the 7th Infantry Division near Baybay, and one of its detachments captured a Japanese aviator, making this epic journey a success.

*　　*　　*

The Americans were finding the Japanese troops on Leyte much better trained and more skillful than those they had encountered in earlier battles in New Guinea. The Japanese usually fought a delaying action and would surrender ground only when forced to, and then they would only fall back to the next line of prepared positions. When Americans bombarded their positions they would go to ground, or withdraw temporarily from the area, only to return to man those positions the instant the American barrage ended. There were few "banzai" charges, wasteful of men and equipment, and rarely successful against experienced troops. The Japanese protected their rear areas and their flanks. The individual Japanese soldier was well disciplined, holding his fire until the enemy was fully exposed and most vulnerable. More often, the Japanese soldier fired late in the afternoon and continued to do so until counterattacks were launched after darkness. These were timed to take best advantage of the Americans' low point in energy, ammunition and food after a hard day of attacking fortified positions.

As was already seen in the Central Pacific Campaigns, the Japanese on Leyte employed the tactic of reverse slope defense with considerable skill. Caves and any natural cover, such as the heavy foliage and dense forests of Leyte, were utilized by the Japanese to strengthen their line or be used as spur-of-the-moment defenses when necessary. As always, the Japanese camouflaged their fortifications with their usual expertise. So devoted where they to this principle that it was not unusual for them to sacrifice good fields of fire in order to improve the camouflage of their positions. Their counterattacks were usually well conceived but often were launched with too few men to accomplish the mission. Communications was the bane of the Japanese, with orders between units being critically delayed or not received at all. Japanese expertise at infiltration of enemy lines was as good as ever, but on Leyte it was far less effective against the experienced troops they faced there. Another weakness was the effectiveness of Japanese artillery. Rarely did they strike critical areas and almost never was Japanese artillery massed to do maximum damage to American forces or installations. Gunnery techniques were inefficient by American standards, and the use of individual guns rarely caused serious damage to the attackers. Here again, the Japanese valued concealment over good fields of fire, which further negated their artillery support.

Nevertheless the Japanese soldier on Leyte was strongly motivated, well trained, and possessed a strong personal sense of duty. Few surrendered, even when circumstances were desperate, and most fought to the death. For the Japanese, the American firepower was the overriding factor which they could not overcome. That and the concise and firm American planning, with the flexible following of that plan, were the factors that the Japanese would later claim defeated them.

Indeed, Japanese planning was one of the problems that plagued their defense of Leyte. The Japanese delayed planning for the island's defense until American forces landed on Morotai in September 1944. The landings, and Japanese expectations that aircraft flying from Morotai would seriously hamper their efforts to prepare the Philippines for defense, brought to their attention the weakness of their aerial defenses there. *Fourteenth Army* was only upgraded to *Fourteenth Area Army* in August 1944, barely two months before the Americans landed. The defender of Leyte, *35th Army*, was organized at the same time. *Imperial General Headquarters* only declared the Philippines as the "decisive battle area" on September 22nd, one month before the Americans landed. Attachments to the *Fourteenth Area Army* only then began to be assigned to it, some from as far away as Manchuria and Tokyo.

Even then disputes continued. One, for example, was an argument between *Imperial General Headquarters* in Tokyo and *Southern Army*, now again at Saigon, over whether to instruct the air forces to attack warships or troop ships in the attacking convoy. Another was over when to launch the joint decisive battle, the battle that went down in history as the Battle of Leyte Gulf.

Another serious disruption to the defense of Leyte was the repeated changes of command which occurred immediately prior to the American invasion. General Yamashita was appointed to command *Fourteenth Area Army* on September 29th, but did not reach Manila until October 6th, exactly two weeks before the Americans landed on Leyte. Lieutenant General Muto, his Chief of Staff, did not arrive until the day the Americans landed, and had to jump from his plane into a watery ditch under American air attack, upon arrival. Reportedly he was the staff officer who, when advised of the Leyte invasion, replied, "Very good, but where is Leyte?" Most of the staff of the *Fourteenth Area Army* were new to the islands and only five of the entire staff of Lieutenant General Kuroda remained behind after his departure.

The *35th Army* had responsibility for the entire Southern Philippines and its forces were disposed to fulfill that assignment. While the *16th Infantry Division* was on Leyte, the *102nd Infantry Division* was in the Visayas, and the *100th Infantry Division* was on Mindanao with the *30th Infantry Division*. The *54th Independent Mixed Brigade* was at Zamboanga, Mindanao, and the *55th Independent Mixed Brigade* on Jolo Island. The newly assigned *1st Infantry Division* was in Korea. None of these units had worked together before, and most were inexperienced or had not seen combat in years. Several were newly organized. But others, like the *1st Division* and the *26th Division*, were rated as excellent and combat-ready units by both the Japanese and the Americans.

Finally, the Japanese did not intend Leyte to be the decisive battle as far as its army was concerned. While the Navy and Air Corps would defend Leyte by destroying the American fleet when it landed there, the army intended to fight its defensive battle on Luzon after the Americans had been sufficiently weakened to make a Japanese victory possible. This was predicated on the assumption that the Americans would land their main force on Luzon, not any other Philippine Island.

The inflated results reported by the *Imperial Japanese Navy* after the naval Battle of Formosa caused the Japanese command to rethink its plans. Acting on unconfirmed reports, admittedly inflated, from the Navy and Air Forces, the review resulted in a reversal of the decisive battle location. Instead of Luzon, it was now to be Leyte. That this decision was made two days after Americans had already established a beachhead on Leyte is difficult to credit. On October 22nd, Field Marshal Count Terauchi ordered, over his protests, General Yamashita to conduct the decisive land battle on Leyte, when the fight was already two days old. All that was immediately available was General Makino's *16th Infantry Division*, a unit which had spent the last two years in garrison in the Philippine Islands. General Suzuki, the army commander assigned to conduct the decisive land battle, couldn't even get to Leyte until November 2nd, two weeks after the battle had been joined. Even their air resources dwindled faster than expected when the suicidal kamikaze program was begun, since aircraft were lost at a much faster rate than they would be with normal tactics. To further aggravate that situation, American air power often ambushed Japanese aircraft replacements while en route to the Philippines. That same American air power routinely destroyed the transportation resources which the Japanese had counted on to reinforce and resupply Leyte. About all the Japanese had going for them was that Manila was a major hub in their supply line and had significant resources in the way of arms and ammunition. It is hard to picture how the Japanese could have been more unprepared for the Leyte campaign.

There is no question that every effort was made to ensure success within limited resources. *Imperial General Headquarters* ordered up additional units to *Fourteenth Area Army,* and added the *1st Raiding Group* to the *4th Air Army*, but few of these units would arrive in time to take part in the Leyte Campaign.[31] General Yamashita would have to rely on what he had at hand to conduct this decisive battle.

*   *   *

General Krueger was more fortunate in that he had more resources coming. One of these was another unit unique to the Pacific War, the 11th Airborne Division. One of only five American airborne divisions created during World War II, it was the only one sent to the Pacific Theater of Operations.[32] It had been activated February 25, 1943, at Fort Bragg, North Carolina. After training and maneuvers it had left San Francisco May 8, 1944, and arrived in New Guinea on May 25. It was now on its way to join Sixth Army on Leyte. Like the Japanese, American reinforcements had to run a gauntlet of enemy air opposition, albeit not as effective as the American air cover. One of the transports bringing the 11th Airborne Division to Leyte was the *Calvert*. As one observer reported "The tail of the convoy, miles back, was welcomed by an attack from three Zeros, one of which was shot down by ack-ack and the others pursued to the westward by our P-38's. The Navy made no bones about wishing to be rid of us, and our loads, and in a hurry. This unseemly haste was engendered by the frequent attacks by Japanese suicide plans on the hundreds of ships now jamming the Gulf."[33]

However, not all of Sixth Army's expected reinforcements arrived as planned. As mentioned, General Krueger was very desirous of landing a division behind the Japanese at Ormoc in order to cut off additional enemy reinforcements and to destroy the Japanese supply base there. He had earlier selected for the assault the 77th Infantry Division, commanded by Major General Andrew D. Bruce. It had recent amphibious assault experience through its participation in the difficult campaign to retake Guam in the Mariana Islands. He was very nearly disappointed. "I had expected right along that the 77th Infantry Division, which was on Guam when it had been designated as part of Sixth Army reserve, would join us on Leyte. But I found that GHQ had released it on 29 October without informing me and that it was now on its way to New Caledonia for rest and rehabilitation. When I brought this to General MacArthur's attention he directed that the convoy carrying the division, although then nearing Bougainville, return and proceed via the Admiralties to Leyte. It arrived on 23 November."[34]

Nor was this the end of the troubles with reinforcements. When the 77th Infantry Division did arrive General Krueger found that "the division had left much of its equipment on Guam and brought with it only a limited supply of rations and ammunition, it reached Leyte short of many things."[35] While the arrival enabled General Krueger to continue with his planned amphibious flank assault, it delayed execution and stressed further his already strained supply lines and space problems on Leyte. So difficult was the situation, that in order to fully supply the new arrival, some equipment and supplies had to be pulled from other units on Leyte.

General Krueger's problems just kept on coming. Earlier he had moved his army headquarters to the vicinity of Tanauan on November 4th, after the U.S. Fifth Army Air Force had assured him that the area was unsuitable for airfields and that they would not be using it. Now, a few weeks later, he received a message from General MacArthur that, contrary to earlier assurances, the Fifth AAF did want to use the area around Tanauan either. General MacArthur was understanding about the situation, telling Krueger that he was not ordering him to move his army headquarters but was leaving the decision up to him, although MacArthur would appreciate his relocating. With all his other concerns and issues this was simply one more which had to be resolved. General Krueger did so in his usual cooperative fashion. Sixth Army Headquarters moved to a beach near Tolosa. By November 28th, the engineer units which had found the San Pablo and Buri Airstrips unsuitable were busy working on a new field at Tanauan.

General Krueger did get one break when General MacArthur postponed the coming invasion of Mindoro, which General Krueger was also to command. This was important as well to the Leyte operation because the same shipping that was to be used to transport the assault troops in the Mindoro invasion were the very same ones he planned to use for his amphibious end run around General Suzuki's *35th Army*. The delay allowed him to rearrange his resources. Insufficient air support was the cause of the ten-day Mindoro delay, but at this point General Krueger welcomed any reprieve.

The 77th Infantry Division was assigned to the XXIV Corps and based in the Tarragona-La Paz area until it could organize itself for the next mission. Held as Corps reserve in the interim, one regiment, the 306th Infantry,[36] was assigned to the 11th Airborne Division in order to release the 17th Infantry Regiment which was then badly needed by its parent 7th Infantry Division on the west coast.

Indeed, XXIV Corps also had its plate full. The 7th Infantry Division was on the west coast above Baybay about to conduct the critical Battle of Shoestring Ridge. The 96th Infantry Division, after eliminating enemy resistance in its front, had moved into the mountains southwest of Dagami and was patrolling the area between Mount Laao to Mount Lobi. The newly arrived 11th Airborne Division was concentrating southwest of Mount Majunag on the Burauen-Albuera trail and on the slopes of Mount Lobi. The 77th Infantry Division was organizing itself in preparation for another amphibious assault.

*   *   *

At sea, the U.S. Navy continued to interdict enemy reinforcements shipped to Leyte. The *Imperial Japanese Navy* had a great deal of experience in supplying their garrisons which were either surrounded or in desperate need of reinforcements and supplies, which could not be sent through an American blockade in the normal fashion. Ever since Guadalcanal in late 1942, the *IJN* had used improvisation to get men and supplies to the besieged garrisons. Leyte was now at the top of their list and they used all of their ingenuity and experience to facilitate the shipment of men and material there. One such method was the use of submarines. This resulted in an encounter near Ormoc Bay on November 27th, when Destroyer Division 43 was sent to sweep the area under the command of Captain Robert Hall Smith, commander of Destroyer Squadron 22.

The ships passed through Surigao Strait without opposition. They arrived at Ormoc Bay and proceeded to bombard the shoreline with their five-inch guns, and then moved out into the Camotes Sea. As they did so, a Navy patrol plane reported sighting a Japanese submarine approaching Ormoc Bay. The destroyer squadron was cruising near Ponson Island looking for the approaching enemy sub when the USS *Waller* (Commander H. L. Thompson, Jr.) made radar contact with a target on the surface about 10,000 yards away. The *Waller* fired star shells and lit up the sea and sky. The destroyers headed directly for the contact and opened fire on the radar coordinates. For some unfathomable reason, the enemy submarine remained on the surface and returned the fire. One submarine against four American destroyers!

The submarine's aim was poor, but not so the Americans'. Hits were registered on the submarine while its return fire remained ineffective. As USS *Waller* set a course to ram the submarine, Captain Smith decided that rather than damage one of his own ships, the division would shoot it out with the obliging enemy submarine using guns. Passing as close as fifty yards the American destroyers pounded the Japanese with 40mm armor-piercing shells into the conning tower and pressure hull. Soon the Americans noticed that the submarine was beginning to glow, indicating internal fires and severe damage. Explosions within the submarine were noticeable. Just as the *Waller* returned for a second run, the target's bow rose up against the sky and the submarine slid to the bottom of the sea. As the destroyers cruised around trying to confirm the kill, a number of Japanese sailors were seen swimming in the dark waters. Attempts to rescue them were discouraged when they made threatening gestures and showed that they held grenades in their fists. Captain Smith, under orders to leave the area before daylight, ordered his squadron back to Leyte Gulf. Behind them they left the survivors of the enemy submarine *I-46* to make their own way to Leyte.[37]

Vice Admiral Thomas C. Kinkaid,[38] commanding the Seventh Fleet in direct support of the Leyte Operation, was having problems of his own. Although his ships had successfully repulsed the main Japanese *Combined Fleet* at the Battle of Leyte Gulf, those same ships, after two weeks of combat and a month at sea, were low on fuel, ammunition, replacements, planes and food. In order to maintain his beachhead protection force, Admiral Kinkaid ordered all the ships he could spare back to the main base at Ulithi, leaving Rear Admiral George L. Weyler[39] with three battleships, four cruisers and thirteen destroyers as the guard for Leyte Gulf. This force's main mission was to protect the gulf from any attempts by survivors of the *Combined Fleet* to enter Leyte Gulf and attack the vulnerable beachhead.

Meanwhile, General Krueger continued to hear of enemy landings at Ormoc. He was pleased to learn that one Japanese convoy of seven freighters was sighted on November 28th by the Fifth Army Air Force and attacked. The fliers claimed four of the ships sunk and the other three forced to offload their cargoes at Palompon. That night, however, a much larger convoy of fifteen ships reached Ormoc Bay safely and unloaded much of their cargo before being caught by the Fifth Army Air Force in daylight, when the pilots claimed all fifteen ships destroyed. Yet, another convoy landed during the night of December 2–3 undetected. Although attacked by destroyers of the Seventh Fleet, only a Japanese destroyer was sunk, the transports escaping. In addition, there were nightly landings by small boats and barges. These were under constant attack by Patrol Torpedo (PT) Boats of the U.S. Navy, but many managed to escape detection by the PT boats and landed their cargoes safely. Every effort was made to block this traffic, but it continued. Four U.S. destroyers were kept on station in the Camotes Sea ready to attack any Japanese shipping reported at Ormoc Bay, but because of Japanese air attacks they could not enter the bay during daylight. Even with this precaution some of them became victims of the Japanese.

Lieutenant Commander Noriteru Yatsui landed at Ormoc Bay with one of these convoys on November 1st, and described the experience. "We anchored near and to west of Ormoc Pier. . . . On 2 November, shortly after dawn, P-38s commenced attacking and continued all day, both strafing and dive-bombing. No serious damage but quite a number of casualties to men on deck and material damage to guns and equipment on deck were sustained. At about 1400, three groups of 8 each of B-24s bombed from high level concentrating on *Noto Maru* which was sunk at anchor. Ninety per cent of her cargo had been unloaded. No other ship was hit. All cargo was unloaded from other ships. . . . The three remaining ships of the convoy and escort sailed from Ormoc at sunset 2 November and returned to Manila without further incident."[40] In addition to receiving troops shipped from Manchuria and Manila, Ormoc also was the terminus for a shuttle service set up by the Japanese for troops of the *35th Army* whom General Suzuki had ordered to Leyte from other islands under his command. A regular run was established, for example, from Cebu.

The landing on the evening of December 2, 1944 was opposed by the three American destroyers of Destroyer Division 120 (Commander J. C. Zahm) which left Leyte Gulf and passed through Surigao Strait headed for Ormoc. The mission was to interdict Japanese reinforcements entering Leyte through Ormoc Bay. As they entered the bay, the USS *Cooper* (Commander Mel A. Peterson),[41] a new ship barely six months out of the shipyard, made a radar contact with two targets 12,000 yards away. Together with the USS *Allen M. Sumner* (Commander N.J. Sampson) and USS *Moale* (Commander W.M. Foster), the force opened fire. For nine minutes the three ships fired at the radar contact until suddenly a fire was seen in the target area, illuminating what appeared to be a Japanese destroyer.[42] As the ship appeared to be sinking, the USS *Cooper* shifted fire to a second target but, as she opened fire, the *Cooper* was struck by a Japanese torpedo. A huge explosion knocked the destroyer over on her side and water swept over the superstructure. Within seconds the ship broke in two, with survivors swimming away from the ship in water, oil and fire.

Commander Zahm was faced with a terrible decision. He could risk his other two ships in searching for survivors in the face of enemy air attacks and shore batteries. Or he could save his remaining two ships by pulling out without searching for the survivors from the USS *Cooper*. One of his remaining ships, the *Moale*, was already damaged by gunfire from the *IJN Take*, a second Japanese destroyer which had been hidden in the darkness behind its sister ship. He pulled his ships out of Ormoc Bay, calling for Air-Sea Rescue to send their planes in the morning to search for survivors. These gallant pilots and their crews rescued 168 of USS *Cooper's* crew, but another 10 officers and 181 men went down with her.[43] These survivors had the rather unique experience of conversing with survivors of the enemy ship they had just sunk while both groups floated in the dark sea, awaiting rescue.[44]

*   *   *

General Suzuki, meanwhile had his own problems. Every time he made a move to launch his long cherished counterattack against U.S. Sixth Army, some new problem arose. His own *35th Army* had still not gained the start line positions from which his planned attack was to be launched and, despite significant reinforcements, he was still unable to reach these initial goals. The latest issue was that during his concentration on the battle in the northern mountains to keep the Americans away from Ormoc, another enemy force had suddenly appeared in his rear, around Baybay, which was the western terminus for one of his avenues of attack on the Americans. At first believing that these were simply reconnaissance forces, he soon learned that there was a strong American force coming north from there. Instead of attacking east from Baybay, General Suzuki now first had to secure the area before his attack could even get started. Much as he hated to divert limited resources, he now had to send the *26th Infantry Division* to the south to open up the way across the island to the Buri vicinity. His decision, reinforced by orders from General Yamashita, put the new amended plan into motion. The *26th Infantry Division* was to clear out any opposition around Baybay and then move over the mountains, where they would participate in a coordinated attack on the American rear areas. By November 22nd the entire division, led by the *13th Independent Infantry Regiment*, was well on its way to the Albuera area where the advance elements of the enemy force were known to be located. Leading elements soon became aware of a series of hills and ridges to their front, which the Americans would soon be calling "Shoestring Ridge."

CHAPTER 6

INTO THE MOUNTAINS—
SHOESTRING RIDGE

B esides their new innovation of the *kamikaze*, or suicide attack, the *Fourth Air Army* made other contributions to the defense of Leyte. Indeed, for several days in November while the U.S. Third and Seventh Fleets were either bombarding Luzon or returning to distant bases for replenishment, the Japanese actually had air supremacy over Leyte. The U.S. Army Air Force could not bring enough planes to Leyte to prevent constant Japanese air attacks on the American Fleet offshore and the ground installations on the island. With airfield construction nearly at a standstill, due to weather and terrain obstacles, the Japanese enjoyed a few days of triumph.

In order to take advantage of this shortage of American air support, the *Fourth Air Army* decided to take a more direct hand in the ground battle. The *Kaoru Airborne Raiding Detachment* was originally formed as a multi-company guerrilla unit, and one company of this unique unit was on Luzon during the Leyte operation. The men, recruited from the Takasago tribe on Formosa, were rated as courageous and skilled jungle fighters. Led by Japanese officers, technicians and medical personnel, the unit had been trained by the *Nakano Intelligence School* staff in guerrilla and infiltration tactics. The *Fourth Air Army* decided to put these specialist troops to use on Leyte.

Under the command of Lieutenant Shigeo Naka, the *1st Guerrilla Company* was quickly trained in air-landing operations. The objective was the American airfields on Leyte. The plan was for the guerrillas, carrying demolition charges, to use transport aircraft to crash-land on the American fields where they would destroy as many enemy aircraft as possible before melting into the jungle and conducting guerrilla operations against the Americans. Given the code name *Operation Gi,* the plan was scheduled for late November.

On November 26th four transports, each carrying ten raiders, took off from Lipa Field, south of Manila on Luzon, and headed for the two airfields at Burauen. Flying low to avoid enemy interception, the planes headed southeast to Leyte. Two hours later they reported back to *Fourth Air Army* that they were over their targets. No further word was ever received from the raiders. When the next day no American aircraft appeared over Leyte, Luzon or Ormoc Bay, the raiders were credited with a success.

Unfortunately for the Japanese, that was not the case. One transport landed in the sea near Dulag Airfield. An American patrol from the 728th Amphibian Tractor Battalion went to their assistance but, when fired upon, returned the fire and killed two of the raiders. The others fled into a nearby swamp. A second plane crashlanded on Bito Beach and nearby American paratroops killed one raider before the survivors vanished into the jungle. According to the history of the 11th Airborne Division, an antiaircraft crew was on the alert for enemy aircraft when a plane crashed nearby. As the plane came to a stop, the gun crew yelled over to the plane's occupants asking if they needed any help. Supposedly, the Japanese answered in English, "No, everything O.K." and the gun crew went back to scanning the sky for enemy planes. The third plane did, in fact, reach Burauen field, but before it could land, it was shot down and all occupants killed. The fourth and final plane missed its target completely, landing near Ormoc where the occupants joined up with Japanese ground troops. After that, the fate of the *1st Guerrilla Company* is not recorded.[1]

*   *   *

The advance of the *13th Independent Infantry Regiment* of the *26th Infantry Division* did not go unnoticed by General Arnold at 7th Infantry Division headquarters. Fortunately, the units of his division, which had been assigned to secure the Burauen area, were just then being relieved by newly arrived 11th Airborne Division units. As the relief was being completed on November 22nd, the freed-up units of the 7th Infantry Division were ordered to move in force to the west coast. In the interim, General Arnold had ordered Colonel Finn to move his 32nd Infantry Regiment north to the Damulaan-

General Douglas MacArthur (center) with Lieutenant General Walter Krueger (right), commanding Sixth U.S. Army, and Brigadier General Julian W. Cunningham (left) on Goodenough Island, 3 February 1944. *Signal Corps/NARA*

General Douglas MacArthur wades ashore during the initial landings on Leyte, Philippine Islands, 20 October 1944. This became a well-known photograph of the general which appeared often in books, newspapers and magazines supporting his career. *Signal Corps/NARA*

General MacArthur at Tamahermerah, Dutch New Guinea, with Major General Robert L. Eichelberger, commanding Eighth U.S. Army, Rear Admiral Daniel E. Barbey, commanding Northern Attack Force and Major General Frederick A. Irving, commanding 24th Infantry Division. *Signal Corps/NARA*

Lieutenant General George C. Kenney (right), commanding Allied Air Forces, Southwest Pacific Theater with Major General Ennis C. Whitehead, commanding Fifth U.S. Army Air Force, somewhere in New Guinea, 14 March 1944. *Signal Corps/NARA*

Technician 4th Class Warren Miller of Company "A", 3rd Engineer (Combat) Battalion, 24th Infantry Division, injured by a sniper in the back and neck while repairing a bridge destroyed by the retreating Japanese near Carigara, Leyte Island, is aided by buddies, 11 November 1944. *Signal Corps/NARA*

Staff of the 2nd Battalion, 19th Infantry Regiment, 24th Infantry Division on Leyte. L to R: Lieutenant Joseph Malon, Captain James W. Robinson, Lieutenant Colonel Robert B. Spragins (Battalion Commander), Major Charles H. Isackson, Captain Walter R. Bridgeforth and Captain Edwin L. Crosdale, on 5 October 1944, just before the Leyte Campaign, when the battalion was to seize Hill 522 and later Hill 1525 behind enemy lines on Breakneck Ridge. *Signal Corps/NARA*

Major General Frederick A. Irving, who commanded the 24th Infantry Division during the first month of the Leyte Campaign, 20 February 1944. *Signal Corps/NARA*

Members of the 34th Infantry Regiment, 24th Infantry Division, examine antitank gun put out of action by Japanese mortar fire on the road north of Jaro, Leyte, P.I., 31 October 1944. The jeep driver lies dead besides his vehicle. *Signal Corps/NARA*

Lieutenant Colonel Frederick R. Weber, commander and later executive officer of the 21st Infantry Regiment, 24th Infantry Division at Leyte, taken prior to that campaign, 20 February 1944. *Signal Corps/NARA*

Natives unloading Buffaloes at Consuegra, Leyte, P.I., 24 November 1944. This supply depot was critical to the maintenance of the American forces on Kilay Ridge. *Signal Corps/NARA*

Officers of the 6th Ranger Battalion at Sixth Army Headquarters near Tacloban, Leyte, P.I., 17 December 1944. *Signal Corps/NARA*

Tankers of the 706th Tank Battalion, attached to the 77th Infantry Division, conduct maintenance on their vehicle and observe Japanese barges burning along Ormoc Bay Beach, Leyte, P.I., 16 December 1944. *Signal Corps/NARA*

Corporal Robert W. Viken of Long Island, New York and Corporal Willard Trumbell of Los Angeles, both members of the 96th Infantry Division, hunt a Japanese sniper in a demolished cemetery at Dagami, Leyte, P.I., 22 October 1944. *Signal Corps/NARA*

Less than 200 yards from enemy lines, amid the forward patrols of Company "F", 34th Infantry Regiment, Major General Franklin C. Sibert, commanding X Corps, holds a conference with Major General Frederick A. Irving, commanding 24th Infantry Division, Leyte Island, P.I., 22 October 1944. *Signal Corps/NARA*

Men of the 77th Infantry Division make an administrative landing at Terragona Beach, Leyte Island, after being diverted from a planned rest and rehabilitation base. *Signal Corps/NARA*

Cerilino Bening, a 16-year-old guerrilla, is attached to Company "B", 96th Filipino Infantry, at Consuegra, Leyte Island, P.I., 25 November 1944. *Signal Corps/NARA*

Recently promoted Major General Hugh J. Casey at his desk, 14 March 1944. General Casey was the Chief Engineer Officer, Southwest Pacific Theater of Operations. General Casey had innumerable problems with the terrain and climate of Leyte after the invasion. *Signal Corps/NARA*

Vice Admiral Thomas C. Kinkaid, commanding Seventh U.S. Fleet, which supported the Leyte invasion forces. *NARA*

Members of Company "C", 85th Chemical Mortar Battalion, direct fire from a nearby ridge into a defile between Hill 1525 and O.P. Hill near Carigara, Leyte, 12 November 1944. *Signal Corps/NARA*

Lieutenant General Walter Krueger (left), commanding general, Sixth U.S. Army, congratulates Colonel John F. Bird upon the award of the Legion of Merit for his service in the Southwest Pacific Theater of Operations. No date. *Signal Corps/NARA*

General Tomoyuki Yamashita (right), commanding 14th Japanese Area Army. General Yamashita opposed the decision to make Leyte a decisive battle but was overruled by Imperial General Headquarters. He was tried after the war and executed as a war criminal. *NARA*

Lieutenant General Sosaku Suzuki, commanding the 35th Japanese Army, defenders of Leyte, 1944. General Suzuki was killed in action later in the Philippines campaign. *NARA*

Japanese troops fording a river in the Philippines, no date. Captured Japanese war photo. *Signal Corps/NARA*

Field Marshal Count Hisaichi Terauchi, commanding Southern Army, Imperial Japanese Army, 1941–1945. He commanded Japanese Army operations throughout the entire Southeast Asia area. Accused of war crimes, he died of natural causes soon after the cessation of hostilities while under house arrest in Malaya. *NARA*

Private First Class
George Benjamin, Jr.,
of Carney's Point,
New Jersey and
Company "A", 306th
Infantry, 77th Infantry
Division, earned a
posthumous Medal
of Honor near Ormoc
on 21 December, 1944.
Signal Corps/NARA

Private First Class
Leonard Bostrom, of
Preston, Idaho and
Company "F", 17th
Infantry, 7th Infantry
Division earned a
posthumous Medal of
Honor near Dagami,
28 October 1944.
Signal Corps/NARA

Major General William H. Gill (right), commanding general, 32nd Infantry Division at Leyte with his aide, Captain William F. Barres, on Luzon in 1945. *Signal Corps/NARA*

Exactly three years after she fired the first American shots of the Pacific War, the USS *Ward* (DD139), Lieutenant R.E. Farwell, USNR, was sunk while covering the amphibious landings of the 77th Infantry Division at Ormoc Bay, Leyte, 7 December 1944. *U.S. Naval Institute*

The USS *Mahan* (DD364), Commander E.G. Campbell, hit by three kamikaze planes, was another victim of the naval battles in Ormoc Bay, 7 December 1944. *U.S. Naval Institute*

The USS *Cooper* (DD695), Commander Mell A. Peterson, was sunk while intercepting a Japanese resupply convoy in Ormoc Bay, 3 December 1944. Her survivors had the unique experience of sharing the dark waters of the bay with Japanese survivors from sunken ships of the reinforcement convoy. *U.S. Naval Institute*

Caridad area along the west coast in preparation for the advance on Ormoc. His other regiments were busy clearing the rear areas of the division, along the east coast, and until that was complete, he could not move them to Baybay.

Those clearing operations were occasionally difficult, as when Company F, 17th Infantry, was crossing a cornfield and ran into heavy fire coming from an enemy strongpoint consisting of pillboxes, connecting trenches and spider holes. The company suffered heavy losses until Private First Class George T. Retzlaff, an automatic rifleman, took aggressive action. On his own initiative, he attacked a trench containing at least twenty-five Japanese soldiers, emptying two magazines into the crowded trench. As he was inserting his third magazine, he was hit three times in the right wrist, falling to the ground. Despite his serious wounds, Retzlaff tossed three grenades into the enemy trench, using his left hand. He did this to draw fire upon himself, allowing the rest of Company F to reorganize and renew their advance against the entrenched Japanese. The native of Tinley Park, Illinois, survived to wear his Distinguished Service Cross.[2]

Not far away, Company K, 382nd Infantry Regiment, 96th Infantry Division, was also fighting to clear the remaining Japanese forces from east of the mountains. As First Lieutenant Cledith W. Bourdeau led his company forward, it was stopped by a blast of small-arms, machine-gun and mortar fire from hidden Japanese forces. Wounded in the initial blast of fire, First Lieutenant Bourdeau continued to deploy his assault platoon into position. He then led a supporting platoon into action, fully exposing himself to enemy fire. As he did so, he spotted two enemy machine guns that were holding up Company K's advance. Bourdeau crawled to within fifteen yards of the concealed guns, from where he destroyed both of them. After crossing another fifteen yards of ground completely exposed to the enemy, he knocked out another machine gun. The fleeing gun crew was killed by members of Company K. By this time, Lieutenant Bourdeau, from Presidio, California, realized that his strength was fast ebbing away and as his command was facing superior odds, ordered Company K to withdraw while he remained behind to cover the withdrawal. When he noticed a soldier receive wounds during the withdrawal, Bourdeau went to his aid, advancing seventy-five yards under enemy fire to reach him. After applying first aid, he assisted the wounded man back to the company. For his inspiring leadership and personal courage on 18 November 1944, Lieutenant Bourdeau was promoted to captain and received a Distinguished Service Cross.[3]

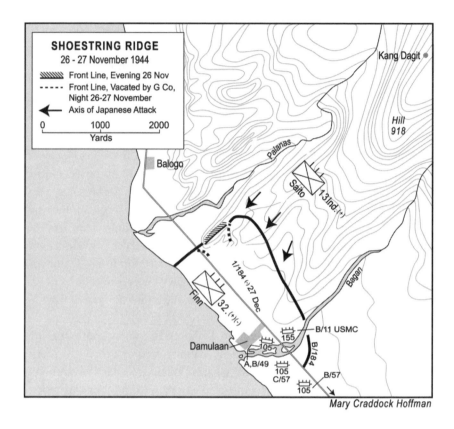

SHOESTRING RIDGE
26 - 27 November 1944

▨▨▨▨ Front Line, Evening 26 Nov
---- Front Line, Vacated by G Co,
    Night 26-27 November
◄— Axis of Japanese Attack

0   1000   2000
         Yards

Kang Dagit

Hill
918

Balogo

Palanas

Saito

13 Inf. (-)

1/184 (-) 27 Dec

Finn

32. (+)(-)

Bagan

155

105

B/11 USMC

B/184

Damulaan

A,B/49

105
C/57

105

B/57

Mary Craddock Hoffman

The 96th Infantry Division's fight continued throughout November. On 19 November, Captain George W. Carter, the executive officer of the 1st Battalion, 382nd Infantry, had taken the lead in an infantry company struggling through jungle terrain when it was hit by enemy fire. Captain Carter moved forward, struggling through dense undergrowth, until he spotted an enemy pillbox from which machine gun fire was directed at the infantrymen. He charged the pillbox and used grenades to knock it out. As he looked around, Captain Carter realized that his command was outnumbered by the enemy. Deciding to return to the company, he had begun the return journey when he was struck by enemy fire in the foot. Under direct sniper fire, he disregarded his painful wound and directed an artillery barrage on the enemy positions he had identified. Hearing a cry for help from a wounded man, Captain Carter, from Memphis, Tennessee, himself now wounded a second time, went to his aid. After applying first aid while under fire, Carter carried the wounded man, despite his own severe wounds, to safety before allowing the medical staff to treat his own wounds. For his outstanding leadership of this rifle company, Captain Carter was promoted to major and awarded a Distinguished Service Cross.[4]

*   *   *

The 32nd Infantry, less its 1st Battalion at Panaon Strait, was along the Palanas River. Facing them were the advance elements of the *26th Infantry Division*, which General Suzuki had sent south to push the Americans out of his way. The Americans had established their defenses along a series of ridges that ran alongside the Palanas River. That river runs southwest between them and ends at the roadside. The heights drop sharply towards the river and a narrow valley separates them. Colonel Finn established his defense line on the southern ridge line where its north face dropped steeply into that valley. Dense bamboo thickets lined the riverbanks, while the ridge itself was covered by cogon grass mixed with palm and bamboo. The gullies on the ridge were particularly well covered with undergrowth. The north end of the ridge is marked by Hill 918 and the southern end by the rice paddies, between the road and the sea. From Hill 918, the Americans could see the entire coastline between Baybay and Ormoc. Off of Hill 918, a T-shaped finger ridge, cut by ravines, sloped down to the low ground. This area came to be known as Tom and Dick Hills. The entire ridgeline would soon be known to the Americans as "Shoestring Ridge."

Colonel Finn had many concerns about his position while awaiting the bulk of the division to join his advanced regiment. Enemy barges were landing troops in plain sight of his men while Japanese destroyers cruised offshore, past his position, unhindered. General Arnold feared that the Japanese might be planning a counter-landing at or near Baybay which would not only cut off Colonel Finn's regiment, but close the western terminus of the only road available to his division to join the 32nd Infantry. The road to Baybay was both the only line of communication and the only supply route to Colonel Finn's forces. Once again, the steady rain and mud already made communication, supply and troop transfers difficult, slowing American operations significantly. It was only through the strenuous efforts of Company B, 13th Engineer Combat Battalion, that the road remained useable. In addition, to support the six thousand men around Baybay, the division had been allocated only twelve trucks and five DUKWs. These vehicles were in constant use over the narrow, often single-lane, trail and fourteen old bridges to Baybay. A Japanese landing would make these operations impossible.

Knowing that he could not quickly reinforce Colonel Finn over the single supply road, General Arnold had Lieutenant Colonel Charles A. Whitcomb's 3nd Battalion, 32nd Infantry back the 2nd Battalion on Shoestring Ridge by establishing defensive positions to the south of it. However, concerned that the Japanese might either flank the American defensive line or break it, he ordered the 2nd Battalion, 184th Infantry, recently arrived, to be held back in a reserve position to counterattack any such enemy advance past Shoestring Ridge. His order stipulated that this battalion was not to be committed without his express permission.[5] He then brought up his strength, the artillery of Batteries A and B of the 49th Field Artillery Battalion, and Battery B of the 11th 155mm Gun Battalion, USMC. These guns were set up near Damulaan in support of the 2nd and 3rd Battalions, 32nd Infantry. To join them, he added the regimental cannon company's two guns. The fourteen guns were barely 1,500 yards behind the front lines, and the heavy Marine Corps guns were placed so that they could shell Ormoc. (See Map 5)

Protecting his line of communication was a platoon of the 7th Reconnaissance Troop, which patrolled the road between Baybay and Damulaan. A platoon of light tanks, from the 767th Tank Battalion, was also stationed at Damulaan. No other tanks were available on the west coast. While making these preparations, the Americans were receiving information from Filipinos, who were moving south away from the battle, that large enemy forces were massing on the opposite side of the Palanas River. They were reportedly digging in field guns and building trenches. These were subsequently identified as the *1st* and *2nd Battalions, 13th Independent Infantry Regiment,* and two battalions, one each from the *11th* and *12th Independent Infantry Regiments,* all from the *26th Infantry Division.* Included was the entire artillery force of the *26th Infantry Division.* Led by Colonel Saito, these forces had been sent south by General Suzuki to keep the Americans away from Ormoc, while the Japanese built a new trail from Albuera over the mountains to Burauen. General Suzuki still believed his long delayed counterattack could be launched.

General Arnold had an inadequate number of troops to defend every foot of Shoestring Ridge. As a result, there were gaps in the line where it was believed that either terrain or thick undergrowth would discourage any enemy advance. The main defenses were along the highway and on that part of the ridge that overlooked the artillery base. Companies F and G manned a line 1,500 yards wide along the flat land between the ridge and the sea. Barricades of dirt and sandbags were created at seventy-five yard intervals and the area in front mined. Company E and guerrillas from the 94th Philippine Infantry, attached to the battalion, were on a ridge that extended to Hill 918. Guerrillas outposted areas between Companies G and E.[6] On the night of November 23rd, Thanksgiving Day, the Marines of Battery B opened fire on Ormoc from their positions at Damulaan.

* * *

Meanwhile, overhead, the Army Air Force continued to fight to gain air supremacy over the island of Leyte, if not the entire Philippines. Continued Japanese reinforcements frustrated these efforts, but the army fliers continued their effort. One of the leaders was a dashing twenty-four-year-old in the Army Air Forces, Major Richard Ira Bong. He had been fighting with the Fifth Army Air Force since the early days in New Guinea, and had already earned a reputation as a superb flier and shooter. For the past eight months Major Bong had been relieved of his command responsibilities, and pretty much allowed do as he pleased. A favorite of Lieutenant General Kenney's, he had been given the freedom to fly when and where he chose. Competition between the Pacific and European Air Forces was a prominent factor in this assignment, for Major Bong was the top-scoring ace in the Far Eastern Air Forces. The major had already earned the Distinguished Service Cross, two Silver Stars and seven Distinguished Flying Crosses along with fifteen air medals when he took off from Dulag, on December 7th, with a flight of four Lockheed P-38J fighter aircraft.

Flying with Major Bong were other top scoring army aces in the Pacific, Major Thomas B. McGuire, the operations officer of the 475th Fighter Group, and two wingmen, Major Jack Rittmayer and First Lieutenant Floyd Fulkerson of the 431st Fighter Squadron. The foursome took station over Ormoc Bay, and soon Major McGuire shot down a Mitsubishi "Sally" bomber,[7] raising his total of "kills" to twenty-nine. Not to be outdone, Major Bong spotted another Mitsubishi and dove after the Japanese plane. Within seconds he had shot it down over Bohol Island for "kill" number thirty-seven. Half an hour later a torpedo plane was shot down by Major Rittmayer. Flying at 3,000 feet, the four-plane formation was suddenly aware of five Japanese planes attacking. Major Bong downed one, the other pilots finished off the remaining four.

Five days later, Major Bong was again over Leyte flying with a group from the 9th Fighter Squadron based at Tacloban. Before he did so, he was stopped by General MacArthur personally who reportedly stated, "Major Richard Ira Bong, who has ruled the air from New Guinea to the Philippines,

I now induct you into the society of the bravest of the brave, the wearers of the Congressional Medal of Honor of the United States."[8] Major Bong's actual citation for the Medal of Honor cites him "for conspicuous gallantry and intrepidity in action above and beyond the call of duty in the Southwest Pacific area from 10 October to 15 November 1944,"[9] and goes on to state that although he was not expected to fly combat missions he volunteered to do so over Balikpapan, Borneo and Leyte, which resulted in the downing of an additional eight enemy aircraft during the period.

*　　*　　*

As if the opening salvo by the Marines was the signal he had been awaiting, Colonel Saito launched his attack against Shoestring Ridge the same night that the Marines began firing. Japanese artillery opened return fire and early rounds fell in the vicinity of Battery A, 49th Field Artillery Battalion. Enemy mortars joined in, and the fire shifted to the front lines of the 32nd Infantry. The American gunners of Battery B of the 49th Field Artillery instituted counter-battery fire, and for a while silenced the Japanese artillery. Nevertheless, the Japanese again opened fire and cut all communications between the advanced 2nd Battalion and regimental headquarters. Later, a relay through the 3rd Battalion was established.

Additional shelling hit Companies F and G. This lasted for some two hours, until in the bright moonlight the infantrymen spotted enemy soldiers moving in orderly lines across the Palanas River. As they approached the lines of the 2nd Battalion, 32nd Infantry, Japanese artillery fire began to pound the American foxholes. Soon enemy mortars and machine guns joined in the onslaught. It soon became apparent that the main enemy effort was directed at Company E on the right of the line.

Captain John J. Young, commanding Company E, had orders to withdraw in the face of superior enemy forces. Estimating the attacking force as two companies, he waited fifteen minutes and then ordered his men to withdraw over previously planned routes to new positions. But the heavy fire slowed the execution of his orders, delaying some units who were late in getting the order. The withdrawal became uncoordinated and confused. Soon, Company E was a series of small groups or individuals seeking to find safety as best they could. Despite the confusion, Captain Young assembled his company before daylight and led them to new positions on low ground behind a height known as Jean Hill.

Meanwhile, Company G had been attacked by large enemy patrols with grenades, but had retained its positions. When Captain Roy F. Dixon of Company G learned that Company E had withdrawn, he posted his two right squads to move to Jean Hill and reestablish contact with Company E. This part of the American lines now faced east towards Hill 918 instead of north. The battle continued throughout the night. Only one enemy group managed to penetrate the lines, by a gap in the right flank. This group passed through the American defenses and appeared headed for Damulaan, but for unknown reasons soon disappeared. On the low ground, Company F had been harassed by small patrols, but no major attack developed.

November 24th dawned with the Japanese holding Hill 918 and Tom and Dick Hills. Colonel Saito had seized the high ground, but he had neglected to pierce the American line. Colonel Nelson immediately reformed his battalion. While sending patrols from Company F to the Palanas River, he had his three companies form for an attack on Hill 918. When his patrols reported no Japanese forces along the river, he had his battalion dig new positions facing the main enemy threat. Behind them patrols cleaned up enemy stragglers who had penetrated the lines during the night. Colonel Finn had requested permission to send up Companies K and L to join Colonel Nelson's force, and permission came from General Arnold immediately. These companies were placed in an extension of the line facing east, while Company F faced north. In effect, the reinforced 2nd Battalion, 32nd Infantry, now occupied a "fishhook position," not unlike that held by Union forces at Gettysburg in the Civil War.

Reinforcements in the form of Battery C, 57th Field Artillery Battalion, arrived during the day and joined the perimeter defenses. It had taken this unit four full days to cross over the island from the west coast on the road to Baybay. It established itself across the road from Battery B, 49th Field Artillery, and just south of the Bucan River. There were now five infantry companies and two reinforced artillery batteries defending that perimeter. American patrols went out to try and locate the enemy artillery positions, while the American artillery used its fire to probe likely locations. As they did so, a Japanese plane flew over the area and most probably pinpointed the American artillery positions for the Japanese.[10]

Colonel Nelson's attack regained some of the lost ground but did not push on to Hill 918. The rest of the day was spent bringing up supplies, particularly artillery and mortar ammunition, and sending patrols to ensure that the Japanese were not trying to infiltrate large bodies of troops around the American position towards Baybay.

*   *   *

It was the supply situation that concerned Colonel Finn the most, and from which the battle was to get its name. The artillery, which was the backbone of the defense, used up ammunition at a prodigious rate, and at the end of the first night's battle had almost exhausted its original supply. The next day a resupply arrived, which would be all but used up the next night. Any interruption in the supply of ammunition, particularly artillery and mortar ammunition, would have doomed the defense. As Colonel Finn was later to remark, "The old slogan, 'too little and too late' became 'Just enough and just in time' for us."[11] Aware of their precarious situation, the troops of the 32nd Infantry soon dubbed their fight the "Battle of Shoestring Ridge."

The resupply of ammunition that arrived allowed the American artillery and heavy mortars to probe Japanese lines during the day. The mortars of Company L shelled a group of Japanese assembling on a hill directly to its front, and although the Japanese dispersed they did not leave the hill. Nor did this deter the Japanese who, aided by a full moon, attacked again that night with the heaviest artillery barrage the Americans had yet experienced. While the enemy artillery fire kept the Americans' heads down, Japanese soldiers methodically moved into their attack positions. As on the day before, this was to be a well-organized and well-controlled assault. A reinforced battalion was used in the ground assault, while large combat patrols probed Companies G and F to keep them from reinforcing at the point of assault. Covered by machine guns, the Japanese attacked Company L, which suddenly found itself fighting some fifty Japanese who had managed to work in close to the company. Another Japanese company moved into a small draw on Jean Hill, which defined the boundary between Companies L and K. Here, they set up machine guns and began to fire on the two company flanks.

The draw was the responsibility of a platoon of Company K. After more than a month of fighting on Leyte, the platoon, like all other American units, was severely under authorized strength, down to nineteen men. These men now faced a company of enemy troops armed with machine guns and well supported with mortars and artillery. The American machine guns, which until now had remained silent so as not to reveal their positions to the Japanese artillery, opened fire. This fire roared just behind the nineteen men of Company K in the draw. They could not easily withdraw, nor could they hold their position. In moments they were in the fight of their lives, using grenades, bayonets, knives and fists to hold their position and not be overrun. The situation seemed hopeless.

Behind the trapped platoon lay an outpost of Battery B, 11th 155mm Gun Battalion, USMC. A Marine Corps machine gunner in the outpost, described as "a big nineteen-year-old Marine from Elizabeth, New Jersey," opened fire with his heavy machine gun, firing over the heads of the infantry and directly into the attacking Japanese. He traversed up and down the draw, and soon had all enemy fire against the trapped platoon silenced. With their lives suddenly returned to them, the platoon survivors moved to previously prepared positions from which they could cover the draw with their own fire.[12] From there they covered the draw so effectively that the Japanese soon gave up that avenue of attack.

Company L managed to push the Japanese away from their positions, inflicting heavy casualties on the attackers. Company K, also significantly under authorized strength, managed to retain its defense line as well, all but wiping out the attacking force. Every weapon was used, including artillery, mortars, machine guns, grenades and rifle fire. The Japanese did not give up, however, and spent the remainder of the night probing for weak points in the American line. Enemy mortars and machine guns did not cease fire, and kept the American lines under constant bombardment throughout the night. One group of about twenty-five Japanese did succeed in infiltrating past the American front and moved to within fifty yards of the battalion command post. Here, they set up two machine guns and opened fire on the headquarters and supply personnel. A combat group was hastily formed of headquarters, medical and engineer troops, who eliminated this enemy threat.

The group of Japanese who had been repulsed by Company L was regrouping for another attack. Company L did not have an artillery forward observer with them this night, but First Lieutenant William C. Bentley of the Regimental Cannon Company was on hand and immediately assumed that role. Taking two men and a field telephone, he crawled fifty yards forward to a vantage point where he directed artillery fire on the Japanese. Three times the Japanese attempted to renew their attack on Company L, and three times the artillery fire drove them back. They then tried a flanking attack, which ran afoul of the Company E mortars and two of the battalion antitank guns. The mortars and canister shells from the cannons convinced the Japanese to give up the idea.

The Japanese artillery did manage some success during the night, however. They directed heavy counter-battery fire at Batteries A and B, 49th Field Artillery Battalion. Whether the accuracy of this barrage was due to the Japanese plane which had over flown the position earlier is a matter of conjecture, but this night the Japanese artillery was on target. Before the fire ceased, Battery B had all four of its 105mm guns knocked out. By using the parts of the four destroyed guns, the determined artillerymen had one gun operational by morning.

Colonel Finn reviewed the night's events and took immediate steps to strengthen his positions, eliminating weak points revealed by the most recent attack. He moved up the seventy-nine men of Company I, from Baybay, into that draw between Companies K and L to prevent any more penetrations, like the one that had only been stopped the night before by the Marine machine gunner. He also sent out strong patrols in front of his lines to prevent the Japanese from assembling for more attacks too close to his own lines.

With the 2nd Battalion, 184th Infantry now defending Baybay, Colonel Finn brought up Major Whitcomb's 3rd Battalion, 32nd Infantry, headquarters group to command his own battalion, most of which was now on the front lines. General Arnold, also closely monitoring the battle, released the 1st Battalion, 184th Infantry to Colonel Finn, who in turn moved its Company B up to Tinagan to watch for any Japanese attempt to outflank the Shoestring Ridge position. The 7th Reconnaissance Troop took over responsibility for the coast between Baybay and Damulaan. Headquarters and Battery B of the 57th Field Artillery moved up to Camulaan to add additional firepower to the American defense. The remaining gun of Battery B, 49th Field Artillery, was moved to a new position in the hope of avoiding detection.

But once again, ammunition resupply was the most critical concern. The night's battle had all but exhausted the resupply brought up the previous day. Every vehicle and every soldier not needed on the line was put to work bringing up more artillery and mortar ammunition. Soldiers who had spent the night awake fighting off the Japanese now spent the day without sleep bringing up supplies. It was backbreaking work, making tired men exhausted, and resulted in additional casualties from fatigue and illness.

* * *

The night of November 25–26 was a repeat of the previous night. Japanese artillery opened fire after dark, and soon afterwards a reinforced battalion assaulted the draw between Company K and L. This time Colonel Finn was prepared, and the Japanese now faced Company I, 32nd Infantry. Another company-strength force hit Company G where the fishhook curved, now called "The Bend" by the soldiers. Here, they encountered Staff Sergeant Walter B. Kellogg and the six men of his squad, who were protecting a machine gun position. Under the cover of artillery and mortar fire, the Japanese attacked the gun position. Within minutes, three of Staff Sergeant Kellogg's men were killed and the other three seriously wounded. Ordering his three wounded men to the rear, Staff Sergeant Kellogg determined to hold the position alone. Armed only with his rifle, the non-commissioned officer held the position against overwhelming numbers of enemy attackers. At times using grenades, his bayonet and even a knife, Staff Sergeant Kellogg was eventually mortally wounded while protecting the vital machine gun. Despite his wounds Kellogg remained at his post, defending the machine gun, until dawn. As the sun began to come up and the Japanese withdrew, Staff Sergeant Kellogg died at his post. For his selfless gallantry in protecting a vital position within the defense, he received a posthumous Distinguished Service Cross.[13]

Both attacks were beaten off with much less difficulty than on the preceding night. But once again, the Japanese managed a small success when a group of eight men, led by an officer, moved unnoticed along the Bucan River, which ran about a mile and a half south of the Palanas River. Again the victim was Battery B, 49th Field Artillery, which was hit by a barrage of grenades. Unable to determine from where these grenades had come, the artillerymen were confused. Using the cover of night, the Japanese scrambled out over the riverbank and tried to place satchel charges on the American guns. Only one succeeded, and he knocked out the gun permanently. All of the Japanese were killed by the artillerymen or the squad of Company I, which moved down the ridge and joined in the fight. In the morning, the ravaged Battery B was combined with Battery A, 49th Field Artillery. A platoon from Company B, 184th Infantry moved into the artillery positions to prevent future infiltrations.

The daylight hours of November 26th were used to again replenish ammunition, move the positions of automatic weapons to avoid Japanese artillery, and relocate the exhausted men as best they could. There were not enough troops on the west coast to relieve the exhausted soldiers of the 32nd Infantry, so no large group could be taken off the front lines. Despite this, Colonel Finn had established a rest camp at Caridad, where serious exhaustion cases and non-battle casualties could be treated and allowed some rest. Wounded were being evacuated over the same miserable supply road that brought ammunition and food forward. The wounded were first carried by DUKW to Baybay, but only after dark to avoid air attack from enemy planes, which often flew overhead. The 7th Medical Battalion had an advanced station there for emergency treatment of serious wounds. But the wounded who needed hospital care still had to be transported over the long, twisting, muddy road to the east coast. It usually took an ambulance two full days to make the journey.

*　　*　　*

A platoon of Company B, 184th Infantry had been left at Tinagan when the bulk of the company had moved to the Bucan River to protect the artillery. On November 26th, this platoon reported that small groups of Japanese were finally moving beyond the flank of the 32nd Infantry Regiment. While this concerned Colonel Finn and General Arnold, they were still required to hold the line along Shoestring Ridge. Patrols sent forward to the Palanas River reported that the main force of the Japanese were still there, indicating that the flanking force was scouting, but not attacking, around the flanks. Repeated requests by Colonel Finn for air support went unanswered, and no such protection was available to the 32nd Infantry.

Colonel Saito was busy during the day, too. He brought up two fresh infantry battalions to launch his massive counterattack on the night of November 26–27. As usual, the Japanese artillery opened the battle after dark. Some fifty enemy machine guns pounded the Americans while the two battalions moved by companies down Tom Hill and up the slopes of Jean Hill toward "The Bend." American artillery replied immediately, ignoring counter-battery fire for the moment. As the Japanese came up the hill, Companies G and E opened fire with all of their weapons, cutting down the attackers as they appeared. Casualties on both sides were heavy. Nevertheless, the Japanese kept coming and soon reached the American line, where the fighting became hand-to-hand. Just at the moment when it appeared that the Japanese attack was succeeding, a series of flares roared up over the Japanese lines and the attackers melted away.

Colonel Saito had recalled his attacking force. Leaving their wounded on the slopes of Jean Hill, the Japanese withdrew for a renewed attack. Colonel Finn, using the lull, sent up more infantrymen to fill the gaps created in the line by the first assault. Company E had no officers left and was now led by its noncommissioned officers. All that remained of Companies E, G and H at "The Bend" were some thirty men still holding their positions. Technical Sergeant Marvin H. Raabe, of Company H, took command of the group. Supplies of ammunition were also sent up to the line. The American mortars continued to fire to prevent the enemy from reorganizing.

Technical Sergeant Raabe ordered his supporting mortars to keep firing at the draw which led to the two hills at "The Bend." He then placed his few remaining men in position from which they could cover the approach with their fire. As he did so, barely an hour after they retreated, the Japanese returned.

Without artillery fire, but with mortars and machine guns blazing, the attack came on again. This attack led directly into Sergeant Raabe's fire zone. The attack was less well directed than the earlier one, but still the Japanese came up the hill. A large group of the attackers tried to slip around the flank, while others drifted to the left and tried to infiltrate to the ridge top. A few of these managed to reach the foxholes which Sergeant Raabe's men had left when they changed position. When he discovered this, Sergeant Raabe led his men in a bayonet charge on their former positions, which cleared the ridge top of Japanese. This attack, however, left the opening between the hills uncovered and the Japanese were beginning to move through it. Sergeant Raabe turned his few men around again and attacked down the hill. Savage hand-to-hand fighting took place before Sergeant Raabe's small force cleared the hill of enemy troops.

There now occurred a lull in the battle and Sergeant Raabe organized his men yet again. Japanese wounded covered the hill and were crying out for assistance. The Americans with Sergeant Raabe were physically and mentally exhausted, their nerves on edge, expecting at any moment to be killed or wounded. Many of the men bore wounds which they ignored to stay in the fight. One enemy soldier in particular got on the nerves of the soldiers. After what seemed a long time of him alternately crying out for help and singing in Japanese, an American soldier put him out of his misery.[14]

The Japanese kept up their fire at the Americans on Shoestring Ridge. Using mortars, machine guns and grenade launchers, they kept the Americans under an accurate pounding. This soon annoyed Staff Sergeant Leroy R. Soderholm, a mortar section leader, who began to roam around the ridge spotting enemy positions and then directing his mortar crew in destroying them. He was credited with destroying eleven enemy positions.

Meanwhile, Sergeant Raabe had placed a machine gun on his extreme left flank. This weapon was kept busy keeping the Japanese from outflanking Jack Hill to the north. As they did so, however, the gun suddenly jammed. Under fire and with Japanese all around them, Staff Sergeant Lewis V. Pulver, and his assistant, Private First Class Dee Taylor, took the weapon apart at the bottom of the muddy foxhole, repaired it, reassembled it and then opened fire again. While they worked, Private First Class Rufus F. Pate stood over the hole, keeping the Japanese from getting to the critical weapon and its crew. He threw so many grenades at approaching Japanese that he soon lost count. These men were credited with saving the left flank of the Shoestring Ridge line. Slowly the Japanese attack petered out, with no formal withdrawal, no flares, and no command. The Japanese had exhausted their resources at Shoestring Ridge. For his actions this night, Technical Sergeant Raabe would receive the Distinguished Service Cross and be promoted to second lieutenant.[15]

Colonel Saito's other battalion hit the section of the line held by Companies E, L, I and K. Although the fight was determined, there was never the crisis that had occurred in front of "The Bend." But as on previous nights, the greatest Japanese success did not come at the point of their main attack, but elsewhere. The groups of Japanese which had been deflected away from "The Bend" and Jean Hill had moved off to the north slope of Jack Hill, where it slopes down to the Palanas River. Here a small piece of high ground jutted out over the coastal plain. This hill was covered with a bamboo thicket which obscured fields of fire. Once the Japanese had established themselves within the thicket and opened fire, the Americans realized that a strong enemy force had penetrated their perimeter.

Company G, less one platoon at "The Bend," had covered Jack Hill. Because of its low strength and commitments elsewhere, Company G's commander, Captain Dixon, had only placed a three-man listening post within the bamboo thicket. Initially, Company G was little involved, but soon noted large groups of Japanese assembling at the bottom of the promontory on which the thicket resided. Two platoons of Company G tried to drive them off, without success. An outpost on the hill, under Staff Sergeant Lester C. Jackson, requested permission to withdraw from the new company commander.[16] The runner reached Lieutenant Wolfe and received permission, but faced strong enemy fire on the return trip. Unsure if he could reach the outpost, the runner yelled out that it was OK to withdraw. Unfortunately, the order was heard by most of Company G, and soon men were pulling off the hill under the impression that they were conducting an authorized withdrawal. More and more men from Company G joined the withdrawal, each believing it was approved. Within forty-five minutes, the two platoons of Company G and attached heavy weapons platoon were calmly marching down the highway near Damulaan, heading south. Here, they were met by First Lieutenant Robert E. Engley of Company H, who quickly realized what had happened and ordered the men back to their positions. Lieutenant Wolfe, the new company commander, had remained on the hill unaware of the situation.

The Japanese quickly capitalized on this mistake. Enemy troops worked their way up to the bamboo grove and took over empty foxholes. From there they could fire directly upon the headquarters and artillery positions in the Damulaan Area. Fortunately for the Americans, however, the Japanese did not fully realize their good fortune and did not push through the huge gap in the American perimeter. Instead, they developed the hilltop for defense and prepared to repulse the inevitable American counterattack.

Company G returned to the hill, where one platoon was able to get back into its old position without difficulty. But the other platoon found that they could not get near the Bamboo Thicket where they had previously been dug in. Some two hundred Japanese and twenty machine guns now occupied the thicket. Colonel Finn and Colonel Nelson could not get enough information immediately to determine a next move. When Company G reported that the Japanese were dug in on the hill, Colonel Finn asked General Ready,[17] the assistant division commander, for additional authority to restore his lines using the 1st Battalion, 184th Infantry. Meanwhile, Company F turned one platoon towards the thicket and across the highway, protecting its flank and rear areas. A squad of Company G, which had never left its position, was also turned to face the thicket with orders to prevent the Japanese from expanding their hold on the hill. A platoon of Company I was rushed up to aid this squad.

Meantime, First Lieutenant Desmond M. Murphy, an artillery forward observer, was still in an observation post at the edge of the thicket where he had been before the withdrawal. He didn't see the infantry leave the hill and so stayed in position, still spotting targets for the artillery. So close were the Japanese that he whispered his directions into the phone and repeatedly ordered his battery not to call him back, as the phone ring would alert the enemy to his presence. As the Japanese entered the thicket, he directed artillery fire on them, barely yards from his own position. Soon, four infantrymen who had also missed the withdrawal order, joined him in silent observation. It was these men who counted over two hundred Japanese and twenty-two machine guns in the Bamboo Thicket.

Colonel Finn now had the authority to use additional troops to plug the threatening gap. Even before daylight on November 27th, Lieutenant Colonel Daniel C. Maybury moved his battalion up on trucks from Caridad.

He already had Company B at Damulaan and two platoons of his Company C were patrolling in the foothills to the east. The rest of the battalion moved up while behind them the 2nd Battalion, 184th Infantry, moved into Caridad from Baybay. Colonel Finn and Colonel Maybury conferred and decided to move the battalion to Jean Hill, and then along the rear of Companies L and E at "The Bend." That way, the attack to recapture Jack Hill would be launched toward the west. Colonel Maybury intended to attack with Companies A and B abreast, but terrain soon limited the attack to a one-company front, so Company A led the assault. As Captain Norville H. Smith, commanding Company A, looked at the terrain, he quickly realized that it was too narrow even for a company. Instead he had to attack in a column of platoons, one platoon at a time. First Lieutenant Robert L. Gary sent his platoon in as skirmishers, but was pinned down quickly. Enemy fire was just too heavy and accurate to push forward.

A mortar barrage preceded a second attack, during which Staff Sergeant Arthur D. Morales stood up in plain sight of the enemy to direct his squad. Ten casualties later, this attack also stalled. Captain Smith pulled the platoon back to its start line and asked for an artillery concentration on the Bamboo Thicket. Colonel Finn reluctantly explained that because, as usual, the artillery had expended its ammunition during the night attack and resupply had not yet reached them, no artillery support was available. Once again the "shoestring" aspect of the Shoestring Ridge battle took a hand in operations. Finally, the two officers decided that of the five hundred rounds remaining to the 105-mm guns, some two hundred would be expended on the Bamboo Thicket. Colonel Finn also authorized that the last sixty rounds of mortar fire be made available to be used in the bombardment. Finally, four hundred rounds of 81mm mortar ammunition were allocated to the preparation.

The bombardment lasted twenty minutes. The entire amount of shells from the artillery and mortars were fired into the Bamboo Thicket, and as the last shell exploded, Captain Smith ordered his company forward. Five hours of bloody fighting resulted in renewed American possession of the vital hill. Company A immediately dug new defensive positions and tied in its flanks with Company F, 32nd Infantry on the left and Company G, 32nd Infantry on the right.

The hill had been recovered just in time. That night, November 27–28, the Japanese came on again. Although the attack came in with the usual flair, the entire event was anticlimactic. No Japanese reached the American foxholes and no part of the line was threatened with penetration, despite the best efforts of the Japanese. The American troops noticed that the light of battle seemed to have gone from the attacking Japanese, and the energy they had displayed on previous nights was no longer there. As evidence of the lack of enthusiasm by the enemy this night, the 32nd Infantry suffered casualties of only one killed and nineteen men wounded.

Only the recently arrived Company A, 184th Infantry, had some troubles this night. Enemy machine guns firing from across the Palanas River pinned down the Americans as the Japanese climbed the hill. Some of these men reached a position at the juncture between Company A and Company G, 32nd Infantry, on the right. Enemy grenades, rifles and machine guns placed accurate fire on the Americans. So intense was this fight that Privates First Class Philip A. Frusto and Paul Mann, each firing a light machine gun, fired their guns steadily until the barrels burned out from the heat of constant firing. As these men tried to replace their gun barrels, they were overrun by the attacking Japanese. To fill this hole, First Lieutenant Arthur Duchow, Private First Class Silvester H. Sueper, and Sergeant Charles Tolan jumped into the gap. They closed a dangerous breach at the cost of their lives. But the Japanese did manage to gain a foothold on a small part of Jack Hill. Their success had cost Company A, 184th Infantry, eight men killed and forty-nine wounded.

Both sides in the Battle of Shoestring Ridge were now exhausted. Colonel Saito had no more men, certainly not enough men, to renew his attack with any prospect of success. He had committed six infantry battalions against the Americans, of which an estimated three-fourths had fallen. And on the other ridge Colonel Finn's 32nd Infantry was exhausted, short of men and supplies, and barely able to defend themselves. But the Americans had other units at hand, at last, and early on November 28th Colonel Finn learned from General Arnold that the 184th Infantry would be relieving the 32nd Infantry on Shoestring Ridge. Colonel O'Sullivan soon had his men up on the ridge and concentrated his firepower on the small hold the Japanese had on Jack Hill. Ammunition stocks were, for the first time, up to American expectations, and these were used to good effect. The night was quiet, with no Japanese attack for the first time in four nights. Infiltration attempts by elements of the *13th Independent Infantry Regiment* were easily beaten off.

At dawn on November 29th, Company A, 184th Infantry was relieved by Company C which attacked Jack Hill. Supported by Company F, the attack was designed to clear the Japanese off the hill. As they advanced it seemed as if the Japanese had gone, but one pocket of about ten enemy soldiers held the extreme tip of the hill. As darkness came down, these, and about forty others who had come up the hill, staged the last Japanese attack on Shoestring Ridge. They were killed. The Battle of Shoestring Ridge was over.

* * *

General Suzuki had not been idle during the Battle for Shoestring Ridge. He still cherished the idea of a decisive counterattack against the American airfields, which he believed existed around Burauen. With these in Japanese hands, the Americans would lose their air support and be unable to bring in supplies and troops as easily as they had been doing. He had dispatched Colonel Saito and his detachment from the *26th Infantry Division* precisely to keep open his flank movement across the mountains from Albuera toward Burauen. While he sent some of his staff south to supervise Colonel Saito's attack, he busied himself with details of his coming counterattack.

The problem was that the Americans, besides not relying on the airfields around Burauen, were about to attack themselves. With Shoestring Ridge securely in their hands, the 184th Infantry was directed to continue the attack north towards Ormoc, General Suzuki's staging area. The 17th Infantry, relieved by elements of the 11th Airborne Division, was moving to the west coast and would support the coming attack. The entire 7th Infantry Division was about to be assembled on the west coast for the move north.[18]

Colonel O'Sullivan briefed his commanders on the plan after receiving his orders from General Arnold. After relieving the 32nd Infantry, the regiment would clear any remaining enemy stragglers from the area before moving up the highway. The front lines now were almost exactly the same as they had been before the Battle of Shoestring Ridge, and Colonel Saito's detachment still barred the way north. Moving Colonel Saito out of the way became what the Americans termed the "Battle of The Ridges."

As mentioned earlier, the ridges were a series of sharp hills and spurs heavily overgrown with bamboo thickets and high cogon grass. They rose from the coastal plain to the central mountain range. The most important tactically was Hill 918, which had briefly been in American possession before the Battle of Shoestring Ridge. Another high point was Hill 380, which lay between the Palanas River and the Tabgas River. General Arnold ordered his division to attack with two regiments abreast. To do this, he had to await the arrival of the 17th Infantry, which appeared on December 3rd. General Arnold then ordered a renewal of the attack for December 5th. The 17th Infantry would attack on the right and the 184th Infantry on the left. He also ordered Lieutenant Colonel O'Neill K. Kane to move his tanks of the 776th Amphibian Tank Battalion to a position west of Balogo, a mile north of the front lines. The tanks were to move out on the 5th to fire on the town and the enemy positions in the hills above it. Coordinating with the two assault regiments, the tanks were to lead off the battle.

That the tanks were available at all was due to American ingenuity. Because the bridges along the Abuyog-Baybay Road would not support the heavy American tanks, and the Camotes Sea still was insecure due to forays by the *Imperial Japanese Navy,* the decision was made to use the amphibian tanks, which Colonel Kane volunteered to lead, by sea around Leyte to assist the 7th Infantry Division's attack. While General Hodge at XXIV Corps was skeptical, General Arnold favored the idea and implemented it.[19] As a result, the 7th Infantry Division had tank support for the Battle of the Ridges.

Colonel Kane sent his tanks forward at dawn of December 5th. They moved offshore successfully until within two hundred yards of Balogo. From there they fired over 2,500 rounds of 75mm ammunition into Tabgas and the northern slopes in front of the attacking 7th Infantry Division. Colonel Kane then took his tanks further north and reconnoitered the area around Calingatgan before turning south again. Not wanting to waste ammunition, Colonel Kane ordered his tanks to land 500 yards south of the Tabgas River and fire their remaining ammunition before returning to American lines. No enemy opposition hindered the move of Colonel Kane's tanks.[20]

Behind the tanks the two infantry regiments attacked. Enemy opposition was fierce. The Japanese had prepared their defenses with their usual thoroughness. Using reverse slope tactics, they were able to fire on the advancing infantry while relatively safe from American artillery and mortar fire. Once again, supply over the hills and in deep valleys on trails covered by enemy fire was difficult and deadly. Nevertheless, the 17th Infantry went after Hill 918 led by Lieutenant Colonel William B. Moore and his 2nd Battalion.

Company G went from Jean Hill directly up a long ridge to the crest of Hill 918. Even as they left Jean Hill, enemy artillery inflicted twelve casualties on the company. Enemy machine guns wounded more as the company advanced. One gun covered the approach that the company had selected, so Captain Schade ordered Technical Sergeant William A. Flint to take his 3rd Platoon around to the south and knock it out. Although Flint found the way difficult, with poor visibility due to the undergrowth, the *2nd Battalion, 12th Independent Infantry Regiment,* atop Hill 918, had a good view of the whole American attack. Soon the 3rd Platoon was pinned down.

Captain Schade advised Colonel Moore that he would hold his position until Company E made the crest of Hill 918 and knocked out the enemy gun. That company attacked from the Bucan River and encountered only stragglers as they moved up the slopes of Hill 918. It was the undergrowth and steep hillsides that slowed the advance of Company E. Their advance was slowed to a crawl, about two hundred yards in an hour.

Meanwhile, Captain Schade had noticed that small groups of Japanese were trying to get between him and the 1st Battalion to the right. Colonel Moore rushed up two platoons of Company A to cover the exposed flank and ordered Captain Adams to move his Company F between G and E Companies, and attack Hill 918 through a depression that seemed to offer better access to the crest. By now, Captain Hughes and Company E had reached the crest of Hill 918 and could see no Japanese. Apparently their approach had not been seen by the enemy. Captain Hughes settled down to await the arrival of Company F, which finally reached the crest shortly before dark.

While Captain Hughes was waiting, he planned a joint attack across the crest of Hill 918 to clear it of the enemy. Captain Adams agreed, and just before darkness the two companies charged across the top of the hill. They did well until reaching a small knoll in the center from which six enemy machine guns and mortars opened fire. But Captains Hughes and Adams were prepared for this and had placed their own supporting mortars and machine guns in position to support the attack. These now opened fire and quelled the Japanese fire. Casualties of four men killed and seventeen wounded, all by the guns on the knoll, were evacuated under cover fire. As the company commanders reported to Colonel Moore, he ordered them to dig in for the night and renew the attack in the morning.

*   *   *

Meanwhile, the 1st Battalion, 17th Infantry was battling for the series of ridges which ran off Hill 918, including Tom and Dick Hills. Lieutenant Colonel Albert V. Hartle had separated his two companies during the attack and enemy infiltration was attempted between them, but insertion of Company H into the gap stopped this attempt. Little in the way of opposition was encountered, although the Japanese had a good view of the area. As the battalion came to a steep ravine in front of Dick Hill they opened fire. Five machine guns supported by mortars and small arms fire pinned both Companies A and B to the ground. Several men were wounded and lay in the open. Colonel Hartle ordered Company D's heavy weapons to open fire. This they did to good effect, eventually silencing the enemy guns.

December 6th saw Company C, 17th Infantry, working their way up a spur ridge which led to Hill 380. Little enemy fire was encountered at first. Patrols had reported that the ridge ran around a huge depression, called an amphitheater, and led to the top of Hill 380. The 1st Platoon led the way along the top of the cliff. As they came out on a trail, an enemy machine gun opened fire. Twenty men were immediately hit and all but two fell off the cliff into the gorge below. Half of these men were killed while eight of the others managed to crawl back to safety. Sergeant James H. Gatlin had a broken leg and could not move. He managed to splint his broken leg and waited until darkness when a patrol sent out to find him brought him to safety.

Technical Sergeant Hanford B. Lauderdale was commanding the 1st Platoon, Company C, during the attack. After reaching the crest of the steep ridge, heavy fire from Japanese machine guns halted all further advances. Lauderdale rushed forward to take charge of the leading elements, and as he did so was struck down by shrapnel. Refusing to stop for medical aid, he remained in command, and together with Second Lieutenant Keith D. Penry, directed the attack until hit again with another serious wound. Realizing that a withdrawal was now necessary, Technical Sergeant Lauderdale ordered his platoon's second-in-command to move the wounded down the ridge. With Lieutenant Penry dead and realizing that he himself was too severely wounded to withdraw, he remained behind to cover the withdrawal until wounded for the third time, this time mortally. For his self-sacrifice on 6 December, Technical Sergeant Hanford B. Lauderdale was awarded a posthumous Distinguished Service Cross.[21] The company withdrew under the cover fire of Private First Class Philip Dorame and his BAR. Despite four wounds he held off the enemy until he, too, fell mortally wounded.

First Lieutenant Rolland L. Steele led two platoons of Company B forward, only to fall under more enemy fire. The two platoons were now trapped as before. Colonel Hartle ordered Captain Robert P. Brust, commanding Company A, to knock out the enemy guns. He suggested sending a platoon around the left flank to Tom Hill and then firing on the backs of the Japanese on Dick Hill. Two such attempts failed in the face of strong enemy automatic weapons fire. Colonel Hartle now ordered his two companies off the hill to allow artillery fire to strike the Japanese. The withdrawal was as dangerous as the attack, and during it Lieutenant Steele was killed.

An artillery forward observer with Company B had spotted the guns which had killed Lieutenant Steele. American artillery soon knocked out some of them. Several enemy positions were seen to have been destroyed. The battalion pulled its casualties off the hill. The day had cost it more than seven killed and fifteen wounded. That night the battalions reorganized for another attack on December 7th.

The patrols sent out early on December 7th reported no enemy contact. Swiftly Colonel Pachler ordered his two battalions back up the hills. There they found but twelve Japanese soldiers who were too shell-shocked to put up a fight. Colonel Saito had pulled out during the night. The next objective was Hill 380, across the Palanas River.

The 184th Infantry Regiment was already across the river. Its 1st Battalion had met little opposition as it advanced along the flat ground along the coast. The 2nd Battalion in the nearby hills encountered more opposition and was slowed, but not stopped. While the 2nd Battalion dealt with that opposition, the 3rd Battalion come up and passed around the 2nd Battalion to continue the joint advance across the Palanas River and to a point some six hundred yards north. This battalion was now faced with taking Hill 380.

Like the others in the Battle of the Ridges, Hill 380 was covered with thick grass and deep and tangled ravines. The Japanese covered all approaches with machine-gun and mortar fire. First Lieutenant William F. Leonard led Company I up the hill until it was pinned down by enemy guns. Lieutenant Leonard set up his own machine guns to knock out the enemy guns. One of them destroyed a hut, in which at least one enemy machine gun was placed. But by the time this was accomplished, darkness was fast approaching and, rather than move over strange ground in the dark, the company dug in for the night. Behind them Company L tied the line in with the rest of the 3rd Battalion, 184th Infantry.

Nearby, Company B had moved on Hill 380 as well. Thick undergrowth apparently concealed their approach from the Japanese. As they neared the crest, the firing against Company C broke out and the company rushed to aid their comrades. The leading scouts suddenly stumbled into several Japanese in trenches. All were intent on Company C and never heard Company B's approach. The scouts did not fire, but instead sent back word to the company commander who organized his attack carefully. As he scouted the enemy, however, the company commander was wounded by yet another group of Japanese. But now the company knew the locations and strength of both enemy forces on Hill 380. Using the machine guns of Company D, most of the enemy positions were knocked out. The surviving enemy troops gathered for a counterattack against Company C, which was unprepared. However, Captain William R. Davis, the battalion operations officer, spotted the group from across the river while using his binoculars to watch the fight. He immediately directed the fire of Company D's heavy machine guns on the attackers and shattered the attack before it could hit Company C.

The next day, Colonel Moore's 2nd Battalion, 17th Infantry took up the attack on Hill 380. Enemy opposition stopped Company E, but Colonel Moore sent Company G around it to the crest of the hill before the Japanese realized what was happening. An attempted counterattack by about fifty Japanese was beaten off, and then the two companies coordinated their attacks on the remaining Japanese defenders of Hill 380. By noon the hill was in American possession. A prisoner taken later reported that five hundred Japanese had been assigned to hold the hill.

One soldier who was instrumental in the success of the attack against Hill 380 on 7 December was Private Fred W. N. Boardman of Company E, 17th Infantry. When the Japanese opened fire, he volunteered to flank and eliminate the enemy positions. Despite the cautions of his platoon sergeant and with no regard for his personal safety, Private Boardman, from Phoenix, New York, crawled forward about one hundred yards under concentrated machine gun, rifle and mortar fire until he reached grenade range of the enemy guns. He then jumped into the enemy position and overpowered the gunners, threw the machine gun out of the emplacement and opened fire with his rifle on the remaining Japanese. He used his rifle and bayonet to eliminate the gun crew and its protecting infantrymen, allowing Colonel Moore's battalion to conquer Hill 380. For his important contribution to this victory, Private Boardman received a Distinguished Service Cross.[22]

Colonel O'Sullivan had, in the meantime, pushed his 1st and 2nd Battalions up Highway 2 towards Ormoc. As they went, the next major hill was 606, which loomed over the road ahead. By nightfall on December 7th, the regiment was preparing to assault the hill which was believed strongly held by the Japanese, since it was the last big hill before Ormoc. The next day, December 8th, the Americans attacked, only to find that not only had the Japanese pulled out, they had not even left delaying forces behind. Colonel Saito was gone.

*   *   *

The 7th Infantry Division had achieved what the Japanese thought impossible. They had crossed the central mountain range over the miserable

Abuyog-Baybay Road and had held back the strong enemy counterattack along Shoestring Ridge. Then it had managed to attack north toward Ormoc where the Japanese had their main base on Leyte. It had decimated the right flank detachment of the *26th Infantry Division*, and seriously reduced the strength which General Saito had counted on for his cherished counterattack at Burauen. They had also reduced the number of troops that the Japanese had to defend Ormoc.

The Japanese were running out of time on Leyte. They had determined that this was to be the decisive battle, and yet it was not going according to plan. General Suzuki had for weeks been planning his counterattack, but events kept delaying its execution. With *Imperial General Headquarters* in Tokyo demanding victory and refusing to accept reality as it existed on Leyte, General Suzuki had to find some way to regain the initiative.

Once again General Suzuki turned to his favored counterattack plan. Although it had to be significantly modified thanks to the American advance to Albuera, he received assistance from the *4th Air Army* with his planning. Apparently impressed with the illusionary success of the earlier suicide mission, the *4th Air Army* proposed that they contribute to the counterattack by sending another, albeit stronger, airborne attack to coordinate with General Suzuki's ground attack. This proposal had the *2nd Raiding Brigade* of the *4th Air Army* flying suicide aircraft to the Dulag and Tacloban airfields carrying demolition teams which would then destroy American planes and installations at these locations. Then two paratroop companies would drop on the Burauen airfields, in coordination with the *35th Army's* ground attack, to further disrupt American defenses. The loss of the airfields would cripple the U.S. Sixth Army and force it to withdraw or surrender. The attack was scheduled to begin December 5th.[23]

General Krueger was not happy with his progress either. He still wanted to secure Ormoc Valley and drive the remaining Japanese troops into the mountains of the west coast where they could do no harm and escape only by sea. While they did, American infantry would mop up the area until it was cleared. The progress of the 1st Cavalry and 32nd Infantry Divisions in driving south to Ormoc Valley had been slow due to strong enemy resistance. He had these two divisions driving south and the 7th Infantry Division driving north, but there were still strong enemy forces between them, and progress would continue to be slow and costly. Like his opponent, General Suzuki, General Krueger returned to his original plan. He would launch another amphibious landing behind the enemy force, landing just below the port of

Ormoc. This would have the benefit of dividing the *35th Army* as well as knocking out its major port of supply, halting reinforcement and hopefully shortening the entire campaign. Up until recently, he had neither the troops nor the amphibious shipping necessary for this attack.

Now, however, General MacArthur had postponed the Mindoro landings, freeing up the necessary amphibious shipping. And the diverted 77th Infantry Division had arrived on Leyte. In conversations with the Navy, he learned that they were cautious about the proposed operation, citing the strength of Japanese air power in the area and the vulnerability of their ships to kamikaze attacks. Nevertheless, Admiral Kinkaid agreed to provide the necessary shipping for the planned assault.

Accordingly, General Krueger issued a Warning Order to his commands on December 1st, and followed up on December 4th, ordering his two Corps to make a strong effort against the enemy in Ormoc Valley and along Highway 2 in support of the coming operation. General Hodge, commanding XXIV Corps, was to coordinate its planning and execution, as he had troops already on the west coast and the 77th Infantry Division was to be assigned to his command once it had landed. In effect, both commanders, General Krueger and General Suzuki, were planning to attack each other at about the same time.

*   *   *

Meanwhile, the struggle at sea continued as the Japanese continued to reinforce the *35th Army*. But increasingly, this effort was coming under American attack. One such attack came from the USS *Flasher* (Commander G. W. Grider), who had a notable war patrol for an American submarine. *Flasher* had been a part of an American submarine wolfpack when she was directed to intercept a Japanese convoy in the sea between Palawan and Indo-China. Positioning himself on the convoy's track, Commander Grider waited while the Japanese steamed towards his ambush point. When they appeared, he took his sub on a direct path to the convoy, but suddenly a cloudburst obscured the entire enemy convoy. Undeterred, Commander Grider continued forward toward the last sighted position of the target. And as suddenly as it appeared, the cloudburst vanished, leaving Commander Grider and USS *Flasher* facing an oncoming Japanese destroyer. Coolly waiting for a good shooting position, *Flasher* was within 1,100 yards when Commander Grider gave the order to fire four torpedoes. His aim was right on the mark, and down went the *IJN Kishinami*.[24] Once the destroyer was out of the way, the

Flasher lined up on a large tanker behind the sinking enemy warship. As they did so, however, another enemy destroyer started a run on the American's periscope. Commander Grider, out of position for a shot, took his submarine deep but not before firing more torpedoes at the tanker. As the submarine dived, two distinct explosions were heard coming from the direction of the target tanker.

In the meantime, the USS *Flasher* was undergoing a severe anti-submarine attack. Enemy depth charges exploded close aboard, and while the submarine was well shook up, no damage was done. After he felt a safe time period had passed, Commander Grider brought the submarine up to periscope depth and looked around. The tanker was sinking and not far off so was the enemy destroyer. Escorts were picking up survivors and looking for the *Flasher*. Commander Grider ordered his crew to reload the torpedo tubes while preparing to go in to finish off the two crippled ships. Despite renewed rain squalls, the USS *Flasher* lined up the two targets and fired four torpedoes. Two were designed to run deep, to pass under the destroyer and hit the sinking tanker. The other two were to run shallower, designed to hit the destroyer. All four torpedoes found their mark.

The remaining Japanese escort ships took off after the *Flasher*. For the next half hour, Commander Grider and his crew suffered under repeated depth charge attacks, some of which were too close for comfort. Yet when this attack was over Commander Grider brought his ship to periscope depth and looked around. The sinking enemy destroyer was gone. The tanker was burning from stem to stern. The rest of the convoy had left except for a couple of escort ships circling the tanker. Soon they, too, departed, leaving the burning ship alone in the darkening sea. Commander Grider now had to finish off the tanker, for although she looked like a total loss, it was possible she could be salvaged. Closing to within 300 yards of her, he lined up a torpedo and a camera, hoping for a photograph for posterity.

Unfortunately for posterity, the shot was lost. The torpedo hit dead center and as it did, it blew out the fires aboard ship, plunging the whole area into darkness. The photograph showed nothing but darkness. All Commander Grider had to show was the confirmed sinking of two Japanese destroyers and the ten thousand-ton tanker, *Hakko Maru*.[25]

December also saw the Far East Air Forces busy with preparation for the Luzon invasion. Heavy bombers raided various places on Luzon and Halmahera while fighter sweeps were conducted over Leyte and the Netherlands East Indies. Fighter bombers supported ground operations in the Central Philippines and at Mindanao. Some of the latter hit enemy storage areas at Palompon, on Leyte. Enemy airfields were a priority target for all of these sweeps. Japanese barges, communications facilities and defensive positions were also targeted.

*   *   *

While Generals Hodge and Arnold had been securing the Sixth Army's hold on the west coast of Leyte at Shoestring Ridge, General Krueger had been planning for his next phase. When General MacArthur postponed the Mindoro invasion for ten days, the amphibious shipping assigned to that operation became temporarily available for General Krueger's amphibious landing plan. He had finally received the 77th Infantry Division, designated to make the assault, after its diversion into the Pacific. With the troops and shipping now available, it was time to make the attack. If he waited any longer he would lose his amphibious shipping and the troops would no doubt be used up in the ground attack continuing on Leyte.

That the latter was entirely possible was evidenced by the fact that even while the 77th Infantry Division was en route to Leyte, General MacArthur had diverted one of its infantry battalions to work as stevedores unloading ships at the Mindoro invasion. Assigned to General Hodge's XXIV Corps, the division was to assemble on Leyte and then mount up for the assault against the Japanese rear at Ormoc.

General Hodge issued the orders for the 77th Infantry Division to land at Deposito, just south of the main Japanese port at Ormoc. In doing this, he ordered General Arnold's 7th Infantry Division to drive north to the Panilahan River where they would be in a position to join General Bruce's division after it had landed. In order to facilitate command and control, General Arnold also ordered that once his division had landed, General Bruce would command both the 7th and 77th Infantry Divisions. Since both Generals Arnold and Bruce had commanded their divisions in previous amphibious landings, General Krueger objected to this arrangement and had General Hodge amend his orders. Each division commander would control his own division, while General Hodge controlled the overall operation as corps commander.

Once these details had been agreed upon between the commanders, General Krueger issued Field Order Number 46 of December 4, 1944, which directed XXIV Corps to make the main effort with its left flank, the 7th Infantry Division, while at the same time making an amphibious landing at

Ormoc on December 7th, using the 77th Infantry Division. It was also to relieve the battalion of the 32nd Infantry Regiment, at Panaon Strait, with units of the 9th Philippine Military District. The order also specified that General Sibert's X Corps was to make its main effort with its right, the 32nd Infantry Division, also beginning December 5th, by advancing south along Highway 2 in support of the XXIV Corps attack. The 1st Cavalry Division, meanwhile, was to complete the clearance of Samar, and on Leyte clear up enemy defenses in the Cananga and Bagacay areas in the north. Both the 11th Airborne and 96th Infantry Divisions were to continue in their missions of clearing up enemy opposition along the mountain barrier between the Leyte and Ormoc Valleys.

Still concerned about moving his troops quickly enough between threatened areas due to road conditions, General Krueger also requested of General MacArthur's headquarters that all or part of the 38th Infantry Division[26] be made available to him in the event that a need for additional ground troops arose. The 38th Infantry Division was staging on Leyte for future operations and had not originally been a part of the Sixth Army's troop list for Leyte. Headquarters agreed to loan General Krueger the 149th Infantry Regiment[27] and a battalion of the 152nd Infantry Regiment,[28] pending its need for the projected operation. General Krueger quickly attached two 149th Infantry Battalions to the small 11th Airborne Division, while using the 152nd Infantry Battalion to relieve a battalion of the 77th Infantry Division, which had been detached to Samar. That battalion rejoined its parent division at Ormoc.

By December 6th, all of General Krueger's plans for the amphibious attack he had been planning since before the Leyte operation began were in motion. The XXIV Corps was attacking up the west coast and the X Corps was attacking from the north towards the same objective, Ormoc Valley. The amphibious landing was in motion, with the convoy carrying the 77th Infantry Division already in route towards Ormoc. But as night fell, General Krueger learned some disquieting news. A large number of hostile planes were reported over Leyte. Some forty-nine had been shot down, but a fleet of enemy transports had been seen dropping hundreds of Japanese paratroopers at the north end of San Pablo airstrip in the Burauen area. Others were reported in different locations. General Whitehead, commanding the U.S. Fifth Army Air Force, called to report that his headquarters was under heavy ground attack, and that paratroopers had dropped in his area. General Suzuki had struck first.

CHAPTER 7

THE "OLD BASTARDS" LAND

The barrio, or village, of Deposito was located about three and a half miles southeast of the main Japanese port of Ormoc on Leyte. The eastern shore of Ormoc Bay offered several good landing beaches which could be used by the Americans. Usually, the beaches were formed of hard sand and gravel that could readily accommodate landing craft and the vehicles they carried. With the experience of the landings in San Pedro Bay behind them, the planners chose Deposito because of this hard sand. There were several roads which led off the beach toward Highway 2 inland, therefore making the swamps around the area less likely to block the advance off the assault beaches. Highway 2 was only about half a mile inland from the beach, and since this was to be the main route of supply and communication, the beaches nearest it were those chosen for the landings. The minor promontory of Panalian Point blocked a direct beach view to Ormoc.

Rear Admiral Arthur D. Struble[1] was assigned to command Task Group 78.3 which was to carry and land the 77th Infantry Division at Ormoc. Once landed, it was to remain and support the landings until relieved. With an escort force of only twelve destroyers, Admiral Struble was to lead eight transports, twenty-seven landing craft, twelve medium landing ships and a minesweeper unit to the area between the Baod and Bagonbon Rivers, where the troops were to be landed on assault beaches White One and White Two. The line of departure was set at 2,000 yards off the beach, but if enemy fire proved too dangerous it could be moved back another thousand yards. Rocket-firing landing craft would bombard the beach prior to the attack.

The Fifth Army Air Force was to provide air cover for the attack. They were to have air cover over the beach area day and night for the convoy's trip from San Pedro Bay to Ormoc Bay, and to cover the return trip as well. Bombers would be held on call to attack enemy air bases or targets of opportunity, should they be needed. Seventeen night fighters and seventy-two day fighters would fly cover for the trip. On the day of landing, this would be increased to nineteen night fighters and ninety-six day fighters. Ten flights of forty bombers each would cover the actual beachhead, while six flights of twenty-four bombers each would cover the convoy on its return journey to Leyte Gulf. These planes included twenty-four P-47s for interception of enemy aircraft and ground support, sixteen P-40s for ground support, and thirty-four Marine Corps F4Us for top cover and interception.[2]

Meanwhile, as plans were being made, the "Old Bastards" were organizing themselves on the beach at Tarragona. They called themselves that because they were older on average than the usual age of the American soldier in World War II. When the Marines, alongside whom they had fought the battle of Guam, had noticed that, they awarded themselves this new title, one they had made respected by those same Marines who rated their division as "almost as good" as a Marine division. Officially they were known as the "Statute of Liberty Division" from their shoulder sleeve insignia, and from the fact that they had originated as a division of the New York State Army Organized Reserve.[3]

The 77th Infantry Division had a history by the time it landed on Leyte. During World War I, they had fought in France and, among other things, produced the legend of the "Lost Battalion." They were one of the first three Army Reserve divisions activated for World War II and had trained cadres for other divisions which later fought in Europe. They had also enjoyed some notable division commanders during their tenure to date. Among these were Major General Robert L. Eichelberger, now commanding U.S. Eighth Army, and Major General Roscoe B. Woodruff, who rose to corps command.[4] Unlike many of the other divisions fighting on Leyte, the 77th had been trained in amphibious operations while awaiting shipment overseas.[5] Then it shipped out for Hawaii where, after more amphibious training, it joined the III Amphibious Corps for the invasion of Guam.

Their odyssey after Guam has already been related. Upon reaching Leyte, the division had lost a detachment of some 1,300 officers and men for the Mindoro landing. Then the 306th Infantry Regiment[6] was assigned to assist the 11th Airborne Division, which was relieving elements of the 7th Infantry

Division. The position of the regiment was so isolated that while attached to the 11th Airborne Division, its supply and evacuation was the responsibility of the 96th Infantry Division, its artillery support provided by elements of the 7th Infantry Division, and its transportation provided by a battalion of Marine Corps artillery nearby.

Within hours of first landing at Leyte, Company K, 306th Infantry, was in contact with the enemy. A large patrol had moved out from Burauen when they ran into a group of Japanese. One was captured and twenty others killed. As the patrol continued, it came under fire again, and one squad was pinned within fifty yards of a Japanese machine gun. The squad leader and the BAR operator were killed trying to attack the enemy position. Then the platoon leader, 2nd Lieutenant Clarence P. Dow, tried to attack, only to be killed as well. The company executive officer, 1st Lieutenant Lemuel Goode, grabbed an automatic rifle and charged the gun, knocking it out, but was severely wounded in the process. A platoon of Japanese was then seen outflanking the company, and an all-around defense was immediately established by 1st Lieutenant Stan Kurland and Staff Sergeant Carl G. Puryear. Company I came forward and attacked the Japanese who were flanking Company K and drove them off. Eighty-five enemy dead were counted. After an artillery preparation the 3rd Battalion, with Company G attached, returned to the attack on this position and counted 150 enemy dead when they cleared it. Several machine guns and a 70mm artillery gun were captured. It was quite a welcome to Leyte.

Meantime the 307th Infantry Regiment[7] was ordered to send its 2nd Battalion to Samar to protect a naval base there. The division's 302nd Engineer Combat Battalion was already hard at work maintaining the roads and bridges within the division sector. It was assisted by the long-attached 242nd Engineer Shore Battalion. When the Japanese air landing occurred on November 26–27, elements of the 77th Infantry Division took part in the search for enemy infiltrators. Five of these were later killed by the division.

When General Krueger issued his warning order December 1st for the assault landing at Ormoc, the division was dispersed from Baybay on the west coast to Tarragon on the east coast. Elements were on Mindanao and Samar. Other parts of the division were under command of the 11th Airborne Division and XXIV Corps. Very quickly, General Bruce began to collect his division for the coming mission. Here, as always on Leyte, transportation was the problem. Two battalions of the 306th Infantry were up in the mountains of Burauen and had yet to be released by the 11th Airborne Division.

The 307th Infantry Regiment had the farthest to go and the heavy rains choked the roads with mud, making passage by vehicles all but impossible. Only the 305th Infantry[8] was near the beach at Tarragona, and even its 2nd Battalion was all the way across the island at Baybay supporting the 7th Infantry Division. Muddy roads, heavy rains and broken bridges slowed the assembly of the division considerably.

Nevertheless, the "Old Bastards" somehow managed to get themselves to the beach at Tarragona by the end of December 4th. Some were still not actually at the beach, but they were on their way and closing fast. Tanks, anti-aircraft weapons, chemical mortars and light artillery were grouped and ready to load. The 232nd Engineer Shore Battalion remained with the 307th Infantry, clearing its route to the beach over treacherous roads. Tracked vehicles did yeoman duty in pulling other vehicles along the roads until they could proceed on their own, then went back and pulled others forward. It was long, hard, backbreaking work, but it was done. Finally the loading began on the night of December 5th, with the 306th and 307th Infantry Regiments still coming in to the staging area.

The Navy had instructed the division that the support and transport ships would only remain off the beaches at Ormoc for two hours, because the Americans did not have control of either the waters or the skies along the west coast of Leyte. This meant that all troops, equipment and supplies for the first two days of the landings had to be unloaded in two hours. Everything had to be mobile. Instead of loading the troops onto the many vehicles that the division would be landing at Ormoc, the supplies were packed into the 269 vehicles of various descriptions that would land at Ormoc that first day. The troops would be carried on landing craft and would have to walk ashore instead of the usual ride in armored vehicles.

Once ashore, the division was to turn north and drive on Ormoc. XXIV Corps would have the 7th Infantry Division cover the division's rear and southern flank by pushing north to meet with the 77th Infantry Division at or near Ormoc. The 11th Airborne Division was to continue to push over the Central Mountain Range and likewise join up somewhere nearby. On the east side of the mountains, the 226th Field Artillery Battalion[9] was to place its big 155mm artillery guns to support the division by firing over the mountains. Meanwhile the X Corps would fight south down from Carigara Bay to close the ring around General Suzuki's *35th Army*.

*　　*　　*

General Suzuki had not waited for General Krueger to get all his pieces in place. He had no intention of standing still while the Americans surrounded him and slowly but surely killed off his army. Instead, he seized the initiative by finally launching his long delayed counterattack. The need for this attack was far-reaching. Japan was slowly but surely starving to death. Its supplies of food, oil and other needs to continue the war, while feeding and caring for its own people, were fast being cut to starvation levels. The American submarine effort, as evidenced by the USS *Flasher* and many other submarines, was cutting the flow of supplies to Japan from the Netherlands East Indies and other resource areas. With the war increasingly using up resources, Japan needed to maintain its lines of supply. By October of 1944, the line to the Netherlands East Indies was all but cut.

If American naval and air power was securely based within the Philippines, the lines to the resources in the southwest Pacific would also soon be cut. If significant American air forces were based in the Philippines, any hope of supplies from the Southeast Pacific was destroyed. Therefore, the American air bases on Leyte had to be knocked out, and Leyte recovered so as to prevent them from ever being re-established. In contrast, if the Japanese could not only knock out the American bases on Leyte, but take them over and use them for their own air forces, they might be able to prevent any additional invasions of the Philippine Islands.

To emphasize this point to General Suzuki, General Yamashita sent a liaison officer from *Fourteenth Area Army Headquarters* to Leyte in late November. The message conveyed to Suzuki was that the prevention of the establishment of American air bases on Leyte was critical not only to the Battle for Leyte, but to the continued well being of Japan as well. General Suzuki was told that the conquest of the Burauen airfields and the destruction of the Tacloban and Dulag airfields was a critical mission for the *35th Army*. Simply put, the Japanese had to eliminate American air power on Leyte, or lose the war.

General Suzuki was already intent on regaining the airfields, which the Japanese remained convinced were in operation around Burauen. He refined his counterattack plan into a coordinated effort between ground and air forces to seize the airfields. For four days the air forces were to fight to eliminate American air power on and over Leyte. On the night of November 26th, just as this air campaign should be reaching its climax, specially trained demolition troops were to crashland on the Dulag and Tacloban airfields and put them out of commission. Others would seize the Burauen fields and hold them for the coming ground attack. These were the *3rd* and *4th Airborne Raiding Regiments* who would fly from Luzon and drop on the Burauen airfields.

While this was taking place, the *16th Infantry Division*, the *26th Infantry Division* and the *68th Independent Mixed Brigade* of the *35th Army*, would infiltrate through the Central Mountain Range and capture the Burauen airfields with the help of the paratroopers who, by then, should have gained a foothold. These were the orders which took Colonel Saito and his detachment of the *26th Infantry Division* off the ridges in front of the 7th Infantry Division and turned him to the east, leaving the way to Ormoc relatively open. Colonel Saito's targets were the San Pablo and Bayug Airfields. If all went well, the Japanese hoped that they could continue with their attack all the way to Dulag airfield, and eventually to the shores of Leyte Gulf.

As usual, General Suzuki was having trouble gathering his assets for the planned attack. He originally scheduled the attack to begin on December 7th, but General Yamashita disapproved this schedule and ordered that the attack begin on December 5th. However, a bad weather report convinced General Yamashita that a one-day postponement was necessary, and so the attack was to begin on December 6th, one day before General Krueger had scheduled his amphibious attack on the Japanese rear. Yet once again, Japanese communications failed them. The postponement message was sent to the two leading assault forces, the *16th* and *26th Infantry Divisions*, but General Makino at the *16th Infantry Division* never received the postponement order.

Not that it was going to make much difference. The Japanese continued to underestimate the strength of the American forces on Leyte. The U.S. Sixth Army now had two corps, eight divisions and many thousands of service and support troops on Leyte. In addition thousands of Army Air Force troops and Services of Supply troops covered the rear of Sixth Army, supporting the air effort and preparing for future amphibious invasions. General Makino, whose *16th Infantry Division* was now well under one thousand men, organized the remnants of his division into one infantry battalion and attacked as originally planned. On December 1st, taking personal command of the attack and leaving a small rear guard at Ormoc, General Makino led the way towards Burauen through the mountains. Unknown to them, all work on their target airfields had been stopped by General Krueger on November 25th, after writing them off as useless.

*   *   *

The Americans had not planned for a Japanese counterattack this late in the campaign. Instead, they were concentrating on their own coming attack, which was intended to finally trap the enemy in a pocket which the Sixth Army could destroy at its leisure. However, the stiff fight put up by the Japanese, once they decided to make Leyte the decisive battle, changed plans. The 11th Airborne Division had not been on the Sixth Army's original troop list. But necessity and availability resulted in its being assigned at just the right time. General Swing's paratroopers had relieved the 7th Infantry Division to allow the latter unit to move to the west coast. This left the paratroopers holding the eastern edge of the Central Mountain Range, precisely where the Japanese intended to attack. By November 28th, the 11th Airborne Division was in place to block all the known exits from the Central Mountain Range, and the 7th Infantry Division was attacking the Japanese right flank at Shoestring Ridge. Additionally, General Swing had left small security forces at the now abandoned airstrips. The area was mostly swamp, sometimes as deep as five feet, with some 800 yards completely open. The San Pablo, Bayug and Buri airstrips lay within this area.

Prisoner interrogations and Ultra radio intercepts indicated to Sixth Army intelligence officers that the Japanese were planning some type of counterattack. It was also known, from Ultra, that this was to be a coordinated effort between Japanese ground and air units and would be directed at the Burauen airfields. But not unlike the Japanese, the American intelligence officers did not believe that the Japanese had sufficient resources to actually initiate the planned attack, and so little was done to prepare for it. No new trails were found around Burauen, and the old ones showed no signs of recent activity. As far as the Americans were concerned, they had blocked all the available trails leading from the west over the mountains. Although an airborne attack was considered feasible, again the Americans did not believe that the Japanese had sufficient assets left to them to make a real threat. Nevertheless, General Hodge of XXIV Corps, in whose area the airfields lay, issued alert orders against the possibility of an enemy airborne attack on the fields. He also ordered a company of the 77th Infantry Division attached to the 11th Airborne Division and assigned it to protect Dulag Airfield. Another battalion of the 306th Infantry and Companies A and B of the 767th Tank Battalion were stationed north of Burauen in case an attack was actually launched. Orders were also issued for infantry forces to prepare to defend the headquarters of the Fifth Army Air Force, which was in place near the airfields.

The truth was that, despite the fact that the airstrips were no longer in full use, the area contained valuable American installations. Chief Warrant Officer William G. Nelson of the 1st Battalion, 187th Glider Infantry Regiment, recalled the sights when his battalion reached the area. "As had the troops of the 2nd Battalion, we of the 1st goggled at the wide variety of service units, glumly settled into the mud of countless bivouacs along the Dulag-Burauen Road. Long since we have learned that there were more than a hundred such camps . . . and they were all immobilized, scarcely able to meet their own supply needs. Moreover, the fighter squadrons of the 5th Air Force were moribund, trapped in the ooze of their operations fields. The only planes still functioning in the San Pablo area seemed to be our little resupply 'cubs' which puttered in and out on their vital supply missions. Protection of this entire service area fell to the responsibility of the 11th Airborne Division, and the First of the 187th [Airborne Infantry Regiment] was the single infantry battalion immediately available in [sic] the Division commander for the task. Weakened by detachments, we numbered at the time exactly fourteen officers and two hundred and ten men."[10]

But no one told this to General Makino. Leading his battalion-strength *16th Infantry Division* over the mountains, he managed to reach the outskirts of the Buri Airstrip undetected. Unaware of the postponement order, General Makino not only made the difficult march but arrived on time, December 6th, 1944. The *26th Infantry Division*'s detachment had much more difficulty and fell several days behind schedule, as we shall see.

*   *   *

While the Japanese infantry on Leyte marched over the Central Mountain Range to strike at the rear of the Sixth Army, the airborne part of the operation took off from Luzon. Soon after midnight on November 27th, the first group of suicide demolition teams made the attempt already described. While completely unsuccessful, it did serve two purposes. It convinced the Japanese that it had, in fact, been successful and that the American airstrips could be taken from the air and held if they received timely ground support. Second, it alerted the skeptical Americans that the Japanese could and would send airborne strike forces behind their lines. As a result, the defensive preparations around the useless airfields were made soon after the failed first attack. Both General Krueger and General Hodge issued warning orders to their troops to be on the alert for an airborne attack. But as usual in such cases, the lull between the first and second attacks relaxed security as time passed.

The second airborne strike was quickly assembled. This was organized as *Operation Te*, a corresponding plan coordinated with the ground forces' *Operation Wa*. The assault force was to be drawn from the recently arrived *2nd Raiding Brigade*, a sub-unit of the larger *1st Raiding Group*, the rest of which remained in Japan. Commanded by Colonel Kenji Tokunaga, it used the code name "*Takachiho*" after the area in Kyushu from which it drew inspiration. Sometimes called the "*Takachiho paratroopers*," it consisted of two parachute regiments, each numbering about 700 officers and men. The brigade had only been ordered to the Philippines on October 25th, and had fully arrived November 30th, less than a week before the planned operation. It had suffered no losses during the trip to Luzon.

The airborne plan called for Major Tsuneharu Shirai's *3rd Raiding Regiment,* reinforced with part of Major Chisaku Saida's *4th Raiding Regiment,* to board Type 100 Heavy Bombers[11] and crashland on the Burauen, Dulag and Tacloban Airfields. The raiders were then to attack their priority targets, American aircraft and supply dumps, with demolitions. Other paratroopers would jump from Type 100 Transports[12] to engage any security forces, destroy antiaircraft defenses and destroy any other facilities they found. About 250 paratroopers were assigned to the Buri Airstrip, 72 to the Bayug Airstrip, 36 to the San Pablo Airstrip, 104 to the Dulag Airstrip and 44 paratroopers to the Tacloban Airstrip. The transports to carry the paratroopers only arrived at Clark Field on Luzon on December 5th, the day before the assault. As they prepared for their mission, General Tominaga handed the commanders a battle flag inscribed in Japanese, "Exert your utmost for your country" and signed by the general.[13]

At 1540 Hours on December 6th, 35 transports and four heavy bombers lifted off from Clark Field headed for Leyte. As they arrived overhead, American anti-aircraft fire opened up a heavy barrage on them. Although most of the transports reached their assigned areas over the airfields, the heavy American fire confused many of the pilots, and as a result most of the paratroopers were jumping over the San Pablo Airstrip. Major Shirai and about sixty of his *3rd Raiding Regiment* troopers did jump over Buri. The transports bound for Dulag and Tacloban, the only operational strips on the Japanese schedule, were all shot down before they could release their paratroopers. Only 17 of the original 35 transports returned to Luzon, and most of these were damaged. A second echelon, scheduled for the following night, took off in eight transports and two heavy bombers, but bad weather forced them to abort the mission.[14]

*   *   *

The 11th Airborne Division had landed on Leyte on November 18, at Bito Beach. As was usual for American airborne division of the period, it contained a much smaller number of troops than the standard infantry division of the time, and its 8,000 men unloaded their equipment and supplies quickly under the threat of Japanese air attacks.[15] The advance echelon under the assistant division commander, Brigadier General Albert Pierson,[16] found that the beaches were blocked by unfordable rivers and was itself very narrow. Beyond the beach lay a bottomless swamp. Vehicles could not exit the beach until the engineers had built roads. But General Swing was not concerned, for at this time his understanding was that his division was only staging on Leyte for a future invasion of Luzon.

As they finished unloading their ships, the men of the division got their first taste of combat on Leyte. An enemy aircraft was seen flying over the beach headed directly for a group of paratroopers unloading supplies. As they watched, fascinated, the plane turned towards the transports they had just unloaded and despite accurate antiaircraft fire, crashed directly into the bridge area of the ship. A few hours later the blazing wreck sank beneath the waters of Leyte Gulf. Soon the constant fighting between enemy aircraft and the P-38s of the Fifth Army Air Force became regular entertainment for the work crews.

But the work had to be completed, and the paratroopers worked day and night to get it done. The night work was performed under floodlights, which had to be turned off each time a lone Japanese reconnaissance plane, derisively called "Washing Machine Charley" from the sound of its misaligned engines, flew overhead. He would circle for a while, drop the occasional bomb, and then turn for home.[17] Only once did he do any damage, when his bomb hit a causeway that had just been completed by the 127th Airborne Engineer Battalion. Soon after the division finally settled itself on Leyte came the orders from General Krueger to General Swing that his division was now assigned to Sixth Army for the Leyte Campaign.

General Swing quickly got his first assignment. The 11th Airborne Division would push across the island through the Central Mountain Range to keep the Japanese bottled up between the X Corps in the north and XXIV Corps in the south. The paratroopers were to hold the eastern door to this trap closed. General Hodges' Field Order 28 directed the paratroopers to relieve the 7th Infantry Division and attack along the line Burauen-La Paz-

Bugho. General Swing dispatched Colonel Orin D. Haugen's 511th Parachute Infantry Regiment[18] into the mountains. Moving one battalion at a time, the regiment was assembled at Burauen for the move into the hills. Patrols were soon moving among the hills, scouting a way for the rest of the paratroopers to follow. As they did so, General Hodge held a meeting with General Swing and added the protection of the Corps and Army Air Force rear areas to the missions assigned to the 11th Airborne Division.

The selection of the 11th Airborne to march over the hills was not made randomly. The paratroopers were probably in the best physical shape of any combat group on the island and they were trained to operate in lightly armed groups, on foot and surrounded after dropping behind enemy lines. These skills would be useful in the rugged, difficult mountain range. The problem that would arise, however, was that precisely because they were lightly armed,[19] when they met determined enemy resistance they had less in the way of support than did standard infantry companies.

To better control his division, General Swing moved his headquarters to San Pablo, the small town outside of Burauen. His remaining two regiments, each only two battalions strong, were assigned flank protection and security missions throughout the area, but enemy strength in the mountains soon had Colonel Harry D. Hildebrand's 187th Glider Infantry Regiment[20] alongside the 511th Parachute Infantry. Behind the lines, the 152nd Airborne Antiaircraft Antitank Battalion, under Lieutenant Colonel James Farren, moved up to protect the division and corps installations around Burauen. Several units of Lieutenant Colonel Douglas C. Davis' 127th Airborne Engineer Battalion were also in the area.

Up in the mountains, Lieutenant Colonel Ernest LaFlamme's 1st Battalion led the difficult way to a major guerrilla camp. Without meeting any enemy opposition, the battalion made its way in the usual rain and deep mud to the camp where it set up its own base alongside the guerrillas. But following the battalion, the regimental commander, headquarters company and Captain Thomas Mesereau's Company C had no such luck. At the recommendation of a guide, Colonel Haugen took what he was told was a shortcut, and marched directly into a Japanese ambush. A platoon of Company C attacked the ambush and killed twenty of the enemy at a cost of eight of their own, but was forced away from the rest of the American force and withdrew. Several attempts by Company C and Headquarters Company to attack the main enemy force across a stream were unsuccessful, until one final effort succeeded. The two forces battled in hand-to-hand combat. Although they had succeeded in crossing the stream, the Americans now found themselves surrounded. Small groups became separated and one such group found its way back to the division headquarters, where it reported the rest of its group wiped out. Due to the poor maps of the area, they could not even pinpoint the area of the ambush. Artillery observation planes were ordered up to try and locate the lost companies.

Lieutenant Colonel LaFlamme was ordered to move from his bivouac area and locate the trapped companies behind him. A platoon was sent out and located the rear of the Japanese force that had Company C pinned down, but the platoon commander was killed and the enemy force was far too large to be taken on by a platoon-sized patrol. After getting these reports, General Swing ordered Lieutenant Colonel Harry Wilson and his 2nd Battalion, 511th Parachute Infantry Regiment, to move up to Burauen and replace Lieutenant Colonel Norman Shipley's 3rd Battalion, which in turn he sent into the mountains to rescue the trapped company.

Up in the mountains, Company C, new to combat, was firing off its ammunition much faster than experienced troops would have done, and stocks became critical. They had also no food with them, but they learned quickly. In order to conserve their grenade supply, for example, they became adept at catching and throwing back incoming Japanese grenades. But they spent the night under attack, no relief column yet being able to reach them. Then, on the morning of November 28th, a group of Japanese demanded their surrender. These Japanese were led by the very same Filipino guide who had led the company into the ambush. Colonel Haugen ordered his men to kill the Filipino guide and answered the Japanese demand with gunfire.

That night, Colonel Haugen took eight men and crawled out of the company's perimeter. He sent six of the men to Colonel LaFlamme, to guide his battalion back to the ambush site, while he took the other two men and traveled to division headquarters to report to General Swing. Even as he traveled, 1st Lieutenant Donald E. Neff, a liaison pilot of the 675th Glider Field Artillery Battalion,[21] had located the ambush site. Flashes from mirrors had attracted his attention and then he had heard the gunfire from the ground. Yet he could still see nothing through the thick jungle. Instead, he marked a landmark tree in his mind and reported back to division headquarters. Colonel Shipley was immediately advised of the suspected location of the lost company. General Swing next ordered Lieutenant Colonel Norman E. Tipton, executive officer of the 511th Parachute Infantry, to make a jump onto the bivouac area of the 1st Battalion, and lead them to the trapped company. Once on the ground, he was to assume command of the regiment and clear up the ambush problem. Meanwhile, the 3rd Battalion would move up the mountain to the 1st Battalion's bivouac area.

While the scouts searched for the lost companies, the division personnel officer, Lt. Colonel William Crawford, had liaison planes begin to drop food and ammunition to the spot Lieutenant Neff had identified as the ambush site. These supplies did, in fact, land in the clearing, but enemy fire kept Company C from recovering any of them. The next day Colonel Tipton made his jump from a tiny liaison plane. He landed successfully, assumed command, and began his move to rescue Company C. Back at division headquarters, Colonel Haugen agreed that the location of the trapped company was as indicated by Lieutenant Neff. But word had to be brought to the 2nd Battalion, and it needed a guide. A paratrooper, one of the two who had come out of the mountains with Colonel Haugen, volunteered to make another jump to the 2nd Battalion and lead it to the ambush site. But there was a price. The paratrooper's boots were worn out after only a few days on Leyte. But it so happened that the division's intelligence officer, Lt. Colonel Douglas Quandt, had the same size boots. The deal was made and the scout, with new boots, jumped to guide the 2nd Battalion to the trapped company.[22] Soon thereafter the Japanese, attacked in the rear by Company G and from the front by 1st Battalion, retreated.

On November 27th, with Company C still trapped in the mountains, the first of the Japanese airborne operations landed on Leyte. As earlier related, one of the planes landed on Bito Beach in the division's rear area. The gun crew thought it was a friendly aircraft and offered assistance. All but one of these Japanese suicide demolitions men escaped into the swamps. But by daylight, the men of the 11th Airborne Division were alert to the possibility of an airborne attack.

Meanwhile, the paratroopers in the hills found, like the infantrymen before them, that communications and supply in the difficult terrain was a major problem. But they had one advantage: eleven small liaison planes, which soon became daily sights flying over the far-flung columns, supplying them with messages, supplies, orders, and even the division's daily newspaper. One of the reasons this worked so well was that General Swing had set up a series of radio relay stations to guide the planes and pass on their communications. These, in turn, were guarded by security teams drawn from the 152nd Antiaircraft Antitank Battalion. Technical Sergeant Alexander Ruzycki commanded one of these four-man teams outside of Burauen. One morning, Sergeant Ruzycki spotted two enemy soldiers crawling toward his radio relay station. He calmly shot them both, and then reported the incident. A few minutes later three more Japanese appeared. These he also killed, but not before sustaining wounds to his hand and thigh. Once again he reported the incident, this time suggesting that a combat patrol might want to check out the area for more enemy soldiers. By the time the combat patrol arrived, Sergeant Ruzycki and his team were involved in a firefight with over twenty Japanese. Between the two groups, twenty-two Japanese were killed and the radio relay station preserved. Sergeant Ruzycki received a Silver Star.[23]

Behind the front, elements of the 187th Glider Infantry Regiment were still clearing the rear areas of small Japanese groups, including some from the earlier air-landing episode. Assisted by elements of the separate 503rd Parachute Infantry Regiment,[24] the hunt was long, tiring and difficult. But several of the Japanese, who had landed at the airfields, had been found and eliminated. Leaving the rest to the 503rd Parachute Infantry, the 1st Battalion, 187th Glider Infantry, moved to an assembly area near the San Pablo Airstrip on December 2nd.

Up in the mountains, the 511th Parachute Infantry was still fighting a large enemy force which they believed was protecting some kind of Japanese installation. But as everywhere on Leyte, evacuation of the wounded was a problem. General Swing determined that with his light planes, he could fly the wounded out of the mountains instead of carrying them, sometimes for days, over the rough terrain. The only problem was that there was no airfield up in the mountains. General Swing ordered the division engineer, Lieutenant Colonel Davis, to build one. And so, a platoon of the 127th Airborne Engineer Battalion jumped from the liaison planes to the original bivouac area with shovels, axes, saws and picks to clear an area for a landing strip. In the interim, the light planes dropped in medical personnel from the 221st Airborne Medical Company, including surgical teams and technicians to treat casualties.

The success of this scheme was best illustrated by the experience of Captain Thomas Brady, who commanded Company A of the 511th Parachute Infantry. He was seriously wounded in the head during a skirmish, and carried by litter into the newly established base. There, the battalion surgeon performed a skillful brain operation that saved his life. For three days, he was treated in the makeshift "hospital" and then, on the road to recovery, he was flown to the Dulag General Hospital where, after more treatment and rest, he was flown to the United States.

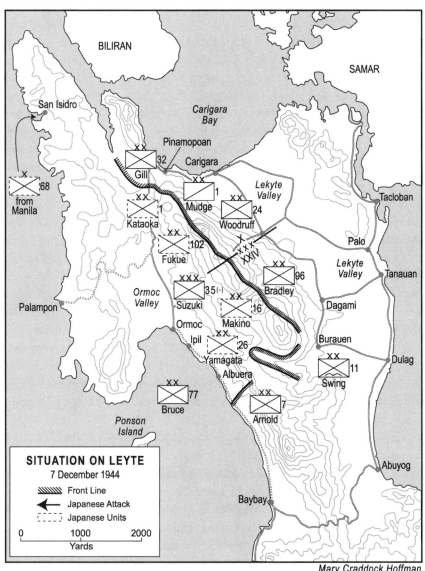

BILIRAN

SAMAR

San Isidro

Carigara
Bay

Pinamopoan

XX
32
Gill

Carigara

Lekyte
Valley

Tacloban

X
68
from
Manila

XX
1
Mudge

XX
24
Woodruff

XX
1
Kataoka

Palo

XX
102
Fukue

X
XXX
XXIV

Lekyte
Valley

Tanauan

Ormoc
Valley

XXX
35(-)
Suzuki

XX
96
Bradley

Palampon

Dagami

XX
16
Makino

XX
26
Yamagata

Ormoc

Ipil

Burauen

XX
11
Swing

Dulag

Albuera

XX
77
Bruce

Ponson
Island

XX
7
Arnold

Abuyog

SITUATION ON LEYTE
7 December 1944
///// Front Line
← Japanese Attack
⌐ ¬ Japanese Units

0   1000   2000
Yards

Baybay

Mary Craddock Hoffman

* * *

The 287th Field Artillery Observation Battalion[25] had a small detachment of 47 men stationed near the Buri Airstrip on December 5th. Along with a hundred or so service men from other units, they were the first Americans to see the *16th Infantry Division* emerge from the mountains. It had been a difficult journey to the foothills outside Dagami, and of the five hundred men who had started, some two hundred had been killed by American artillery fire or air attacks. The remainder moved into a deep gully some 6,500 yards southwest of Dagami and organized for the attack, which they still thought was scheduled for December 5th. Their target was the airstrips where they expected to join up with the paratroopers from Luzon and eliminate American air strength on Leyte. From prisoners, it was learned that morale in this force was low and that wounded men had to be left behind. Food had been off the land, usually bananas and coconuts. Relations between officers and men, never good in the Japanese Army, was much lower than usual. Despite all these difficulties, General Makino led his remnants towards Buri Airstrip.

Earlier, there had been at least three infantry battalions guarding the airfield area.[26] But when days had passed with no more airborne attacks, these had been sent on other missions. At dawn on December 6th, the remnants of the *16th Infantry Division* came out of the gully and attacked. Spotted by the men of the 287th Field Artillery Observation Battalion, the information quickly reached XXIV Corps Headquarters. The attacking Japanese crossed the main road and then disappeared into a swamp which lined the airfield. A machine gun was set up in a shack 300 yards west of the highway. Led by a Filipino, the Japanese force then moved to launch its attack on the Buri Airstrip.[27]

Their first targets were the bivouac area of the Fifth Army Air Force Bomber Command. Many sleeping men were killed in their bunks, but soon the others were firing back at the oncoming Japanese. So much firing, in fact, that the nearby 11th Airborne Division units soon complained of receiving "friendly fire" from the excited Air Force service troops. Clearing the airstrip, the Japanese then dug themselves into a wooded area just to the north.

Learning of the attack, General Hodge had ordered General Bradley to turn over control of the 1st Battalion, 382nd Infantry to General Swing for the defense of the airfields. Another battalion was to sweep the Dagami-Burauen road to ensure there were no more attacks coming. Lt. Colonel Robert MacCleave and part of the regimental headquarters of the 187th

Glider Infantry, and Lt. Colonel George Pearson's 1st Battalion, 187th Glider Infantry, moved up from Bito Beach to the San Pablo Airstrip. General Swing then ordered a platoon of the 187th Glider Infantry flown to Buri in the liaison planes, while the rest of the battalion followed on foot. The only other units nearby were a battalion of Marine Corps artillery and a battalion of tanks, both mired in mud.

Upon arrival at the airstrip, Colonel Pearson had to calm down the airmen before he could get any information. Once he did, he left behind a security squad, and with the rest of his battalion began to comb the surrounding area for the Japanese. Even now, Colonel Pearson was unaware that he was in the midst of a major Japanese counterattacking force. When his patrols returned they reported encountering groups of Japanese in the woods and swamps, having killed several and driving the rest off. But as the numbers of Japanese in these reports climbed, Colonel Pearson realized that this was no small harassing patrol, but a force of considerable size. He gathered the 180 men of his battalion[28] and prepared to attack.

The attack began in darkness, into dense jungle growth which included thick bamboo, sago palms and dense rain forest growth. Forming lines of skirmishers with two-yard intervals, the men attacked to the northeast. Within five minutes, they were in firefights with Japanese soldiers. Many of these were at point-blank range due to the limited visibility. Sometimes they came to rice paddies where they could see the enemy and eliminate them. Several Japanese pretended to be dead, but when prodded came suddenly alive, only to be made dead again. After two hours of this, Colonel Pearson called a halt and took stock of his situation. His officers reported killing eighty-five enemy troops while suffering only two wounded.

As Colonel Pearson paused, General Swing arrived at Buri. He ordered Colonel Pearson to place his battalion along the Dagami-Furauen Road and keep it open. He was also advised to keep alert for another attack from the west. Colonel Pearson set up his two companies and a section of heavy machine guns along a rise that overlooked the road. Since he had expected only to perform a reconnaissance, he had left his men's packs, heavy equipment and mess equipment behind. His mortar section had no guns, but the platoon leader went into the service area and found two mortars with ammunition he could "borrow." A patrol was sent out to contact the 382nd Infantry.

As he waited along the road, Colonel Pearson and his men identified "several hundred" Japanese coming from a hill to the west. A patrol sent out confirmed that this was an enemy force, and artillery fire was placed on it as it advanced. However, the artillery fire was soon lifted because the target area was on a divisional boundary and there was a probability that friendly forces might be hit. Despite this, the 1st Battalion, 187th Glider Infantry had cleared Buri Airstrip of all but a few pockets of Japanese. Under sniper fire, they continued to protect the airfield pending further orders.

*   *   *

That night, as the glider men rested and prepared a meager dinner, a flight of planes appeared over the field. Many of the Americans stood transfixed as they watched the spectacle of bombs falling, antiaircraft guns firing and planes disintegrating overhead. They ran for their weapons and foxholes, ducking blazing falling debris as they went. Some were strafed by the escorting fighters. Men began yelling that they had seen parachutes coming down. These were quickly identified as Japanese paratroopers. The *2nd Raiding Brigade* had arrived.

One of the first to see the new arrivals was Private Mort Ammerman, a trooper in Company B of the 188th Glider Infantry Regiment.[29] He "saw many aircraft flying overhead—at their altitude and in the subdued light conditions we assumed that they were C-47s and recall that we thought some unit of the 11th AB was making a night jump . . . ."[30] Private Ammerman thought no more about it and went to sleep, as best he could, in the rain. Sometime later he was awakened by the sound of firing and felt a pain in his leg. He had been wounded. In the pitch darkness he could see nothing, but quickly rolled over, searched unsuccessfully for his rifle, and took cover. Armed only with a trench knife, he listened while a friend, who had also been shot, slowly died in the darkness nearby. Later, one of his friends found Private Ammerman and pulled him to safety.

Private Holloway and his squad were guarding a bridge on the road near the airstrips. One survivor ran for help and brought back Company B of the 188th Glider Infantry, who cleared the area and sent the wounded men to a hospital. Nearby, the staff of the 11th Airborne Division was just sitting down to supper when they, too, heard the aircraft overhead. At first thinking they were friendly, they counted the planes and the paratroopers they dropped. Over 250 jumpers were counted.

The Japanese paratroopers used a system of bells, whistles and horns to assemble after the drop. Several spoke in loud voices, repeating phrases in English, such as "Everything is resistless, surrender, surrender" or "Hello, where are your machine guns?"[31] Once organized, the Japanese moved toward their objectives, the airfields. There they set fire to a number of the small liaison planes of the 11th Airborne Division, and then moved to the bivouac area and destroyed it. Some of them came up against local defenders like Captain Felix H. Coune, who with some men from the Headquarters, 11th Airborne Division Artillery, blocked one path. One of the liaison pilots was caught in a ditch and spent fourteen hours hiding while the Japanese walked past, over and around him. At San Pablo, the Japanese destroyed more small planes, a jeep, and several tents and blew up a gasoline dump. They threw ammunition into the blaze to destroy that, as well.

The area held a mix of units, including airborne engineers, an airborne signal company, a Quartermaster Company[32] and an ordnance company. These men fought for their lives, and a vicious firefight was soon in progress. Lieutenant Paul J. Pergamo and his platoon of the 127th Airborne Engineers set up three machine guns on a knoll and fought off three attacks on their position during that night. At the 1st Battalion, 187th Glider Infantry's Battalion Aid Station, Captain Hans Cohn, the Battalion Surgeon, was working on a wounded man. Japanese fire shot a plasma bottle out of his hand. Undeterred, Captain Cohn lowered the wounded man into a nearby slit trench and continued his work. By dawn, most of the Japanese paratroopers who lived moved off to the north and linked up with the surviving elements of the *16th Infantry Division.*

General Swing quickly realized that this was no mere suicide attack to destroy a few airplanes. Deciding he was in the midst of a counterattack designed to retake the airfields, for which his division was now responsible, he ordered Lt. Colonel Lukas E. Hoska, Jr., to bring the men of his 674th Glider Field Artillery Battalion[33] up from Bito Beach armed as infantry. Leaving their guns behind, the Glider Artillery Battalion reported in to General Swing at the airfield. General Swing, in the meantime, had organized Lieutenant Colonel James Farren's detachments of the 152nd Airborne Antitank Antiaircraft Battalion, to defend the division command post. Lieutenant Colonel Davis' Engineers were also pulled in along with several stray detachments they had found along the way. As daylight broke on December 7th, Colonel Davis led the attack to clear the airstrip. It reminded one member of a Civil War charge, with the engineers lined up on one side and alongside the artillerymen, also lined up, both ready to move across the flat ground against the enemy.

Under the personal observation of General Swing, Colonel Davis led the charge across the airfield, pushing the Japanese back some three hundred yards and relieving his own Company A, which had been pinned down by the airborne attack. As soon as the strip was reasonably clear, although still under sniper fire, the liaison planes that survived began to take off and deliver their supplies to the paratroopers up in the mountains. That night the two groups, engineers and artillerymen, formed a defense line at the north end of the strip and dug in for the night. There they would stay for the next few days.

At Buri Airstrip, there were no defenders, for the field was abandoned. Seizing the arms and ammunition abandoned by the fleeing Air Corps and Service Troops, the Japanese dug themselves in to hold the field until their own ground elements arrived. But General Krueger had already learned of the airborne attacks and requested more troops from General MacArthur. Once again, a unit staging on Leyte for future operations on Luzon had recently arrived, and General Krueger was given the 149th Infantry[34] of the 38th Infantry Division,[35] for his temporary use in clearing up the Japanese counterattack. Two battalions of the regiment were immediately ordered to the Burauen area.

Major Martin C. Grigg brought his 1st Battalion, 149th Infantry up along the road to Burauen. As he marched, he was greeted by General Swing, who introduced himself by saying, "Glad to see you. I am General Swing of the 11th Airborne Division. We've been having a hell of a time here. Last night approximately seventy-five Jap paratroopers dropped on us of which we have accounted for about fifty. Fifteen hundred yards from here on an azimuth of 273 degrees is another airstrip just like this one. Between here and there are about twenty-five Jap troopers. It is now 1400. I want that strip by nightfall."[36] With this rather abrupt introduction to battle on Leyte, Major Grigg led off his battalion as ordered by General Swing.

Wading through a swamp that was shoulder deep in places, Company A arrived at Buri before darkness. Company C, on the other hand, ran into opposition and was delayed for an additional ninety minutes. Although not securing the strip, and having encountered more opposition than General Swing had expected, the battalion dug in for the night.

The 382nd Infantry of the 96th Infantry Division also entered the fight December 7th. Private First Class Dencker had only recently been pulled of the lines and enjoyed a Thanksgiving dinner of "salty ham, fried eggs and apples" when his 3rd Battalion was ordered to clear up some enemy paratroopers at the fields. His Company L was given twenty minutes to load up arms and ammunition and move out toward the airfields. Loaded into trucks they moved over bumpy, muddy roads, traveling along with no idea of where they were going other than in the direction of the airfields. After creeping along at fifteen miles an hour due to road conditions, they were dismounted and told to march down the road. Soon they came upon the 116th Station Hospital, whose large tents stood out in the growing darkness. Company L immediately established a defensive perimeter around the hospital. In the not too far off distance they could hear the sounds of battle. The next morning some of the men of Company L began to teach the hospital staff how to operate M-1 rifles and carbines.[37]

The 1st Battalion, 382nd Infantry had moved earlier and had managed to link up with the 1st Battalion, 149th Infantry, near the airstrip. Three battalions of three different divisions now were set to clear the Japanese from Buri Airstrip.[38] But the Japanese were by no means defeated. During the night they brought up additional machine guns and placed them directly in front of Company A, 382nd Infantry. When the battalion began its attack on the morning of December 8th, these guns immediately pinned down the company. Private First Class Warren G. Perkins risked his life to locate the enemy guns and direct mortar fire on them. The resulting barrage knocked out the guns and stunned the Japanese.

Private Ova A. Kelley of Norwood, Missouri was a member of Company A's Weapons Platoon. According to his platoon leader, 1st Lieutenant Robert Jackson, Private Kelley "just got mad" and launched a one-man attack on the Japanese. He left his foxhole with an armload of grenades and charged the Japanese. Throwing the grenades with great accuracy he moved forward, killing five of the enemy and forcing the rest to retreat. Then, using an M-1 Rifle he emptied it at the disorganized Japanese fleeing his attack. Three more enemy troopers fell to his fire. With the rifle empty, he picked up a discarded M-1 Carbine and opened fire, killing another three Japanese. Behind him Company A came forward, inspired by Private Kelley's example and destroyed the rest of the two officers and 34 enemy soldiers who had held them up earlier. Two heavy and a light machine gun were captured. Still not satisfied, Private Kelley led the attack across the airstrip, leading Company A in securing its objective. As he did so, he was mortally wounded by sniper fire and died two days later. For his conspicuous gallantry and leadership on December 8, 1944, Private Kelley was awarded a posthumous Medal of Honor.[39]

*   *   *

The Battle of the Airstrips began to go to the Americans on December 9th, when the 1st Battalion, 149th Infantry attacked with all three companies on line. They crossed the airstrip under enemy fire. These guns were placed on the high ground to the north of the airstrip and, although the field was now clear of the enemy, the battalion was forced to withdraw to the southern edge of the field to avoid the fire from the ridge. Another fifty enemy dead had been counted during the day. Meanwhile the 1st Battalion, 382nd Infantry sent out patrols to clear the surrounding area. This left behind only a few mortar men and headquarters personnel. As darkness fell, about 150 Japanese attacked this small group. Fighting back with their weapons, the infantrymen killed fifty of the enemy while losing seven of their own.

December 10th saw a half-hour artillery barrage before the 1st Battalion, 149th Infantry attacked again. The three assault companies cleared the area of individual Japanese riflemen and destroyed small pockets of resistance. By late afternoon, the battalion was in a defensive perimeter around the Buri Airstrip. As darkness fell, however, another Japanese attack hit the administration buildings of the Fifth Air Force. Major General Ennis C. White-head[40] was at his desk in his office when a bullet came through the wall. After ducking, he ordered his aide to find out who was responsible for the casual shooting. The staff officer contacted Lt. Colonel Pal V. Kaessner of the 8th Aviation Signal Battalion by telephone. The following conversation is reported in the army's official history: "Colonel," he said sternly, "you've got to stop that promiscuous firing down there immediately!" "Like to, Sir," answered the Colonel, "but the Japs . . ." "Japs" shouted the staff officer, "that can't be Japs. That fire is coming from our fifties." "That's right . . . and the Japs are doing the shooting!" "Where in the hell did the Japs get our machine guns?" "How in hell should I know, sir?" "The bullets are coming right through the general's quarters." "Tell the general to get down on the floor. Incidentally, that yelling you hear is a banzai raid on our mess hall."

The attack pushed the defending Air Force personnel back until they reached the hospital area, where they held. A counterattack soon drove the Japanese off, leaving thirty dead behind them. The Japanese army's major counterattack on Leyte was finally over.

Only about one battalion of the *26th Infantry Division* had reached the battlefield and it was quite disorganized. General Makino's *16th Infantry Division* had been all but wiped out in this final burst of offensive spirit. And just as the attack got underway, General Suzuki learned that an American force had landed below Ormoc, threatening his own rear areas. Since Ormoc was essential to the survival of the *35th Army,* he immediately called off the counteroffensive and ordered all remaining troops back to Ormoc to defend his own lines of supply. The advance elements at the airfields now struggled back the way they had come. The trip was, if anything, worse than the trip in the other direction. Those that managed to make it back to Ormoc made it as individuals, all unit integrity having been lost in those terrible mountains between the Leyte and Ormoc Valleys. Behind them they left failure. Aside from a few small planes, a gasoline dump and many dead Americans, they had not achieved anything strategic. The Leyte Campaign would continue as planned. The Sixth Army was now at the northern and southern entrances to the Ormoc Valley, the last Japanese stronghold on Leyte. The logistical situation of the Japanese was now dire, with their main port of Ormoc endangered by the Americans to their rear.

*　　*　　*

Having completed the exhausting work of loading aboard their transports at Tarragona Beach, the 77th Infantry Division had set sail on the morning of December 6th. Before they sailed, however, minesweepers had cleared the channel between Leyte and the Bohol Islands repeatedly, on November 27th and again on December 4th, and 6th, but no mines were found. At noon, the convoy left San Pedro Bay and rendezvoused off Tarragona. Escorted by destroyers, the ships sailed undisturbed, although several unidentified planes were observed overhead. As they sailed into the darkness another group of eighteen bombers was seen over the convoy, but these paid no attention to the ships and flew off in the direction of Tacloban. These were probably the first wave of Japanese paratroopers in General Yamashita's counteroffensive.

Ahead of the convoy, three destroyers entered Ormoc Bay and prepared themselves for a pre-invasion bombardment. The destroyers, the USS *Barton*, USS *Laffey* and USS *O'Brien*, were straddled by some near misses from a shore battery, but return fire soon silenced this opposition. As December 7th, 1944 broke warm and calm, these destroyers opened fire on the planned beach area. As they fired, the landing craft left their destroyer transports and headed for beaches White One and White Two, three and four miles southeast of Ormoc. As the 25-minute bombardment ended, the landing craft hit the beaches a few minutes after 0700 Hours. The Japanese *35th Army* was now surrounded.

As the troops moved ashore, enemy planes appeared overhead, but as the men looked for cover they realized that there were no foxholes on ship or shore. Landing in knee-deep water on good beaches, the landings proceeded as planned. The 307th Infantry, less its 2nd Battalion on Samar, met only slight resistance on its right flank, but quickly moved to its beachhead line and captured intact the bridge over the Boad River. Behind them, the 902nd Field Artillery Battalion[41] came ashore to provide support. Alongside the artillery, Company A, 776th Amphibian Tank Battalion, set up to protect the beachhead from any counter-landing from the sea. With support behind them, the men of the 307th Infantry moved forward and by mid-afternoon had captured the barrio of Ipil from the *12th* and *13th Independent Infantry Regiments.* Eighty-three enemy were killed and one prisoner taken. Several Japanese trucks were captured and put into immediate use hauling supplies up from the beach. The 305th Infantry Regiment also landed easily and soon had strong patrols to the south, where they found and destroyed three enemy supply dumps. By mid-afternoon the division headquarters was established in Deposito. The 7th Infantry Division was seven miles south and pushing north to join forces with the 77th Infantry Division.

Aboard the convoy, however, Admiral Struble received word of an enemy convoy bound for Ormoc Bay ninety minutes after the first troops landed on the White Beaches. Aircraft of the Fifth Fighter Command flew off to intercept the Japanese ships, which included six transports and seven escort vessels. The result was one of the fiercest aerial battles of the campaign as planes of the 341st and 347th Fighter Squadrons dropped bombs and strafed the enemy vessels. Marine Corps Fighter (VMF) Squadrons 211, 218 and 313 joined in with the land-based aircraft and destroyed two cargo ships and two passenger transports. Southwest Pacific Headquarters later estimated that the entire convoy was wiped out and that 4,000 Japanese troops had drowned.[42]

While the air battle raged eighteen miles away, near San Isidro, Admiral Struble had more news. Enemy aircraft were spotted on radar approaching Ormoc Bay. Twelve bombers escorted by four Japanese fighters were headed for the convoy, which lay stationary in the restricted waters of the bay. An interception by P-38s of the Fifth Army Air Force broke up the formation, although some planes kept coming.

Lieutenant R.E. Farwell, USNR, commanded the destroyer transport USS *Ward*, which on December 7th, 1941 had fired the first American shots of the Pacific War when she opened fire on a midget Japanese submarine trying to sneak into Pearl Harbor. Now the old ship had been converted into a destroyer transport with many additional battles on her record. At Ormoc the *Ward* was patrolling near Ponson Island as antisubmarine protection with the destroyer USS *Mahan* (Commander E. G. Campbell) and two minesweepers when several enemy planes attacked. These planes came in swiftly in a torpedo attack chased closely by P-38s. The destroyer had to check its fire so as not to hit the friendly aircraft. The *Mahan*, nevertheless, knocked down three enemy planes and damaged two bombers. The two damaged planes immediately converted to kamikazes and dove on the ships below. The first damaged plane hit the sea barely fifty yards short of the *Mahan*. Three others did the same, but number five hit the destroyer just behind the bridge. Number six hit her at the waterline, and another plane crashed on the forecastle. Plane number seven, apparently deciding the ship was finished, merely strafed the length of the ship before it was shot down by the ship's gunners. Two more attempts to crash the ship were stopped by the P-38s and AA fire.

Commander Campbell kept his ship at full speed while racing toward the other ships on the picket line. Damage control parties worked to squelch the many fires aboard. It was quickly realized that full speed only fanned those fires so Commander Campbell stopped his ship. When the fires cut off the flooding controls, which allowed the magazines to be flooded, thus preventing the ship from blowing up, Commander Campbell ordered all boats lowered and abandoned ship. Destroyers USS *Walke* and USS *Lamson* were soon picking up the *Mahan*'s survivors. Ten sailors had been killed and 32 others were wounded. When everyone was clear, the *Walke* fired torpedoes to sink the *Mahan*, as ordered by Admiral Struble.[43]

Meanwhile, Lieutenant Farwell had seen the USS *Mahan*'s problem, but was too busy with his own. Three enemy planes broke away and came after the USS *Ward*. They came directly at the ship and despite an emergency left turn, the leading plane hit the *Ward* just above the waterline on the port side. This plane went through the ship's side into the boiler room. A huge explosion followed. The second plane strafed the ship before being shot down some 200 yards away. The third plane was also shot down. With the threats dealt with, the *Ward*'s crew set about fighting the huge fires that had resulted from the hit. The ship lost all power with its boilers knocked out and, without power, the fires could not be brought under control. Like the *Mahan*, Lieutenant Farwell worried about uncontrolled fires reaching his ammunition magazines. Abandon ship was ordered while the destroyer USS *O'Brien* and destroyer transport USS *Crosby* stood by to help. Admiral Struble had no choice but to order the veteran destroyer sunk, which was accomplished by the *O'Brien*'s gunfire.[44] Ironically, the skipper of the *O'Brien* was Commander William W. Outerbridge who, as a young lieutenant, had been the captain of the USS *Ward* on December 7th, 1941.

Admiral Struble waited for another hour while some stranded landing craft tried to back off the beach, but reports of additional aircraft coming in prompted him to order the stranded ships to make their own way back to San Pedro Bay after dark. With his surviving ships and escorts, the convoy left Ormoc Bay shortly after 1100 Hours. As they did, the USS *Smith*, a destroyer, shot down a plane diving on it. More planes appeared and one dove on the destroyer USS *Hughes* and missed, being shot down. Another went for the destroyer transport USS *Cofer*, but was shot down before reaching the ship. Still another went after the destroyer USS *Liddle*, but was also shot down. As the *Liddle* tried to clear flaming debris from that plane, another attacked from dead ahead and crashed into the bridge, wiping out the ship's combat information center and killing the captain, Lieutenant Commander L.C. Brogger, USNR. Lieutenant R.K. Hawes, USNR, took command and led the ship out of Ormoc Bay with the rest of the convoy. On the way, they treated the 22 wounded and buried 36 killed. The entire trip back was punctuated by these attacks. The USS *Edwards* was damaged, as was the USS *Lamson*. The USS *Flusser*, escorting the damaged *Lamson*, ran out of ammunition while protecting herself and *Lamson*, but managed to get herself and her sister ship safely back to Leyte Gulf. Records later showed that fifty-five enemy aircraft had been counted making sixteen different raids on the convoy. It wasn't until darkness started to settle over Task Group 78.3 that its sailors could breathe a sigh of relief.

*   *   *

Back at Deposito, the 77th Infantry Division, the "Old Bastards," had landed without casualties. More than 2,000 men were ashore, division headquarters set up, artillery support in place and a company of tanks on the beach. The experienced division had adapted to a speedy landing in order to reduce the risk to themselves and their naval covering force which, due to enemy air superiority over the beachhead, could not linger to support them as they had been used to in the Central Pacific.

General Suzuki had not expected a landing behind him at Ormoc, or anyplace else for that matter. Until the middle of November, he had not even erected a single defensive position there. Believing that the U.S. Navy was a damaged force, he did not anticipate its amphibious capabilities would be available on Leyte for some time. And since the Japanese Navy maintained a naval base on nearby Cebu, he felt that the threat of that base would protect his rear from any amphibious threat. However, as the 7th Infantry Division reached the west coast and more and more American aircraft and ships were seen in Ormoc Bay, he conceded the "possibility" that some sort of landing might be possible. To address this possibility he created the *Ormoc Defense Headquarters* under a Colonel Mitsue, who was the commander of the *35th Army Shipping Unit*. The *Shipping Unit* formed the nucleus of the new force, but antitank and antiaircraft units were added to its troop list as was an automatic gun company. General Suzuki also ordered that any units which happened to be in Ormoc would come under Colonel Mitsue's command in time of crisis. As usual the plan of defense was simple. Any attack was to be met with the full force available and then counterattacked and destroyed. But the Japanese were late and slow to build defenses in the area, busy with shipping reinforcements and supplies to the *35th Army* then about to counterattack the Sixth Army's rear areas. When the Americans did land, Colonel Mitsui had only a few trenches and some field fortifications to use in defending Ipil. He was able to add one infantry company and a machine gun company from a battalion of the *30th Infantry Division*, which happened to be in Ormoc at the time of the landing, to his meager forces. Believing he faced only one American infantry regiment, Colonel Mitsui set about doing battle.

The battle Colonel Mutsui sought would be initially against the 1st Battalion, 307th Infantry. It had already moved some 300 yards north of Deposito and then another 500 yards in the afternoon. Colonel Mitsui's *Shipping Unit* began to oppose this advance with machine guns and cannon, using dugouts along the route, but the Americans pushed into Ipil where they halted when the Japanese blew up one of their ammunition dumps in the face of the Americans. As the explosions settled, the infantrymen cleared the barrio and by nightfall had a perimeter at its northern edge. An estimated sixty-six enemy had died and one had been taken prisoner. Japanese medical supplies, a bivouac area and numerous documents had also been taken.

On the other end of the beachhead, the 305th Infantry sent patrols south to try and make contact with the advancing 7th Infantry Division. They, too, found enemy food dumps and a pillbox, all of which they destroyed. Within the beachhead, a few bombs were dropped by enemy planes, but no damage was done. By nightfall, the 77th Infantry Division had established a beachhead two miles wide, from Ipil in the north to the Bagonbon River on the south, and had pushed inland over a mile. The plan remained the same, to push north quickly and capture Ormoc. Then General Bruce would march north to meet with the X Corps coming down from the north, hopefully around Valencia.

But General Bruce had only his own division and had yet to make contact with either the 7th Infantry Division or any other friendly forces. Moving north would stretch his already limited resources and expose his division to attacks all along his lengthening front. As he moved, his line would stretch to the breaking point. But General Bruce was a student of military history and had remembered the campaign of Confederate General Thomas "Stonewall" Jackson in the Shenandoah Valley where, surrounded by enemy forces, he had maintained his small army by keeping his troops together with their supplies and support. And that is precisely what General Bruce decided to do. Each day he would "roll up his rear" and form a new defensive perimeter each night. Patrols would be out constantly to warn of any threats from Japanese forces outside the moving perimeter. The 307th Infantry would lead the push north and the 305th Infantry would protect the rear. In the middle the artillery, engineers and tanks, along with the supplies, would move forward each day.

Colonel Mitsui had established some strongpoints north of Ipil. These consisted of two coconut log bunkers, several trenches and foxholes. Behind these were riflemen and machine gunners on the banks of every stream between Ipil and the next barrio, Camp Downes.[45] Dug into the base of trees and along the wooded ridges that extended from the northeast toward the highway, other guns and riflemen waited. The highway itself was nine feet wide with three-foot shoulders and surfaced with either coral or gravel. At Camp Downes, a reinforced company dug itself in for a last-stand defense with the *Ormoc Defense Headquarters.* Here they had set up thirteen machine guns, two 40mm antiaircraft guns and three 75mm field guns, some dug into the foundations of the buildings. Riflemen protected the entire area. The *12th Independent Infantry Regiment* sent two of its companies to assist the *Shipping Unit's* defense until the main body of the regiment could arrive.

Colonel Stephen S. Hamilton led the 307th Infantry north the next morning, December 8th. As it moved north of Ipil, it encountered enemy opposition at the Panalian River at noon. General Bruce ordered the regiment to push north regardless, and to reach a position south of Camp Downes by evening. All of the division's reserves were made available to Colonel Hamilton, including the 2nd Battalion, 306th Infantry, the 902nd Field Artillery Battalion, Company A of the 776th Amphibian Tank Battalion, and Company A of the 88th Chemical Weapons Battalion. Behind these units, the 305th Infantry, reinforced with the 77th Reconnaissance Troop, would move north and defend the beachhead.

The first move was made by a platoon from Company A of the 776th

Amphibian Tank Battalion, which went into the water and traveled up toward Camp Downes. As the platoon reached Panalian Point, it received enemy fire. The platoon returned to report the location of the enemy guns and the 902nd Field Artillery Battalion took them under fire. Up front, the 307th Infantry continued to push forward against determined enemy opposition. Rifles, machine guns, mortars and light artillery fire opposed the American advance. The Japanese had dug temporary positions, but the American fire drove them steadily back. As they advanced, the Americans captured considerable quantities of small arms and artillery ammunition. Behind the front, an enemy company attacked Company A, 88th Chemical Weapons Battalion, but were twice driven off with high-explosive and white phosphorus shells. By darkness, the leading battalion had advanced about 2,000 yards. Colonel Vincent J. Tanzola's 305th Infantry continued to protect the southern and southeastern flanks of the division as it moved north. At night the regiment was around Ipil but still had some units as far south as the Baod River.

*　　*　　*

The Japanese defense had suffered severely from the attack of the 307th Infantry on December 8th. One battalion commander was severely wounded and many of his men killed. As a result, the two battalions of the *12th Independent Infantry Regiment* that were to have reinforced the line in front of Camp Downes were, instead, ordered to dig in north of Ormoc on the night of December 9th. The *1st Battalion, 12th Independent Infantry Regiment,* and elements of the regiment's *3rd Battalion,* would be left to delay the Americans while additional forces were rushed to the defense of Ormoc. In addition, elements of the *30th Infantry Division,* a paratroop unit of eighty men, a ship engineer unit of 500 men, and 750 naval troops, a total of 1,740 Japanese troops, were placed in front of the advancing "Old Bastards."

But the Americans themselves were being reinforced. A convoy brought the division's other regiment, the 306th Infantry, during the night of December 9th. This regiment would protect the eastern, or inland, flank of the division as it moved north up the coast of Ormoc Bay. The division now had one regiment on its northern, eastern and southern flanks. Ormoc Bay itself guarded the western flank.

The attack on December 9th was launched with the 1st Battalion, 306th Infantry, and 3rd Battalion, 307th Infantry. Almost as soon as the attack began, after an artillery bombardment, it was apparent that the Japanese had been reinforced during the night. Enemy forces on the ridges and high ground, which overlooked the approaches to Camp Downes, were well positioned to hit any approaching force. Intense artillery and small-arms fire hit the leading troops. Fire from the 902nd Field Artillery and the newly arrived 305th Field Artillery Battalion[46] was called upon to support the attack and the assault went forward. As if the ground resistance wasn't bad enough, the leading battalions were also strafed by Japanese planes that appeared over the "moving" beachhead during the day. But the "Old Bastards" kept moving forward. At one position, which was dubbed the "Battle of Bloody Hill," they captured eleven heavy machine guns, two 40mm antiaircraft guns and three 75mm field guns. As the day wore down, the leading elements entered Camp Downes and set up their night perimeter.

General Bruce now altered his dispositions. He left the 2nd Battalion, 305th Infantry at the south end of the perimeter at Ipil and moved up the regiment's other two battalions to Camp Downes to establish a strong all-around perimeter. He also moved his forward command post into Camp Downes as night fell. When they arrived, they had a brief skirmish with some Japanese who disputed ownership of the new site until they were driven off. The attack would continue on December 10th.

The 306th and 307th Infantry Regiments would attack together that day. This time, the objective was the port town of Ormoc, with its concrete pier, which allowed easy unloading of reinforcements and supplies. While the 307th continued to attack up the highway, the 306th was to move to the northeast and try to envelop the defenders and force them out of Ormoc. Fighting against the same type of opposition they had encountered all the way north from Deposito, the leading infantry regiments moved up, searching out each hidden position and destroying it with hand weapons. Their continued success worried General Suzuki, who ordered additional units from the *12th Independent Infantry Regiment* to Ormoc's defense. Yet it was too little and too late. At 0900 Hours, December 10th, Company A of the 776th Amphibian Tank Battalion moved into Ormoc, the first American troops to do so. Fighting among the streets, they sent their 75mm shells into the buildings from which the Japanese fired at them, from basements and rooftops. Out in Ormoc Bay, Admiral Kinkaid had stationed some landing craft which also fired into the city, using machine guns and rockets. These sailors cleared the pier of its defenders before they were forced to withdraw, out of ammunition.

The battalions of the 306th Infantry, which had moved out to the northeast, had encountered opposition as well. This, however, was less intense than that along the highway, and the infantry moved steadily. By mid-afternoon, the 1st Battalion, 306th Infantry was at a bridge on Highway 2 north of Ormoc. The 3rd Battalion was nearby. But along the highway, the 307th Infantry was stopped at a ravine in front of Ormoc where the Japanese had established their defense line. Using bayonets, grenades and mortars, the ravine was cleared, and surprisingly American casualties remained light. Hitting the *Shipping Unit* and the *12th Independent Infantry Regiment* hard, the 307th entered Ormoc to find a "blazing inferno of bursting white phosphorus shells, burning houses, and exploding ammunition dumps" from all the fire it had received in the past days. Against an enemy dug in on all sides, the regiment fought through rifle and machine guns dug in under houses. Using mortars, machine guns and self-propelled field guns to clear the way, the infantry cleared Ormoc, street by street, house by house. Amazingly, in all this chaos the Americans suffered only thirteen casualties in the clearing process.

One of those casualties was 2nd Lieutenant Tracy W. Young of the third platoon, Company K, 306th Infantry Regiment. On 11 December 1944, Lieutenant Young was leading his platoon in an attack against a company of Japanese dug in at a bamboo thicket atop a steep ridge near Ormoc. Despite intense machine-gun fire and exploding enemy grenades, he moved ahead of his platoon, killing seven of the enemy with his rifle at point-blank range. His platoon followed and eliminated eighty Japanese soldiers holding the bamboo thicket position. But then, enemy reinforcements from behind the ridge attacked and Lieutenant Young led a determined defense with bayonets. Young moved from squad to squad, shouting encouragement and leading the defense. But now ammunition was running low, and the Japanese were still attacking. Rather than losing the gain his men had made at considerable cost, Lieutenant Young ordered his men to fix bayonets and led a charge against the oncoming Japanese. He led the attack from the front and suffered a mortal wound just as his men secured the ridge for which so much blood had already been shed. For his dauntless leadership and personal courage in capturing the vital ridge, 2nd Lieutenant Tracy W. Young was awarded a posthumous Distinguished Service Cross.[47]

Meanwhile, one of the supporting units was in a fight of its own. The 305th Field Artillery Battalion had taken up a position to support the 306th Infantry, but had no infantry support of its own. As it fired on Ormoc, a Japanese force came out of the east and occupied a hill just 500 yards from the battalion and along the division's main supply route. Immediately, all the battalion's cooks, drivers, mechanics and clerks were assembled under Captain Loomis, the Battalion Communication Officer, and prepared to assault the hill. While they armed themselves, Battery C turned its 105mm howitzers on the hill and blasted away. When Captain Loomis' group attacked the hill, they drove off the Japanese and established defensive positions there.

General Bruce now reported to General Hodge. He advised him that he had taken Ormoc and outlined his future plans. His men had killed 1,506 Japanese and taken 7 prisoners. His own losses were 123 men killed, 329 wounded and 13 missing. He asked that his division's southern boundary be brought north to the Boad River and that the 7th Infantry Division take the area south of it. He wanted to continue his advance towards Valencia, while the 7th Infantry Division moved up and took control of Ormoc and Camp Downes. He was also looking for protection for his exposed eastern flank by the 11th Airborne Division, when he concluded his report with the phrase, "Have rolled two sevens in Ormoc. Come seven, come eleven."

They were coming. On December 7th, the 7th Infantry Division moved north using the 184th and 17th Infantry Regiments to attack up Highway 2. With Shoestring Ridge now cleared and most of the enemy forces off either attacking the airfields or defending at Ormoc, the route was lightly defended. Only the necessity of moving over ridges and streams slowed the drive north. On the night of December 9th, the division came up against a group of Japanese who were caught between the 7th and 77th Infantry Divisions, forcing them into the mountains. On December 11th, an advance patrol of the 2nd Battalion, 184th Infantry Regiment reached Ipil and made contact with the 77th Infantry Division.

But the Japanese had not given up defending their vital rear areas. When Company K, 17th Infantry Regiment, was moving forward near the Panilahan River, the lead squad, under Sergeant Joseph N. Medina, came under heavy sniper fire. Ordering his men to seek cover, Sergeant Medina crept forward through the tall grass until he came within range of the bamboo thicket in which the snipers were hiding. He tossed a grenade into the thicket and then charged into it, killing three enemy snipers. He signaled his squad forward and then proceeded ahead some two hundred yards where he came under machine gun fire. A nearby hut erupted with additional rifle fire directed at Sergeant Medina. Disregarding the personal risk, Medina rushed forward alone and managed to escape all the incoming enemy gunfire until he reached a point near a small structure. He threw a grenade into the hut and, after the explosion, rushed inside, killing two Japanese, but finding two others charging him with fixed bayonets. He shot both attackers with his rifle but one of the wounded Japanese continued to attack, forcing Sergeant Medina to kill him with the bayonet. With his squad now up and clearing the hut, Medina jumped out the window and went seeking the enemy machine gun. This he quickly located and destroyed with grenades. For his bold leadership on 13 December 1944, Sergeant Joseph N. Medina was awarded a Distinguished Service Cross.[48]

The XXIV Corps now had complete control of the eastern shore of Leyte at Ormoc Bay. The Japanese forces on Leyte were now divided, and the remnants of the *26th Infantry Division* and attached units were surrounded. All enemy reserves had been committed, and obtaining additional reserves was made far more difficult due to the loss of Ormoc. A juncture of X Corps and XXIV Corps, thereby encircling the entire *35th Army*, was now far more likely to occur. Highway 2, the last major road on Leyte, was also now denied to the Japanese. In effect, the Japanese were pinned in Ormoc Valley.

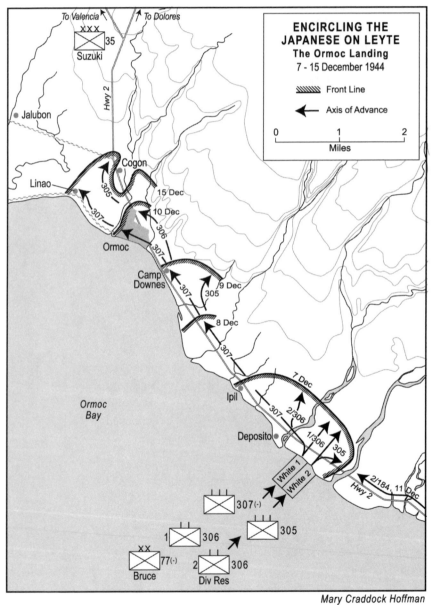

ENCIRCLING THE JAPANESE ON LEYTE
The Ormoc Landing
7 - 15 December 1944

///// Front Line

◄— Axis of Advance

0   1   2
Miles

To Valencia   To Dolores

XXX 35
Suzuki

Hwy 2

Jalubon

Cogon

Linao

15 Dec

10 Dec

305

306

307

Ormoc

307

Camp Downes

307

305

9 Dec

8 Dec

307

7 Dec

Ipil

307

2/306

Ormoc Bay

1/306

305

Deposito

White 1
White 2

Hwy 2

2/184, 11 Dec

307(-)

1 306

305

XX 77(-)
Bruce

2 306
Div Res

Mary Craddock Hoffman

CHAPTER 8

THE LAST VALLEY

W hile the "Old Bastards" were busy clearing the west coast of Leyte along the shores of Ormoc Bay, the U.S. Navy was bringing up more supplies and equipment to help them continue the job. No amphibious assault ever succeeded without supplies and reinforcements arriving in good time. On December 11th, just as General Bruce was moving north out of Ormoc, Task Unit 78.3.8, under Captain J.F. Newman, Jr.,[1] set out from Leyte Gulf with six destroyers[2] and thirteen landing craft. They left Tarraguna and sped through Surigao Strait at dusk on December 11th. As they passed through the strait near Limasawa Island, a flight of sixteen enemy aircraft attacked. The convoy had been provided meager fighter cover of just four Corsairs[3] of Marine Fighter Squadron 313, and these were directed by the USS *Smith* (Commander F.V. List), equipped as a fighter-director ship, to the oncoming enemy where they knocked down two of the planes.

The Corsairs protecting the Ormoc convoy reported being attacked by 16 enemy fighters, carrying 500-lb bombs under each wing. They shot down the two planes described above, but the others continued on. Four more enemy planes were shot down by the destroyers' antiaircraft fire. Their targets were the USS *Caldwell* (Commander D.R. Robinson, USNR) and the USS *Reid* (Commander S. A. McCornock). Four more enemy planes were hit, but not downed, by the antiaircraft fire. But the Japanese were not deterred. Four of them went after the *Reid*, with devastating results. The first Japanese pilot tried to crash-dive the ship, but only succeeded in hooking his wing on the

245

ship's starboard whaleboat before colliding with the waterline. But as he hit the ship, the bomb he was carrying exploded, causing fearsome damage. Without pause, a second enemy plane came in and hit the Number 3 Gun and an antiaircraft position. These explosions set off the ship's ammunition magazines and set her ablaze. She soon heeled over on her side and sank by the stern. Within two minutes of the hit by the first suicide plane, the USS *Reid* was underwater.[4] Loss of life was heavy and only 152 of her crew, about half of her complement, were saved. The veteran destroyer, which had been in the war since the first attack at Pearl Harbor, a ship with 13 invasions, 12 enemy planes and one submarine to her credit, was gone.

But Captain Newman and the surviving ships continued on to Ormoc Bay, which they reached about midnight. Although continually stalked by enemy aircraft, they delivered the vital supplies and then departed, once again having to make the return run in broad daylight. Again, enemy planes harassed the convoy and it was soon involved in a full-scale aerial assault. After a conventional attack by enemy bombers, the suicide planes showed up and began their deadly attack. The USS *Caldwell* took a hit in her radio room, losing 29 dead and 40 wounded, four of whom later died. Although the blast knocked out her forward guns and started a fire which consumed her forecastle, these were extinguished by the damage control teams, and the ship managed to return to Leyte Gulf under her own power.

Indeed, sometimes between the American and Japanese reinforcing convoys, Ormoc Bay seemed like Grand Central Station at rush hour. When the American convoy first entered Ormoc Bay on December 11th a small group of ships, the USS *Conyngham* and two Landing Ships, Medium, were detached to land at Caridad, 15 miles to the south. But as the convoy proceeded to Ipil, they ran into a Japanese convoy trying to unload troops and supplies at the same time and place. Two Japanese ships and a barge were about to land their cargoes near Ipil. The USS *Coghlan* (Commander B.B. Cheatham) spotted these ships on its radar at seven miles distance and opened fire. The Japanese tried to retreat along the west side of Ormoc Bay, but *Coghlan*'s radar showed a sudden flash and then one of the targets disappeared from the radar screen.[5] The *Coghlan* shifted fire to the other target, which made off at high speed. This target was later identified as the *IJN Yuzuki*, which was sunk by aircraft off San Isidro later in the campaign. The barge apparently escaped.

Other convoys were actively supporting the American forces at Baybay, further south along the west coast of Leyte. Task Unit 78.3.10 (Captain

W.M. Cole)[6] consisted of four destroyers and eleven landing craft carrying supplies to Baybay. Arriving undetected, the convoy unloaded without difficulty and then set out to return to San Pedro Bay. It was still dark over the sea when an enemy bomber dropped a near miss on the USS *Drayton* (Commander R.S. Craighill), killing two men and causing minor damage. Things heated up when daylight came. Before noon, eight enemy bombers came out of the clouds, undetected by radar, and attacked. Aided by two destroyers on antisubmarine patrol nearby,[7] this attack was beaten off with the Japanese losing two planes to the American antiaircraft fire.

But the Japanese were not done with this convoy just yet. They returned in the afternoon and one suicide plane made a run on the USS *Mugford* (Commander M.A. Shellabarger), first strafing her and then crashing into the port side. Two men died immediately and eight others soon after while another sixteen were horribly burned. The hit set the destroyer afire but excellent damage control work soon had these under control. The *Mugford* made San Pedro Bay under her own power. Nearby, the USS *Hughes* (Commander E.B. Rittenhouse) was on patrol off Dinagat Island when she was attacked by five planes. One crashed into her port side killing eighteen sailors and wounding another 22. The *Hughes* also caught fire and suffered severe damage. The remaining Japanese planes circled overhead, apparently trying to determine if the blazing American ship was worth another suicide dive to sink her. Satisfied that she was done for, they flew off to find other targets. But they were wrong. Although heavily damaged and unable to move under her own power, the *Hughes* called for fighter cover and a tow. That evening the USS *Laffey* and tug USS *Quapaw* arrived and escorted the destroyer to the safety of San Pedro Bay.

The Marine pilots had disregarded their own Navy's "friendly fire" and flew into the antiaircraft fire to try and save the ships. They claimed five additional enemy planes shot down, including two by 1st Lieutenant Clyde R. Jarrett. But it was a costly day for the Marine Air Group, with six Corsairs shot down by friendly fire or enemy aircraft. Three Marine pilots were killed[8] and eight more Corsairs were written off as too badly damaged to repair.[9]

One of the downed Marine Corps pilots, 1st Lt. Walter D. Bean, had been listed as missing but showed up nine days later with an interesting tale. He had been shot down by an enemy plane and landed in the sea. Neither his life preserver nor his inflatable life raft would work, and he nearly drowned before grasping a coconut log and holding onto it throughout the night. He was drifting toward two enemy destroyers when some Filipino canoes happened by and picked him up. At first suspicious that he might be Japanese, they were pleased when he reported himself as an American pilot. Given first aid, food and rest, he was taken to an island northwest of Cebu where he was the first American the islanders had seen since the Japanese invasion of 1942. He was treated royally and transported back to Leyte in stages. At one point, the natives brought in two Japanese pilots they had captured when their plane was shot down. These prisoners were made to run a gauntlet of bolo knives, bats and stones. They were promised that if they survived, they would be freed, but as they fled they were shot instead. Clearly, the Japanese claim that they were working for the benefit of all Asians had not taken hold in the Philippines.

The Marine Corps Fighter Squadron (Night) 541 had other problems. Used to flying all night vectored by radar to intercept enemy planes, they were instead assigned to fly the dawn and dusk patrols only, at the request of the Army Air Forces who advised them that this was necessary because their own army pilots were not trained in dawn and dusk landings. As a result, much of the special skills of Marine Night Fighter Squadron 541 were wasted. But on December 12th, Captain David W. Thomson's flight was making one of these dawn patrols when they were vectored to another American convoy en route to Ormoc. Nearby, another four-plane flight was flying cover for some PT boats patrolling Carigara Bay.

As these air patrols were following their respective ships, their radar operators on Leyte reported a large Japanese air formation heading for the Ormoc convoy. Captain Thomson took his three planes[10] and headed for Ponson Island to find themselves facing 33 enemy aircraft. Outnumbered eleven to one, the Marines nevertheless dived into the enemy formation. Marine 1st Lieutenant Fletcher D. Miller, Jr., brought his four planes from above Carigara Bay to join in the fight. Captain Thomson's group claimed five enemy planes, and more importantly broke up the enemy formation, sending it into confusion. When Lieutenant Miller's group showed up, they knocked down another six enemy planes and disrupted the Japanese even more. The convoy, observers of the entire episode, later radioed the Marines, "Nice show, boys, thanks a million."[11]

These losses and the still strong Japanese opposition to any American convoy on the west side of Leyte, prompted the Navy to suggest to General Krueger that supplies for XXIV Corps, and particularly for the 77th Infantry Division, be hauled overland from Abuyog to Baybay and then from there carried by landing craft to Ormoc. General Krueger, who had personally examined the route from Abuyong to Baybay, disagreed that such a plan was feasible and prevailed upon the Seventh Fleet to continue with its resupply convoys directly to Ormoc. Fortunately, there were few more such battles as that of December 11th.

The Japanese, meanwhile, were also still sending troops and supplies to Leyte, although not through Ormoc anymore. On December 11th, the same day opposing convoys battled in Ormoc Bay, another enemy convoy of three transports and five destroyers was identified heading toward Leyte. The convoy also had an escort of some thirty fighter planes. Once again, Marine Air Group 12 dispatched Fighter Squadrons (VMF) 211, 218 and 313 to stop this latest reinforcement attempt. As the convoy crossed the Visayan Sea on approach to Leyte's west coast, the Marines delivered a devastating dive-bomber attack through intense enemy antiaircraft fire and fighter opposition. Eight planes targeted the largest enemy transport[12] and dropped a thousand-pound bomb each. The battle took place about 40 miles east of Panay Island. A transport and a supply ship were reported damaged with eight enemy planes shot down. That afternoon, another 30 Marine planes and 16 Army Air Corps P-40s attacked again. By this time, the convoy was within five miles of Palompon. A "large troop transport" was reported sunk, and VMF-211 also claimed two destroyers and another transport sunk. VMF-218 claimed additional hits on another destroyer and a transport, while VMF-115 claimed damage to a transport. Post-war evaluation credits only two cargo ships of 8,700 tons sunk during this battle. As the Marines left the scene, the ship was blazing fiercely and had a huge hole in her side. They reported this ship and two other transports sunk. It was believed that a full Japanese infantry battalion had been lost.

A few hours later a joint flight of Marine and Army Air Corps planes returned and found the remnants of the convoy, barely thirty miles from Leyte. Another freighter was reported sunk and two others set ablaze. These latter ships beached themselves on a small island west of Palompon where their troops and supplies, those that survived, were stranded. Unfortunately, the remainder of the convoy did reach Leyte and discharged the remaining troops and supplies.

*   *   *

When General Bruce and his "Old Bastards" captured Ormoc and closed off the bay to enemy reinforcements, they had eliminated the last major port access to Leyte for the Japanese. There were other ports, but none capable of handling the volume of troops and supplies which the Japanese now needed if they were going to turn the Battle for Leyte around. The few other ports were also much further away from the site where General Suzuki planned his new defense, Ormoc Valley. Essentially, the landing of XXIV Corps at Ormoc and the breaking of the Yamashita Line by X Corps had trapped the *35th Army* in Ormoc Valley, the last valley available to them on Leyte.

The landing at Deposito had encouraged General MacArthur that the annoying Leyte Campaign, which was delaying his other conquests in the Philippines, was almost at an end. He sent to General Krueger a message which read, "Please extend to your command my hearty congratulations on the success of the Ormoc Operation. It was well executed with that cool courage, resolute determination and indomitable will for victory which has so characterized our forces in all campaigns."

As early as December 7th, and probably earlier than that, the Japanese were using San Isidro as a receiving port for troops and supplies. A convoy of fourteen ships was seen that day entering the small port and, despite strong American air intervention they successfully landed a full regiment there. It was this landing that diverted the tired 34th Infantry Regiment to the area to clear it of these newly arrived Japanese.

Meanwhile, XXIV Corps and X Corps were now ready to deal directly with the remaining forces of the *35th Army*. General Arnold's 7th Infantry Division had made contact with the 77th Infantry Division on December 10th at Ipil, and now moved into the mountains between the shore and Ormoc Valley to deal with the *26th Infantry Division*. Across the valley, General Swing's 11th Airborne Division was also facing the *26th Infantry Division* while pushing its way towards the 7th Infantry Division on the other side of Ormoc Valley. Behind them the 38th and 96th Infantry Divisions cleared up the remnants of General Suzuki's counterattack by eliminating the remaining elements of the *16th Infantry Division* and *2nd Raiding Brigade*.

To the north, X Corps had the 32nd Infantry Division pushing south into Ormoc Valley from Breakneck Ridge. Opposition remained strong from the *1st Infantry Division*, and isolated enemy pockets remained to be mopped up behind the lines. The 1st Cavalry Division was busy clearing the enemy from Mount Catabaran and around Bonbongan. To speed up this task, the Cavalry had been given the 151st Regimental Combat Team from the 38th Infantry Division. Over on Samar, the 8th Cavalry Regiment had almost completed clearing that island's coast of enemy troops. The next major step was for General Bruce to capture Valencia, which would finally close off the entrances to Ormoc Valley and trap General Suzuki once and for all.

* * *

General Suzuki had finally launched his long-desired counterattack against the Americans, directed particularly at their airfields. He had high expectations and had even gone forward to the headquarters of the *26th Infantry Division* in the mountains near Lubi to personally supervise the operation, while some of his staff directed the defenses against the Americans at Shoestring Ridge. His Deputy Chief of Staff, Major General Yoshiharu Tomochika, took command of the remaining elements of *35th Army* at Ormoc.

The failure of this attack and the success of the American landing at Deposito completely changed things for General Suzuki. He reacted quickly as the news reached him of the counterattack's failure and the American landing, ordering a Colonel Imahori[13] to organize a defense in the Ormoc sector based upon the *12th Independent Infantry Regiment,* reinforced with four additional rifle companies, and the rear area troops available around the critical supply base. Then he moved to have the *16th* and *26th Divisions* withdraw to the west and establish a defense of Ormoc Valley. The *16th Division* was by now all but destroyed, having only 200 men left with the division's colors. These men were attached to other units and the *16th Division* ceased to exist.

The efforts of the *26th Division* to withdraw through the mountains were severely restricted by General Swing's 11th Airborne Division which, despite the attack to its rear, had continued its attacks west from Burauen into the mountains between the Leyte and Ormoc Valleys. Even as the Japanese tried to move, the American paratroopers were attacking Lubi, General Suzuki's advance headquarters. This attack caused the general's staff to disband and scatter to save themselves. General Suzuki himself had to infiltrate through American lines to reach his command post at Huaton, four miles north of Ormoc. This he managed to do by December 13th, his chief of staff arriving the following day. Upon arrival there, he learned that his *35th Army Headquarters* had lost all communications with the *26th Division.* It would not be heard from again until early March, nearly three months away.

Quickly reassessing his situation, General Suzuki had his Chief of Staff, General Tomochika, prepare new plans. He had just been told by a staff officer of the *1st Infantry Division,* fighting the 32nd Infantry Division, that his unit was on the verge of collapse. General Suzuki ordered it to go on the defensive, halting all counterattacks. Colonel Imahori reported that he had already lost the equivalent of one battalion at Ormoc and was pulling his remaining forces back into prepared defenses north of the city.

Realizing how drastically the situation on Leyte had changed for the Japanese, General Yamashita had sent to General Suzuki about four hundred paratroopers of the *4th Air Raiding Landing Unit,* but with the proviso that they be kept near Ormoc for its defense. General Yamashita also provided the *5th Infantry Regiment,* an artillery battalion, a company of engineers, and a transportation company drawn from the *8th Infantry Division.* He also sent a *Special Naval Landing Force* of 400 men, with light tanks and sixteen trench mortars. Meanwhile, General Suzuki sent a battalion (less two companies) of the *58th Independent Mixed Brigade* and an artillery battalion to protect the Camotes Islands, hoping that their presence would keep the waters of the Camotes Sea open to his reinforcement convoys. The former were the troops which were on the transports attacked by the Marine Corps planes and which suffered so much damage that only the troops of the *Special Naval Landing Force* arrived safely on Leyte. Other transports were forced to stop at Palompon on the west coast, considerably delaying their arrival at the front. On December 9th, the *77th Infantry Regiment* also landed at Palompon, the last major reinforcement the *35th Army* would receive during the Battle for Leyte. General Suzuki, optimistic as ever, hoped to organize these units into a counterattack force. He hoped to launch his attack on December 17th.

*   *   *

General Bruce, still calling upon his knowledge of military history, advanced his 77th Infantry Division on December 10, using what he referred to as blockhouse tactics, a development of 18th-century warfare. Each of his units would advance each day with their supplies and food, and each night would establish an all-around defensive perimeter. That way there was no supply line for the Japanese to cut and he could keep his division relatively intact as it moved north. During the day, armed convoys would travel from unit to unit carrying resupply and other needs. Filipino guerrillas were used to guard the bridges and bring in intelligence of the enemy. By nightfall on December 10th, the 305th and 307th Infantry Regiments were north of the city.

General Bruce planned only a limited attack on December 11th in order to straighten out his division's lines and get everyone in place for the push to Valencia. After a thirty-minute artillery preparation, the leading elements of the 306th and 307th Infantry Regiments began to push across the Antilao River, but were stopped by heavy small-arms and machine gun fire from a position across the river. The enemy position was on the north bank at the barrio of Cogon. It blocked Highway 2 and was on a slightly raised plateau which covered the river banks. It was protected by rice paddies on each of its own flanks. An estimated reinforced battalion with machine guns, antitank guns and field pieces defended this position. Colonel Imahori had chosen well.

The defenses themselves consisted of innumerable spider holes reinforced with coconut logs hidden under brush and dirt. The center of the defense was a three-story concrete building, which had been converted into a mini-fortress. Aside from the building, every other *12th Independent Infantry Regiment* position was hidden in the undergrowth or expertly camouflaged. None could be seen beyond ten feet and then only if you knew where to look. Although the Americans could bypass this strong point, it blocked Highway 2, which would be their main line of communication and supply.

The 1st Battalion, 306th Infantry attacked, only to be stopped by heavy machine-gun fire at the bridge over the Antilao River. The Americans replied with point-blank fire from self-propelled howitzers and other field pieces. Infantry weapons supported the barrage, but no apparent dent was made in the Japanese defenses. But during the fighting, Company A, 306th Infantry, managed to get across the river and about one hundred yards into the Japanese defense. They found enemy machine guns every five or ten yards, each with short but deadly fields of fire. Only when the attacking infantry came within point-blank range would these guns open fire, ensuring many casualties among the attacking Americans. Although rifle fire and hand grenades eliminated several of these positions, the cost to Company A was too great and it withdrew.

The 3rd Battalion, 306th Infantry made some progress on the beach flank, but after moving about 1,000 yards, they hit a well-organized enemy position on a steep ridge protected by an equally deep ravine. A moat of 800 yards of rice paddies also protected it from a flank attack by the 1st Battalion. With only one and a half companies available to him, Lt. Colonel Gordon T. Kimbrell, the battalion commander, decided to attack despite the strong defense.[14] After an artillery preparation, the battalion attacked and managed to advance through heavy fire to a foothold on the ridge, but they could not reach the crest. The battalion commander was deciding what to do next when the Japanese decided the issue with a strong counterattack. For an hour the two forces fought fiercely for the ridge, and although the counterattack was beaten off, the battalion could not remain in its exposed position. The 3rd battalion withdrew for the night.

That afternoon, the 2nd and 3d Battalions of 305th Infantry came up from Ormoc and moved into a position between the 306th and 307th Infantry Regiments. As night fell, the 77th Infantry Division was in position to renew its attack the next morning with the 305th taking over the lead. That night came the attempted Japanese landing in Ormoc Bay earlier described. The units on shore were alert and as soon as the enemy barge came into range, every available weapon fired on it. The 7th Antiaircraft Artillery Battalion joined with the tank destroyers, amphibian tanks and Cannon Company weapons of the 307th Infantry in the defense of the division's rear. The barge immediately burst into flame and some reported that the Japanese, who evidently still thought their forces held Ormoc, climbed on the gunwales and shouted, "Don't shoot!" Another, unidentified, vessel was then seen discharging troops to the northwest of the town. The antitank guns of the 307th Infantry immediately took this vessel under fire while forward observers of the 902nd Field Artillery Battalion directed artillery fire on the landing area. As this vessel tried to leave, it began to burn fiercely and soon sank. About 150 men, eight amphibious tanks,[15] a number of rifles, mortars and machine guns and some ammunition had been unloaded before the vessel's destruction, but the other supplies, including four trucks loaded with ammunition, went down with the ship. Indications of a third ship unloading farther to the west were responded to with an artillery barrage. At dawn, the third ship was revealed attempting to leave Ormoc Bay, but heavily damaged. American planes later sank this vessel. Prisoners taken later confirmed that the Japanese of this reinforcement group believed that their own forces still held Ormoc. They also reported that casualties amongst them had been heavy.

While the front and rear areas were under attack, the supply lines were under construction. The 77th Infantry Division had found itself in the situation of a more or less "bastard" unit, a situation having nothing to do with their nickname. Having been diverted to Leyte after the heavy battles on Guam, they had not been fully re-equipped and supplied. Although General Krueger had made every effort to rectify this situation before the division went into combat at Ormoc, many things were still lacking. The division had only a few trucks to haul its supplies. The shipping schedule was erratic and subject to changes due to enemy air opposition. Unloading remained slow and difficult, and there were not enough men to handle it. So the 132nd Engineer Combat Battalion worked on the cross-island road while men of the 706th Tank Battalion and 292nd Joint Assault Signal Company loaded ships and trucks at San Pedro Bay for the trip to Ormoc. Even infantrymen who had recently recovered from wounds and were in the rear areas were put to work loading ships and trucks. Everyone understood that without supplies, the 77th Infantry Division would be overwhelmed.

* * *

After the hectic day and night of December 11th, General Bruce decided to give his "Old Bastards" a day of rest. Positions were consolidated, supplies brought forward, artillery placed closer to the front lines and patrols sent out to learn as much as possible about the enemy positions the division now faced. The artillery conducted harassing fire on the enemy position across the Antilao River throughout the night.

General Bruce renewed the attack on December 13th, with the objective of seizing the road junction north of Cogon and then continuing the attack to the north. The 305th Infantry was to lead off in the center right down Highway 2, while the 306th Infantry protected its right. Behind them, the 184th Infantry of the 7th Infantry Division would relieve the last two of the division's infantry battalions protecting Ormoc and take over that job, while the 77th's battalions moved to the front.

The attack began with a fierce but brief bombardment by all four of the division's artillery battalions. So severe was this fire that the Japanese defenders were stunned by it, some so severely that they stumbled into American lines in an effort to escape it. These unfortunate soldiers were shot down as they approached the American positions. However, the fire seemed to do nothing to the concrete building or its defenders inside.

Bruce had placed Colonel Paul L. Freeman, a War Department observer, in charge of a special attack force, which included Companies E and L of the 305th Infantry. This group was ordered to attack the concrete building. The 2nd Platoon of Company A, 88th Chemical Mortar Battalion, knocked out two enemy machine guns on the approach to the building. The Americans attacked into heavy enemy fire, which was in part neutralized by close-in friendly artillery fire. The 3rd Battalion, 305th Infantry attacked with Company K in the lead. They managed to use a draw to move up to the ridgeline within 500 yards of the concrete building. Just as they reached the ridge, however, they were hit with the first of five counterattacks. Losses on both sides were severe. One American platoon lost 41 men out of 52 in a matter of minutes. Mortar and machine guns stopped the attacks. At this moment, the situation was at a stalemate, with the Japanese holding one end of the ridge and the Americans holding the other. Neither could move forward and neither was willing to withdraw.

One of the men in Company K was Technical Sergeant Glen E. Tweed, who was in a leading platoon. When the enemy counterattack hit his company, his platoon leader was killed and two leading non-commissioned officers seriously wounded. Realizing that the platoon was badly disorganized by the loss of its leaders, Tech Sergeant Tweed assumed command in the middle of the violent counterattack and deployed the platoon to repulse that charge. His men blunted the Japanese attack. But more attacks came against the platoon and heavy casualties were suffered. Both of the platoon's light machine guns fell silent, their crews killed or wounded. Sergeant Tweed seized one of the machine guns from its mount and, exposing himself regardless of the deadly situation, advanced toward the enemy, firing the machine gun from the hip. Seven Japanese soldiers charged the sergeant who was delaying their attack, but Tweed quickly cut them down with automatic weapons fire. An enemy machine gun then took the sergeant under fire from a nearby bamboo grove. At this point, Tweed turned into the grove and sprayed the entire area with his machine gun until the enemy was killed and the machine gun silenced. Sergeant Tweed continued to lead his platoon throughout the day until he was killed in action later that evening. For his resolute leadership at the risk of his own life, Technical Sergeant Glen E. Tweed was awarded a posthumous Distinguished Service Cross.[16]

Company I relieved the depleted Company K and held the American half of the hill. Lt. Colonel Edward Chalgren, Jr., commanding 3rd Battalion, also lost men due to heat exhaustion, but a rest area was set up several hundred yards to the rear in a sheltered area where the men were given cold water and allowed to rest. Nearly all of these men insisted on returning to their units and continuing the fight.

As the fight petered, out Captain Louis Hinson, commanding Company I, noticed a group of men in a draw to the left of his company. Permission for supporting mortars and artillery to fire on these men was at first denied, as Colonel Chalgren had sent a patrol out into that general area. But when Captain Hinson called that he could identify Japanese soldiers with his binoculars, the fire order was granted. Mortars, 37mm guns and machine guns fired up and down the draw. Later some 350 enemy dead were counted in that draw. The sixth counterattack against the Americans on the ridge never materialized. Meanwhile, an air observer from the 305th Field Artillery Battalion had uncovered an enemy position which was completely hidden from ground observation. He blasted the concealment off these positions and then conducted an observed shoot by his battalion, which knocked many Japanese out of action. When the 3rd Battalion, 305th Infantry later occupied this area, they counted more than two hundred enemy dead.

Thursday, December 14th, opened with an attack by the 305th Infantry to envelop the Cogon strong point from the west. While Company E made a frontal attack, the rest of the battalion moved past the strongpoint and concrete building and continued on another 1,000 yards to the north of the vital road junction. Meanwhile, Company E slowly and painfully dug the Japanese out of their spider holes. Fighting was often hand-to-hand and self-propelled guns were brought up to fire point-blank at stubborn Japanese positions. Protected by the infantry, these guns knocked out one position after another, while the accompanying infantry dropped grenades into nearby spider holes. Armored bulldozers manned by the division's own 302nd Engineer Combat Battalion plowed through the underbrush, burying many of the Japanese in their holes. Captain James E. Carruth, of the engineers rode the lead bulldozer and leaned out of his cab, killing any escaping Japanese with his carbine. To increase their protection while still killing Japanese, some crews of the self-propelled guns drove over enemy holes and dropped grenades into them through the armored vehicles' bottom escape hatch. Shortly after noon, the position was cut off and surrounded.

Colonel Freeman's special attack force was, at first, unable to move forward. The enemy in the concrete building remained. They fought on, with no hope of escape or victory, until they were killed. Another small isolated group remained defiant north of the concrete building until they, too, were wiped out. Colonel Freeman's force attacked under cover of artillery and mortars, knocking out two pillboxes as they advanced, slowly and carefully, to the building. Using flamethrowers and tank destroyer guns to cover their advance, they managed to get close enough to use rifles, bayonets and hand grenades. First Lieutenant Robert P. Nett was leading Company E, 305th Infantry, in the attack. Advancing against heavy machine gun and other automatic weapons fire, Lieutenant Nett led the attack from the front, charging against the strongpoint. Using his rifle and bayonet, he killed seven enemy soldiers who were entrenched in front of the building. Despite being seriously wounded, Lieutenant Nett refused medical treatment and continued to lead the assault. Waving his men forward, he was hit and seriously wounded a second time. He pressed ahead, leading his men, until the final assault on the concrete building was ready. This final assault he personally led, and once again he was wounded. Only when the attack had been successful did Nett agree to turn over command of Company E to his subordinate and retire unaided for medical treatment. For his gallant leadership on December 14th, Lieutenant Nett was awarded the Medal of Honor and promoted to Captain.[17]

Nearby, Company L advanced through heavy jungle and used flamethrowers to burn the Japanese out of their defenses. It was the bitterest fighting the division had encountered since landing at Ormoc. By the end of Friday, December 14th, the Cogon defense position of Colonel Imahori was no more. Six hundred and thirty-three dead Japanese soldiers were counted in and around the destroyed concrete building. Additional enemy dead had been buried by the bulldozers or lay uncounted in the jungle.

*   *   *

While the west flank of XXIV Corps had been advancing steadily, if with difficulty, around Ormoc, the eastern flank was still struggling through the Central Mountain Range. General Arnold's division was a mere seven miles away, after clearing Shoestring Ridge, and managed to make the link in a few days. General Swing's 11th Airborne Division, however, was strung out in the mountains and defending the airfields under enemy attack. But they moved ahead anyway. Suffering daily rains, cloudy weather and poor visibility, the paratroopers and glider soldiers struggled through the same jungle and mountain conditions as had hampered the 24th and 32nd Infantry Divisions to the north. Even their ubiquitous small liaison planes were often grounded because of rains, poor visibility or low clouds. This left the combat battalions short on food, ammunition, medical supplies, socks, boots and uniforms, all of which quickly disappeared in the heavy jungle. Socks lasted only a few days, rotting quickly in equally rotting boots. At night the troops suffered from the cold, especially those sleeping in muddy foxholes in wet clothes. Men tried to steam dry themselves by wrapping themselves up in ponchos and letting their own body heat dry them out.

The 511th Parachute Infantry was struggling to fight its way through a pass southeast of Mahonag.[18] Lt. Colonel Harry Wilson's 2nd Battalion had relieved Lt. Colonel Norman M. Shipley's 3rd Battalion. Both units were trying to find the Japanese supply trail that they believed led through the mountains and which had brought the enemy counterattack force to attack the airfields. Fighting nearby was the 2nd Battalion, 187th Glider Infantry. Chief Warrant Officer Nelson remembered the fighting well. "There was just one trail, so the battalion was strung out in single file. Every inch of the trail was slippery and the going was hot and tough as we crossed the flooded rice fields west of Burauen. This part of the move was pleasant strolling compared to the mountain trail we were about to encounter. Once in them, it was a nightmare of climbing straight up the sides of sheer cliffs, cutting footholds as we went, pulling ourselves up by the vines along the trail. Foot by foot we scaled the greasy heights and a slip would have plunged one to his death on the rocks below. Reaching the crests, we'd catch our breath, then slip and slide down the other face of the height only to be met with the necessity of crossing a raging mountain river in the canyon below."[19]

Under such conditions, fast movement was all but impossible. Men moved forward in small groups, sometimes only a squad at a time, until they could regroup in some small flat space deep in the mountains. By the afternoon of December 3rd, the 2nd Battalion, 187th Glider Infantry reached Anonang, a clearing in the middle of the jungle with one grass shack. There was a known Japanese position below the plateau on which Anonang lay. Captain George Ori and Company F were ordered to occupy an old outpost and observe the Japanese. Arriving at the outpost, Captain Ori found a telephone wire from the previous occupation still operational. He quickly called for mortar fire on the Japanese. That night the Japanese attacked Company F, but were repulsed without American losses.

The next day Captain Ori decided to test the Japanese defenses. A platoon went down to see what they could of the Japanese, but they were hit by enemy machine-gun fire as soon as they came out in a clearing before the main Japanese position. The Japanese on the hill sent in a counterattack which cost the platoon its commander and two others wounded, one of whom would die later that night. The Japanese position soon earned the name "Purple Heart Hill." Later, on December 5th, the Japanese tried to counterattack the 3rd Battalion, 511th Parachute Infantry at Mahonag, but were repulsed. That same day the battalion reported that it was completely out of food and low on ammunition, oil and signal supplies. A transport plane and two of the liaison planes dropped the vital supplies under sniper fire. The battalion mortars fired whenever the planes made a pass over the drop zone, to keep the sniper's heads down, and the drop was successful.

It was the next day that the 3rd Battalion's Intelligence Officer led a patrol which discovered the Japanese supply trail. It was just north of Manonag and across a river at the base of Mount Mahonag. It was a foot trail which had been widened enough for small vehicles like a jeep. It had been corrugated with three- and four-inch logs to form a road. But the Japanese suffered from the constant rains as much as did the Americans. By the time it was discovered, it had sunk to a foot below the surface of the mud. The trail ended just north of Lubi from origins on the west coast, just above the Talisayan River. A branch ran to the north along the west coast of Leyte.

On December 7th, just as the 77th Infantry Division was landing at Deposito, the 2nd Battalion, 511th Parachute Infantry began to march up the trail. The rest of the regiment followed along a smaller trail to the south. Behind, they left Captain Hobert B. Wade and his Company E as the battalion rear guard. They were to follow the battalion the next day. As Company E prepared to move out on December 8th, the Japanese attacked. The company was still in its prepared positions and opened fire. First Lieutenant Norvin L. Davis' platoon was holding its position when one of its members, Private First Class Elmer Fryar, became dissatisfied with his view of the attacking Japanese. He got out of his foxhole and climbed to an elevated position behind a log in front of the machine gun protecting his platoon. From that exposed position, he directed the machine guns and mortars, while killing individual Japanese with his rifle. He quickly became the objective of the attacking Japanese, who realized Private Fryar was the cause of their heavy losses.

As he lay there firing and directing others' fire, he noticed that one of the company's sergeants had been struck in the head by a bullet and was wandering aimlessly toward the Japanese. Private Fryar arose from his position and ran to the stumbling, wounded sergeant. He dragged him back to safety and then dressed the sergeant's wounds. By this time Company E was beginning to withdraw from the position to follow orders and join its battalion. The Japanese mistook this movement for a retreat and renewed their assault. Fryar turned over the wounded sergeant to the company aid men and returned to his exposed position, directing fire on the attacking Japanese. As the Japanese again withdrew, the platoon moved back and began to march down the trail to rejoin its battalion. Private First Class Fryar and Lieutenant Davis marched in the middle of the platoon column. As it moved along, a Japanese sniper arose from a hidden position and aimed directly at Lieutenant Davis. Without hesitating, Fryar threw himself between the sniper and Davis, taking a burst of automatic weapons fire in his chest. Mortally wounded,

Fryar continued his fight, tossing a grenade at the enemy sniper, killing him. Private First Class Fryar, of Denver, Colorado was, at age 32, the oldest American paratrooper to win the Medal of Honor in World War II.[20]

The 511th Parachute Infantry marched along the trails. As one participant later stated, "The trail was even more difficult than the one from Manarawat to Mahonag. The heavy rains had made it ankle deep in mud in some spots and dangerously slippery in others. At some places it was necessary to pass the parts of the mortars up to a man on a ledge above, and then the men had to help one another over the ledge. Frequent breaks were necessary and the movement of the column was very slow."[21] Deserted Japanese campsites, some large enough for a regiment, were discovered along the way. In one instance, the 2nd Battalion found one and attacked from two sides, killing "hundreds" of Japanese troops. Searching the camp after the attack, the battalion found "Japanese flags were strewn about, maps, diaries, code books, and cooking utensils lay on the mossy ground of the village among the dead Japanese. Awe-inspiring above all was the sight of the Japanese wounded, deserted in caves and lean-to's on the side of the canyon. Gagged and bound and left to die, these pitiable creatures would have inspired the revolted pity of the fiercest soldier."[22]

Later that day, the 2nd Battalion was marching along the trail when it was hit by an artillery barrage. Although it was never confirmed, this was believed by many to have been friendly fire, since artillery observation planes were flying overhead immediately before the barrage hit the battalion.

The 511th continued their march and soon reached a high hill on which the Japanese had defenses. Colonel Lahti ordered his 3rd Battalion to attack, which they did, seizing the hill after a bloody fight. As they stood on the position, which they named "Rock Hill,"[23] they could see off in the distance, perhaps six miles away, Ormoc Bay. This was a welcome sight to the exhausted paratroopers who knew that Ormoc was the objective of their march. But before they could get there they faced more hard fighting, and more hills and jungle. To begin with, the Japanese launched a series of counterattacks to regain "Rock Hill" that night against Company H, each of which was repulsed.

The next day, Captain Pat Wheeler led his Company G off the hill along the Japanese supply trail. Enemy machine-gun fire stopped the attack shortly after it was begun. Three men were wounded, and an officer and enlisted man were missing. Colonel Lahti called the company back to "Rock Hill." As they returned, more enemy attacks struck the 3rd Battalion, aided by mor-

tars and machine gun fire. The battalion was blocking the enemy's main supply route, and they wanted it back. The next morning, December 10th, the
1st Battalion and regimental headquarters reached "Rock Hill" and reinforced
the embattled 3rd Battalion. Colonel Lahti's battalion, meanwhile, had "lost"
its Company G when it set off on a mission to contact the 77th Infantry
Division around Ormoc. Shortly after the company left the perimeter, all
contact was lost and the company disappeared into the thick jungle-covered
mountains. Then the battalion was attacked from all sides by the Japanese.
It was now surrounded on "Rock Hill." Attempts to move the unit's eighteen
seriously wounded to safety were blocked by the enemy. Its men had not
eaten for four days and their ammunition supply was running low, particularly
in hand grenades, which were the weapon of choice in the jungle. Finally on
December 13th, the battalion received an airdrop of rations and medical supplies.

Colonel Haugen ordered the new commander of the 2nd Battalion,
Major Frank S. Holcombe, to attack from the west to relieve the 3rd Battalion. The attack was unsuccessful in the face of strong enemy resistance at
"Maloney Hill," between the 2nd and 3rd Battalions. But good news finally
arrived on December 17th when elements of the 32nd Infantry Regiment,
7th Infantry Division contacted Company G, still trying to reach the west
coast. Captain Wheeler's men had gone ten days without food and many
were suffering from malnutrition. Often surrounded by Japanese and unsure
of the proper direction, Company G had finally established itself at a position
they named "Starvation Hill," where they hoped to be seen by patrolling aircraft. Recognition panels were set out and they watched as the rest of the
battalion received their airdrops without any sign that they had been seen.
The only food available was that taken from Japanese bodies, usually rice.
They also dug up edible roots and passed those out. Soon they were making
soup out of palm and banana trees. Water was not a problem, as the company
had set up near a stream at the hill's bottom. At some point Captain Wheeler,
still determined to accomplish his mission, asked for volunteers to try and
contact the 7th Infantry Division. At least fifty men volunteered and five
were selected for the patrol that day. These men actually made it all the way
to the beach at Ormoc Bay, but their weakened physical condition made the
trip so slow that by the time they did, the company had already been found.
A second patrol had made contact with the 7th Infantry Division and supply
drops soon followed. Company K, 32nd Infantry Regiment, soon arrived to
escort the exhausted paratroopers to safety.

On December 18th, Colonel Haugen used his attached heavy Marine Corps artillery battalion to bombard "Maloney Hill," which they did to good effect. Company B then walked to the top of the hill against no opposition. Scores of dead Japanese were found there, in blasted and crushed emplacements. An ambush, which Colonel Haugen had set out behind the hill, caught more than one hundred of the retreating Japanese and cut them down along their own supply route.

Meanwhile, the 2nd Battalion, 187th Glider Infantry still faced "Purple Heart Hill." For nine days, between December 2nd and 11th, the battalion engaged in vicious firefights with the Japanese, trying to find a weak spot in their defenses. Finally the assistant division commander, Brigadier General Pierson, ordered an attack on "Purple Heart Hill." Lt. Colonel Arthur H. ("Harry") Wilson sent Companies F and G into the attack. Supported by Battery A of the 457th Parachute Field Artillery Battalion,[24] the attack went slowly because it was difficult to identify the Japanese positions. Company F seized Ori hill and was working its way down the reverse slope toward the main enemy position by 1300 Hours. But American artillery blocked further advance, and the observers were still having great difficulty in spotting the Japanese.

The attack continued the next day, but an urgent call from one of the radio relay stations of the 152nd Airborne Antiaircraft Battalion caused Colonel Wilson to divert Company F to their rescue from attacking Japanese. Meanwhile, a platoon patrol under 1st Lieutenant Harrison I. Merritt, ran into fierce enemy resistance and Captain George Walters brought up the rest of Company G to assist. The company attacked what was a strong Japanese position, losing several men including Captain Walters. Lieutenant Merritt took command and called in mortar fire. The Japanese scattered and Company G cleared the position. That afternoon aid arrived in the form of the 1st Battalion, 187th Glider Infantry. Colonel Wilson's men, who had run out of food and were existing on roots and green corn patches, were sent to block the Japanese supply trail, while Colonel Pearson and his 1st Battalion took over "Purple Heart Hill."

General Swing now decided that his southern area, patrolled by the 188th Glider Infantry, was relatively clear of enemy troops. He ordered the 188th Glider Infantry to move north and assist in clearing the Japanese Main Supply Route, along with the other two regiments. Concerned about evacuation of the wounded, General Swing also sent the 127th Airborne Engineer Battalion to Baybay on the west coast with orders to find the western terminus of the Japanese supply route and to widen it as far as possible to accommodate ambulances and trucks. The 408th Quartermaster Company was also ordered to set up supply points in the Ormoc area to be ready for the arrival of the exhausted, starving and nearly naked paratroopers. This resulted in the engineers locating the exact end of the Japanese trail, which was radioed to Colonel Haugen, who in turn directed his 511th Parachute Regiment to a more correct course of advance. Originally, he was advancing two ridges away from the correct end of the trail.

The battle continued this way until December 23rd, when Colonel Wilson received orders to take "Rock Hill" and then make a breakthrough to the coast. With General Swing near the head of his column, the 2nd Battalion, 187th Infantry moved out, shooting a few Japanese who blocked their way. Leading was Company G's 2nd Platoon under 1st Lieutenant Joseph Giordano. Time and again the platoon ran into small groups of Japanese, who either fought or fled the Americans. Machine guns positions were outflanked and overrun. Small groups of Japanese infantry were killed or driven off into the jungle. Soon the platoon was on the west side of a high mountain from which they could see the sea. Here, Lieutenant Giordano stopped his platoon and fired off a violet smoke grenade. As they watched anxiously, on a ridge some five hundred yards away, Lieutenant Giordano saw the answering violet smoke. The 11th Airborne had at last made contact with the XXIV Corps forces on the west coast. And in the process, they had all but destroyed the *26th Infantry Division*.

*   *   *

When the 128th Infantry of the 32nd Infantry Division had captured Limon on November 22nd, it could be said that the Battle of Breakneck Ridge had ended. Perhaps the battle had ended but the fighting continued for some time. The loss of Limon had severed contact between the *1st Infantry Division* and the *102nd Infantry Division*, both of which were holding the *35th Army's* northern flank while General Suzuki prepared for his counterattack. Lieutenant General Tadasu Kataoka,[25] commanding the *1st Infantry Division*, was forced, due to losses, to consolidate units and redistribute his forces in order to hold his line against the attacking 32nd Infantry Division. His command had lost over 3,000 men killed or wounded, and one-third of the infantry weapons of his division were destroyed or inoperable. Grenades and ammunition were in short supply and his men were suffering from the effects of constant battle and living in jungle conditions. He was, after the loss of

Limon, out of communication with all other units except *35th Army Head-quarters* and even that connection was often lost. The division's *1st Division Transport Regiment* found it impossible to supply food or ammunition to the *1st* and *57th Infantry Regiments* or the *1st Artillery Regiment*.

General Kataoka decided to regroup his division along Highway 2, in the Limon-Pinamopoan area, which would block the continued American advance south. In order to strengthen this new position, he sent his *1st Reconnaissance Regiment*, a unit he formerly commanded, to attack the flank of the 32nd Infantry Division. The regiment set off to make the attack, but along the way were themselves attacked by a much larger American force and never arrived at their attack jump-off point. The Limon sector was assigned to the remnants of the *57th Infantry Regiment* while the *1st Infantry Regiment*, reinforced by elements of the *49th Infantry Regiment*, was to defend the area south of Limon. These positions were to be supported by the *1st Artillery Regiment*. The *1st Engineer Regiment* and other divisional support troops were issued infantry weapons and ordered to defend Highway 2.

These were the Japanese dispositions as General Gill's 32nd Infantry Division renewed its attack to clear Highway 2 of the Japanese. With his 127th and 128th Infantry Regiments attacking together, the "Red Arrow" division pushed off down Highway 2. They immediately ran into prepared enemy positions consisting of well-camouflaged foxholes, ten-foot-deep spider holes and connecting trenches. Like the other attacking American units in X Corps, they found themselves in a maze of deep ravines, steep hills and thick jungle. Constant rainfall only made the situation that much more difficult. Each enemy position required a costly attack to reduce it, and the Americans had to be on constant watch for a Japanese counterattack.

One such attack occurred on December 5th, when Company M, 126th Infantry Regiment, was preparing its defenses. A machine-gun crew consisting of Privates First Class William A. McWhorter, William D. Brooks and George O. Panzer were bringing up ammunition to their position when the Japanese attacked. Private First Class McWhorter, from Liberty, South Carolina, was a veteran of previous battles in New Guinea, including Aitape, Saidor and Morotai. The enemy attack was almost beaten off when a Japanese soldier threw something into the gun emplacement. Private Brooks later related, "Just as they quit, I saw an object come flying through the air and land inside our position. As I realized it was a block of TNT with a fuse attached, McWhorter rushed to it and picked it up. There was no time to do anything with it and he hugged it to his chest and bent over and turned away from us. As he did so it exploded. He had deliberately given his life for mine."[26] For saving the vital machine gun and its crew at the cost of his own life, Private First Class William A. McWhorter was awarded a posthumous Medal Of Honor.[27]

The 3rd Battalion, 127th Infantry also found rough going past Limon. It was assigned to seize Hill 400, which was a major position in the defenses of the *1st Infantry Division.* Automatic weapons, mortars, artillery and small-arms fire combined with difficult slopes on the hill's approach, and dense undergrowth made the mission very difficult. Supported by the heavy weapons of Company M, Companies K and L attacked. For the next eight days a vicious battle raged, alternating between American attacks and Japan-ese counterattacks. At one point the battalion was forced to withdraw tem-porarily, but it soon returned and renewed the battle. Wounded men refused evacuation and fought on. Medical officers and aid men treated casualties in the front lines, both to save lives and because many wounded refused to leave the battle. Finally, on the eighth day the battalion made a charge across two hundred yards of ground that had been made barren by all the explosives it had absorbed, to reach the main Japanese positions where they engaged in hand-to-hand combat until the position was overrun. For its gallant efforts to seize Hill 400, the 3rd Battalion, 127th Infantry received a Presidential Unit Citation.[28]

By December 14th, the 32nd Infantry Division had cracked the Yama-shita Line completely and reached positions a mile south of Tolibaw. The advance was pushed by Colonel Raymond G. Stanton's 126th Infantry and Colonel Frederick R. Stofft's 127th Infantry Regiments. Every bend in the road was lined with foxholes dug into the banks of the road, and spider holes dug underneath the roots of trees and logs on the hillsides. It remained a bit-ter, close, hand-to-hand fight, and because of the steepness of the terrain and denseness of the tree growth, the inaccuracy of maps and the nearness of adjoining units, artillery and mortar fire could not be used to full advantage to reduce these positions. Once again, the individual rifleman had to go in at great personal risk and do the job.

One such infantryman was Sergeant Leroy Johnson of Company K, 126th Infantry. A squad leader who had already earned a Silver Star award in Papua, he led his nine men on a patrol near Limon to scout out Japanese defenses. The ridge, which was their objective, was held by a particularly effective, well-entrenched enemy machine gun. Sergeant Johnson spotted the gun's position and ordered his men to wait while he went forward. He managed to get within six yards of the gun when a Japanese soldier rushed to man it. Sergeant Johnson quietly withdrew and reported the situation to his commanding officer. Ordered to destroy the gun, Johnson took three other men and returned to the enemy position. Together the men knocked out the gun and began to assault the position when another enemy force attacked their flank hurling grenades. As they rushed for cover, Sergeant Johnson noticed that two enemy grenades had fallen among his men. Knowing that they would be killed or severely wounded while the Japanese continued their attack, he deliberately threw himself on the two grenades and absorbed the full blast with his own body. Fatally wounded by the blast, he died soon after. The Louisiana soldier was awarded a posthumous Medal of Honor.[29]

The battle still raged as the 32nd Infantry Division continued to press the *1st Infantry Division* back away from the Yamashita Line. Private First Class Dirk J. Vlug was another veteran of the division, having joined it in training at Camp Livingston, Louisiana. The twenty-nine-year-old soldier was now with the 126th Infantry at a roadblock along Highway 2. Technician 4th Grade James J. Madigan was with Private Vlug at the roadblock when enemy tanks suddenly attacked. As Madigan later recalled, "My battalion had set up a roadblock along the Ormoc Road to prevent the Japs from getting behind our lines. In the afternoon . . . we saw five Jap tanks coming down the road. The first tank was laying a smoke screen to conceal their movements. They started firing at us with heavy machine guns and 37mm cannons. All of us took cover except Private Vlug, who grabbed a rocket launcher and about six rounds of ammunition. I saw him move out toward the road by himself. The Japs in the lead tank started to direct heavy machine gun fire at him."[30]

Captain James K. Sullivan picks up the story. "With one accurately fired round, he knocked out the first tank, killing its occupants. The second one stopped. Nip soldiers came out to attack Vlug. Using his pistol, he instantly killed one of them and forced the rest to return to the tank. Before they could get it moving, he used his launcher to demolish the vehicle. Meanwhile three more Jap tanks were moving up the road. Sighting Vlug, they immediately opened fire with their machine guns. Maneuvering to one side, he succeeded in putting the third tank out of action with a shot from his launcher. Despite the hail of enemy bullets, he pressed the attack against the remaining two tanks, which were now at close range. He destroyed still another of these tanks with his bazooka. Using his last round of ammo, he hit the last tank as it was trying to move around the burning wreckage of the other tanks, putting it out of control and causing it to swerve off the road and fall down a steep embankment."[31] For his stalwart solitary defense of the roadblock position in the face of five enemy tanks, Private First Class Vlug was awarded a Medal of Honor.[32]

December 15th was a busy day for the 32nd Infantry Division beyond Limon. Company C, 127th Infantry Regiment was also on the Ormoc Road that day, blocking the supply and escape route of a large group of Japanese trapped within American lines. As they moved into the blocking position, a strong enemy force, including ten tanks, attacked. This attack was well supported by 75mm and 150mm artillery fire from the *1st Artillery Regiment*. The Company C men were subjected to point-blank fire from the enemy tanks, artillery and small arms. The numerically superior enemy force attacked fiercely, trying to open an escape route. Despite the odds against them, Company C held its ground and returned fire with accuracy and volume. After a fierce battle, the Japanese were completely routed, two of their 75mm guns knocked out, and one of the 150mm guns as well. Nine enemy tanks were completely destroyed and the other was known to be severely damaged. Once the enemy attack faltered, Company C went over to the attack and completed the rout by driving the Japanese off the field. Only stragglers from the enemy force survived. For its gallant conduct along Highway 2, the Ormoc Road, Company C, 127th Infantry Regiment, was awarded a Distinguished Unit Citation.

It was also on Friday, 15 December, 1944, that Staff Sergeant Leon Byrum of the 32nd Infantry Division distinguished himself. Stationed at the regimental command post, Byrum and the rest of the command were hit by a strong enemy artillery barrage, under the cover of which Japanese soldiers attempted to infiltrate the area. Sergeant Byrum killed one of the infiltrators and wounded a second, who tried to escape. Byrum, from Rockford, Illinois, went after the wounded enemy soldier only to find himself exposed to the fire of two enemy squads. Disregarding his own safety, Sergeant Byrum engaged the two enemy forces with his rifle and pinned both of them down, disorganizing the attack on the regimental command post. He then moved to prevent their escape from the area while continuing to fire. By this time, others of Sergeant Byrum's squad came to his assistance and together they eliminated seventeen of the attacking enemy soldiers. For his actions in saving the regimental command post and preventing enemy disruption of the ongoing attack, Staff Sergeant Byrum was awarded a Distinguished Service Cross.[33]

These types of battles continued until December 19th, when the 1st Squadron, 112th Cavalry relieved part of the 126th Infantry. That same evening, Company B, 126th Infantry rushed the last enemy position holding up the advance and overran it, finding over 200 enemy dead. The next day contact was made with the 1st Cavalry Division and, for the most part, the 32nd Infantry Division was done with the Leyte Campaign.

*   *   *

The *Fourteenth Area Army* had intended to land the *39th Infantry Regiment* and an artillery company from the *10th Infantry Division* near Carigara on December 16th, but with the American landing at Ormoc, this plan was cancelled. General Suzuki took about 100 men from the *102nd Infantry Division* and attached them to the *1st Infantry Division* to give it some strength. The *35th Army* commander was now so poor in resources that a mere 100 men was considered a valuable addition to his depleted units. But the Americans had, by now, seized both the northern and southern entrances to Ormoc Valley. Only the port of Palompon remained available to the Japanese. The *35th Army* was about to be trapped.

General Krueger was still pushing his commanders to close off Ormoc Valley. He wanted General Sibert's X Corps to seize Valencia on Highway 2 while the XXIV Corps' 77th Infantry Division moved north, also directed on Valencia. Once this area had been seized, the jaws of the trap he had designed would be closed, the Japanese trapped within Ormoc Valley. General Krueger had noted that the Japanese were moving supplies, men, ammunition and artillery to the Valencia area and concluded that this was where General Suzuki intended to make his last stand on Leyte.

The lack of opposition west of Highway 2, as the 77th Infantry Division made its way north, caused General Bruce to prepare a plan to take advantage of this opening. He recommended to General Hodge, at XXIV Corps, that he be allowed to put pressure on the enemy retreating up Highway 2 while he organized another attack coming from the west. General Hodge agreed with this plan and gave his permission to execute it, if circumstances permitted. So on December 16th, 1944, just as the German Winter Counteroffensive hit the Allied Armies in Western Europe, the 305th Infantry Regiment advanced from Cogon north along Highway 2. The 1st Battalion advanced on the left of the road and the 3rd Battalion on the right. The 2nd Battalion was kept in reserve.

Resistance was sporadic. By enveloping the enemy positions as they revealed themselves, the regiment continued to advance north and established positions north of Cogon. Meanwhile, the 307th Infantry started its part of the plan to envelop Valencia in a column of battalions led by the 2nd Battalion. Its route crossed rice paddies and waist-deep rivers, so all vehicles had to be left behind. All supplies, equipment and ammunition were hand-carried. Native carriers were organized to assist with this effort and the movement met only scattered resistance as it moved forward. As the column reached San Jose, two platoons of Japanese tried to defend the barrio but these were quickly eliminated. By 1600 Hours, San Jose was within the American defense perimeter. The regiment had covered eight difficult miles during the day. The 307th Infantry was now on the flank of Valencia and its airfield.

When the infantry had passed, the engineers came forward to bridge the rivers and make the path more manageable. One of these engineers was Captain James E. Carruth, a division engineer officer who had earlier fought in the front lines, and who now found that the infantry company he was to support was halted at the Antilao River by camouflaged enemy positions across that river. Seeing the numerous casualties caused by the enemy fire from spider holes and hidden gun emplacements, Captain Carruth called forward a bulldozer, climbed up into the exposed cab, and directed the driver to ford the river and overrun the enemy positions. Time after time, as the vehicle moved about, ripping the cover off hidden enemy positions, Captain Carruth leaned out of the cab and fired an automatic rifle into the exposed positions, killing the occupants. Despite the personal risk at his exposed position, he kept this up for some time. A Japanese officer and two men saw the danger presented by Captain Carruth and charged the bulldozer with an explosive charge. These men he killed with his automatic rifle. Then he calmly directed the destruction of more of the enemy defenses. Almost singlehandedly, Captain Carruth overran a strong enemy defensive position and allowed the infantry to advance with minimal casualties. For his valiant initiative in destroying such a strong enemy position, the Houston, Texas native received a Distinguished Service Cross.[34]

The 306th Infantry also moved forward behind the 307th Infantry. It later swung to the north and advanced, without difficulty, during the day. It was a hard march physically due to terrain conditions and the need to carry all supplies and equipment. Machine guns, mortars, mortar ammunition, hand-grenade cases, extra radio batteries, litters and blood plasma were all hand-carried, in addition to the infantrymen's normal combat load, plus three days rations. The regiment marched over five miles of rice paddies under a broiling tropical sun, on a rare day without clouds. Usually, the men walked ankle deep in soft earth or mud. Sometimes the mud, despite the warm day, was knee-deep. Occasionally, a soldier would sink up to his shoulders with all the heavy gear driving him deeper into the thick mud. It could take a squad of men to pull the trapped soldier out of the sucking mire. Despite all these difficulties, the regiment arrived at Cabulaban and dug in for the night.

With all three infantry regiments out in front, the division's artillery batteries had been assigned to support them as needed. They were also told that they would have to defend themselves should enemy attacks on their positions develop. Although some of these units had proven that they could defend themselves quite well, no enemy attacks developed at this stage of the march.

The next day, Sunday, December 17th, the artillery pounded Valencia, the road leading to it, and the airfield outside the town. General Bruce had two of his three infantry regiments out on a limb, flanking the enemy-held area with just the supplies they could carry. Only the 305th Infantry, attacking up Highway 2, had a supply line, and even this was susceptible to enemy attacks. If the 305th Infantry did not open the way to Valencia, the other two regiments would be left stranded well ahead of the main American position with limited supplies.

The 305th Infantry attacked up Highway 2 again on Sunday. Resistance continued to be spotty, usually small enemy groups holding an isolated position. But as they came up to the village of Tambuco, the march came to a halt. The approach was narrowed by swamps and marshes to either side, and the Japanese had dug in under the huts of the village with a strong point on either flank. Self-propelled guns were sent in, but made little dent in the enemy defenses. Once again, excellent Japanese camouflage meant that the Americans had to get as close as ten feet before they could identify the enemy positions. The commanders decided to try and blast the estimated 200 Japanese defenders out of Tambuco with all the artillery they could muster, while mortars fired white phosphorus to burn down the huts under which they had their main defenses. Following the self-propelled guns, the infantry then attacked, using grenades and automatic weapons fire to clear the Japanese from the village. The attackers cleared the village until they reached the north end where enemy resistance stiffened again.

The regiment was falling behind schedule. They had expected to reach the high ground north of Tambuco that night, but were not yet in sight of that objective. Every time Colonel Tanzola was asked about setting up night defenses, he replied, "Hell, we've only started this fight, just give me one more half hour."[35] Behind the infantry, the artillery battalions were waiting to move up and establish new supporting positions. Lt. Colonel Elbert P. Tuttle came up alone, and armed only with his pistol began searching for a new location for his 304th Field Artillery Battalion.[36] Despite sniper fire directed at him as he moved behind the infantry, he directed his batteries into their new firing positions. Some of these were within 100 yards of the firing line. The amphibian truck companies, manned by Negro drivers, also came under fire as they drove up with artillery ammunition for the newly established gun positions. Some men of the 304th Field Artillery were wounded as an enemy ammunition dump exploded within fifty yards of the battalion's new command post. In fact, some batteries were so close to the front line that they actually formed a part of it, all the while firing support missions for the attacking infantry.

The 306th Infantry attacked from the west and soon ran into opposition from Japanese paratroopers. These men had arrived by air, as previously described, and had been held in reserve by General Yamashita's orders until now. They were concealed in huts but had not dug positions, which made them easier to eliminate. A coordinated attack was launched with the 2nd Battalion leading. Intent on the attack from the front, the Japanese missed the rest of the battalion as it came in from the flank. Surprised, the Japanese were soon overrun. Cabulaban was in American hands before dark.

During this fight, the 3rd Platoon, Company B, 306th Infantry, pushed hard against the enemy led by a squad under Sergeant Frederick J. Jezyk. The soldier from Wake, Massachusetts repeatedly exposed himself to enemy fire in order to locate the enemy and direct his squad's fire on them. He led the way across a wide, muddy ditch, tossing grenades to good effect. Once across, he led a group of his men into a new position when an enemy grenade fell among them. Shouting to his men to take cover, Sergeant Jezyk threw himself into a position between the missile and his men. His swift actions caused him severe wounds, but saved his squad from injury. Undeterred by his serious wounds, Sergeant Jezyk then calmly directed his squad in a withdrawal and was the last man to leave the advanced position, carried by his two scouts. For risking almost certain death to save his men, Sergeant Jezyk received a Distinguished Service Cross.[37]

That night a supposed Japanese tank attacked down Highway 2 and, despite a hit by a rocket, went right through the defenses of Lieutenant

Colonel Kimbrell's 2nd Battalion. Colonel Kimbrell ordered his men to make sure the tank did not get away again when it returned and, when it did, the men of Company L smothered the vehicle with rockets, machine guns and ten automatic rifles. The vehicle burst into flames and exploded with a deafening roar. Daylight revealed that this was not a tank, but an enemy truck loaded with soldiers, all of whom were killed in the fight.

It was during these battles that Private First Class Fred M. Ghents of Company G, 306th Infantry, fell to enemy fire. Earlier, near Ipil, he had been with Company G when they had attacked a high enemy-held ridge. An automatic rifleman, Private Ghents moved forward alone, despite heavy enemy fire directed at him, to reach a point near one of the enemy positions. He suddenly jumped up and began firing in short bursts and charged that position, killing eleven Japanese occupants. His squad attempted to follow, but were pinned down by two enemy machine guns. Without hesitation, Private Ghents ordered two men to accompany him and, under the cover of their fire, he advanced alone against the enemy machine guns, killing the crews. His courageous one-man assault so dispirited the defenders that they abandoned their remaining defenses and, leaving behind twenty-five dead, withdrew. For these actions, Private First Class Ghents would receive a posthumous Distinguished Service Cross.[38]

General Bruce became increasingly concerned about his wounded. Not only did they need better medical care than they could get at the front, they required four men to carry them and another four to guard them, since the Japanese refused to respect the Red Cross insignia. Together with Lieutenant Colonel Charles L. Davis, the division's operations officer, General Bruce developed a plan to speed up the advance. A massive artillery bombardment from all available division and corps artillery battalions was placed on Valencia and its approaches. The barrage continued all morning and ceased only after noon. The 307th Infantry attacked two hours later against stiff resistance by Japanese paratroopers, who appeared in good physical condition and who were well equipped. Nonetheless, by dusk, the regiment was on the edge of the airstrip and within a thousand yards of Valencia.

Meanwhile, the artillery liaison planes had responded to General Bruce's concerns about his wounded. They flew to makeshift landing sites within the 306th and 307th Infantry Regimental zones and airlifted the more seriously wounded back to division hospitals. Back at division headquarters, an artillery barrage unexpectedly struck the headquarters area. These enemy guns were located around Dayhagan. They were quickly silenced after artillery observers spotted them, but not before General Bruce's personal latrine was demolished.

Monday, December 18th, saw the renewal of the attack by the 305th Infantry. Resistance was light and by mid-afternoon, the regiment had seized Dayhagan. That same morning the 307th Infantry renewed its own attack on Valencia and its airstrip. Again, the Japanese paratroopers fought stoutly, but were pushed back. By mid-morning, the town and the airfield were captured and some 369 enemy dead counted. Several enemy tanks were discovered, destroyed by the massive artillery preparation fired the day before. Colonel Smith's 306th Infantry also moved forward, noting that after a day and a half the enemy resistance seemed to "collapse," after which the regiment had a "field day" moving into Cabulahan. Over 1,000 enemy dead were counted in this area after the battle. Sixty sabers, indicating a high percentage of officers, were counted among the spoils. By dusk, physical contact had been made with the 307th Infantry and the leading elements of the 305th Infantry. The 77th Infantry Division had seized Valencia.

Immediately armored columns, which had been waiting for this moment, began to move forward escorting supply vehicles past bypassed enemy pockets to the advanced infantry. The remaining wounded were evacuated by the same method. General Bruce reported his success to General Hodge and requested permission to continue with his advance until he could make physical contact with X Corps.

*　　*　　*

Meanwhile, the purpose for which Leyte was being seized was still foremost in General MacArthur's mind. As a result, he continued to direct efforts to neutralize Japanese defenses on other Philippine islands, most especially Luzon, his next major objective. As a result of this, much of the Army Air Force effort was redirected at Luzon and its supporting bases. Late in December, Major Thomas B. McGuire was once again in the air. His competitor, Major Bong, had been returned to the United States for the award of his Medal of Honor, giving Major McGuire a chance to catch up to his rival for top ace of the Pacific Theater. He, too, had earned many awards for gallantry and a Purple Heart for wounds received when he was shot down the year before.

On December 25th, he led a squadron of fifteen P-38 fighter planes over Luzon to escort American bombers which were to neutralize Mabalacat Airdrome. As they approached for the attack, they were faced by about twenty enemy fighter aircraft. Immediately, Major McGuire led the 475th Fighter Squadron into battle, shooting down one fighter with a deflection shot during the opening round of the fight. Then his wingman was hit and had to withdraw from the battle. More enemy fighter aircraft appeared. Enemy antiaircraft fire filled the skies. The B-24 bombers began their run over the airfield, under attack by Japanese fighters. Some enemy planes dropped phosphorous bombs in the midst of the American bomber formation, hoping to set some afire. Another American fighter pilot reported himself on fire and abandoned the fight.

More Japanese fighters appeared and went in after the bombers. There were now well over fifty enemy fighters opposing Major McQuire's reduced protective force. Nevertheless, the twenty-four-year-old pilot remained in the fight, taking on several Japanese fighters. Then his guns stopped firing. His rapid maneuvers had damaged the feeding mechanism of his guns, leaving him defenseless in the enemy-filled skies. Undeterred, the young pilot began making "dry" runs against enemy fighters, diverting them from attacking the bombers. Four times he did this, each time forcing an attacking Japanese fighter plane to abort its run on an American bomber. Somehow, Major McQuire survived the battle, and after fifty interminable minutes, the fight was over.

The next day, Major McQuire was once again in the air over Luzon. He shot down another four enemy planes now that his guns were repaired, making his total thirty eight "kills." He had only two more to go to catch up to his rival, Major Bong. There seemed a good chance that McQuire would even the score, since Bong was no longer in combat. For his heroic efforts to save the bombers when his guns were inoperative, and his constant heroism in leading his squadron in attacks against the Japanese, Major McQuire would be awarded the Medal of Honor.[39]

On January 7th, 1945, Major McGuire again led a strike against the Japanese. While flying over Negros Island, he spotted an "Oscar"[40] attacking one of his men, Major Jack Rittmayer. McGuire engaged the enemy plane but, anxious to improve his score, made dangerous maneuvers to engage the enemy. As he made a pass on the Japanese fighter, his plane stalled. Too low to bail out and with no room left to maneuver, Major McGuire crashed into the trees, his plane exploding on contact. Major Rittmayer was also shot down, probably by a second enemy plane.

The loss of the second highest scoring Ace in the FEAF did not discourage the American flyers. The young pilots continued to fly and fight whenever the opportunity arose. For some, the rise to glory came unexpectedly. One such individual was Captain William A. Shomo. The twenty-six-year-old had been flying in the Southwest Pacific for eighteen months when he was promoted to command the 82nd Tactical Reconnaissance Squadron, 21st Observation Group, Fifth Army Air Force. He had flown in New Guinea and again during the battle for Biak. His job was to fly over enemy areas and photograph defenses, terrain and any other details which might be useful to invading Allied forces. His was not a direct combat role, albeit just as dangerous.

Shortly after his promotion to command the 82nd Tactical Reconnaissance Squadron, the unit was given new and better equipment. They were issued North American F-6Ds which were photo-reconnaissance versions of the P-51D Mustangs heavily used as fighters in Europe. After a brief time to get used to the new planes, Captain Shomo took up a flight over the Philippines on January 9th, 1945. The following day he was again over Luzon and shot down his first plane in fourteen months. Up again the next day, January 11th, he and his wingman were over Tuguegarao Airdrome and flying just above the treetops when they spotted several enemy aircraft above them. Without any idea how many enemy aircraft were opposed to him, Captain Shomo turned his and his wingman's plane into the enemy formation. They quickly identified a dozen enemy fighter planes, Kawasaki KI-61 "Tony" fighter aircraft.[41] Despite odds of thirteen to one against them, Captain Shomo didn't hesitate, but went immediately for the leading enemy aircraft.

With his opening burst, Captain Shomo flamed an enemy plane. He moved to one side and flamed another "Tony" with another burst from his guns. The Japanese formation exploded in confusion. Nearby, Captain Shomo's wingman, 1st Lieutenant Paul Lipscomb, shot down a third enemy plane. Captain Shomo kept up the pressure, moving in for more kills. Next, he went after a bomber, which the enemy fighters had been escorting. Flying underneath the Japanese, he sent a burst of fire into the plane's belly, setting it afire. The plane hurtled into the ground. As he pulled out of this fight, another enemy fighter approached head on. He hit this plane and then dived on another group of Japanese flying just below him. After dropping the leader of this group out of the sky, Captain Shomo chased after a "Tony" who was fleeing the battle, and shot him down as well. Turning to look behind him, Captain Shomo saw more enemy planes coming to the fight. Calling for Lieutenant Lipscomb, who claimed another three enemy planes shot down, the two men headed for home.

Once back on Leyte, Captain Shomo and Lieutenant Lipscomb were debriefed. The fight was duly recorded and the two men, who were not supposed to fight but to take pictures, were credited with several planes each. Captain Shomo, credited personally with seven enemy planes in one morning over Luzon, was promoted to Major and awarded the Medal of Honor.[42] Unlike his two compatriots who won the medal by fighting in the Philippine skies only to be killed before the end of the war, Major Shomo survived the war and retired, as a Lieutenant Colonel, to his home in Pennsylvania.

CHAPTER 9

THE JAPANESE RETREAT

When the 77th Infantry Division's three regiments converged on Valencia, the last exit from the Ormoc Valley was denied to the Japanese. General Yamashita had planned to reinforce the *35th Army* with the *Takahashi Detachment*, which included the *5th Infantry Regiment*, an artillery battalion, an engineer company and a transport company from the *8th Infantry Division*, along with another *Special Naval Landing Force*. They were to move from Luzon to Ormoc. Now, they had to be moved to Palompon instead. The last major reinforcement had been the *77th Infantry Regiment*, which landed at Palompon about December 9th. Coming from Cebu, it had assembled on Leyte and moved to Huaton, the latest headquarters of the *35th Army*. Hauton was a small barrio on Highway 2, some three and a half miles north of Cogon.

General Suzuki arrived there on December 13th, after his long and difficult trip from Burauen, where his long-cherished counterattack had failed to disrupt the American offensive. But still undeterred, the aggressive Japanese commander planned another attack, this time against the Americans at Ormoc. Assembling the remnants of the *12th Independent Infantry Regiment*, *4th Airborne Raiding Regiment, Mitsui Shipping Unit, Ito Naval Landing Force*, and the newly arrived *77th Infantry Regiment*, he planned to use them to attack, on December 17th, the advancing 77th Infantry Division.

As had happened often before in General Suzuki's Leyte Campaign, events moved faster than his planning. The loss of Cogon and the envelopment of his force from the west forced another change in plans. The 305th

Infantry had overrun a battalion of the *12th Independent Infantry Regiment* and also badly hurt portions of the newly arrived *77th Infantry Regiment*, all before any counterattack could be staged. Realizing that his force was now too weak to successfully counterattack the Americans, he ordered these two infantry regiments to fight a delaying action. But once again the Americans moved faster than the Japanese. Valencia fell to the 77th Infantry Division, which had begun its attack on December 17th, the same day that General Suzuki had expected to launch his own attack.

It appears that Colonel Imahori, of the *12th Independent Infantry Regiment*, failed to receive General Suzuki's change in orders, for he attempted to reach Ormoc on the same day that the Americans launched their attack. He was unsuccessful, and American records fail to record any major enemy attack that date. It was probably artillery supporting Colonel Imahori's "attack" that destroyed General Bruce's latrine.

Meanwhile, General Krueger was also altering his plans. Seeing that the XXIV Corps was making better progress in Ormoc Valley than was X Corps, he ordered, on December 19th, an enlargement of the XXIV Corps zone. This increase placed the barrio of Libongao, just below the juncture of Highway 2 with the road to Palompon, within the XXIV Corps' zone. Accordingly, General Hodge ordered General Bruce to continue north and secure the Palompon road before making contact with X Corps approaching from the north.

Leaving the 305th Infantry to hold Valencia, General Bruce sent the 306th and 307th Infantry Regiments up Highway 2 once again. The 307th was to move along the road to Libongao and then to the junction with the Palompon Road. The 306th Infantry was to move across difficult country and reach the same road to the northwest. The regiments would therefore be making parallel attacks but would be separated by about 2,300 yards of jungle and hills. Once the latter regiment had reached the road near the Togbong River, it would move both west and east, meeting with the 307th Infantry while expanding the advance toward the last Japanese port.

It so happened that General Suzuki and his headquarters were now located at Libongao. Here he had his headquarters guard and a part of the *4th Airborne Raiding Regiment*. A field artillery battalion, an engineering company and a transportation company were also in the immediate area. From Palompon, a battalion of the *77th Infantry Regiment* was still en route along the road. This last unit General Suzuki directed on Valencia, with orders to destroy the Americans there. They were to run head-on into the advancing "Old Bastards."

*   *   *

It quickly became clear to the 307th Infantry when they moved north of Valencia on Tuesday, December 19th, with the campaign now entering its third month, that the Japanese were still fighting. The infantrymen found themselves facing a strong defense force along the highway armed with light artillery, machine guns and mortars. Positions on the ridges flanking the road, held in force by the battalion of the *77th Infantry Regiment*, had clear fields of fire against any approaching force along the road. Japanese light artillery had direct fire views as well. Despite this, the Americans attacked with grenades and supporting arms, and by dark had pushed their way up the road for three miles, reaching Libungao. Here the 2nd Battalion, 307th Infantry came up against a strong enemy position on the high ground north of the Naghalan River. Once again mortars and machine guns blocked the way. Supporting weapons, including artillery, failed to clear these Japanese soldiers off the commanding terrain. Although over two hundred Japanese dead had been counted during the day, there were obviously many more blocking the road ahead. With darkness approaching, the regiment went into night defensive positions.

Behind the advancing infantry, the 302nd Engineer Combat Battalion struggled to make the road passable for heavy equipment, especially the artillery. Two battalions had been ordered to advance to Valencia, but the roads had prevented this until after the engineers could improve it and repair the many broken and downed bridges along the route. The engineers worked day and night, risking enemy snipers while working under lights at night. Once the bridges were fixed they became the responsibility of the attached Filipino guerrillas, who guarded them against enemy sabotage.

General Bruce was anxious for a rapid advance to cross the Tagbong River. To ensure a fast passage, he organized another armored column, consisting of the 1st Battalion, 305th Infantry, self-propelled guns from the 305th and 306th Infantry Regiments, Battery A, 305th Field Artillery, a platoon of the 302nd Engineer Combat Battalion and detachments from the 306th Field Artillery. In support was a detachment from the 718th Amphibious Tank Battalion, with fifty tracked landing vehicles, and another detachment from the 302nd Medical Battalion, with ambulances. Armored cars and a platoon of light tanks completed the force.

Learning from guerrillas that the road and bridges between the road junction and the port of Palompon were in workable condition, the guerrillas also promised General Bruce that they could obtain enough local labor to pave the road with coconut logs should any weak spots be found along the way.

The 306th Infantry was 800 yards from the Tagbong River, at the intersection of the Palompon Road and Highway 2, when they renewed their attack on December 20th. A battalion was assigned to each objective, while the 2nd Battalion remained in reserve. First to attack was the 1st Battalion across the Tagbong River. Fierce enemy opposition from the other bank stopped Company A, after it lost a squad of men. Company C crossed the river but was soon after pinned down. Company B, meanwhile, cleared out the village and held the near side of the bridge across the river. By mid-afternoon, a stalemate had ensued and Company C was withdrawn back across the river.

Nearby, the 3rd Battalion attacked to the east to gain the road junction. Slow and costly progress was made, and by mid-afternoon Company K had reached the objective. Enemy and friendly fire forced a short withdrawal and, soon after, on division's order, the entire battalion was pulled back some 300 yards. That allowed enough space for the 307th Infantry to fire all of its weapons unrestricted against the flanks of the Japanese defenders. The day ended with the 1st Battalion on the Palompon Road and the rest of the regiment within 300 yards of the road junction.

Simultaneously the 307th Infantry attacked, with the 2nd Battalion leading. They, too, hit strong enemy defenses manned by soldiers of the *77th Infantry Regiment*, new to Leyte. Elements of both the *1st Infantry Division* and the *5th Infantry Regiment* of the *8th Infantry Division* were identified. Clearly General Suzuki was throwing everything he had into the defense of Palompon, his last port of entry into, and out of, Leyte. The Americans believed that they faced 2,000 Japanese troops, most of them new to Leyte and well equipped, healthy and well fed. These men launched two counterattacks during the day, with some 200 men in each. They hit Companies E and G, supported by mortars and machine guns. Both attacks were repulsed with all the attackers killed. Other, smaller, counterattacks hit other units, but all were defeated. As the Americans pushed painfully forward, some thirty enemy trucks were captured. Several of these were immediately put to use by the Americans who used them to evacuate wounded and bring up arms and ammunition. The 307th Infantry pushed forward all day, advancing some 2,000 yards and claiming 1,497 enemy troops killed. The regiment ended the day within 1,000 yards of the road junction.

During the day General Bruce kept his armored column at Valencia awaiting an opportunity to advance forward. The 305th Infantry also remained protecting Valencia. Concerned that the drive was losing momentum, General Bruce ordered a full pursuit for December 21st, straight down the road, hoping to link up with the 1st Cavalry Division of X Corps to the north.

*   *   *

Shortly before dawn on December 21st, the men of 1st Battalion, 306th Infantry at the river began to hear sounds from the Japanese which made them suspect a counterattack was imminent. Sure enough, a mortar and artillery barrage hit the American positions, which killed two officers and four enlisted men. Seven others were wounded. After an hour the enemy fire was lifted and an estimated 500 enemy troops attacked. More than a score of them penetrated the perimeter but were killed before they could do much damage. Artillery fire broke up the attack shortly after. When daylight finally came, the battalion counted another 400 enemy dead in and around their position.

Soon after the attack was repulsed the battalion commander, Major Claude D. Barton, received orders to renew the attack. But the fierce dawn attack had depleted the battalion's ammunition supply. Only two boxes of ammunition for each machine gun remained, and there were only fifteen rounds of 60mm mortar ammunition left to the entire battalion. Major Barton requested permission to delay the attack until noon so that he could replenish his ammunition stock.

The battalion then attacked after a ten-minute artillery barrage. Company C again crossed the river as did Company B. The attached Company E was held up by enemy fire at the road. The next objective was to reach the Pagsangahan River. But as the new orders were being issued, Company B erroneously left its hilltop position across the river guarded only by a platoon. The Japanese saw the opening and counterattacked, driving the solitary platoon off the hill and back across the river. The new attack had to be postponed, and cost the battalion another day and a half of hard fighting to retake the high ground they had so briefly held. Major Barton sent Company A back across the river to take the ground.

One of Company A's radio operators was Private First Class George Benjamin, Jr., from Carney's Point, New Jersey. As Company A attacked up a hill strongly defended by the Japanese, he took his place at the rear of the company. A rifle platoon was assigned to protect a light tank assisting in the attack, but hesitated as the tank moved forward. With complete disregard for his own safety, Private Benjamin raced across the fire-swept ground to the tank, waving and shouting for the men of the rifle platoon to follow him. Still carrying his heavy, bulky radio on his back, and armed only with a pistol, he moved forward through heavy machine gun and rifle fire to the first enemy position, where he killed the crew of a light machine gun. He continued to lead the assault, despite the fact that the Japanese had now identified him as a leader of the attack and concentrated all their fire on him. He killed two more enemy soldiers and continued to yell encouragement to the men following him until he was mortally wounded. Even after being shot down and evacuated, he insisted on speaking to the battalion's executive officer, to brief him on the situation at the front line he had done so much to advance. For his outstanding gallantry and leadership, Private Benjamin was awarded a posthumous Medal of Honor.[1]

The 2nd and 3rd Battalions of the 306th Infantry attacked toward Libungao and captured the road junction later that same morning. The 307th Infantry also attacked and soon made contact with the 306th Infantry about 300 yards short of the road junction. For a while the situation was extremely complicated, especially for the supporting artillery. The 304th Field Artillery supported the 306th Infantry and the 902nd Field Artillery supported the 307th Infantry. These two regiments were attacking toward each other and great efforts were made to avoid any "friendly-fire" incidents. As if the situation weren't complicated enough, elements of the 1st Cavalry Division were also approaching the same area, making it that much more difficult. Nevertheless, there were no "friendly-fire" casualties during this operation, a credit to the professionalism of the artillery observers and gunners.

When the 3rd Battalion of the 306th turned to the north to make contact with the Cavalrymen, they hit a strong defense blocking the way. Three hundred yards north of the road junction, the Japanese had dug themselves into a ridge from which they swept the entire area with small arms and mortar fire. Soon after this position was identified, Brigadier General Edwin H. Randle,[2] the assistant division commander, ordered Colonel Hamilton to commit his 2nd Battalion to the east of Highway 2 and attack north to the right of, and in conjunction with, the 3rd Battalion, 306th Infantry. Both attacking battalions fought fiercely. Lt. Colonel Joseph B. Coolidge led the 2nd Battalion, 307th Infantry forward under modest cover from a series of ridges, but Major George T. Larkin's 3rd Battalion, 306th Infantry had no such protection and attacked across exposed rice paddies, suffering from enemy fire. Casualties were heavy and units depleted. Private Harold T. Bevis was the only surviving member of his machine gun squad and carried the machine gun, its ammunition, and tripod and also served as the entire crew of his gun during this attack. By noon little progress had been made by either battalion.

Undeterred, General Randle sent the 2nd Battalion, 306th Infantry on another flanking maneuver. This attack proved more successful and relieved some of the pressure on the other two attacking battalions. But the Japanese remained determined, for this was their last supply route on Leyte and led to their last port. The Americans, on the other hand, had to secure the cross-roads in order to bring up their own supplies and support while evacuating their wounded. The fighting remained savage throughout. Company B, 302nd Medical Battalion, was treating over one hundred wounded by this time, with no means of evacuating them to hospitals in the rear. Both sides needed the junction. Only one could have it.

A partially destroyed bridge was yet another obstacle to the American advance. This bridge was over a small stream thirty yards from the fighting. A group of men from the 302nd Engineer Combat Battalion worked in the open to repair this bridge in the anticipation that once the road was open it would be needed. Despite falling mortar shells and the occasional sniper, the engineers repaired the bridge. As they did so, the quarter-ton ambulances of Companies B and C, 302nd Medical Battalion, ran the gauntlet of fire to evacuate the wounded, some of whom had been hit two days earlier.

The repair of the bridge also allowed passage of the self-propelled guns and light tanks to the front lines. These guns joined with the attacking bat-talions and, by late afternoon, the enemy defenses were overrun. Once again, the Americans moved north against weakening resistance. The river was now the boundary between the 77th Infantry Division and the 1st Cavalry Divi-sion, so elements of the 307th Infantry, which had crossed the river, were pulled back to the south side. That afternoon, at 1630 Hours, the 3rd Bat-talion, 306th Infantry made contact with elements of the 1st Cavalry Divi-sion. X Corps and XXIV Corps had joined hands along the west coast of Leyte. The *35th Army* was trapped.

*   *   *

While the "Old Bastards" had been fighting their way up the west coast, the troopers of the 1st Cavalry Division had been fighting their way down that coast. While the detached 8th Cavalry Regiment cleared Japanese from nearby Samar, the rest of the division, reinforced with the 112th Cavalry Regimental Combat Team, worked its way west and then south along the coast from Carigara. On December 16th, the 1st Squadron, 112th Cavalry observed a large enemy pack train accompanied by over 100 enemy troops, on a high bluff west of the Leyte River. Too far away for carbines, the troopers took the enemy column under fire with rifles and machine guns. Artillery was also called down upon the Japanese soldiers and a later count showed 75 enemy dead on that bluff when the Americans reached it.

The 12th Cavalry Regiment was assembling at the barrio of Lonoy from which they were to launch a renewed attack on Highway 2 to the south. Supplies were provided by airdrop, and new observations positions established. From these OPs, the troopers brought down artillery fire on Japanese observed along the road or in huts, enemy gun positions, a motor park and camp fires. As the troopers moved down from Mt. Cabungaan, Sergeant Henry M. Lowery of Texas took immediate action when his light machine gun squad was pinned down by enemy fire. Two enemy machine guns had the squad in a vicious crossfire. Despite the considerable personal danger, Sergeant Lowery worked his way to the front of the guns and personally destroyed them, releasing his squad.[3] Behind the 12th Cavalry, the 5th Cavalry moved in and finished the mopping up job begun by their predecessors.

Working with the 126th Infantry of the 32nd Infantry Division, the 12th Cavalry pushed through slight enemy resistance and moved southwest to attack Lonoy. The 1st Squadron moved quickly against continuing light opposition and was soon within Lonoy, clearing Japanese snipers and stragglers from the barrio. The 2nd Squadron had a tougher time. Moving through thick tall grass and vegetation, the advance guard was hit by Japanese artillery and machine guns at point-blank range. A number of casualties resulted and the leader of the advance platoon, Technical Sergeant Floyd A. Weaver of Texas, organized his men and placed them in good positions to renew the attack. Led by Sergeant Weaver, the attack overran one of the enemy artillery pieces, only to be hit by fire from a second, previously undisclosed, enemy field gun. Four men were killed and the platoon attack halted. Weaver again organized and led an attack against this gun, which he destroyed. For his courage, Technical Sergeant Weaver was awarded a battlefield commission and a Silver Star.[4]

Behind the advance Troopers, the 1st Collecting Company, 1st Medical Squadron, was set up to treat the casualties resulting from this latest advance. Captain Henry W. Hodde, the company commander, was working on the patients when Japanese artillery began to land in the company's midst. While the others dove for the nearest cover, Captain Hodde remained exposed in the open, moving from casualty to casualty, moving them from the impact area and administering to their injuries. He, too, earned a Silver Star. Despite this sporadic Japanese resistance, the 12th Cavalry secured a line about 150 yards south of Lonoy by darkness.

The following day, December 20th, the 12th Cavalry again attacked, this time towards Cananga. Small groups of Japanese were barricaded in huts or dug in at tactically significant places along the road. But, for the first time in six weeks, the Cavalrymen were out of the mountains and able to maneuver. Using the American army's "fire and movement" techniques,[5] they quickly cleared the opposition, along with the supporting 271st Field Artillery Battalion. This is not to imply that the fighting was anything less than fierce. Private First Class Eugenio Castro led his surviving squad members in an attack across open ground against a hut filled with the enemy that was holding up the advance. Master Sergeant Wayne Locke was killed while directing his platoon from Troop F during an enemy counterattack. Sergeant Theodore J. Denman of New Jersey was pinned down but then crawled forward, under fire, to an enemy position which he destroyed with grenades. Sergeant Denman then led Troop B forward to wipe out the enemy defenders.[6]

To the north, the 7th and 112th Cavalry Regiments moved slowly alongside the 32nd Infantry Division. They remained in densely wooded vegetation, so the advance was necessarily slower. Every inch of ground was disputed by the Japanese, who now realized that they were trapped and had nowhere left to which to retreat. Leading scouts were especially vulnerable in these disputed advances, and when the lead scout of Troop B, 112th Cavalry fell in the open under enemy fire the platoon commander, 1st Lieutenant Warnock D. Harwell of Oklahoma crawled forward in full view of the Japanese. Under their fire the entire way, he managed to drag the wounded scout to safety. Lieutenant Harwell was awarded a Silver Star. In the 2nd Squadron, 7th Cavalry Private First Class Margarito G. Lopez of Texas won himself a Distinguished Service Cross[7] when, as a member of Troop E, his twelve-man patrol was ambushed by the Japanese. The Browning Automatic Rifle-man was seriously wounded. With complete disregard for his personal safety, Private Lopez crawled forward to the side of the wounded man, who lay fully exposed in the enemy's fire zone. He dragged the wounded man to safety and then took the BAR and ammunition, charging against the enemy position that had cut his scout down. His one-man attack killed thirteen of the enemy and captured their machine gun. His patrol was then able to move forward and complete its mission.

On December 21st, the 12th Cavalry launched a coordinated attack on Cananga. Colonel John H. Stadler, Jr., led his regiment in the attack, which was supported by the cavalrymen's own 271st Field Artillery and artillery firing from the 77th Infantry Division. Once inside the town, each and every hut had to be individually cleared of the enemy. While this miserable business continued, Colonel Stadler sent patrols south, where one of them soon contacted the 77th Infantry Division coming up from near the Tagbong River. Back in Lonoy, a patrol unexpectedly came upon an enemy tank, which gave them a few bad moments before they knocked it out and killed its crew.

Like the "Old Bastards," the Cavalrymen had not been able to bring their vehicles over the mountains with them, and so they, too, resorted to using captured Japanese trucks as their own supply vehicles. This provided some gallows humor in one instance when Troopers in a captured Japanese truck took a wrong turn and wound up in an enemy bivouac area. The Cavalrymen looked at the Japanese, who looked back. Neither side reacted violently; the truck quickly turned around and went back the way it had come. Only then did the two sides fire at each other, with unreported results.

In addition, the thick jungle made supply over the ground routes all but impossible, so airdrops were used extensively. The Cavalrymen were especially grateful to come down out of the mountains onto the western coastal plain, where at least they could see the sky and not have to trudge up and down constantly to move forward even to the slightest degree.

Further inland, the 32nd Infantry Division and the 7th and 112th Cavalry continued to push the enemy stragglers from the "Yamashita Line." By December 22nd this was believed to have succeeded, and most of the enemy's artillery and communications had been destroyed by this advance. Most of the enemy had broken contact with the advancing Americans, except in front of the 1st Cavalry and 77th Infantry Divisions around Bagatoon. North of Lonoy an enemy convoy, including two more tanks, was destroyed as they attempted to move along Highway 2, not having been told that it now belonged to the U.S. Sixth Army.

The fighting around Lonoy did not suddenly stop, as Japanese units repeatedly moved into the area on their way to someplace else. In one such instance a platoon was ambushed by the Japanese. Commanded by Technical Sergeant Benton W. Cogswell, the platoon was immediately pinned down by the enemy fire. Sergeant Cogswell quickly realized that his platoon would be destroyed if the ambush wasn't immediately broken up. Grabbing a light machine gun he advanced, firing from the hip. His gallant actions inspired his platoon to join him in knocking out the enemy ambush positions. For his leadership, Technical Sergeant Cogswell was given a battlefield commission.

*   *   *

While the Cavalry and 32nd Infantry continued to clear the mountains and the "Yamashita Line," the 302nd and 232nd Engineer Combat Battalions continued their own war with the many broken bridges along Highway 2, behind the 77th Infantry Division. The men worked day and night, reinforcing the small bridges to allow them to carry the heavier weapons used by the American army. As each bridge was completed, they could handle the two-and-a-half-ton trucks, the self-propelled weapons and tanks. The engineers also worked on the airfield at Valencia, making it possible for army transport planes to land and provide supplies while evacuating wounded.

On December 23rd, guerrillas reported that there was a large group of the enemy, possibly a battalion, at Matagob (also known as Dipi). The 305th Infantry was moving in that direction and so they called for an air strike which started fires, blew up ammunition dumps and caused considerable other damage. Without its 1st Battalion, the 305th Infantry continued its attack and found the enemy positions at Matagob abandoned. Meanwhile, General Bruce had another one of his "end run" tricks up his sleeve, and the regiment's 1st Battalion was withdrawn and sent back to Ormoc for its next assignment.

Despite the fact that it was Christmas Eve, the 305th continued its attack that day. About 200 enemy troops counterattacked their positions around Matagob, but were beaten off. One hundred enemy dead were left behind against not a single casualty for the American infantry. The regiment moved forward as scheduled but progress was slowed by terrain. Small groups of Japanese armed with 70mm artillery guns blocked the advance, but were soon overrun. The artillery was knocked out by counter-fire from Company A, 88th Chemical Weapons Battalion, attached to the division. Attempts to move field artillery to Matagob were frustrated by the continuing problems with the bridges over Highway 2. One 90-foot bridge even collapsed under the weight of an artillery prime mover. A 155mm howitzer and several other pieces of equipment were dropped into the 24-foot-deep river.[8]

General Bruce was now trying to implement his latest scheme, which was designed to close the Palompon Road at its other, seaward, end. To accomplish this, he designated the 1st Battalion, 305th Infantry to make another amphibious landing,[9] the campaign's seventh amphibious assault in barely two months. The Sixth Army was preparing a four-division assault to finish off General Suzuki's *35th Army*, with the 1st Cavalry coming down from the north, flanked by the 32nd and 24th Infantry Divisions, while the 77th Infantry Division held the southern line. Sixth Army had begun the campaign with two corps of two divisions and was ending it the same way. But General Bruce didn't want to push the Japanese off Leyte, he wanted to trap them on the island. In order to accomplish that, he had to close their last escape route, the port of Palompon. He knew he could not keep pace with the retreating Japanese due to the poor road conditions and, most of all, the poor bridges along that road. He had to get ahead of them, and with the 77th Infantry Division's skill in amphibious landings, he believed that one more small landing would close the Japanese off from any escape or reinforcement.

To that end, he prepared another task force centered around the 1st Battalion, 305th Infantry. The Special Task Force would also include the Amphibian Tractor Company; Company A, 776th Amphibian Tank Battalion; a platoon of Company D, 706th Tank Battalion; three guns from the Regimental Cannon Company; 2nd Platoon, Company A, 302nd Engineer Battalion; a detachment from Company A, 302nd Medical Battalion; the 292nd JASCO;[10] the 305th Field Artillery Battalion; and several smaller units.[11] The task force commander was Lt. Colonel James E. Landrum.

General Bruce had made a recommendation to General Krueger through General Hodge that he be allowed to organize and execute this plan. General Krueger then met with Admiral Kinkaid to discuss the possibility of naval support for this venture. He particularly wanted, at least, a destroyer escort for the many small craft that would carry the assault troops from Ormoc Bay to Palompon. This was reasonable considering the recent Japanese naval and air activity in the area. Admiral Kinkaid, whose resources were hard pressed in executing other landings in the Philippines and who was then in preparation for the major landings on Luzon, scheduled for less than a month away, said that the best he could do was provide a PT Boat escort which he believed would be adequate for the mission. General Krueger agreed and authorized General Hodge to have General Bruce execute his plan.

This he did on Friday, December 22nd. While the 2nd and 3rd Battalions, 305th Infantry, fought their way down the Palompon Road from Valencia, the 1st Battalion would make an amphibious landing at the port of

Palompon itself, thus closing the last Japanese port on Leyte. On December 23rd, the 1st Battalion loaded aboard amphibian tractors and landing craft of the 718th and 536th Amphibian Tractor Battalions at Ormoc. Protected by the promised PT Boats and close air support, the convoy sailed unmolested from Ormoc Bay, except for three tractors which sank during the voyage due to mechanical difficulties. They arrived at 0500 Hours on Monday, Christmas morning.[12] Before their arrival, the Fifth Army Air Force had bombarded the port town, and the 77th Infantry Division's artillery had done the same. In addition, mortar-firing landing craft of the 2nd Engineer Special Brigade had accompanied the landing forces and they launched their shells prior to the first infantry landing. The long-distance guns of the 531st Field Artillery Battalion, firing from San Jose, also contributed to the pre-invasion bombardment. By the time the first infantryman landed, the port town was unrecognizable as a habitat.

While the 2nd and 3rd Battalions, 305th Infantry, attacked to the west along the Palompon Road against stubborn resistance, the 1st Battalion came ashore "standing up," as was the expression of the period. No enemy fire was encountered. Meanwhile, General Bruce could barely contain himself with excitement and soon was flying in a liaison plane low over the newly established beachhead, cheering his troops forward. As he watched, a planned armored column struck off up the Palompon Road while the rest of the Task Force cleared the village of Look, where they had landed, and moved quickly on to Palompon, which they captured by noon. The last enemy port on Leyte was now in American hands.

But the fighting on Leyte continued. Back along the road, the two assault battalions of the 305th Infantry faced strong enemy defenses consisting of small-arms, mortar and artillery fire from positions dug into the hills to their northwest. When the 2nd Battalion tried to outflank these, they were unsuccessful and had to withdraw. Attacks against the Japanese went on throughout the day, and additional artillery fire was brought on the enemy. Despite this, additional enemy artillery guns revealed themselves as the Americans continued their attack. One 75mm gun was in a draw about 1,000 yards from Matagob, and with its first round barely missed the regimental command post located in a nearby school house. Fortunately, the second round also missed, but was seen by an artillery observer, who brought down artillery fire on it before the Japanese could get off a third round.

The seizure of Palompon was the occasion for General MacArthur to announce that organized resistance on Leyte had been destroyed. All that remained to be done was mopping up scattered enemy pockets. This announcement did little for the infantrymen, paratroopers and cavalrymen fighting in the coastal plains, jungles and mountains of Leyte, but for the 77th Infantry Division their morale was lifted, at least a little, by General Bruce's insistence that as many of his men as physically possible receive a turkey dinner for the holiday.

*　　*　　*

Despite General MacArthur's announcement, General Suzuki and the remaining men of his *35th Army* did not believe that they were yet merely remnants to be mopped up. The Japanese had covered the area around Matagob with foxholes and emplacements protected with many spider holes designed to stop any American attack down the Palompon Road. To the south, they had fortified caves, gullies and ridges on both sides of the road, and also dug in deeply. Some of these positions were later found to be as deep as eight feet, but barely two-feet wide at the top, to protect the occupants from return fire. Machine guns were protected by coconut log bunkers which usually required a tank or self-propelled gun to knock out. All of these positions were invisible to the advancing Americans until they either stumbled physically over them or were fired upon by them. The Japanese also had excellent observation from the ridges alongside and above the road from which to bring down their fire on the advancing Americans.

The Japanese manning these defenses were from the *5th Infantry Regiment*, along with elements of other Japanese units which had retreated into the area. These included batteries from the *8th Field Artillery Regiment*, the *8th Division Signal Unit*, the *8th Transport Regiment* and the *8th Engineer Regiment*. There was an estimated 2,000 to 3,000 Japanese troops defending the road, although many more were no doubt separated from their units and straggling in the hills.

This resistance and the poor terrain, which prevented close support from the American tanks and self-propelled guns, made the advance down the Palompon Road slow. Because the Japanese positions commanded the road, they could not be bypassed and instead had to be knocked out one after the other. The infantry was supported by artillery and the heavy mortars of the 88th Chemical Mortar Battalion, which were capable of knocking out some, but not all, of these enemy positions once the infantry had identified them. Each night, small enemy counterattacks invariably hit the leading battalion, but were always beaten off.

On Christmas Day, the advance took the day off. Except for the ever-present patrols, no American advance was planned to allow the troops a day of rest and to give them time to enjoy the holiday as much as they could under the circumstances. General Bruce ordered artillery salutes fired into the Japanese lines and permitted bonfires and gatherings for singing songs. In part, these were to improve the soldiers' morale and also to lure unwary Japanese into American lines thinking they were unprepared for a counter-attack. Depending one's your point of view, these ruses were largely unsuccessful.

There was some good news, however. That day a flight of friendly air-craft, which had left from the island of Mindanao, arrived over the 77th Infantry Division short on gas and unable to cross the mountains to Tacloban. Picked up by the 6th Support Aircraft Party at the Division Command Post, they were guided in to the field at Valencia. Lined with jeeps with their head-lights on to form a runway, the emergency field hosted five fighter planes and a medium bomber,[13] all of whose crews were happy that the infantry had secured Valencia before their emergency occurred.

The following day, the 3rd Battalion, 305th Infantry outflanked the Japanese on the left, and after killing 160 enemy soldiers, drove the others off into the hills. Meanwhile General Bruce, impatient with the delay imposed on his advance to Palompon by the strong Japanese resistance, decided to send the 2nd Battalion, 305th Infantry over water to Palompon. That battalion would then attack east along the road while its sister 3rd Battalion continued the attack west. The 1st Battalion would remain securing the Palompon area.

Once again, conferences with Sixth Army Headquarters and the Seventh Fleet resulted in passage of one of General Bruce's infantry battalions to the former enemy port. Arriving on Thursday, December 28th, the 2nd Battalion landed without incident. The following day, the 3rd Battalion launched a new attack to the west but were quickly pinned down for the entire day by heavy Japanese resistance. On the coast, the 2nd Battalion,[14] now labeled the Provisional Mountain Force, moved out of Palompon and took up a position along the road from which it could launch its attack to the east. The Japanese defenders of the Palompon Road were now under attack from front and rear.

By this time the 302nd Combat Engineer Battalion had repaired all of the bridges up to the front lines, allowing supporting forces to join in the battle. The fight continued to be fierce, however. In one instance, the 305th Cannon Company's M-8 self-propelled guns were moving in support of an attack when the lieutenant leading the assault element was hit in the face. He left orders for a continued attack and then went to the rear for medical treatment. A few moments later the Regimental Operations Officer, a Major, jumped up on the lead tank to take over. He lasted a few minutes until he, too, was wounded in the head by an enemy sniper. Finally, another lieutenant came forward and took over, leading the attack forward.

The 77th Reconnaissance Troop had more of a humanitarian mission than usual this day. Reports that there were 3,500 natives who reportedly were being held at Hot Springs resulted in their assignment to bring these people back into friendly lines. Two platoons set off on a march during which they encountered several small groups of the enemy. The artillery observers with the patrol brought down fire on these groups, killing them or driving them off. An estimated twenty-six enemy were killed and the natives were successfully rescued and brought back to Valencia.

On December 30th, both battalions attacked again. The Provisional Mountain Force met scattered resistance until mid-morning, when they came up against well-entrenched enemy troops about four miles east of the port. Strong enemy machine-gun fire stopped the advance for the day. To the east, the 3rd Battalion succeeded in knocking out the enemy position that had stopped it the day before and moved to within 1,000 yards of the barrio of Tipolo. Artillery fire had been placed to fire directly upon the advancing Americans, and one tank had been knocked out by this fire when it rounded a bend in the road to face six enemy field guns, but three of the enemy 75mm guns had been destroyed and two others captured in turn. Back at Palompon, Company C made yet another amphibious landing and conducted a reconnaissance-in-force near Abijao to the north. Japanese mortar fire and small-arms fire opposed the landing, but the town was seized and burned to prevent its use by any returning Japanese. Company C also succeeded in making radio contact with units of the 1st Cavalry Division who were near Villaba.

The next morning, the Americans renewed their attack, only to find that the Japanese had retreated. Opposed only by scattered rifle fire, the two attacking 305th Infantry battalions joined hands along the Palompon Road soon after noon on December 31st, 1944. All organized resistance in and around Palompon had ended, and Highway 2 was now secure for American use from the Ormoc Valley to Palompon. The 77th Infantry Division later estimated that it had killed 5,779 Japanese troops and taken another 29 prisoners in return for 17 Americans killed, 116 wounded and 6 missing in action.

New Year's Day, 1945 saw the tired but successful 305th Infantry bivouacked at Look while the usual patrols scoured the area for Japanese. An emergency supply of ammunition was transported over water to the 1st Cavalry Division at Villaba where, after a heavy firefight, they were in need. Units of the 306th Infantry began to move towards Calubian with orders to relieve elements of the X Corps, slated for the Luzon Invasion, which was only weeks away. Indeed, the remaining days on Leyte for the "Old Bastards" were ones of patrolling, killing small groups of Japanese, and water movements to new patrol areas. But the Japanese were still dangerous, as when on January 12th a group of them attacked the Villaba defenses with satchel and pole charges. The 305th Infantry and their supporting amphibian tractor crews put an end to that attempt quickly. Truck columns continued to be ambushed, and food and weapons stolen from the vehicles. Often the Japanese executed the classic ambush, using the fragile bridges along Highway 2. They would allow the head of a convoy to go over a bridge before they blew it up, trapping the rear of the convoy in their fire zones. Then the bridge at the rear of the convoy was also blown up, preventing it from withdrawing from the ambush. Grenades were thrown into the trucks and machine guns fired at them. Although rarely were the entire convoys destroyed, damage was sometimes severe, as were casualties. American arms began to find their way into Japanese hands in the jungles of Leyte. As late as January 22nd, reports from natives reported large organized groups of Japanese roaming northern Leyte. These men were armed, and although without food, usually stole the natives' food before moving on. Radio intercept stations still reported Japanese headquarters' radios operational on Leyte as late as the end of January.[15] Artillery fire was placed on these whenever discovered, with unobserved results.

On February 3rd, elements of the 164th Infantry Regiment,[16] Americal Division,[17] arrived at Palompon to relieve the 77th Infantry Division. For the "Old Bastards," the Leyte Campaign was over.

*   *   *

As for the 1st Cavalry Division that December, it was still leading X Corps down the coast. It, too, was then directed to the west coast to clear the area of organized Japanese forces. On its right was the 32nd Infantry Division and on its left the 77th Infantry Division. On December 23rd, the division moved west from Highway 2, now in American hands, to clear the coastal plain. Resistance was slight and that night, the 12th Cavalry established a night perimeter on a ridge about 1,400 yards northwest of Kananga. This pattern repeated itself over the next couple of days, with the Americans moving steadily to the west against minimal resistance. The main obstacles were waist-deep swamps and thick vegetation. By December 28th, the 5th and 12th Cavalry Regiments led the way out of the mountains and reached the barrio of Tibur on the west coast. This was about 2,800 yards north of Abijao, where Company C, 305th Infantry made one of its last amphibious assaults of the campaign. Only small, scattered groups of Japanese had been encountered, few of whom had any interest in putting up a stout defense. The 7th Cavalry took the barrio of Tibur and killed thirty-five Japanese defenders. That night, December 31st, the Japanese counterattacked the cavalrymen at Villaba. Using bugle calls to direct their assault, an estimated 500 Japanese struck four times in the early morning hours with mortars, machine guns and small-arms fire. American artillery broke up the attack and they soon dissolved back into the night.

The 32nd Infantry Division had also reached Lonoy and made physical contact with the 7th Cavalry Regiment. The 128th Infantry sent out the usual patrols throughout the Limon area between December 11th and 18th to try and eliminate enemy stragglers remaining along the "Yamashita Line." Several bypassed pockets of resistance were wiped out by these patrols, and by December 20th General Gill ordered the regiment to be prepared to move to the west coast. Beginning Christmas Eve, the 127th and 128th Infantry Regiments conducted a sweep through the mountains to the coast. As they went, they encountered and destroyed additional enemy stragglers or bypassed positions. Once again, as always in the Leyte Mountains, the rain, dense forests and steep cliff-like hills slowed the advance more than did the resisting Japanese. Supplies could only be received by airdrop, upon which the battalions came to depend for survival.

After pulling themselves up one ridge and sliding down the next for days, the two regiments finally reached the flatter coastal plain on Christmas Day. Here, the 1st Battalion, 127th Infantry ran into a strong force of about 400 Japanese which they dispersed. It wasn't until 29 December that the two regiments were able to reach their objectives. The 128th Infantry established itself on the high ground overlooking Tabango and Campopo Bays, while the 127th Infantry took the high ground overlooking Antipolo Point. Once again, patrols were sent out regularly and these soon made contact with the 1st Cavalry Division and the 24th Infantry Division.

The 24th Infantry Division had guarded a rear area and lines of communications after being relieved from Breakneck Ridge by the 32nd Infantry Division. One battalion, Colonel Clifford's 1st of the 34th Infantry, had been sent to deal with a new Japanese landing near San Isidro, about which more will be heard later. Meanwhile, the rest of the division patrolled extensively along the west coast of Leyte to eliminate enemy stragglers and to block any escape attempts by Japanese who wished to flee the island. Companies F and G of the 34th Infantry moved by landing craft to Gigantangan Island, landing at night. Their mission was to clear the island of any Japanese. There were none, and the mission was successfully completed.

Leaving Company F behind, Company G boarded its craft and sailed along the west coast of Leyte in the San Isidro Bay area, 6,000 yards to the south. As the craft sailed past San Isidro itself, they were met with machine-gun fire from the barrio and the hills above it. Instead of the planned frontal attack, they moved south and made their own landing beaches. Getting ashore was difficult as some of the landing craft stuck in the mud a hundred yards offshore, while others got stuck on the beach. The supplies they had come to pick up were loaded with difficulty and they returned to join Company F. The 1st Battalion would seize San Isidro.

On January 1st, 1945, the exhausted 24th Infantry Division was relieved by the 77th Infantry Division and moved to a staging area for its next assignment.

*   *   *

By the time the X and XXIV Corps joined together near Valencia, Japanese morale and physical conditions had deteriorated significantly. Desertion became commonplace. The wounded were unable, or unwilling, to assemble with their units. Without proper medical facilities or supplies, these wounded became a severe burden on the remaining able-bodied Japanese, who often abandoned them, or more often, convinced them to commit suicide rather than further burden their remaining comrades.

Slightly wounded Japanese soldiers marched with their units as long as they were able, for they knew their fate if they fell out of the line of march. Nevertheless, they often could not keep up and became stragglers. And, of course, there were always the deserters. The *35th Army* had already instituted a policy of returning slightly wounded men to battle. But many of the service units, such as the shipping and air corps troops, refused to fight because they had not been trained in infantry tactics. Even some artillery and antiaircraft units refused, saying that they had no infantry training, and that without their guns, now destroyed or abandoned, they were useless.

The poor diet and constant living underground or deep in the jungle had, no doubt, contributed to this slow disintegration of the *35th Army*, and it must be remembered that many of the combat units, in particular the *1st Infantry Division*, retained their military ethics. With the capture of Ormoc by XXIV Corps, the supply of food and other supplies to all Japanese troops on Leyte was cut off. This began their diet of starvation and forced them to live them off the land, something that was difficult to do within a hostile population. Like several American battalions who had made their gallant stands on the hills of Leyte, the men of the *1st* and *57th Infantry Regiments* were soon forced to eat coconuts, grasses, bamboo shoots, the heart fibers of coconut tree trunks and whatever native fruits and vegetables they could forage. Men quickly became weak and sick with various ailments from this miserable diet. Much of the reason the Americans found so much abandoned equipment along Highway 2 was simply that the retreating Japanese were too weak to move it any further. Even General Tomochika, the *35th Army's* Chief of Staff, was forced to leave one of its headquarters naked as the Americans approached, having left his uniform to be cleaned. He did, fortunately, manage to find another one along the way.

At the command levels, things had been settled by December 19th. On that date, *14th Area Army* in Manila had advised General Suzuki that from that date forward the *35th Army* was on its own, left to its own resources, such as they were, and that it could continue to operate within its own operational area[18] without succor from Manila. On that same date, General Suzuki ordered a conference of commanders and staff officers of the *1st* and *102nd Infantry Divisions*. At the meeting, he sent the *1st Infantry Division* to the north around the Matagob area and the *102nd Infantry Division* to the southern sector in the same vicinity. Once again, the aggressive Japanese commander told his subordinates to organize and prepare for another counterattack. Each division was left to its own devices as to how and when to relocate to its new base area. General Suzuki then moved his headquarters yet again, to a location north of Palompon.

Both Japanese divisions began their withdrawal on December 21st. With about 2,000 men left to it, the *102nd Infantry Division* failed to gain contact with General Suzuki or his staff, and so decided to move to the west coast near Villaba, ten miles north of Palompon. Here it made contact with the *1st Infantry Division*, the *68th Independent Mixed Brigade* and the *5th Infantry Regiment*. During its own withdrawal, the *1st Infantry Division* had run into the newly arrived *68th Independent Mixed Brigade* which, blissfully unaware that the Americans owned Highway 2, were marching down a trail toward that highway. Diverted by the infantrymen, the brigade turned and marched with them to the new rendezvous. After much marching and some fighting, which cost them more casualties, the retreating Japanese finally assembled under orders from General Suzuki around Mt. Canguipot, two and a half miles southeast of Valencia.

In Japan, the Japanese people were being proudly advised by their government that their forces still held the Burauen and San Pablo Airstrips and were continuing the attack on the American positions. That would have been news to both the Americans and Japanese on Leyte. But a more realistic evaluation of the campaign, as of the end of December 1944, was made by a noted post-war Japanese historian, who commented, "Japanese units were cut to pieces and stragglers scattered to the hills. They were driven deeper and deeper into the jungle by relentless enemy attacks and exhausted from lack of food. The privation and suffering was worse than Guadalcanal; the total defeat was the same."[19]

CHAPTER 10

THE BITTER END

The military phrase "mopping up" is often used to disguise the diffi-cult and dangerous work of clearing up enemy stragglers who, espe-cially during the Pacific War, refused to surrender or retreat. In the Southwest Pacific Theater of Operations, it became a more bitter phrase when General MacArthur, for reasons of ego or professional prestige, often declared a campaign under his direction to be in the mopping-up phase long before organized enemy resistance had ended. For the soldiers who had to conduct these "mopping up" campaigns, their sufferings were made more acute in the knowledge that their commanders didn't think that their accom-plishments were important.

General MacArthur's predilection for declaring campaigns over long before they actually were caused him occasional embarrassment. This, in fact, had begun at his very first offensive campaign when at Buna, New Guinea, he declared the battle in the mopping-up phase only to suffer humiliation when the Japanese blocked his troops from seizing a vital base area. So upset was the general that he called for General Eichelberger, then commanding I Corps, and ordered him to complete the assignment at Buna "or don't come back alive." Fortunately, General Eichelberger knew his trade and defeated the Buna defenders.

Such incidents were repeated time and again as the Southwest Pacific Theater moved up the north coast of New Guinea. At Aitape, the battle was declared over weeks before the Japanese *18th Army* launched a massive coun-terattack along the Drinumor River, which caused the XI Corps some serious moments before it was finally repulsed. Again at the island of Biak, General Eichelberger had to be called forward to take over a failing fight, despite the fact that communiqués from General MacArthur's Headquarters proclaimed that the fight was all but over.

Nor was New Guinea the end of the pattern. Within weeks of the Sixth Army's landing on Leyte, communiqués were again going out stating that the campaign was in the mopping-up phase and "all but over." This just as the 24th Infantry Division was fighting and dying on Breakneck Ridge, and days before the 7th Infantry Division fought for its life at Shoestring Ridge. It was all very discouraging to the infantryman, tanker, engineer, medic and others who fought and died while "mopping up."

The infantryman's acidic sense of humor was one thing that sustained him. As the new commander of the 24th Infantry Division later recorded, "Most of this fighting is in inconspicuous little actions which nobody hears about—mopping up. In Europe when we advance we really capture something. Out here we just capture another island, important enough though it may be, that looks much like all other islands. As one doughboy remarked after we had cleaned out a small objective—'Well, there's another half million coconuts'."[1]

The usual method of true "mopping-up" was the use of the combat patrol. It consisted of a patrol leader and any number of riflemen, sometimes accompanied by machine gunners, mortar men and engineers. If larger forces were expected to be encountered, then artillery forward observers would accompany the patrol. On rare occasions tanks or light-armored vehicles went along. The terrain in which these patrols were conducted was usually the worst in the area, good hiding places for the enemy who expected to remain hidden, gathering his own food, until his forces returned to the island and destroyed the Americans.

In the Pacific, as nowhere else, the mopping-up phase was often bloody and frustrating. The Japanese soldier had long been indoctrinated that surrender was dishonorable. If he ever surrendered for any reason he could never return home to Japan. So by and large the Japanese soldier did not surrender, even when it was obvious to all concerned, including him, that his situation was hopeless. Mopping up in the Pacific War was one of the most difficult, heartbreaking and bloody assignments a unit could get.

*   *   *

This task first fell to the 34th Infantry Regiment of the 24th Infantry Division. The regiment had last been discussed during its battles along Breakneck Ridge in November. While the rest of the division rested before moving on to another Philippine Island invasion, the 34th Infantry was left behind to mop up. Their assignment was the Leyte Peninsula, jutting out north of the island between Carigara Bay and Cebu. It was a bad assignment.

Early on, First Lieutenant Benjamin H. Wable of Helena, Montana led a combat patrol deep into the mountain country around Sinayawan. For twenty-five days the men searched for stray Japanese while existing on cold rations. It rained almost all of the time, and when it didn't the mist made it feel like rain. Sixteen times Lieutenant Wable's group was attacked by Japanese, and sixteen times it fought them off.

Another combat patrol was led by Sergeant Thomas Martin of Hawaii. Searching the area around Capoocan and Mount Minoro, the patrol discovered a fork in the trail they were following. Unsure, Sergeant Martin split his patrol, sending one group to the right while he led another to the left. After moving along in the quiet for a while, a sudden burst of firing hit the patrol. Rifles and machine guns opened fire on Sergeant Martin's section. The scout fell to the ground. He looked to see the source of the enemy fire, but could not. He wriggled forward to a small knoll where he spotted the enemy. There was an enemy observer hiding in a bunch of wild bananas. Further along was a company of Japanese moving along the trail. By this time the scout had been spotted, and after a brief exchange of fire with the enemy observer, he withdrew and reported to Sergeant Martin. Realizing that he was outnumbered ten to one, Sergeant Martin had to think fast. He knew that the Japanese had to be stopped or they would ambush the other half of his patrol. He immediately ordered his section to establish a trail block. With all the weapons they carried the Americans opened fire up the trail. In the meantime, Sergeant Martin sent a messenger to bring back the other section of his patrol. After the skirmish, eleven enemy dead were counted. The Americans didn't lose a man.

Later that night, this group of Japanese attacked the patrol base at Sinawayan. After five hours of fighting, eighteen enemy bodies were counted. On November 11th, another patrol was hit by the same group. The Americans were in a bad spot for defense and very quickly their BAR man was wounded, allowing the Japanese to move closer. Private Leo Gomolchak, of Pittsburgh, grabbed the BAR, stood upright, tossed grenades and then opened automatic fire. His determined stand saved the patrol from being overrun.

A few days later, civilians reported that a force of Japanese had established themselves along the Colasian-Ormoc Road. They had captured several civilians and bayoneted others who had tried to escape. They ordered the natives, upon pain of death, to bring them food. A patrol from Company G was sent out to investigate. The lead scout, Private Marvin Edge of Georgia, crawled up a jungle-covered slope to within fifty yards of the Japanese. Even then, he could not pinpoint their exact location. So he stood up and yelled, "Hey," then dropped to the ground. Immediately, machine guns and grenades answered his hail. Now knowing exactly where the Japanese had established their trail block, he reported in and mortars destroyed the position. Twenty-three dead Japanese were later found in the area.

But that was not all of them, apparently. As another patrol walked the area a day later it was hit by enemy fire. The lead scout went down on the trail, wounded. The patrol leader crawled up to the wounded man and began to pull him to safety, but was also wounded. Despite his own injuries, the patrol leader pulled his scout out of the line of fire and into the bushes.

These incidents had aroused the interest of the Americans. Company E sent out a stronger force to find out what this enemy group was up to in the jungles. They wanted particularly to destroy the group's automatic weapons. But as they moved up the trail, the lead scouts were fired on by machine guns. The patrol leader identified the location of the guns and then ordered a withdrawal. But the lead scout was trapped under the enemy machine guns. Private Kenneth Foldoe of Minnesota decided he would help. Going forward, he worked his way through burnt kunai grass to a point from which he could bring his BAR to bear on the enemy gun crew. Busy firing at the trapped scout, the Japanese were surprised when Private Foldoe opened fire on them. They quickly swung their gun to fire at the BAR man. He engaged them in a gun duel long enough to allow the trapped scout to scurry to safety, and then Private Foldoe took off at the run. The patrol reported back that the enemy on the trail had four machine guns and about seventy-five men.

Now Company E sent out a stronger patrol to deal with this stubborn enemy force. As they moved toward the enemy, snipers killed one man. Then, while seeking the position of the machine guns, the patrol discovered that the experienced Japanese had moved them, knowing there would be some follow-up by the Americans. A completely new reconnaissance became necessary. It was conducted by Private Kelcie Odom of Colorado. He crawled into the vicinity of the Japanese and then stood up to draw their fire, which he quickly did. Before falling to the ground he noted the new position of the enemy guns. The Japanese were well aware of what Private Odom was doing and sent a sniper to dispatch the inquisitive American. But Private Odom saw him coming and shot him down before he could do any damage. After he reported to his patrol leader, the Americans attacked the Japanese from three sides. It was a bitter, vicious and deadly fight, but when it was over, the enemy group no longer threatened anyone. Most of the Japanese were killed and the few survivors melted into the jungle. Several more American soldiers were killed while "mopping up."

And still the Japanese appeared. One small group somehow popped up near Colasian, well within the American-controlled coastal area. They saw a battery of howitzers passing along the coastal road and waited for darkness to attack. The initial attack wounded two artillerymen, and they fell on the road. The section leader, Sergeant William Hammock of Alabama, ordered his convoy to "keep moving." While the section moved up the road, Sergeant Hammock dropped off his vehicle and fought to protect the two wounded men on the road. He managed to do so until help arrived.

The vast area to be covered and the shortage of trained infantry forced commanders to use expedients to accomplish their missions. To this end, the regimental antitank company was assigned a sector to patrol. Borrowing rifles, carbines and machine guns, the company set out to clear its assigned sector. They discovered a Japanese bivouac and attacked. Facing rifles, machine guns and knee-mortars, the attack was beaten off twice. Undismayed, the antitank gunners dragged mortars up the hill and put down a mortar barrage. They followed this up with another attack up the hill. Japanese bodies lay throughout the bivouac area, and there were additional signs that many wounded had escaped into the jungle.

The next day the gunners did it again on a ridge to the south. Using mortars they drove the Japanese off the hill, but once the barrage lifted, both sides raced for the top. The Japanese got there first, but the Americans put up an all-day fight, at the end of which they owned the hill. Then they did it once again to the third ridge south. Even as they did so, several Japanese filtered past them and reached the coastal road, where they had to be individually routed out and killed.

Other groups or individual Japanese continued for weeks to strike unexpectedly at American troops. Instances were noted where they dressed in U.S. uniforms, no doubt stripped from the dead, and tried to get into American positions. A few were found dressed as women, again hoping for naive Americans to have sympathy enough to let them get in close enough to kill one or two before they themselves died. It remained a bloody, brutal business.

Sometimes the Japanese watched while American truck convoys moved over a road, then mined the road so that when the trucks returned, they would roll over the mines. Japanese snipers were a constant problem, shooting into American bivouac areas, particularly at night, to keep the soldiers on edge. Others mined foxholes alongside a trail and then moved up the trail. When an American patrol arrived, the enemy would fire on them, hoping one or more Americans would jump for cover into the mined foxholes. Still others left tracks of Japanese footwear along a trail. A patrol would follow those tracks into a pre-planned ambush zone where machine guns were waiting for their targets to arrive. Small fires were left burning to attract patrols, who naturally thought they were about to surprise a group of Japanese having dinner. Instead, they themselves were ambushed by waiting Japanese.

One such ambush had a single Japanese sniper fire down a trail deliberately, revealing his position. What it didn't reveal was that two machine guns were flanking the trail and waiting for the American patrol to walk into its ambush. A patrol from Company F did just that late in November. One of the members was Private John Lomko of Chicago, who despite protocol had insisted on carrying along a light machine gun. He immediately set up the gun and covered the patrol while it withdrew. Then Private Lomko slowly withdrew down the trail himself, dragging the gun behind him and pausing every few yards to return the enemy's fire. He was killed in action.

Another patrol under Sergeant Jack Wheat of Kentucky walked right over disguised Japanese spider holes and continued on until the Japanese opened fire at their backs. Two men fell under the Japanese fire and the remainder were pinned to the ground. Sergeant Wheat fired back. But then the Japanese made a mistake of their own. They came out of their holes and launched a bayonet attack. Sergeant Wheat's fire kept them at bay until the patrol could organize and vanish into the jungle.

And so it went. A patrol from Company E found Japanese dug in on a hill overlooking the coastal road. It took an artillery barrage and three ground assaults before Company E could claim possession of the hill, but it cost them eleven men killed to do so.

It wasn't only the Americans that were out hunting. When Company E went looking for an enemy observation post that was directing artillery fire from single guns hidden in the jungle, they succeeded in knocking it out. But that night the Japanese counterattacked. Suicide detachments crawled through ravines and reached the coastal road where they installed machine guns in the swamps and on a nearby ridge. The first convoy at dawn was ambushed. The lead truck was disabled and the last truck knocked out by mines tossed by the Japanese. Men were killed defending the convoy. There was no way out, the road blocked both east and west. A call for a boat to take the wounded men to safety was made, but when it arrived, the Japanese drove it off with machine-gun fire from the dominating ridge. Finally, two courageous American infantrymen used an amphibious truck to evacuate the wounded under direct enemy fire, while others obtained an armored weapons carrier and saved other wounded.

Company E then went after the machine gun on the ridge. Five times they attacked up the hill, and five times the machine gun fire drove them back down to the road. Enemy sharpshooters protected the machine gun position, so getting close enough to knock it out was unusually difficult. In addition, the steep slope directly in front of the gun not only gave it a clear field of fire but prevented assault teams from reaching it. Mortar and machine-gun fire from the road did no harm to it. The coastal road and the beach were closed to American traffic.

The next day a decimated platoon from Company E attacked for the sixth time. The platoon numbered only fourteen men, led by Staff Sergeant Michael Blucas of Pennsylvania. Blucas was an experienced infantryman, and ordered his men to move up the hill in short rushes. He understood that a rifleman needs about three seconds to aim and fire his rifle. If the targets, the men in his platoon, were out of sight within those three seconds, they would not be hit. Rushing forward in short two- to ten-yard moves, the platoon reached the crest of the ridge. Now they had to find the gun. Visibility atop the ridge was barely five yards. To see farther you had to stand up, and standing up would get you killed. Nevertheless, Sergeant Blucas and Private Louis H. Baker of Iowa stood up. The enemy gun fired and revealed its position. Both men dived for cover, but now the gun also knew where the Americans where and fired into their area. In order to allow the platoon to advance, the machine gun had to be distracted. Private Baker stood up again and opened fire with his rifle. He killed three enemy soldiers before he himself was cut down. Sergeant Blucas tried to lead his men forward only to be killed. The platoon withdrew. It would take a seventh assault on the ridge before the gun was knocked out and the road opened once again.

*   *   *

General Suzuki had not waited around to participate in the American "mopping up" of his remnant *35th Army*. With all but a few thousand of his troops now dead or hiding in the jungles and mountains of Leyte, trying to survive, he followed the orders of General Yamashita. He set about preparing to withdraw his army headquarters to another island where it would take control of the other units in the Southern Philippines. From there he would continue the fight against the Americans. Orders had been sent to him from Manila confirming that he was to leave Leyte with his headquarters and move to the south to control future battles expected there. But poor communications between Manila and Leyte, combined with the fact that *35th Army Headquarters* was by this point a fugitive, had failed to elicit a reply. Messages with these orders were first sent December 14th, and they were repeated on the 19th, 25th and 26th. Still, *Fourteenth Area Army's* staff remained unsure that General Suzuki had received any of them.

General Suzuki had, in fact, only received one of these messages, and even it was incomplete. Nevertheless, he was able to make sense of the message and, in any case, he had little choice, his army having been largely dispersed on Leyte. Another message was also sent, this one a personal message from General Yamashita, whose chief of staff General Suzuki had been earlier in their careers. This message evidenced concern for the welfare of General Suzuki and his army. In the two months since Leyte had been invaded, Yamashita wrote, the *35th Army* had "waged many a heroic battle against superior enemy forces and in the face of numerous difficulties."[2] General Yamashita went on to say that General Suzuki and his army had dealt a great blow to the Americans, denying them freedom of action. He also mentioned the delay that the Japanese on Leyte had inflicted on American plans. But the enemy had "increased his material power and war potential" and "solely on the strength of his material superiority" these Americans were now threatening Luzon. Because of this "we shall seek and destroy our enemy on Luzon Island, thereby doing our part in the heroic struggle of the army and avenging many a valiant warrior who fell"[3] on Leyte.

Concerned that the surviving Japanese would prefer suicide over a continued losing fight, General Yamashita also included a passage encouraging continued resistance. "I cannot keep back tears of remorse for tens of thousands of our officers and men fighting on Leyte Island. Nevertheless, I must impose a still harder task on you. Please try to understand my intentions. They say it is harder to live than die. You, officers and men, be patient enough to endure the hardships of life, and help guard and maintain the prosperity of the Imperial Throne through eternal resistance to the enemy, and be ready to meet your death calmly for our beloved country. I sincerely instruct you on the above."[4] It is known that this message was received by General Suzuki.

General Suzuki now tried to organize the remnants of his army on a high plateau near Villaba, his latest headquarters location. In early January, he issued a new order to his troops that called for "independent operations to the end," and it apologized "that the situation should have come to such an unfavorable condition."[5] He advised his men of his deep gratitude to them for their sacrifices during the campaign, and remembered those who had fallen in battle. The army's assignment now, General Suzuki wrote, was to keep as many American troops busy as possible to ease the battle on Luzon. He noted that the operation was to be continued to the last man to protect the Imperial Throne.

The Japanese headquarters near Villaba was on a high plateau which was largely protected from American observation by high rocky hills and heavy woods that covered the area. Occasionally American artillery shelled the heights, but it was usually unobserved harassing fire. Nevertheless, more Japanese soldiers were killed and wounded. The wounded were in particularly bad shape because all of the medical supplies had been lost, captured or abandoned as the army withdrew from the attacking Sixth Army. Food was less of a problem, and the Japanese stole food from native fields while establishing several gardens of their own. But the main item on General Suzuki's agenda was escape from Leyte.

In accordance with Yamashita's orders, General Suzuki began to plan for his army's escape. The wounded and those still lost in the jungles and the mountains, fighting the Americans who were "mopping up" would, of course, be abandoned. The troops most fit and best equipped would be sent out first, to other islands still held by the Japanese, in order to further delay the American conquest of the Philippines. General Yamashita aided as best he could, sending several barges to Leyte early in January for their transportation. The remnants of the *1st Infantry Division* were sent out on these barges to nearby Cebu. General Kataoka at first declined to go, stating that he had lost so many officers and men on Leyte that he wished to remain and fight on to the death. He suggested that the relatively intact *68th Independent Mixed Brigade* go to Cebu instead. But General Suzuki insisted, so General Kataoka and the last 800 remaining troops of the *1st Infantry Division* left Leyte for Cebu in three groups in January.

The repeated transport of the Japanese off Leyte soon caught the attention of the American naval forces patrolling to prevent just such an occurrence. They were soon aware of the evacuation and cut the routes which the Japanese used to move their troops off Leyte. From January forward, only a few hundred men managed to make their escape successfully. General Suzuki soon learned that many of these were actually deserters, having abandoned their units and left without permission. Some were later captured, court-martialed, and executed by Japanese commanders on the islands on which they sought safety. One who did not, however, was Lieutenant General Shimpei Fukue,[6] commander of the *102nd Infantry Division*. This unit had five infantry battalions, supporting units and division headquarters on Leyte. Late in December 1944, he informed *35th Army Headquarters* that he intended to evacuate the remnants of his units to Cebu, if he could find transportation. Ordered not to do so, and to report personally to General Suzuki at his headquarters, General Fukue refused to comply and, with his staff, set out for Cebu. Upon arrival there, he was relieved of his command and charged with desertion in the face of the enemy. Due to a technicality in Japanese military law, he was never tried and, in fact, was reinstated to his command. After the war he was tried and executed as a war criminal.

In the meantime, General Suzuki sent a staff officer to Manila with his report on the Leyte Campaign. Several other staff officers were sent to Cebu to establish a new *35th Army Headquarters*. Many officers and men suffered the fate of General Tomochika, who waited on the beach time and again for boats that never arrived. Not until March of 1945 did General Suzuki himself decide to depart Leyte. On March 17th, a barge took his staff, including General Tomochika, to Cebu where an American invasion was expected any day. General Suzuki left on March 23rd, five months after the Americans invaded Leyte.

Left in command of the stragglers on Leyte was the original Japanese commander in the campaign, General Makino. Too sick himself to even say goodbye to General Suzuki, he remained as the senior Japanese commander on Leyte. General Makino had, under his command, the remnants of his own *16th Infantry Division* and the newer *68th Independent Mixed Brigade,* along with several smaller units. These forces were centered in the area around Villaba where many spent their days waiting for transportation that never came. Slowly, steadily, these men disappeared into the jungles or mountains of Leyte. He and the handful of men who remained around him disappeared in the final Leyte mop-op operations of late March–April, 1945.

General Suzuki had a difficult time after leaving Leyte. In early April he decided to move his headquarters to Mindanao, which held the largest number of his troops in the southern Philippines. Under constant threat of Allied air and naval attack, the general and most of his staff risked the passage. Sailing on April 10th in four different groups, the commander and staff of the *35th Army* set out from Cebu. General Tomochika and his group of staff officers made the journey successfully, only to learn upon arrival on Mindanao that General Suzuki and his group had been attacked and destroyed by American aircraft on April 16th, 1945.

*   *   *

The mopping-up operations on Leyte were conducted under the auspices of Lt. General Robert L. Eichelberger and his Eighth Army. As noted earlier, General Eichelberger was an experienced commander in the southwest Pacific, having first engaged the enemy in 1942 at Papua where he took over a faltering campaign and brought it to a swift and successful conclusion. Now he was relegated to a mopping-up role while General Krueger and his Sixth Army moved on to the invasion of Luzon. Indeed, General Eichelberger was very quickly to have his hands full, as not only was he responsible for clearing Leyte of organized Japanese resistance, he was also to invade Luzon near Manila. While assisting General Krueger's army in establishing itself on Luzon, General Eichelberger was simultaneously to conduct literally dozens of amphibious operations to clear the southern Philippines of Japanese.

Most of the supporting naval craft had left Leyte by this time, to move in support of the other Philippine operations General MacArthur was conducting. The PT boats and the 2nd Engineer Special Brigade craft remained to support the Eighth Army operations on Leyte. These devoted themselves to interdicting the many routes over which the Japanese tried to escape to Cebu, the nearest large island which held Japanese forces. The escaping enemy boats were bombed from the air and torpedoed by the PT boats. The Philippine guerrillas often reported on Japanese preparations for escape, and the planes and boats stood waiting off shore until the attempt was made. Guerrillas on Cebu also reported arrivals and where they landed. The next Japanese group usually found the PT boats or Corsairs of Marine Air Group 12 waiting to welcome them to Cebu.

Reports that the Japanese were still in the Camotes Islands, between Leyte and Cebu, and that they were torturing the native population, caused General Hodge to dispatch an infantry battalion to clear those islands. Loading the battalion in amphibian tractors and Landing Craft, Medium, four PT boats under Lieutenant (j.g.) Weston C. Pullen, USNR, landed on Ponson Island on January 15th, to find no Japanese left there. They quickly moved on to Poro Island where they encountered serious resistance. After the Americans had destroyed much of the remaining Japanese on these islands, mopping-up operations were left to the local Filipino guerrillas.

The support provided by the PT boats and the 2nd Engineer Special Brigade craft were crucial to these continued operations. Operating usually at night, the PT boats cut the enemy's lines of evacuation, stranding them on the beaches and forcing them back into the hills and jungles of Leyte where they were eventually killed. Based now at Ormoc, the boats often traveled as far as Cebu where they harassed that Japanese garrison, and again intercepted Japanese who thought that their escape had been successful. Two large freighters and uncounted barges were credited to the PT boats between December 1944 and May 1945.

*　　*　　*

Colonel Clifford and his battalion had been relieved after their battle at Kilay Ridge and ordered to Calubian. Instead of rest, they were given the mission of finding out what had happened to the reported three thousand Japanese who had landed earlier near San Isidro.[7] That barrio lies five miles due west of the village of Calubian.

Colonel Clifford had about one hundred men left in his battalion after the Kilay Ridge battle, but he still had some guerrilla officers of the 95th Philippine Guerrilla Regiment attached to his command. These men promised a force of guerrillas would join his battalion, but it would take a few days to organize them. The local people who lived along the Leyte Peninsula were anxious to clear their land of the enemy and volunteered to accompany Dragon Red in their search for the Japanese. Using captured Japanese rifles, Colonel Clifford armed these volunteers and then sent eight U.S. soldiers to block the road from San Isidro. The patrol was to live with the local civilians and report all developments. If attacked, it was to fight a delaying action.[8]

It was during the "mopping-up" phase of the Leyte campaign that the guerrillas came into their own. They had been of some help during the active part of the campaign, scouting, guiding and providing intelligence on enemy movements. But in the many sweeps during the clearing phase, they eventually bore the brunt of the patrolling, informing and communicating necessary to knock out the smaller groups of Japanese who were hidden in the jungles. Native runners came from the village leaders, informing Colonel Clifford of each and every movement of the straggling Japanese. Armed only with bolo knives, these young runners could cover five miles in an hour and they were used in relays from village to village. Messages were simple and to the point. A panting runner would appear and say, "To Colonel Clifford. Japs here. Hurry."[9] On rare occasions the runners would get sidetracked. In one such case, a runner with a message happened upon a lone Japanese soldier and killed him. Searching him, he found some loot, and then instead of continuing with his mission, went off in search of more enemy to loot. But by and large the runner system worked as well as the American radios in alerting Colonel Clifford to the whereabouts of Japanese hiding on Leyte Peninsula.

For the Japanese, the situation was difficult. While they had a strong force on the peninsula, they had no objective, no resupply and no hope of success. They not only had to provide for themselves, but they were in a hostile country where the natives refused them aid and often killed lone Japanese or small patrols. Security forced them to divide and cover the villages upon which they based themselves. They never could mass their entire force for any purpose.

The first small patrol Colonel Clifford dispatched was led by First Lieutenant Thomas J. McCorlew of Cleveland, Texas. With guidance from local civilians, it entered the outskirts of San Isidro on December 8th, and climbed to a nearby hill. From there, Lieutenant McCorlew spent two full days observing the Japanese movements in and around San Isidro, reporting back to Colonel Clifford every move of the enemy commander. There were five hundred enemy troops, fully armed, and about to march on Calubian.

Colonel Clifford gathered every man available to him and moved to head off the incoming attack. The civilians in Calubian were evacuated, and soon guerrilla runners reported that a force of three hundred enemy troops was fighting the guerrillas at Tobango, five miles south of San Isidro. Calling for reinforcements, Colonel Clifford moved north. By the next day he had a force of about nineteen officers and 368 enlisted men with machine guns, mortars and two field pieces. The leading patrol, under 1st Lieutenant Oakley W. Storey of Los Angeles, had dug in on a grassy knoll when Oakley began to feel that he was under enemy observation. Although all was quiet, Lieutenant Oakley remained uneasy and kept his men alert. Sure enough, at midnight, an enemy force launched a "banzai" attack, surrounding the patrol's perimeter and firing from all sides. Then about one hundred Japanese launched a bayonet charge up the knoll. They had managed to crawl to within fifty yards of the Americans before they revealed themselves with the charge. The enemy ran headlong into the fire of the Americans' automatic weapons, disregarding heavy losses in order to reach those guns and knock them out. Lieutenant Storey was wounded four times during the battle, but he spotted a Japanese captain wielding a samurai sword and encouraging his men forward. Storey and the Japanese captain met face to face. The American's pistol jammed, while the Japanese swung his sword and missed. Lieutenant Storey grappled with the captain, wrenched the sword from his hand, and dispatched him with his own weapon.

Even after daylight the attack continued. Calling for support, Lieutenant Storey was relieved to see Colonel Clifford and the rest of the battalion come up in a counterattack preceded by a rolling mortar barrage. Five times the Americans counterattacked. During the sixth attack, the fighting became hand-to-hand, but the Japanese withdrew. Behind they left seventy-eight dead and much new equipment. Six Americans had died and ten were wounded. Colonel Clifford now held a "front" twenty thousand yards long with 370 men.

The terrain of the Leyte Peninsula is one of low, grassy ridges with some high hills along the coast. There was little in the way of cover for American patrols to move through during daylight hours. So Colonel Clifford changed his tactics. Instead of daylight patrols, the Americans used the knowledge and scouting skills of their guerrilla allies to institute night patrols. The Japanese, reputedly experts at night attacks, were disconcerted by this new tactic on the part of their enemies and never quite adapted to it.

One such night patrol was led by Colonel Clifford's Executive Officer, Major George D. Willets. A former accountant from Seaside Park, New Jersey, Major Willets had only been with Dragon Red since the A-Day landings. But he wanted to get out from under the administrative work, usually the task of an executive officer, and do some fighting. So one morning before light, he took out a patrol of Americans and guerrillas. He was to isolate a group of hills near Taglawan known to be occupied by the Japanese. They reached the hills just at dawn, covered by the inevitable rain, and set up their machine guns. The enemy remained unaware of their presence.

Once everything was set, Major Willets jumped up and shouted for his men to follow him. Covered by the machine guns, Major Willets led the guerrillas to the crest of the first hill. Throwing hand grenades into the enemy foxholes, the Major inspired the guerrillas to take on the rest of the Japanese. A bloody close-quarters fight developed, which so terrorized the unsuspecting Japanese that the survivors fled into the jungle. Bringing up his machine guns, Major Willets led the charge on the second Japanese-held ridge.

The earlier scene was repeated and again the surviving Japanese fled.

Major Willets then spotted two abandoned enemy machine guns in a gully between the ridges. He ordered his guerrillas to go down and bring back the guns, but they refused, citing the possibility of more Japanese on the next ridge. Major Willets went alone into the gully and spotted a dead enemy soldier whom he searched for documents. Bringing back the first enemy gun, he showed it to his guerrillas before repeating his performance. This time, however, the gun and the "dead" Japanese were both gone. Then the Japanese on the ridge recovered and launched a counterattack. With ammunition supplies running low, Major Willets pulled his men back to the first ridge. There they counted 129 enemy dead.

*　　*　　*

Not all of the natives were friendly, however. As we have seen, some cooperated with the Japanese in leading their patrols and informing them of American movements. Even when it became clear that the Japanese had been defeated, some collaborators remained loyal to them. One such individual reported some Japanese at a location which turned out to be an ambush. The patrol was in severe difficulty when Private Donald Ritter of Lewisburg, Pennsylvania pushed a machine gun forward under fire and covered the patrol as it withdrew. Private Ritter saved his patrol at the cost of his own life.

Major Willets was alerted that a large force of Japanese was bivouacked near Mount Banao. Taking a mixed American-Philippine Force and four amphibious tanks, he mounted another night patrol, hoping to strike the enemy at dawn. Following the Nipa River to the general location of the enemy, he surrounded the area, and at dawn the entire force opened fire. Caught cooking their breakfast, the enemy was disorganized and unprepared for the Americans who charged them in their bivouac. Over one hundred were killed while the survivors were tracked down in the jungle and eliminated. A search of this group's belongings showed that they had been active in looting native villages as they moved. Table linen, silverware, jewelry and even women's brassieres were found. One unfortunate Japanese soldier even had a baby's high chair strapped to his pack.

Patrols like these continued throughout December. Colonel Clifford's battalion killed hundreds of Japanese, but others still remained. The exact number will never be known. Then, late in December, Major Snavely's 2nd Battalion, 34th Infantry conducted a sweep of the entire peninsula, using artillery and armored vehicles. Additional hundreds were killed by this sweep, while others killed themselves rather than face capture or death at the hands of the Americans. One or two Japanese surrendered or were captured when they became incapacitated. And even this did not end the "mopping up" which would go on until April, with stragglers coming out of the jungles even after the end of the war. From beginning to end, it was a dirty, dangerous war.

*   *   *

General MacArthur had been waiting impatiently for General Krueger to finalize the Leyte Campaign, for his Sixth Army was to be the spearhead of his long-awaited invasion of the main Philippine island of Luzon. In preparation for this event, Sixth Army had been planning the invasion even while conducting the Leyte Campaign. Unwilling to wait any longer, since the Luzon assault was already scheduled for January 9th, 1945, General MacArthur directed General Eichelberger and his Eighth Army to be prepared to assume command over the Leyte operation. The warning order, issued December 15th, also informed General Eichelberger that nearly all of the existing Sixth Army units on Leyte would remain and come under his control, probably on or about December 26th, 1944. Sixth Army Headquarters and some of its existing units would leave Leyte for the Luzon operation soon after that date.

The air and naval units which had been supporting the Sixth Army would remain in that role after General Krueger departed. Of course, the Seventh Fleet would support the landings at Luzon, so only the supporting forces of the Navy would be available to General Eichelberger. According to these orders, General Krueger turned over command of the Leyte Campaign to General Eichelberger at midnight on December 26, 1944.

General Eichelberger inherited the X and XXIV Corps and the units under their command. Little change was noted by the average soldier on Leyte, since the battle to clear the Japanese from the island continued as before with the same combat units as before. To further ensure that the campaign received no further attention, General MacArthur issued his official announcement that the campaign was over except for mopping up on that same date, December 26th. Ironically, that was the day after General Yamashita had notified General Suzuki that the *Fourteenth Area Army* had written off the Leyte campaign.

Under the command of the U.S. Eighth Army, eight infantry divisions[10] engaged in the mopping-up process on Leyte. Behind them, many other units passed through Leyte staging for other operations throughout the Philippines. General Eichelberger "was told that there were only six thousand Japanese left on the island. This estimate was in serious error, as subsequent events proved."[11] Reports quickly reached General Eichelberger that large numbers of Japanese "well equipped and apparently well fed" were moving into western Leyte. In the first five months of 1945, Eighth Army would claim to have killed more than twenty-seven thousand Japanese soldiers on Leyte.

General Eichelberger also had other duties to perform aside from "mopping up" Leyte. His newly received XXIV Corps actually belonged to the Central Pacific Command and was only there on loan. The time limit for that loan was approaching and the unit, including the 7th, 77th, and 96th Infantry Divisions, had to be returned to Admiral Nimitz for operations in the Central Pacific Theater. The Corps and its component divisions were, therefore, withdrawn from the front lines of western Leyte and staged for the return to the Central Pacific. For General Eichelberger, who had spent his World War II combat career in the Southwest Pacific, "the re-equipping of General Hodge's troops was something of a revelation to the veterans of the old Southwest Pacific Area. Our troops unloaded cargo vessels that came in from the Central Pacific, and, as the stores were brought ashore on the beaches of Leyte, all of us marveled. We had never seen such wonderful gear!"[12] What particularly astonished General Eichelberger and his fellow Southwest Pacific veterans was that every soldier received all completely new equipment, helmet, uniform, underwear, pistols, weapons, boots, vehicles, machine guns, mortars and howitzers. He quickly made an arrangement with General Hodge to accept XXIV Corps' "castoffs" for his own troops.

In return for the loss of XXIV Corps and its three divisions, General Eichelberger received two new combat units, the Americal Division and, later, the 81st Infantry Division.[13] Neither was new to combat, both having fought hard campaigns before being sent to the Eighth Army. Although General Eichelberger had hoped to save the Americal Division for future Philippine operations, the loss of XXIV Corps and the larger than expected numbers of Japanese reported on Leyte, forced him to send it into the front lines where its 164th Infantry Regiment, as we have seen earlier, took over from the exhausted troops of X Corps.

But even to the end of their participation in the Leyte Campaign, the original assault divisions continued to fight for the island. When Company F, 184th Infantry, 7th Infantry Division was mopping up around Biliboy on

3 January 1945, it was stopped by heavy enemy fire and suffered several casualties. But the 1st Platoon continued forward trying to outflank the enemy position. When the platoon was hit again by enemy fire and halted, Private William R. Martin single-handedly assaulted the nearest Japanese position, despite heavy fire and grenades directed at him. Moving over open terrain and through point-blank fire and exploding grenades, Private Martin, from Dayton, Ohio, killed two enemy soldiers hidden in trenches under a house and then turned toward the next building where four more Japanese soldiers fell to his fire. He moved on to a third position, which he destroyed with grenades. His heroic act inspired his platoon to move forward once again and finish off the remaining enemy defenders at Biliboy. For his courageous leadership, Private William R. Martin received a Distinguished Service Cross.[14]

* * *

Major General William H. Arnold[15] brought his Americal Division ashore in mid-January, 1945. The 164th Infantry Regimental Combat Team had been sent forward to relieve tired troops of the original assault forces. Primarily, the Americal Division took over the area held by XXIV Corps between Jaro and Palompon. Early on January 28th, the 1st Battalion, 164th Infantry set off down Highway 2, followed by the 245th Field Artillery Battalion.[16] The following night, Company C of the 164th Infantry was manning the perimeter near Capoocan when three Japanese soldiers attempted to penetrate the defenses. They were the first Japanese soldiers killed on Leyte by the Americal Division.

On February 1, the 3rd Battalion, 164th Infantry moved to Ormoc and then by water to Palompon to relieve troops of the 77th Infantry Division. Meanwhile, in the hills east of Valencia, the rest of the regiment sent out constant patrols to scour the area for hidden Japanese. These patrols added another 24 enemy dead to their total so far. Intelligence reports continued to indicate that there were about three thousand Japanese still within the operational area of the 164th Infantry. These individuals were reportedly grouping themselves into self-defense units for mutual protection and, meanwhile, hopefully waiting for evacuation from Leyte. Several such large groups were reported around the areas held by the Americal Division, some quite large and threatening.

Basing itself around Valencia, the division continued with the patrolling, often eliminating small groups of Japanese found wandering half-naked, poorly armed and starving throughout the area. Colonel William J. Mahoney, commanding the 164th Infantry, decided to make a greater effort to discomfort the Japanese. The regiment's 3rd Battalion at Palompon, less some elements, moved by water from its base to Villaba, only a few thousand yards northwest from Abijao, where a large group of Japanese had been reported. After the landing on February 4th, Company K led the march which was quickly hit by Japanese machine-gun fire even as the infantrymen were unloading from their boats. Company K reacted quickly and the town was soon once again in American hands. That night the Japanese counterattacked but were driven off, leaving 26 dead in front of the American's positions.

Behind the lines, armored patrols moved up and down the roads, protecting convoys and keeping the roads free from harassment by individual and small groups of Japanese. The division's 21st Reconnaissance Troop sent numerous foot patrols into the hills to keep the Japanese off balance. The patrols of the 164th Infantry killed more Japanese and also brought in some prisoners, who were eagerly received by the division's intelligence officers.

The 1st Battalion, 164th Infantry also launched a battalion-sized drive from Dipi to Abijao with the intent to clear the intervening area of all Japanese and any bypassed installations which were still in operation. Enemy bivouacs were also sought out and, when found, destroyed. To the south, the division's 182nd Infantry[17] cleared the area around Ormoc Bay and also sent troops to the Camotes Islands. Few contacts were made at either location.

During the 164th Infantry's move on Abijao, Company A took the lead on 16 February, 1945. Staff Sergeant Sail E. Jackman was the leading platoon guide, and as they moved forward he noticed several Japanese in position in a densely covered draw off their right flank. Quickly selecting three volunteers, Staff Sergeant Jackman moved into the draw to deal with the threat. His objective, to prevent any ambush of Company A, began with the shooting of two Japanese who rose to stop him. Just as he did so, however, he himself was fatally wounded by an enemy grenade. Two of his volunteers were wounded by the same explosion. Sergeant Jackman shouted orders to the other men, and to an aid man who had come forward to help, not to approach him in his exposed position. Nevertheless, after some time and further fighting with the Japanese, Sergeant Jackman was successfully evacuated before he died. For his fearless leadership Staff Sergeant Sail E. Jackman received a posthumous Distinguished Service Cross.[18]

The soldiers of the Americal Division were joined in mid-February by the 2nd and 3rd Battalions, 96th Infantry, Philippine Army. These former guerrillas now stalked the Japanese in the familiar jungles and mountains as well-organized, professional infantry soldiers. The sweeps by the Americans in mid- and late-February resulted in many areas being cleared of Japanese troops and another 288 reported killed. Two prisoners were captured and questioned.

Like most patrols, the ones conducted by the Americal Division were long, tiring and usually dull until that moment of noise and danger suddenly appeared, sending every soldier's heart into overdrive. One such patrol from the 2nd Battalion, 164th Infantry was searching Mount Naguang on February 12th when they ran into a group of the enemy soon after they passed a fork in the trail. One man was wounded and pinned down by Japanese fire. The eighteen-man patrol decided to outflank the enemy position by getting to the rear of the enemy and recovering the wounded soldier. Staff Sergeant Malcolm K. Walsh of Jamestown, North Dakota led a small group through the jungle behind the enemy and blocked their escape route. When the main body heard the firing, they joined in the fight, which resulted in a count of thirteen dead Japanese on the trail. A litter was made for the wounded American and, as the Americans were concentrating on that, Sergeant Walsh spotted a Japanese officer hiding a short distance away. Sergeant Walsh made the count fourteen enemy dead.

Even normally quiet areas could have their dangers. Company I of the 164th Infantry was moving by truck from Palompon to Villaba in order to be relieved by the 21st Reconnaissance Troop. As the troopers motored down the road, one truck hit a mine and exploded. One officer was killed and five enlisted men wounded.

More prisoners were being brought in now that the Japanese were aware that the battle for Leyte was lost. Eleven such prisoners were taken to the division's language officer, Captain James Fogg. As he was interrogating them one at a time, he was startled to hear one of them call him by name in perfect English. A quick conversation revealed that the prisoner had been a student before the war at the University of California, when Captain Fogg had also been a student.

Another incident worthy of note that occurred during the Americal Division's mopping up on Leyte was the first known use of a helicopter to evacuate wounded. In the heavy undergrowth and high mountains, with poor roads and enemy ambushes along any stretch of those roads, evacuation of the seriously wounded remained a concern. On February 16th, a badly wounded man from the 1st Battalion, 164th Infantry was in the aid station in Abijao when a helicopter arrived to evacuate him to a rear base hospital.

Air support also took the form used earlier by the 11th Airborne Division. Americal Division liaison planes often dropped supplies to far-ranging patrols who found themselves far from the nearest supply point. Radio batteries, the lifeline of small patrols out in enemy territory, medical supplies and food were the main staples dropped by this versatile aircraft.

General Arnold had developed a plan of action for clearing the Americal Division's sector of western Leyte. The 164th Infantry would drive up from the south while Colonel Floyd E. Dunn's 182nd Infantry would block any exits for the driven Japanese to the east. To the north, elements of the 164th Infantry and Colonel Claude M. McQuarrie's 132nd Infantry[19] would block the north exit. The intent was to draw a reasonably tight ring around the remnants of the *35th Army* and completely annihilate it.

Supported only by one field artillery battalion and their individual cannon companies, the three regiments moved against the Japanese on February 20th. The drive hit uneven resistance. In one case, the 2nd Battalion, 164th Infantry came up against a company of Japanese holding the barrio of Mansahon. Other battalions pushed through sporadic resistance and kept moving. Not far away, at the outskirts of Abijao, the 1st Battalion hit strong resistance and was counterattacked, forcing the Americans to withdraw to treat their many casualties. But the battles continued and slowly the noose around the remaining Japanese was tightened. By the end of February, the Americal Division had counted more than one thousand Japanese killed during these sweeps.

The Japanese were still strong, though. The 1st Battalion, 164th Infantry, which had been stopped outside of Abijao, was again counterattacked and forced to withdraw inside the Abijao perimeter. Reinforced by Companies E and F of the 2nd Battalion, the attack was renewed on February 22nd, and advanced slowly against strong resistance. Another forty-three enemy dead were counted. These kind of clearance sweeps continued for the remainder of February, and by that time the trap had been closed. At one point the Japanese chose to make a stand on a hilltop when the 2nd Battalion, 132nd Infantry attacked. The battle raged all day and the Americans had to make repeated assaults, but by dark Company G had circled the hill and reached the top, driving off the surviving Japanese. Left behind were more than two hundred enemy dead.

Battles like these were sometimes determined by one soldier. As the division attacked one hill, a platoon detached the squad of Staff Sergeant Lyle V. Stepleton of Pomona, California to watch their flank as they went up the enemy-held hill. Stepleton and six men took position and soon spotted an enemy machine gun waiting to ambush the attacking platoon's flank. Sergeant Stepleton crawled close to the gun, and when within three feet of it, shot the gunner and then killed the assistant gunner with a hand grenade. He then jumped into the position and disabled the enemy machine gun. With two of his men who had come up to help him, the sergeant killed eight other Japanese supporting the machine gun position. The enemy hill was easily captured.

Not far off Company E, 164th Infantry was fighting to hold a hill under Japanese counterattack. Private First Class John L. McInnis of Bossier City, Louisiana was a member of an artillery forward observation party from the 245th Field Artillery Battalion attached to Company E. He had been painfully wounded early in the fight by an enemy grenade, but when an automatic rifleman nearby was wounded, Private First Class McInnis immediately took his place, exposing himself to enemy fire to get the best position from which to shoot at the attacking Japanese. After the rifle was empty, he dropped back into his foxhole and reloaded with one hand while throwing grenades down the slope with the other. He then resumed his exposed position and kept the advancing Japanese from gaining the hilltop in his sector. When the attack was finally repulsed, Private First Class McInnis, too badly wounded to walk, crawled to the foot of the hill for medical treatment. Refusing to be evacuated, he returned to his foxhole just in time for the second enemy attack. Once again he repeated his performance, stopping the enemy attack by his reckless courage, standing up on the exposed hilltop to deliver a withering fire upon the attackers. Not only was he the target of the Japanese, but friendly artillery fire was striking so close to the hilltop that shrapnel from those rounds frequently buzzed over the hill, threatening to maim anyone upright. Despite these dangers, Private First Class McInnis held his position through a third Japanese attack, until dawn came and the enemy withdrew. Only then did he allow himself to be evacuated for medical treatment for the additional wounds he had received. He was awarded a Distinguished Service Cross.[20]

*　　*　　*

The battles to clear western Leyte of organized Japanese resistance continued into March, 1945, although by this time the Eighth Army had moved on to other assignments. Its rear command, the Eighth Army Area Command, still supervised combat operations on Leyte. These continued to be fierce in some instances, as when, during the first four days of March, the 1st Battalion, 164th Infantry, came up against a strong Japanese position built into the crater atop a steep-sided, rocky hill. For four days, the battalion attacked the hill repeatedly, with the rifle companies inching their way up the steep slopes, fighting off small counterattacks and using flamethrowers to clear the dug-in Japanese. At the end, another fifty-four enemy dead were counted while unknown more were buried within their defenses. But the Japanese still held the hill. Americal soldiers later remarked that upon standing near the hill, a terrible stench of death permeated the air. By then the 1st Battalion, 164th Infantry had been diverted elsewhere.

Brigadier General Eugene W. Ridings,[21] the assistant division commander and tactical commander of the sweeps being conducted by the Americal Division, had decided that there was no value in continuing to batter against strong defenses. Instead, he sent the battalion to join in with the others in sweeping western Leyte of Japanese, who were not so safely ensconced in strong defensive positions. The others had been sweeping in accordance with General Arnold's plan to clear western Leyte by trapping the bulk of the Japanese between his regiments. These drives continued to produce results, such as when the 2nd Battalion, 164th Infantry counted a hundred dead Japanese soldiers after sweeping a valley from one end to the other. Attacks by the 132nd Infantry and 182nd Infantry were equally productive. In one instance, Company E of the 182nd Infantry struggled to capture a hill against a fanatically resisting enemy force. Once cleared, the hill turned out to have been the headquarters of some large Japanese unit. The enemy command post was full of footlockers filled with papers and documents. Much in the way of equipment and supplies was left lying in the area. Another 105 enemy dead were added to the count.

Coincidentally, the struggle for Palompon was not quite over yet, either. This port, which the Americans had seized almost two months earlier, was attacked on March 6th by a lone Japanese plane that bombed and strafed it. The attack killed and wounded some civilians, but no American troops were injured and no equipment lost.

Still the battles continued. Small firefights continued to erupt as the Americans continued their sweep of western Leyte. As the circle narrowed, several units were pinched out of the circle and retired to Villaba to await transportation by water to Pinamopoan. The advancing units ran constantly into small groups of Japanese, who were either defending worthless positions or were wandering, seemingly aimlessly, across western Leyte toward some unknown goal. By March 9th the area had been completely swept. All organized enemy resistance between Palompon to Silad had now been eliminated. There was no way Japanese troops could escape Leyte, and there was no way they could organize any defenses. They were trapped and forced to await the Americans' pleasure, provided they didn't starve first.

The 182nd Infantry was now withdrawn from the clearing assignment and ordered to the Capoocan area to await further assignment. The hard luck 164th Infantry Regiment was detached from the Americal Division and placed under the command of the Eighth Army Area Command. They were to continue with clearing operations in western Leyte while protecting American installations in the Ormoc-Valencia sector. But fortunately for the North Dakota regiment, only two days later they were told to get ready to turn over their zone of responsibility to the 108th Infantry Regiment of the 40th Infantry Division.

While they awaited relief, the small battles continued. On March 20th, a patrol was in the bush with Private First Class Albert D. Rojo of Tampa, Florida as lead scout. Leading his patrol, Private First came upon an open field which he began to move across. As he did so, he spotted a Japanese sniper about to fire on him. He dropped quickly to the ground, aimed, and killed the sniper. As he moved on, he came up against six more enemy soldiers. Firing as he marched forward, Rojo killed all six despite the heavy fire they were directing at him. The squad, following behind Private First Class Rojo, simply stared in amazement.

By March 23rd, the 108th Infantry had completed the relief of the remaining elements of the Americal Division on Leyte. These units, in turn, assembled for a new assignment which would take them to Samar and the southern Philippines. Behind them they left an estimated 3,500 Japanese dead and another 68 as prisoners of war.

*   *   *

It could be said that the Leyte Campaign ended when General Suzuki left the island in March 1945. There was no organized resistance left, despite the fact that thousands[22] of Japanese troops remained. But the last recorded mopping-up action occurred on May 5, 1945 and Philippine guerrillas, now officially a part of the newly reestablished Philippine Army, continued to root out hidden Japanese for years afterward.

Nor were American combat units finished with Leyte. Late in April 1945, the 81st Infantry ("Wildcat") Division arrived on the island. Major

General Paul J. Mueller's[23] division had originally been assigned to participate in the invasion of Okinawa. It was being held in reserve on New Caledonia when it was ordered forward to Leyte. The division had fought a hard and bloody campaign under Marine Corps command in the Palau Islands in September, October and November of 1944, and had only recently completed retraining and reorganization in New Caledonia. Leyte was to be used to stage the division to either Okinawa, should it be called there, or to prepare for the invasion of Japan itself, the next major operation. In the meantime, it would train in amphibious and jungle warfare on Leyte.

While training and conducting awards ceremonies for actions in the Palau Islands, the division would also be assigned combat assignments on Leyte. The northwestern hills, again near Villaba and Valencia, were still the scene of active Japanese hostilities. On the 1st of June, 1945, the 81st Infantry Division published Field Order Number 6, which assigned some of its units to participate in clearing these areas of enemy troops. Meanwhile, the division's 306th Engineer (Combat) Battalion was to clear the area of the Valencia Airfield and restore it to American use. The division's 81st Reconnaissance Troop made extensive patrols, mapping the area as it went. From these maps, plans were made for operations against the remaining Japanese on Leyte. Supported by the independent 154th Engineer (Combat) Battalion, the 306th Engineers improved roads and trails into the suspected areas. From these, the division's combat patrols swept the area assigned to them.

In July 1945, reports coming into the division indicated that there were about one hundred enemy soldiers in the 400-square mile area of mountains north of Palompon. Under command of Eighth Army,[24] the division, along with the 1st Filipino Regiment (reinforced), was to clear them out. In turn, each of the division's three regiments was to conduct patrols throughout the zone, particularly around Villaba, to clear out the Japanese stragglers. The first to go was Lieutenant Colonel Dallas A. Pilliod's 3rd Battalion, 321st Infantry Regiment.[25] Reinforced by the 71st Joint Assault Signal Company, the battalion spent a week patrolling throughout the area at the end of July 1945. Nine Japanese were killed with no losses to the Americans, although several cases of malaria occurred.

The battalion was relieved by Major Robert G. Brough, Jr.,'s 1st Battalion, who went to the assistance of the 1st Filipino Regiment, when it reported Japanese within its zone. Over the next several days, Japanese were encountered by the patrols and seven more were killed with two captured. Reports of Japanese molesting Filipino civilians continued to come in, and the Reconnaissance Troop was sent to investigate at the end of July. After patrolling extensively well into August, only one Japanese was located and killed. Additional units were scheduled to begin patrolling in August, when word was received of the pending surrender of Japan. At that time all combat assignments were cancelled and the division settled down to await developments. As it turned out, no further combat missions were necessary on Leyte.

*   *   *

The official United States Army Campaign credit gives the dates of October 17, 1944, when the first Rangers landed in Leyte Gulf, and July 1, 1945, as the start and end dates, respectively, for the Leyte Campaign of World War II. During the busiest month on Leyte, January 1945, there were 257,766 American troops on the island, not all of them, of course, involved in the ground campaign. The U.S. Army reported casualties exceeding 15,500 men. Of these, about 3,500 were killed and almost 12,000 wounded.[26] Japanese figures remain more elusive simply because the *35th Army* was all but destroyed during the battle, and its headquarters and commander were lost soon afterward. Even estimates from American sources vary significantly, as do Japanese sources. General Tomochika, the surviving chief of staff of the *35th Army,* later stated to interrogators that there were anywhere from 59,400 Japanese soldiers and airmen involved in the Leyte Campaign to a high of 61,800. General Tomochika estimated that of these totals, about 13,010 were still alive on Leyte by March 17, 1945, when he left the island. He also guessed that about 49,790 Japanese had been killed during the battle up to that date.

The Americans had set goals for the invasion of Leyte. They needed to establish a foothold within the Philippines for future operations and this they accomplished, although not as strong or useful a base as they had sought. Leyte, with its heavy rains and poor soil, did not provide the number or quality of airfields for the U.S. Army Air Corps to use in supporting additional invasions throughout the islands. These, except for those at Tacloban, were in fact later established on other islands as they fell to the American invasion schedule. Development of Leyte was delayed due to these same adverse conditions and construction on the island never achieved expectations. Leyte never became a major airbase.

The Americans also wanted to reduce Japanese defensive strength in the Philippines by engaging a part of it on Leyte before facing what they believed would be the major battle on Luzon. The Japanese unwittingly cooperated in helping them achieve this goal by deciding, at the last moment, to make

Leyte the decisive ground battle of the war for Japan. They not only risked, and lost, the remainder of their surface fleet but they also diverted significant ground and air resources to the battle on the island. As we have seen, nearly all of these were destroyed or rendered impotent. Further, the transfer and diversion of ground forces from Luzon to Leyte, although cleverly accomplished, crippled the defense of Luzon that General Yamashita had planned. Their loss on Leyte forced him to change his defense of Luzon from an aggressive defense to one more passive, due to the lack of sufficient troops. The Japanese air resources were also depleted significantly, and although the new kamikaze tactic caused great concern among the Americans, it never achieved the goal of turning back or defeating one of the American invasion forces for the duration of the war. It did, however, deplete the air resources of Japan to the point where they had to hoard their remaining planes and pilots for the ultimate defense of Japan.

Perhaps the campaign was best summarized by the enemy commander, General Yamashita, when he testified before the U.S. Military Commission after the war, saying, "After the loss of Leyte . . . I realized that decisive battle was impossible." Leyte, then, had been the decisive ground battle of the war in the Southwest Pacific Theater of Operations.

*   *   *

General Hodge took his XXIV Corps, re-equipped to General Eichelberger's amazement, to Okinawa where they fought the last major battle of World War II. He was promoted to Lieutenant General in June 1945, and retained command of XXIV Corps until 1948, while he oversaw the demobilization of the Japanese Army in South Korea. Then he took command of V Corps in Germany. He next assumed command of the U.S. Third Army in Europe between 1950 and 1952, before becoming Chief of the Army Field Forces from 1952 to 1953. He retired as a general in June 1953, and died on November 12, 1963.

General Sibert retained command of his X Corps throughout additional battles in the Philippines until the end of the war. He retired in June 1946 and died June 24, 1980.

General Walter Krueger took his Sixth Army from Leyte to Luzon, where due to the prolonged resistance conducted by General Yamashita, it remained until the end of the war, in August 1945. At that time, General Kreuger and his army were preparing for the next major battle of the Pacific War, the invasion of Japan. Selected to lead the first invasion, General

Krueger and his staff were relieved instead to be assigned to conduct the occupation of Japan after its surrender in September 1945. Commanding four Corps[27] and thirteen divisions, he took his Sixth Army to Japan and disarmed the Japanese military, established order and protected the Japanese people. Then, after forty-six years as an American soldier, he retired in February 1946. The general moved to a new home in San Antonio, Texas with his wife. They settled down into what they hoped would be a quiet, relaxing life after so many moves during their active military life, but soon financial woes began to plague the general. He had neglected to pay taxes on his income during the war years, and his income tax bill took most of his savings. Friends established a fund to enable them to purchase their dream house. Money remained a problem, however, so much so that he often had to refuse invitations to travel to reunions or other gatherings simply because he could not afford it. Encouraged by friends and well-wishers he soon set upon writing his memoirs, which he found difficult without a staff to help him deal with all the paperwork involved. Rather than feature himself in this memoir, he featured the U.S. Sixth Army and the men he had commanded in World War II. So burdensome was the book that it took him five years to write it, and by the end he said, "Every day I plug away at my book, but progress is slow . . . I often wish I had never undertaken the task."[28]

Although he had served under General MacArthur all during his service in the Pacific, and had disagreed with him on some occasions, and had no doubt been aware of MacArthur's pitting of him against General Eichelberger to get the most of both men, General Krueger remained above the petty post-war squabbles many of the leaders evidenced in their memoirs. His book was, in fact, a history of the Sixth Army in World War II. Even later when General Eichelberger's feelings towards him grew angry and distant, General Krueger never made a derogatory remark about Eichelberger.

Family tragedies dogged the general after the war. His wife, Grace, was in ill health and soon his only son was cashiered from the army for drunkenness. Then, tragically, his only daughter was accused of killing her husband while in Tokyo. A diagnosis indicated that the general's daughter was suffering from mental illness. Despite this, the subsequent court-martial found her guilty and sentenced her to life imprisonment. The general and his ill wife were now left to care for their two grandchildren. In 1955, Grace was diagnosed with cancer and she died the following year. The repeated blows took a heavy toll of the general, and his own health began to fail. He died of pneumonia on August 20, 1967.

General Krueger has been labeled, by one contemporary correspondent, as the "Mystery Man of the Pacific" due to his little-known activities in the Pacific War. Yet, he has also been labeled "MacArthur's Fighting General" and other accolades by those who knew him or studied his campaigns during World War II. Often fighting with inadequate resources, pressed by his commander to move faster than military sense dictated, and never recognized for his accomplishments, General Krueger, nevertheless, delivered victories when they were needed. He did receive acknowledgment from General MacArthur, under whom he had worked for three years in often trying conditions, in the form of personal congratulations, the Distinguished Service Cross and a second Distinguished Service Medal upon his retirement.[29] He was also promoted to permanent Four Star rank.

Many junior officers, who served with General Krueger and then went on to high-level military careers of their own, remembered him with respect. The commander of the 1st Cavalry Division (Airmobile) in Vietnam considered him "one of the great army combat commanders of all time."[30] Another, the commander of the 4th Infantry Division in Vietnam, remarked of General Krueger, "He impressed me always as the finest general around. . . . He was, for many of us, the ideal of a soldier and leader."[31]

Criticized by historians since the war as either too plodding or too aggressive, depending upon the situation, he has also been criticized for not paying enough attention to signals intelligence, or ULTRA. The Leyte Campaign certainly debunks that evaluation, since he relied so heavily upon it that several of his changes in plan were based almost solely upon signals intelligence. But perhaps his long-time commander said it best when he remarked, "The mantle of Stonewall Jackson rests upon his shoulders." General MacArthur's comment, one not often given to others, is illuminating. Still others have compared General Krueger to General George H. Thomas, the Union General of Civil War fame who was known as "Old Slow Trot" for his careful and deliberate moves. Both men never lost a battle they commanded, and both men in the end stood victorious at the head of an army still ready to do battle, if necessary. Neither man ever threw away the lives of their men, while both cared for their soldiers' welfare above all other administrative matters. What is undisputed is that General Walter Krueger served his country faithfully and well, with distinction and skill, albeit with a minimum of publicity. He was certainly one of the premier American generals of World War II.

General Krueger's Sixth Army, as already mentioned, went on to conduct the Luzon Campaign, which was still active eight months later as the war in the Pacific ended. After conducting the occupation of Japan, it was inactivated and its colors returned to the United States. The U.S. Sixth Army was reactivated in Texas on March 1st, 1946, under the command of General Joseph W. Stilwell, and, after General Stilwell's death, General George P. Hays[32] and General Mark W. Clark. It has remained as a training and administrative command throughout the Cold War, Vietnam and the wars in Iraq and Afghanistan.

Appendix I

UNITED STATES FORCES ORDER OF BATTLE
LEYTE, 1944

SIXTH UNITED STATES ARMY

Lieutenant General Walter Krueger, Commanding
Brigadier General George Honnen, Chief of Staff

Colonel George S. Price, G-1   *Colonel Horton V. White,* G-2
Brigadier General Clyde D. Eddleman, G-3   *Colonel Kenneth Price,* G-4

Brigadier General Samuel D. Sturgis, Jr., Engineer Officer
Colonel William A. Hagins, Medical Officer
Brigadier General Philip G. Blackmore, Ordnance Officer
Brigadier General Charles R. Lehner, Quartermaster Officer
Colonel Harry Reichelderfer, Signals Officer
Colonel L. Hoyt Rockafellow, Adjutant General
Colonel Charles W. Mason, Inspector General

32nd Antiaircraft Artillery Brigade
10th Antiaircraft Artillery Group
15th Antiaircraft Artillery Group
94th Antiaircraft Artillery Group
120th Antiaircraft Artillery Group
2nd Engineer Special Brigade
5202nd Engineer Construction
    Brigade (Provisional)
1112th Engineer Construction Group

40th Antiaircraft Artillery Brigade
13th Antiaircraft Artillery Group
25th Antiaircraft Artillery Group
97th Antiaircraft Artillery Group
198th Antiaircraft Artillery Group
5201st Engineer Construction
    Brigade (Provisional)
1113th Engineer Construction
    Group

1118th Engineer Combat Group
1136th Engineer Construction Group
1140th Engineer Combat Group
20th Armored Group
780th Amphibian Tank Battalion
826th Amphibian Tractor Battalion
780th Amphibian Tractor Battalion
727th Amphibian Tractor Battalion
536th Amphibian Tractor Battalion

1122nd Engineer Combat Group
1138th Engineer Construction Group
5209th Engineer Service Group
(Provisional)
776th Amphibian Tank Battalion
632nd Tank Destroyer Battalion
788th Amphibian Tractor Battalion
728th Amphibian Tractor Battalion
718th Amphibian Tractor Battalion

X CORPS
Lieutenant General Franklin C. Sibert, Commanding

X Corps Artillery
226th Field Artillery Battalion, 155mm Gun
465th Field Artillery Battalion, 8-inch Howitzer
531st Field Artillery Battalion, 155mm Gun
947th Field Artillery Battalion, 155mm Howitzer

1st Cavalry Division
Major General Verne D. Mudge, Commanding

1st Cavalry Brigade
5th Cavalry Regiment
12th Cavalry Regiment
61st Field Artillery Battalion
99th Field Artillery Battalion
8th Engineer Squadron
44th Tank Battalion (attached)[1]
1st Medical Squadron

2nd Cavalry Brigade
7th Cavalry Regiment
8th Cavalry Regiment
82nd Field Artillery Battalion
271st Field Artillery Battalion
302nd Reconnaissance Troop
(Mechanized)

112th Cavalry Regimental Combat Team
Brigadier General Julian Cunningham, Commanding

24th Infantry Division
Major General Frederick A. Irving, Commanding (to 18 Nov. 1944)
Major General Roscoe B. Woodruff, Commanding (from 18 Nov. 1944)

19th Infantry Regiment
21st Infantry Regiment
34th Infantry Regiment
13th Field Artillery Battalion
63rd Field Artillery Battalion

3rd Engineer Combat Battalion
24th Reconnaissance Troop (Mecz.)
11th Field Artillery Battalion
52nd Field Artillery Battalion
603rd Tank Company (attached)

XXIV CORPS
Major General John R. Hodge, Commanding
V Amphibious Corps Artillery
Brigadier General Thomas E. Bourke, USMC, Commanding
Headquarters Battery, V Amphibious Corps Artillery
5th 155mm Howitzer Battalion, USMC
11th 155mm Howitzer Battalion, USMC
198th Field Artillery Battalion, 155mm Howitzer
226th Field Artillery Battalion, 155mm Gun
287th Field Artillery Battalion, Observation

7th Infantry Division
Major General Archibald V. Arnold, Commanding

17th Infantry Regiment	13th Engineer Combat Battalion
32nd Infantry Regiment	7th Reconnaissance Troop (Mecz.)
184th Infantry Regiment	31st Field Artillery Battalion
48th Field Artillery Battalion	49th Field Artillery Battalion
57th Field Artillery Battalion	767th Tank Battalion (attached)
2nd Joint Assault Signal Company	

96th Infantry Division
Major General James L. Bradley, Commanding

381st Infantry Regiment	321st Engineer Combat Battalion
382nd Infantry Regiment	96th Reconnaissance Troop (Mecz.)
383rd Infantry Regiment	363rd Field Artillery Battalion
361st Field Artillery Battalion	362nd Field Artillery Battalion
921st Field Artillery Battalion	763rd Tank Battalion (attached)
3rd Joint Assault Signal Company	

SIXTH ARMY RESERVE
32nd Infantry Division
Major General William H. Gill, Commanding

126th Infantry Regiment	114th Engineer Combat Battalion
127th Infantry Regiment	32nd Reconnaissance Troop (Mecz.)
128th Infantry Regiment	121st Field Artillery Battalion
120th Field Artillery Battalion	126th Field Artillery Battalion
129th Field Artillery Battalion	

77th Infantry Division
Major General Andrew D. Bruce, Commanding

305th Infantry Regiment	302nd Engineer Combat Battalion

306th Infantry Regiment
307th Infantry Regiment
304th Field Artillery Battalion
902nd Field Artillery Battalion

77th Reconnaissance Troop (Mecz.)
306th Field Artillery Battalion
305th Field Artillery Battalion
706th Tank Battalion (attached)

STRATEGIC RESERVE
11th Airborne Division
Major General Joseph M. Swing, Commanding

187th Glider Infantry Regiment
188th Parachute Infantry Regiment
511th Parachute Infantry Regiment
674th Parachute Field Artillery
   Battalion

127th Airborne Engineer Battalion
152nd Airborne Antiaircraft Battalion
457th Parachute Field Artillery
   Battalion
675th Glider Field Artillery Battalion

38th Infantry Division
Major General Henry L. C. Jones, Commanding

149th Infantry Regiment
151st Infantry Regiment
152nd Infantry Regiment
139th Field Artillery Battalion
163rd Field Artillery Battalion

113th Engineer Combat Battalion
38th Reconnaissance Troop (Mecz.)
138th Field Artillery Battalion
150th Field Artillery Battalion

ALLIED AIR FORCES

Lieutenant General George C. Kenney, Commanding

22nd Replacement Depot
360th Air Service Group
322nd Troop Carrier Wing
Fifth Air Service Area Command

FEAF Weather Group
FEAF Air Service Command
Fourth Air Service Command
5289th Air Service Area Command
   (Provisional)

U.S. Marine Corps Aviation Units (Attached)

Marine Fighter Squadron 115
Marine Fighter Squadron 218
Marine Fighter Squadron (Night) 541

Marine Fighter Squadron 211
Marine Fighter Squadron 313
Marine Bombing Squadron 611

Fifth U.S. Army Air Force
Major General Ennis P. Whitehead, Commanding

Fifth Bomber Command
308th (Heavy) Bomber Wing
310th (Medium) Bomber Wing
91st Photo Reconnaissance Wing

Fifth Air Force Service Command
309th (Heavy) Bomber Wing
54th Troop Carrier Wing
Fifth Emergency Rescue Group

Fifth Fighter Command
85th Fighter Wing   86th Fighter Wing

Thirteenth U.S. Army Air Force
Major General St. Clair Street, Commanding
Thirteenth Bomber Command   Thirteenth Air Service Command
Thirteenth Fighter Command   Thirteenth Emergency Rescue Group

Royal Australian Air Force
Air Vice Marshal William D. Bostock, Commanding
1st Tactical Air Force   Northeast Area Command
East Area Command   North Command
West Area Command   South Area Command
Northwest Area Command   Netherlands East Indies Air Force

Appendix 2

JAPANESE ORDER OF BATTLE
LEYTE, 1944

IMPERIAL GENERAL HEADQUARTERS

Southern Army
Field Marshal Count Hisaichi Terauchi, Commanding

3rd Maritime Transport Command
Major General Masazumi Inada, Commanding
4th Air Army
Lieutenant General Kyoji Tominaga, Commanding

14th Area Army
General Tomoyuki Yamashita, Commanding (from 9 October 1944)
Lieutenant General Shigenori Kuroda, Commanding (to 23 September 1944)
Lieutenant General Akira Muto, Chief of Staff

35th Army (excluding units not engaged at Leyte)
Lieutenant General Sosaku Suzuki, Commanding
Major General Yoshiharu Tomochika, Chief of Staff

1st Division[1]
Lieutenant General Tadasu Kataoka, Commanding
Colonel Junkichi Okabayashi, Chief of Staff

1st Infantry Regiment
49th Infantry Regiment
57th Infantry Regiment

1st Reconnaissance Regiment
1st Engineer Regiment
1st Field Artillery Regiment[2]

8th Division
5th Regimental Combat Team Only Engaged on Leyte

16th Division[3]
Lieutenant General Shiro Makino, Commanding

9th Infantry Regiment
20th Infantry Regiment
33rd Infantry Regiment
16th Engineer Regiment

16th Signals Unit
16th Reconnaissance Regiment
22nd Field Artillery Regiment[4]
16th Transport Regiment

26th Division[5]
Lieutenant General Tsuyuo Yamagata, Commanding

11th Infantry Regiment
12th Infantry Regiment
13th Infantry Regiment
26th Engineer Regiment

26th Signals Unit
26th Reconnaissance Regiment
11th Field Artillery Regiment[6]
26th Transport Regiment

30th Division (–)[7]
Lieutenant General Gyosaku Morozumi, Commanding

41st Infantry Regiment[8]
74th Infantry Regiment
77th Infantry Regiment
30th Engineer Regiment

30th Signals Unit
30th Reconnaissance Regiment
30th Field Artillery Regiment[9]
30th Transport Regiment

100th Division (Not Engaged on Leyte)

102nd Division[10]
Lieutenant General Shimpei Fukue, Commanding

77th Infantry Brigade
170th Independent Infantry Battalion
171st Independent Infantry Battalion
172nd Independent Infantry Battalion
354th Independent Infantry Battalion
77th Infantry Brigade Signals Unit
77th Infantry Brigade Labor Unit
102nd Artillery Battalion[11]
102nd Signals Company

78th Infantry Brigade
169th Independent Infantry Battalion
173rd Independent Infantry Battalion
174th Independent Infantry Battalion
355th Independent Infantry Battalion
78th Infantry Brigade Signals Unit
78th Infantry Brigade Labor Unit
102nd Engineer Battalion
102nd Transport Battalion

54th Independent Mixed Brigade[12]
Major General Tokichi Hojo, Commanding

360th Independent Infantry Battalion	54th Independent Mixed Brigade Artillery Unit
361st Independent Infantry Battalion	54th Independent Mixed Brigade Engineer Unit
362nd Independent Infantry Battalion	54th Independent Mixed Brigade Signal Unit

55th Independent Mixed Brigade[13]
Major General Tetsuzo Suzuki, Commanding

363rd Independent Infantry Battalion	55th Independent Mixed Brigade Artillery Unit
364th Independent Infantry Battalion	55th Independent Mixed Brigade Engineer Unit
465th Independent Infantry Battalion	55th Independent Mixed Brigade Signal Unit

68th Independent Mixed Brigade[14]
Major General Takeo Kurisu, Commanding

Appendix 3

U.S. ARMY BATTLE CASUALTIES AT LEYTE, 20 OCTOBER 1944–8 MAY 1945[1]

ORGANIZATION	TOTAL	KILLED	WOUNDED	MISSING
Sixth U.S. Army Troops Headquarters	961	141	813	7
Eighth U.S. Army Troops	404	61	340	3
X Corps	7,126	1,670	5,384	72
Americal Infantry Division[2]	731	162	566	3
24th Infantry Division	2,342	544	1,784	14
32nd Infantry Division	1,949	450	1,491	8
38th Infantry Division	272	68	171	33
1st Cavalry Division	931	203	726	2
11th Airborne Division	532	168	352	12
1st Filipino Division	52	14	38	0
108th Regimental Combat Team	53	14	39	0
112th Cavalry Regimental C.T.	160	32	128	0
Corps Troops	104	15	89	0
XXIV Corps	7,093	1,632	5,454	7
7th Infantry Division	2,764	584	2,179	1
77th Infantry Division	2,226	499	1,723	4
96th Infantry Division	1,660	469	1,189	2
Corps Troops	443	80	363	0
TOTALS	**15,584**	**3,504**	**11,991**	**89**

1. Source: Reports of the Commanding Generals, Eighth U.S. Army, Enclosure 1, and
   Sixth U.S. Army, on the Leyte-Samar Operation, p. 155.
2. Includes casualties of the 164th Infantry Regimental Combat Team.

NOTES

CHAPTER 1: DECISION FOR THE PHILIPPINES

1. For details about this and many other contingency plans for a war with Japan, see Edward S. Miller. *War Plan Orange. The U.S. Strategy to Defeat Japan, 1897–1945.* (Annapolis, Maryland: Naval Institute Press, 1991).
2. The August 1944 plan scheduled an invasion of Luzon beginning at Aparri on January 31, 1945, and Lingayen Gulf on February 20, 1945. See Maurice Matloff. *Strategic Planning for Coalition Warfare, 1943–1944. United States Army in World War II.* (Washington, D. C.: Center of Military History, 1994). P. 485.
3. These were the 7th, 77th, and 96th Infantry Divisions.
4. On-scene estimates give the killed as anywhere between "several" to "over three hundred."
5. Colonel Arthur Murray.
6. Major General Harry Schmidt, USMC, Commanding. Units included the 2nd and 4th Marine Divisions and the 27th Infantry Division. The XXIV Corps Artillery supported this campaign.
7. Major General Roy S. Geiger, USMC, Commanding. Units included the 1st (Provisional) Marine Brigade, the 3rd Marine Division and the 77th Infantry Division.
8. For capsule biographies of the ground forces commanders, see Appendix IV.
9. It should be noted, however, that these Cavalry Regiments consisted of only two, rather than the normal three, squadrons.
10. The term "squadron" was another holdover from the division's cavalry days. Infantry divisions had the same units but these were called battalions (for squadron) and companies (for troop).
11. In post-World War II Poland, this area is now Zlotow.
12. General Krueger had originally wanted to use either the 158th Regimental Combat Team or the 112th Cavalry Regimental Combat Team for this and the Panaon Strait area assignment. This way the entire subsidiary operation would be conducted by one experienced independent regiment under the command of a General Officer. How-

ever, neither unit was available because of troop shortages and previous commitments.

13. A-Day, or Attack Day, to distinguish it from D-Day in Normandy. This referred only to October 20th and not the prior landings by detached forces.

14. For details on Japanese signal intelligence which identified Leyte as a target of the advancing American advance, see Ken Kotani, *Japanese Intelligence in World War II.* (New York: Osprey Publishing Ltd., 2009). Pp. 76, 161–162.

15. General Kuroda survived the war.

16. Quoted in A. Frank Reed. The Case of General Yamashita. (Chicago: 1949). Pp. 18–19.

17. Although not at the time official policy, defense in depth had been used earlier at Peleliu and at Biak on New Guinea by the local commanders. The success of these defenses contributed to the change in the official policy, which was first officially used at Leyte. It would be developed into a deadly art at Iwo Jima and Okinawa.

18. That the Americans were coming should have been known to the Japanese commanders. The *Imperial Japanese Navy* code breakers had discerned from signals and direction-finding intelligence that an invasion of Leyte was planned for the near future by the Allies and reported their findings to unspecified ground commanders in the Philippines. What happened to this report in unknown but apparently it never reached General Suzuki. See Ken Kotani, Japanese Intelligence in World War II. op. cit., Pp. 75–76.

19. The USS *Tang* (SS-306) was a Balao Class submarine with a displacement of 1,526 tons armed with ten torpedo tubes (six forward, four aft) and a five-inch deck gun. It carried a crew of 75 and was capable of 21 knots on the surface. It was launched at the Mare Island, California, Navy Yard on 17 August 1943.

20. Committee on Veteran's Affairs, United States Senate. *Medal of Honor Recipients, 1863–1978.* (Washington, D. C.: U.S. Government Printing Office, 1979). P. 645. Commander O'Kane survived his harsh imprisonment and retired a rear admiral to his home in New Hampshire.

21. Arthur D. ("Bull") Simmons would play a key role in the development of the U.S. Army's Special Forces in the post-war Army.

CHAPTER 2: "I HAVE RETURNED"

1. Commander Francis Douglas Fane, USNR (Ret.) and Don Moore. *The Naked Warriors. The Story of the U.S. Navy's Frogmen.* (Annapolis, Maryland: Naval Institute Press, 1956). Pp. 149–156.

2. Lieutenant General Koyji Tominaga was commissioned into the Infantry, December 1913. Graduated War College, November 1923. Attached to Army General Staff, December 1924. Attached to Kwantung Army HQ in Manchuria, December 1925. Assistant Military Attache to Russia, December 1928. Lieutenant Colonel on the Army General Staff, August 1932. Colonel and Section Chief, Army General Staff, August 1936. Commanded infantry regiment in *2nd Imperial Guards Division*, promoted Major General, March 1939. Various staff appointments in Japan and China before promoted Lieutenant General December, 1941. Vice Minister of War, March 1943. Commander *4th Air Army*, August 1944. Refused to move out of Manila as

ordered by General Yamashita and only obeyed after a written order was personally delivered. Ill with fever and deciding that without aircraft his role was defunct, ordered his troops to fight as infantry and escaped to Formosa despite orders from General Yamashita not to leave. Accused of desertion and charged with crimes punishable by death. Overruled by *Imperial General Headquarters* due to his political influence in Tokyo. Captured by the Russians 1945 and held as a prisoner of war until 1955.

3. Cavalryman Sal DeGaetano, B Troop, 12th Cavalry Regiment, quoted in Gerald Astor, The Greatest War. Americans in Combat, 1941–1945. (Novato, California: Presidio Press, 1999). P. 718.

4. The 5th Cavalry Regiment was constituted in the Regular Army as the 2nd Cavalry, March 3, 1855. Re-designated August 3, 1861, as the 5th Cavalry it carries multiple battle honors from the Indian Wars, the Philippine Insurrection, the Civil War, the Mexican Expedition (1916–1917), World War II, Korea and Vietnam. It has been awarded no less than ten (10) Presidential Unit Citations including one for Leyte. The 7th Cavalry Regiment was constituted July 28, 1866, in the Regular Army and carries multiple battle honors from the Indian Wars, Mexican Expedition, World War II, Korea and Vietnam. It has been awarded no less than seven (7) Presidential Unit Citations including one for Leyte. The 12th Cavalry was constituted in the Regular Army on February 2, 1901. It carries multiple battle honors from World War II and Vietnam. It has been awarded no less than seven (7) Presidential Unit Citations including two (2) for Leyte.

5. The 44th Tank Battalion was constituted July 7, 1942, in the Army of the United States as the 44th Armored Regiment and assigned to the 12th Armored Division. Re-designated less elements as the 44th Tank Battalion, on September 15, 1942, it fought in New Guinea, the Bismarck Archipelago, Leyte and Luzon, where it earned two Presidential Unit Citations (Companies B and C each earned a citation).

6. Quoted in Gene Eric Salecker, *Rolling Thunder Against the Rising Sun. The Combat History of U.S. Army Tank Battalions in the Pacific in World War II.* (Mechanicsburg, Pennsylvania: Stackpole Books, 2008). P. 235.

7. The 8th Cavalry Regiment was constituted in the Regular Army on July 28, 1866. It carries multiple battle honors from the Indian Wars, World War II, Korea and Vietnam. It has been awarded no less than six (6) Presidential Unit Citations.

8. Major B. C. Wright. *The 1st Cavalry Division In World War II.* (Tokyo: Toppan Printing Company, Ltd., 1947). P. 75.

9. Ibid.

10. Quoted in Astor, op. cit., P. 709.

11. The 603rd Independent Tank Company was created when the 1st Cavalry Division arrived in the Southwest Pacific without tank support. In a re-organization during the fall of 1943 the Cavalry Division's 7th Reconnaissance Troop was disbanded and its personnel used to organize both the 302nd Reconnaissance Troop and the 603rd Light (later Medium) Tank Troop (later Company). One of the first tank units to see combat in the Southwest Pacific Theater of Operations, fighting in the Admiralty Islands, Biak Island, Wakde Islands, all in New Guinea and later at Leyte and Cor-

regidor islands in the Philippines, the company was often attached to other units. As a "bastard" unit it has no formal military lineage which this author could locate in official sources.

12. Later Colonel Newman, commanding the 34th Infantry, noticed that these flags were being used as an aiming point by the Japanese. He had them taken down until the enemy fire ceased.

13. The 34th Infantry Regiment was constituted in the Regular Army on July 1, 1916. It carries battle honors from World War I, World War II and the Korean War. It has been awarded at least three Presidential Unit Citations, including one for Kilay Ridge, Leyte.

14. Ibid, P. 710. Captain Austin is incorrect about the timing of the death of Captain Wye (Wie). See below.

15. Captain Wai's Medal of Honor was one of 21 awarded fifty years after the war when the Defense Department and Department of the Army reconsidered award recommendations made for dozens of Japanese-American personnel during World War II and upgraded these 21 to the Medal of Honor. Nearly all of the others served in the Mediterranean Theater of Operations or the European Theater of Operations. Letter to the author, United States Senate, Committee on Veteran's Affairs. Congressional Research Service.

16. Astor, op. cit., P. 712.

17. The 19th Infantry Regiment was constituted in the Regular Army on May 3, 1861. It carries multiple battle honors from the Civil War, Indian Wars, War with Spain, Philippine Insurrection, World War II and the Korean War. It has been awarded three (3) Presidential Unit Citations including one for Leyte.

18. Award issued in General Order Number 16, 1945, U.S. Army Forces, Far East.

19. The 13th Field Artillery was constituted in the Regular Army on June 3, 1916, and fought in the Aisne-Marne, St. Mihiel, Meuse-Argonne, Champagne 1918 and Lorraine 1918 Campaigns of World War I as a part of the 4th Infantry Division. Assigned to the 24th Infantry Division during World War II, it fought in the Central Pacific, New Guinea, Leyte, Luzon and Southern Philippines Campaigns. It was awarded a Philippine Presidential Unit Citation for it's part in the liberation of the Philippines.

20. The 63rd Field Artillery Battalion was constituted in the Regular Army on August 26, 1941 and assigned to the 24th Infantry Division at Schofield Barracks, Territory of Hawaii. It fought in the Central Pacific, New Guinea, Luzon, Leyte, and Southern Philippine Campaigns. It was awarded a Philippine Presidential Unit Citation for its part in the liberation of the Philippines.

21. Jan Valtin. *Children of Yesterday. The Twenty-Fourth Infantry Division in World War II.* (Nashville, Tennessee: Battery Press, 1988). P. 39.

22. Lieutenant Dick, of New Brighton, Pennsylvania, had assumed command of C Company when its commander had been killed on the beach. He was also wounded in the shoulder on the beach but refused to relinquish command.

23. Also spelled as Calbasag River.

24. The 383rd Infantry Regiment was constituted in the National Army on September

5, 1918. It saw no combat action until World War II where, as a part of the Organized Reserves, it participated in the Leyte and Ryukyus Campaigns. It was awarded a Presidential Unit Citation for the Okinawa Campaign.

25. Astor, op. Cit., P. 720.

26. Orlando R. Davidson, J. Carl Willems and Joseph A. Kahl. *The Deadeyes. The Story of the 96th Infantry Division.* (Nashville, Tennessee: Battery Press, 1981). P. 21. Sergeant George McFall, another wounded, was one of the first Leyte casualties to reach the States. He received a startling reception at Los Angeles, for one of the city's newspapers misunderstood the advance information and dispatched a galaxy of reporters and photographers to meet the first "lady" (ie: Leyte) wounded of the war.

27. Astor, op. cit., P. 720.

28. Four M3A1 Light tanks of Company D, 763rd Tank Battalion had been converted to flamethrower tanks, known as "Satans." These carried a flamethrower instead of a main gun and internal fuel tanks containing 170 gallons of fuel. When fired, it launched a stream of fire for about 70 yards. Because of the additional equipment within the tank, it carried only a crew of two, the driver and tank commander/gunner.

29. The 382nd Infantry Regiment was constituted in the National Army on September 5, 1918. It saw no combat action until World War II where, as a part of the Organized Reserves, it participated in the Leyte and Ryukyus Campagins. It was awarded a Presidential Unit Citation for the Okinawa Campaign.

30. The 763rd Tank Battalion was constituted March 19, 1942, as a part of the Army of the United States at Schofield Barracks, Oahu, Territory of Hawaii. It was awarded a Philippine Presidential Unit Citation for its performance during the war. It fought at Leyte and Okinawa.

31. This exchange is quoted in Davidson, et. al., op. cit., P. 23.

32. Astor, op. cit., P. 720.

33. Ibid.

34. The 32nd Infantry Regiment was constituted in the Regular Army on July 1, 1916 from personnel of the 1st and 2nd Infantry Regiments at Schofield Barracks, Hawaii. It carried battle honors from the Aleutian Islands, Eastern Mandates, Leyte and the Ryukyus as well as ten more for the Korean War. It earned four (4) Presidential Unit Citations, including two initiated by the U.S. Navy, for World War II and Korea.

35. The 184th Infantry Regiment was originally organized at Sacramento in 1864 as the Sacramento Light Artillery, California Militia. Reorganized as the 4th Infantry in the California National Guard on March 15, 1872 it was again converted to artillery, then back to infantry during various reorganizations within the California National Guard. Upon being federalized on March 3, 1941, it was assigned to the 7th Infantry Division and served with it through the war. It carries battle honors for the Aleutian Islands, Eastern Mandates, Leyte and Ryukyus Island Campaigns of World War II. It was awarded the Philippine Presidential Unit citation for the Leyte Campaign.

36. The 776th Amphibian Tank Battalion was constituted in the Army of the United States as the 1st Battalion, 2nd Armored Regiment, 9th Armored Division, on July 11, 1942, at Fort Riley, Kansas. Reorganized and re-designated on October 9, 1943,

as the 776th Tank Battalion. Re-organized and re-designated, January 28, 1944, as the 776th Amphibian Tank Battalion. It fought in the Western Pacific, Leyte and Ryukyus Campaigns and received a Philippine Presidential Unit Citation for its part in the liberation of the Philippines.

37. The 718th Tank Battalion was constituted November 24, 1942, in the Army of the United States as the 1st Battalion, 9th Armored Regiment and assigned to the 20th Armored Division. It was reorganized and re-designated September 10, 1943, as the 718th Tank Battalion at Camp Campbell, Kentucky, and relieved from the 20th Armored Division. Re-organized and re-designated, April 15, 1944, as the 718th Amphibian Tractor Battalion. It fought in the Leyte and Ryukyus Island Campaigns and was awarded a Philippine Presidential Unit Citation for its role in the liberation of the Philippines.

38. The 767th Tank Battalion was activated January 20, 1943, at Schofield Barracks, Hawaii. It was attached to the 7th Infantry Division for the Marshall Islands campaign and remained with it for the Leyte Campaign. Company A, 767th Tank Battalion, earned a Presidential Unit Citation for the Leyte Campaign between October 23–30, 1944.

39. "Spider holes" was the American term for individual Japanese foxholes which were camouflaged so well that often American troops walked right over them without spotting them until the individual Japanese soldier popped out and opened fire.

40. This account follows the official Army history of the incident. However, the 767th Tank Battalion claims that no tanks were knocked out, but that one tank had its waterproofing material around the 75mm gun set afire by the enemy, which prevented it from continuing its attack.

41. The 17th Infantry Regiment was constituted in the Regular Army on May 3, 1861. It carries multiple battle honors from the Civil War, Indian Wars, War with Spain, Philippine Insurrection, Mexican Expedition, World War II and Korea. It has earned one Presidential Unit Citation for the Leyte Campaign.

42. The 21st Infantry Regiment was constituted in the Regular Army on May 3, 1861, as the 2nd Battalion, 12th Infantry. Re-designated on December 7, 1866, as the 21st Infantry Regiment, it carries multiple battle honors from the Civil War, Indian Wars, War with Spain, Philippine Insurrection, World War II, Korea and Vietnam. It has earned two (2) Presidential Unit Citations.

43. Casualties for A-Day were officially reported as 49 men killed, 192 wounded and 6 missing. M. Hamlin Cannon. Leyte: The Return to the Philippines. Washington, D. C. Center of Military History. 1993. P. 78.

44. The concept of "combat loading" had been established earlier in the war. It required that the supplies likely to be needed first be loaded on each ship last, so as to provide quick and easy access to those urgent supplies. Less important supplies were packed further down in the ship and could be unloaded when urgency was less.

45. The 2nd Engineer Special Brigade was activated at Camp Edwards, Massachusetts on June 20, 1942, as the 2nd Engineer Amphibian Brigade with the 532nd Engineer Shore, 542nd Engineer Amphibian and 592nd Engineer Boat Regiments assigned. After training in Florida and California, it arrived in Australia April 17, 1943, and

participated in the New Guinea and Leyte Campaigns.

46. The 1122nd Engineer Combat Group was re-designated on September 25, 1943, from Headquarters and Headquarters Company, 35th Engineer Combat Regiment at Camp White, Oregon. It served in the Leyte and Ryukyus Campaigns. The 1140th Engineer Combat Group was activated August 25, 1943, at Camp Breckinridge, Kentucky, and served in the Leyte and Ryukyus Campaigns. An engineer group consisted of two or three engineer combat battalions established to perform specific support tasks during operations.

47. The 3rd and 4th Engineer Special Brigades.

48. The DUKW was an amphibious truck. Known as the "Duck" after its military initials, the vehicle was developed in 1942 as an amphibious truck which could transport supplies, or troops, from sea to shore and inland, when necessary. Used widely in most theaters of the war, it was produced in large numbers, 21,147 in total.

49. Quoted in Astor, op. cit., P. 717. The quotation is from an American eyewitness.

50. War Department General Order Number 104, 15 November 1945. Private Moon's automatic weapon was a Thompson submachine gun.

51. For his gallantry during the night of October 21–22, 1944 Private First Class Samuel Jerma was awarded the Distinguished Service Cross and promoted to Sergeant. General Orders 195, General Headquarters, United States Army Forces, Pacific. (25 September 1945). Private First Class John W. Ray also received the Distinguished Service Cross. General Orders 295, General Headquarters, United States Army Forces, Pacific. (2 October 1945).

52. The 361st Field Artillery Battalion had been constituted June 24, 1921 in the Organized Reserves (Portland, Oregon) and assigned to the 96th Infantry Division. It was ordered in Federal Service August 15, 1942, at Camp Adair, Oregon. It served at Leyte and Okinawa.

53. Captain Young was the Company C Commander.

54. The 921st Field Artillery Battalion was constituted in the National Army as the 321st Ammunition Train in 1918. It was re-designated January 30, 1942, as the 921st Field Artillery Battalion and ordered into federal service August 15, 1942 at Camp Adair, Oregon. It fought at Leyte and Okinawa. The 362nd Field Artillery Battalion was constituted in the Organized Reserve (Seattle, Washington) June 24, 1921, and assigned to the 96th Infantry Division. It was ordered into federal service August 15, 1942, at Camp Adair, Oregon. It fought at Leyte and Okinawa.

55. The Alamo Scouts were created in December 1943, by General Krueger who was dissatisfied with the results of other intelligence gathering groups in his area. Officially known as the Sixth U.S. Army Special Reconnaissance Unit, they were a small force, never more than 200 men, who operated behind enemy lines in teams of five or six and were directly under Sixth U.S. Army control. See Larry Alexander, *Shadows in the Jungle. The Alamo Scouts behind Japanese Lines in World War II* (New York: New American Library, 2009); and Lance Q. Zedric, *Silent Warriors of World War II. The Alamo Scouts behind Japanese Lines.* (Ventura, California: Pathfinder Publishing, 1995).

56. General Order Number 89, 1945, U.S. Forces, Pacific.

57. Quoted in Orlando R. Davidson, J. Carl Willems and Joseph A. Kahl. *The Deadeyes.*

The Story of the 96th Infantry Division. Nashville. Battery Press. 1947. P. 28.

58. Ibid.

59. Ibid, P. 31. Colonel McCray received a posthumous Silver Star. Captain Thomas also received the Silver Star.

60. The 381st Infantry Regiment was constituted in the National Army September 5, 1918. Reconstituted June 24, 1921, in the Organized Reserve (Portland, Oregon) and assigned to the 96th Infantry Division. Federalized August 15, 1942, at Camp Adair, Oregon, it served at Leyte and Okinawa.

61. Chemical Mortar Battalions of World War II fired the 4.2-inch Chemical Mortar which was a multiple purpose weapon. Originally designed by the Army's Chemical Warfare Service to fire chemical and gas shells, it was never used for that purpose and soon developed into an artillery auxiliary weapon, firing shells some 3,200 yards. First used to fire smoke shells to provide protection for the infantry, it soon was used to fire high explosive shells for the same purpose.

62. The 780th Tank Battalion was constituted in the Army of the United States as the 1st Battalion, 45th Armored Regiment and assigned to the 13th Armored Division. Re-designated September 20, 1943, as the 780th Tank Battalion and again on April 8, 1944, as the 780th Amphibian Tank Battalion. The battalion fought at Leyte and Okinawa. .

63. General Orders Number 63, General Headquarters, United States Army Forc

CHAPTER 3: INTO THE VALLEYS

1. Interrogation of Major General Toshio Nishimura, 19–22 Nov. 45; as quoted in M. Hamlin Cannon, op. cit., P. 93.

2. Ibid, P. 94.

3. General Walter Krueger. *From Down Under To Nippon. The Story of Sixth Army in World War II*. (Nashville, Tennessee: Battery Press, 1989). P. 162.

4. Unlike some other campaigns in the Southwest Pacific, the Leyte Campaign was the beneficiary of unusually accurate, even timely, radio intercept intelligence on Japanese troop movements, orders of battle, and operations planning. For details see Edward J. Drea, *MacArthur's Ultra, Codebreaking and the War Against Japan, 1942–1945*. (Manhattan, Kansas: University Press of Kansas, 1992). Chapter six deals with Leyte.

5. Ibid, P. 167.

6. This was the attack during which Private Moon received his Medal of Honor, previously described.

7. The 13th Field Artillery Battalion was constituted in the Regular Army as the 13th Field Artillery, June 3, 1916. It participated in five World War I campaigns as a part of the 4th Infantry Division. Assigned to the Hawaiian Division, October 4, 1921. Re-designated as the 13th Field Artillery Battalion and assigned to the 24th Infantry Division, October 1, 1941. It served in the Central Pacific, New Guinea, Leyte, Luzon and Southern Philippines Campaigns in World War II and holds one Presidential Unit Citation for Korea.

8. By this point, Colonel Spragins had been wounded two days in a row, but retained command of his battalion.

9. Similar armor thrusts were attempted, for example, on Iwo Jima by a joint effort of the 3rd, 4th and 5th Marine Tank Battalions and later on Okinawa by the Army's 193rd Tank Battalion (27th Infantry Division) but these were less than successful.

10. General Orders Number 68, General Headquarters, U.S. Army Forces, Pacific.

11. Salecker, op. cit., Pp. 241–242.

12. This unit may have been misidentified in American records. According to Drea, op. cit., P. 167, Table 6.2, the unit was the *1st Company, 6th Armored Regiment.*

13. The Japanese tanks were not identified, but since they were armed only with machine guns they were most likely Type 94 Light tanks. Intended as a reconnaissance vehicle, it had armor so light it could be penetrated by rifle bullets. It carried .30 caliber machine guns and a crew of two.

14. The task force consisted of the 17th Infantry Regiment, Company A, 767th Tank Battalion, 91st Chemical Company, Company A, 7th Medical Battalion, and Company A, 13th Combat Engineer Battalion. For their performance between October 23–30, 1944, these units were awarded a Distinguished Unit Citation. (General Orders Number 32, Department of the Army, 6 July 1949).

15. The 48th Field Artillery was constituted in the Regular Army on October 1, 1933, and re-designated January 1, 1941, as the 48th Field Artillery Battalion. Assigned to the 7th Infantry Division June 1, 1941, it served in the Western Pacific, Aleutian Islands, Eastern Mandates, Leyte and Ryukyu Campaigns. It earned a Presidential Unit Citation for the Inchon Campaign during the Korean War.

16. General Orders Number 62, General Headquarters, United States Army Forces, Pacific. 20 July 1945.

17. General Orders Number 107 General Headquarters, United States Army Forces, Pacific. 14 August 1945.

18. Colonel Logie had believed that he had authority to withdraw his contact patrols with the 96th Infantry Division if the terrain was too difficult. He withdrew the patrols on October 23rd. The next day the assistant Division Commander, Brigadier General Joseph L. Ready, visited Colonel Logie and learned of the loss of contact. He immediately ordered contact re-established which was done. The following day the Division Commander visited Colonel Logie and after some discussion, replaced him as commander of the 32nd Infantry Regiment.

19. The 49th Field Artillery was constituted in the Regular Army on October 1, 1933, and re-designated as the 49th Field Artillery Battalion and assigned to the 7th Infantry Division on June 1, 1941. It served in three World War I campaigns and in the Aleutian Islands, Northern Solomons, Eastern Mandates, Leyte and Ryukyu Campaigns of World War II.

20. Regimental Cannon Companies were armed with the Howitzer Motor Carriage M8. Basically a 75mm Pack Howitzer mounted on a Light tank M5 carriage in an open-topped fully-traversable turret, it carried a crew of four, had a speed of 37 miles per hour, and a travel range of 99 miles.

21. It took two additional days for the engineers to clear the runways and dispersal areas of the Japanese mines.

22. These included the Regimental Cannon Company, a platoon of the Antitank Com-

pany, a platoon from the 13th Combat Engineers, the 767th Tank Battalion and part of the 91st Chemical Company.

23. There is some discrepancy over these tanks. Salecker, op. cit., describes these as three Medium tanks of Company C, 767th Tank Battalion. However, Love, op. cit., describes them as Light tanks. Cannon, op. cit. states only "tanks" without further description. Further, both Cannon and Salecker state that the tanks lost one to antitank fire ahead of the infantry and that another was stalled, later abandoned, with only one tank returning to friendly lines. Love states that all three returned to friendly lines. The narrative follows Love's description as it is taken from first person accounts, although there is no reason to discount the others.

24. War Department General Orders Number 104, 15 November 1945.

25. War Department General Orders Number 58, 19 July 1945.

26. Love, op. cit., P. 235.

27. For this reason he had detached the 21st Infantry for the Panaon Strait assignment instead of one of the 1st Cavalry Division's regiments.

28. Quoted in Drea, op. cit., P. 169.

29. The *1st Infantry Division* was identified from an order captured by the XXIV Corps.

30. General Orders Number 97, General Headquarters, United States Army Forces, Pacific. 7 August 1945.

31. Brigadier General Kenneth Frank Cramer was born in Gloversville, New York on October 3, 1894, and received his Literary Bachelor's Degree from Princeton in 1916, and his Master's Degree in 1917. He was commissioned in the Infantry, Officers Reserve Corps in 1917, and served with the infantry in France at the St. Mihiel and Meuse-Argonne offensives. He was wounded in action and captured on November 5, 1918. Joined the Connecticut National Guard in May 1931. Called to active duty February 1941. Brigadier General July 1942. Assistant Division Commander, 24th Infantry Division 1941–1946. Major General July 1946. Commanded 43rd Infantry Division, 1946–1947. Chief, National Guard Bureau, 1947–1954. Awarded 4 Silver Stars, Bronze Star and Purple Heart.

32. This incident is related in Valtin, op. cit., P. 98.

33. From the *102nd Infantry Division.*

34. Known as the *Tempei Battalion.* Japanese units often took the name of their commanders when detached from a parent unit.

35. Krueger, op. cit., P. 159.

36. Molotov Cocktails were gasoline filled containers, usually bottles, filled with gasoline and with some sort of fuse attached. Tossed on a tank, it would set the vehicle afire, forcing the crew to abandon the vehicle and usually knocking it out of action.

37. General Orders Number 29, 1945, U.S. Army Forces In the Far East. Colonel Newman returned to the division as its Chief of Staff some months later, where in 1945, he guided it during the Mindanao Campaign.

38. This incident is related in Valtin, op. cit., P. 99.

CHAPTER 4: INTO THE MOUNTAINS—BREAKNECK RIDGE

1. In order to accommodate this new field, General Krueger had to move his Sixth U.S.

Army Headquarters from Tanauan to Tolosa to provide the space needed.

2. LSTs were Landing Ships, Tank. The versatile craft were originally designed to carry heavy armored vehicles to beachheads. More than 1100 were built during the war and several were converted to hospital ships, headquarters ships and even small aircraft carriers capable of launching small observation planes over a beachhead.

3. Medical units assigned to the Leyte Campaign included the 110th Portable Surgical Hospital (supporting the 6th Ranger Battalion), the 16th, 19th and 27th Portable Surgical Hospitals, the 38th and 58th Portable Surgical Hospitals, all in X Corps and the 41st and 52nd Portable Surgical Hospitals in XXIV Corps. The 394th, 644th and 645th Medical Collecting Companies and the 69th Field Hospital were also assigned to Leyte. The 7th Portable Surgical Hospital was attached to the 21st Infantry Regiment while at Panaon Strait.

4. C rations were small cans of meat and vegetables (meat & beans; meat and vegetable stew; meat and spaghetti; ham, eggs and potatoes; meat and noodles; meat and rice; frankfurters and beans; pork and beans; ham and lima beans; chicken and vegetables) distributed to the troops which were easily carried. They included jam, crackers, powdered drinks, sugar, cereals, etc. Originally developed for paratroopers the K ration was packed as breakfast, lunch or dinner meals and contained such delicacies as a fruit bar, sugar, crackers, ham and eggs, cheese, meat, orange or lemon powder, chocolate and chewing gum.

5. General Orders Number 195, General Headquarters, United States Army Forces, Pacific. (25 September 1945).

6. "Victory" Division was a nickname for the 24th Infantry Division.

7. War Department General Order Number 17, 11 February 1946.

8. When discussing Japanese plans and intentions during the Leyte Campaign it must be remembered that their intelligence about American positions on Leyte was seriously lacking. Throughout the campaign, for example, they believed that the Americans were utilizing the many airfields that they had abandoned earlier in the campaign, when in fact only Tacloban, Tanaoen and Dulag were operational, the latter minimally.

9. I have been unable to find any trace of this attack in available records, but it was not unusual at this stage of the war for submarines to fail to record attacks on small boats.

10. Hasting, Max, *Retribution. The Battle for Japan, 1944–1945.* (New York: Albert A. Knopf, 2008). P. 175.

11. This was incorrect, of course. The Japanese had seized Wake Island against opposition from the 1st Marine Defense Battalion and a counter-landing was attempted on Bougainville against the 3rd Marine Division.

12. This is the same Colonel Verbeck who had earlier saved the General's life when he was unarmed and attacked by a stray Japanese soldier.

13. The 112th Cavalry Regimental Combat Team was an independent combat unit within Sixth U.S. Army. It had fought on New Guinea and the Bismarck Archipelago before Leyte. Constituted February 20, 1920 as the 1st Regiment, Texas Cavalry, Texas National Guard it was reassigned as the 112th Cavalry and assigned to the 23rd Cavalry Division July 20, 1921. In 1939 it was reorganized as a three squadron

cavalry regiment before it was inducted into federal service November 18, 1940. It was re-designated as the 112th Cavalry Regiment, Special, October 1, 1944. It would later serve on Luzon where it was at the war's end.

14. Salecker, op. cit., Pp. 249–250.

15. The 226th Field Artillery Battalion was organized as the 1st Battalion, Field Artillery, New York National Guard on February 23, 1908. It was expanded and re-designated as the 2nd Field Artillery on May 28, 1912. It served on the Mexican Border and then in France during World War I. It was reorganized as the 105th Field Artillery and assigned to the 27th Infantry Division, New York National Guard June 1, 1921. It was detached and designated the 226th Field Artillery Battalion, September 1, 1942. It fought at Leyte and the Ryukyus Island Campaigns. The 465th Field Artillery Battalion was organized October 15, 1921 in the Organized Reserves and assigned to the 65th Cavalry Division. During the Leyte Campaign it fired 8-inch towed howitzers and was assigned as Corps Artillery.

16. The 128th Infantry was organized as the 1st and 2nd Wisconsin Volunteer Infantry Regiments in 1861 and served in fourteen Civil War Campaigns. Repeated reorganizations in the inter-war years until the 1st, 2nd and 3rd Wisconsin Infantry Regiments were consolidated on July 15, 1917 as the 128th Infantry Regiment and assigned to the 32nd Division. It participated in five World War One campaigns and fought in the Papua, New Guinea, Leyte and Luzon Campaigns of World War II. It holds a Presidential Unit Citation for Papua and two for Luzon.

17. The 32nd Infantry Division was organized on July 18, 1917 as the 32nd Division, National Guard of Michigan and Wisconsin. It fought in the Aisne-Marne, Oise-Aisne, Meuse-Argonne and Alsace Campaigns of World War I. Demobilized August 26, 1917 it was recalled into Federal Service October 15, 1940 as the 32nd Infantry Division. It fought in the Papua, New Guinea, Leyte and Luzon Campaigns, earning a Presidential Unit Citation for the Papua Campaign and Luzon.

18. "Hourglass" was a nickname of the 7th Infantry Division derived from the shape of its shoulder sleeve insignia.

19. General Order Number 79, General Headquarters, United States Army Forces, Pacific. (30 July 1945). The quotation is within the citation.

20. Later known as "Bloody Ridge," "Suicide Ridge" or "Dagami Heights" depending upon which account is used as reference.

21. 382nd Infantry Unit Report 14, 2 November 1944 as quoted in Cannon, op. cit., P. 241.

22. General Order Number 45, 1945, Pacific Ocean Areas.

23. General Easley, still leading from the front, was killed on Okinawa.

24. Donald O. Dencker. *Love Company. Infantry Combat against the Japanese, World War II.* (Manhattan, Kansas: Sunflower University Press, 2002). P. 108.

25. Private First Clss Greenback was awarded a Bronze Star. There is no record of an award to Priate First Class Hartzer.

26. The Mindanao operation was deferred, later cancelled.

27. This was the *26th Infantry Division* landing at Ormoc.

28. Krueger, op. cit., P. 162.

29. During the Leyte Campaign Sixth U.S. Army would receive a total of 336 officer and 4,953 enlisted replacements. By December 20th the Army was short 21,000 men, the equivalent of an infantry division with attachments.

30. Constituted November 12, 1942 in the Army of the United States, the 11th Airborne Division was activated at Camp Mackall, North Carolina February 25, 1943 and participated in the Airborne-Troop Carrier Maneuvers of December, 1943. Transferred to the Regular Army it departed San Francisco May 8, 1944 and arrived in New Guinea May 25, 1944. It arrived on Leyte November 11, 1944. It participated in the New Guinea, Leyte and Luzon Campaigns. It earned a Presidential Unit Citation for the Manila Operation.

31. Constituted August 5, 1917 in the National Army the Division fought in the Oise-Aisne, Meuse-Argonne, Champagne and Lorraine Campaigns of World War I. It was the parent unit of the famous "Lost Battalion" of the Argonne Forest. It was reconstituted June 24, 1921 as a unit of the Organized Reserves from New York State. It was activated at Fort Jackson, South Carolina March 25, 1942 and provided the cadre for the 94th Infantry Division. It participated in the Louisiana Maneuvers in 1942 and trained at the Desert Training Center in California. The 77th Infantry Division left San Francisco March 24, 1944 for Hawaii. It participated in the Guam, Leyte and Ryukyus Campaigns. Its first commander was Major General Robert L. Eichelberger, who on Leyte commanded the Eighth U.S. Army.

32. American tactical radio procedure of the era gave every unit headquarters a call sign, or name, by which it was known. The 19th Infantry's call sign was "Doughboy" and each of its battalions was known by adding a color, red for the 1st Battalion, white for the 2nd and blue for the 3rd.

33. Knee mortar was actually a misnomer. The Japanese Army used a grenade launcher which most Americans thought was fired from the knee. Actually the weapon was fired from the ground as the recoil from the blast could easily break the operator's knee.

34. General Order 123, U.S. Army Forces in The Far East, 1945.

CHAPTER 5: INTO THE MOUNTAINS—KILAY RIDGE

1. Maj. Gen. William H. Gill, as told to Edward Jaquelin Smith. *Always a Commander. The Reminiscences of Major General William H. Gill.* (Colorado Springs, Colorado: Colorado College, 1974). P. 74.

2. Colonel Hettinger had been General Gill's Chief of Staff and had recently requested a combat assignment. Leyte would be his first combat as a regimental commander.

3. The 1st Battalion, 128th Infantry was originally commanded by Lieutenant Colonel William A. Duncan, but Colonel Burns commanded during most of the Breakneck Ridge battle. See Major General H. W. Blakeley (Edward T. Lauer, Historian*), 32nd Infantry Division in World War II.* (State of Wisconsin: N.P., N.D.) P. 185.

4. The 120th Field Artillery Battalion originated as the 2nd and 3rd Squadrons, 1st Wisconsin Cavalry in May 1917 and entered Federal Service August 5, 1917. In September 1917 the 1st Squadron was consolidated with the first two squadrons and redesignated as the 120th Field Artillery and assigned to the 32nd Division. It fought

in the Aisne-Marne, Oise-Aisne, Meuse-Argonne, Alsace, Champagne and Lorraine Campaigns of World War I. It was again inducted into Federal Service October 15, 1940 and served in the New Guinea, Leyte and Luzon Campaigns. It earned a Presidential Unit Citation at Aitape (New Guinea).

5. General Orders Number 137, General Headquarters, United States Army Forces, Pacific. (26 August 1945).

6. Page 59, as quoted in Cannon, op. cit., P. 225–227.

7. War Department General Order 21, 1945.

8. Landing Vehicle, Tracked. These were amphibious vehicles used to transport troops from transports to beachheads. Lightly armored and armed, they could move over land or water at slow speeds carrying troops and/or supplies.

9. Later, on 21 November during the siege of Kilay Ridge, Sergeant Mason's platoon was cut off from the main body of the battalion. With only 20 men left in the platoon, he led a determined defense which repulsed all attacks despite being severely wounded himself. After his force had been relieved, and only after he had personally briefed his replacement on the situation, did Sergeant Mason allow himself to be evacuated for medical aid. For his intrepid leadership of his platoon on 12 and 21November 1944 Technical Sergeant Donald P. Mason was awarded the Distinguished Service Cross. General Orders Number 147, General Headquarters, United States Army Forces, Pacific (3 September 1945).

10. As noted in a previous chapter, this was the battalion's call sign; Dragon for the 34th Infantry and red for the 1st Battalion.

11. Colonel Clifford would win a second DSC on Luzon where he was killed in action, June 1945.

12. It is unclear if the ridge was named after Henry Kilay because he was killed there, or as one source reports, because he was the owner of the ridge. Jan Valtin, Children of Yesterday, op. cit., P. 247 states that he told Colonel Clifford he was the owner of the ridge.

13. Valtin, op. cit., P. 259.

14. General Orders Number 99, General Headquarters, United States Army Forces, Pacific (8 August 1945).

15. General Orders Number 195, General Headquarters, United States Army Forces, Pacific 20 October 1945).

16. War Department General Order 30, 1945. Company A of this battalion would also receive another Presidential Unit Citation for its part in the seizure of Corregidor during the Luzon Campaign, 1945.

17. Krueger, op. cit. P. 176. The official records place the relief on November 18th, not the 17th.

18. Major General J. Lawton ("Lightening Joe") Collins.

19. In August 1945, General Irving took command of the 38th Infantry Division.

20. General Woodruff retained command of the 24th Infantry Division until November 1945.

21. Major General E. M. Flanagan, Jr. (Ret.). *The Angels. A History of the 11th Airborne Division*. (Novato, California: Presidio Press, 1989), states (P. 112) that General Irving

was relieved "ostensibly for failing to take Breakneck Ridge on schedule. General Irving took over the rather innocuous job of commanding the Leyte Garrison Force, the unit that would hold Leyte after completion of the operation." Yet even here the use of the word "ostensibly" raises questions.

22. The 826th Amphibian Tractor Battalion was organized December 3, 1941 at Camp Roberts, California as the 826th Tank Destroyer Battalion. Converted to an amphibian tractor battalion April 18, 1945 and assigned to the Organized Reserves. It participated in the Bismarck Archipelago, Leyte, Luzon, New Guinea and Southern Philippines Campaigns.

23. Wright, op. cit., P. 80.

24. The 126th Infantry was organized between 1855 and 1859 as independent militia volunteer companies around Grand Rapids, Michigan. As such they participated in ten Civil War campaigns. Reorganized in 1874 as State Troops they became a part of the National Guard. Designated the 32nd Michigan Volunteer Infantry they were federalized in May 1898 but did not go overseas. Mustered into Federal Service again on July 1, 1916 for the Mexican Border incident they were released in 1917 only to be called up again that same year. Combined with elements of the 31st Michigan Volunteer Infantry they were re-designated as the 126th Infantry Regiment, Michigan National Guard. As such they served with the 32nd Division in the Aisne-Marne, Oise-Marne, Meuse-Argonne ad Alsace Campaigns of World War II. After World War I they were released until October 15,1940 when again Federalized they served with the 32nd Infantry Division in the Papua, New Guinea, Leyte and Luzon Campaigns. The regiment was awarded a Presidential Unit Citation for Papua.

25. The 82nd Field Artillery Battalion was organized June 3, 1916 in the Regular Army as the 24th Cavalry. Re-designated as the 82nd Field Artillery November 1, 1917 it did not go overseas during World War I. Assigned to the 1st Cavalry Division March 17, 1930 it served in the New Guinea, Bismarck Archipelago, Leyte and Luzon Campaigns during World War II. The 99th Field Artillery Battalion was organized in the Regular Army as the 99th Field Artillery (Pack) on October 1, 1933. Re-designated as the 99th Field Artillery Battalion December 16, 1940 and assigned to the 1st Cavalry Division March 2, 1943 is served in the New Guinea, Bismarck Archipelago, Leyte and Luzon Campaigns. It was awarded a Presidential Unit Citation for its participation in the Los Negros Island battle.

26. War Department General Order 58, 1945. Private First Class Steinbach was awarded a Silver Star.

27. General Orders Number 105, General Headquarters, United States Army Forces, Pacific (18 August 1945).

28. Davidson, op. cit., P. 43. It was standard American operating procedure that at night no one left their foxholes for any reason. Thus anyone above ground at night was automatically the enemy.

29. Private First Class Crandall received a posthumous Silver Star. Private First Class Abrego received a posthumous Bronze Star.

30. Lieutenant Blair received the Silver Star.

31. These included the *10th, 23rd and 19th Infantry Divisions. The 1st Raiding Group*

was a unique unit consisting of parachute units, forced-landing (Glider) units and supporting elements. It was formed from two original regiments of the *Airborne Brigade* in November 1944 and arrived in the Philippines in December 1944. Some of its units participated in the main Japanese counterattack in December 1944 on Leyte.

32. It should be noted, however, that there was another airborne unit, the 503rd Regimental Combat Team, in the Southwest Pacific Theater which took part in the New Guinea and Luzon Campaigns.

33. Quoted in Lieutenant General E. M. Flanagan, Jr., op. cit., P. 105. The P-38 Lightening was one of the premier American fighter planes of the war. A twin engine, twin tail boom single seat fighter plane with counter rotating propellers it was armed with four fifty caliber machine guns and one twenty millimeter cannon. Both of America's highest scoring fighter aces (Majors Richard Bong and Thomas McGuire) flew these planes in the Pacific.

34. Krueger, op. cit., P. 177.

35. Ibid.

36. The 306th Infantry Regiment was organized in the National Army on August 5, 1917 and assigned to the 77th Division at Camp Upton, New York. It fought in World War I and after the war was assigned to the Organized Reserves. It was ordered into Federal Service on March 25, 1942 and inactivated March 15, 1946 at Hokodate, Japan. It fought in the Oise-Marne, Meuse-Argonne, Lorraine and Champagne Campaigns of World War I and the Western Pacific (Guam), Leyte and Ryukyus Campaigns of World War II. It holds a Presidential Unit Citation for Ie Shima in the Ryukyus and another for Okinawa in the same Ryukyus Campaign.

37. In addition to the USS *Waller* this sinking is credited to the USS *Renshaw* (Commander G. H. Cairnes), USS *Saufley* (Commander D. E. Cochran) and USS *Pringle* (Lieutenant Commander J. L. Kelley, Jr.). While agreeing with the date and place, Japanese records credit the USS *Helm* (DD-388) with the sinking. Other Japanese submarine losses in this period around Leyte include the I-26 sunk by the USS *Richard M. Rowell* (DE-403) east of Leyte on October 25th; the I-54 sunk by the USS *Helm* (DD-338) and USS *Gridley* (DD-380) on October 28th; the I-45 by the USS *Whitehurst* (DE-634) on October 29th; the I-38 by the USS *Nicholas* (DD-449) on November 12th off Palau and the I-41 by the USS *Lawrence C. Taylor* (DE-415) and naval aircraft on November 18th.

38. Thomas Cassin Kinkaid was born in Hanover, New Hampshire, April 3, 1888, and graduated Annapolis 1908. Commissioned 1910 and served aboard the USS *Arizona* during World War I. Graduated Naval War College 1930. Commanded Cruiser USS *Indianapolis* 1937–1938. Naval Attache at Rome, then Belgrade 1938–1941. Promoted Rear Admiral November 1941 and led naval task forces during the Gilbert, Marshall, Wake, Bougainville operations. Fought in the battles of the Coral Sea, Midway and Santa Cruz Islands. He commanded naval forces in the North Pacific before taking command of the Seventh U.S. Fleet and being promoted to Vice Admiral 1943. Served as MacArthur's top naval commander until the end of the war. Promoted Admiral April 1945.

39. George Lester Weyler, born May 24, 1886 in Emporia, Kansas and graduated from Annapolis 1910. Commissioned 1912 and commanded various destroyers during World War I. Received his Law Degree from Georgetown University Law School in June 1922. Commanded destroyers before being assigned as Naval attaché in Peru. Graduated from the Naval War College May 1938. Commanded Naval Station at Guantanamo Bay, Cuba September 1940–March 1944. Rear Admiral in August 1942 and Commander of Battleship Division Three March 1944–August 1945. Promoted Vice Admiral upon retirement November 1946.

40. Quoted in Samuel Eliot Morison, *History of United States Naval Operations In World War II, Volume Twelve, Leyte, June 1944–January 1945.* (Boston: Little, Brown & Company, 1984). Pp. 351–352.

41. Morison, Ibid, gives Commander Mel A. Peterson as the commanding officer of the USS Cooper. This agrees with Theodore Roscoe, *United States Destroyer Operations in World War II.* (Annapolis, Maryland: Naval Institute Press, 1953). P. 444. However, Roscoe gives a submarine attack as the cause of the USS *Cooper's* loss, rather than an enemy destroyer. Commander Peterson survived the sinking.

42. This was the IJN *Kuwa* which was sunk in Ormoc Bay at 10-50N, 124-36E.

43. The USS *Cooper* went down in Ormoc Bay at 10-54N, 124-36E.

44. Some of the USS *Cooper's* survivors swam ashore to Leyte where they were hidden by Filipinos until returned to American custody. Apparently there were several Japanese survivors from the *IJN Kuwa* who spoke English and the groups exchanged remarks, although they did not mix together.

CHAPTER 6: INTO THE MOUNTAINS—SHOESTRING RIDGE

1. Gordon L. Rottman and Akira Takizawa. *Japanese Paratroop Forces of World War II.* (Oxford, U. K.: Osprey Publishing Ltd., 2005). Apparently the Americans were unaware of the fourth plane since no mention of it is made in the official U.S. Army history of this episode.

2. General Order Number 89, General Headquarters, United States Army Forces, Pacific. (3 August 1945).

3. General Order Number 352, General Headquarters, United States Army Forces, Pacific. (26 November 1945)

4. General Order Number 402, General Headquarters, United States Army Forces, Pacific. (17 December 1945)

5. General Arnold held the 3rd Battalion at Caridad, to be in a position to prevent an outflanking attack through the mountains by the Japanese. He held the 2nd Battalion, 184th Infantry, at Baybay to prevent a counter landing by the Japanese from the sea.

6. General Arnold received orders from Sixth U.S. Army early in the battle that the guerrillas were not to be given missions beyond their capabilities. As a result he withdrew the guerrillas on the defensive line but retained those manning outposts.

7. The Mitsubishi "Sally" bomber was a twin engine medium bomber armed with four light and one heavy machine gun. It could carry a bomb load of up to 4,000 pounds.

8. Quoted in Barrett Tillman, *Above and Beyond. The Aviation Medals of Honor.* (Washington: Smithsonian Institution Press, 2002).

9. War Department General Order Number 90, 8 December 1944.

10. It should be noted that the 155mm guns of the Marines were never located by the Japanese and never suffered from counter-battery fire. As a result, their fire on Ormoc was consistent.

11. Colonel John M. Finn, "Shoestring Ridge," Infantry Journal, LVII, 3 (September 1945). P. 47.

12. This incident created one of the mysteries of the Leyte Campaign. The Marine has never been identified. The description in the text is taken from Love's The Hourglass, History of the 7th Infantry Division, op. cit., but does not name the Marine. Similarly Cannon's op. cit., official history mentions the incident and notes that the Company K "platoon leader, a technical sergeant, insisted that the Marine gunner either transfer to the Army or he would have to transfer to the Marines, as he couldn't get along without him" but notes that a check of Marine Corps records and interviews with Marine Corps historians and Colonel Finn failed to reveal the name or rank of the Marine.

13. General Order Number 72, General Headquarters, United States Army Forces, Pacific. (27 July 1945)

14. Love, op. cit., P. 260.

15. Ibid, P. 261.

16. Captain Dixon had been mortally wounded by this time.

17. Joseph Louis Ready was born in Brighton, Massachusetts on November 17, 1895 and commissioned into the Infantry in 1917. Served in the Philippines 1919–1920. Served in China 1920–1922. Professor of Military Science and Tactics at the University of Maine 1923–1928. China service 1931–1933 before graduating the Command and General Staff School 1936. Graduated Army War College 1939. Member of the Infantry Board 1939–1942. Brigadier General August 1942. Assistant Division Commander, 7th Infantry Division 1943–1945. Retired as Colonel, March 1946.

18. The 1st Battalion, 32nd Infantry, remained at Panoan Strait.

19. The journey of the 776th Amphibian Tank Battalion, reinforced with a company of the 718th Amphibian Tractor Battalion, around southern Leyte is a minor epic in itself.

20. Japanese records indicate that one of the amphibian tanks was set afire and that the 184th Infantry attack was repulsed.

21. General Orders Number 72, General Headquarters, United States Army Forces, Pacific. (27 July 1945)

22. General Orders Number 299, General Headquarters, United States Army Forces, Pacific. (30 October 1945)

23. The *2nd Raiding Brigade* was a part of the larger *1st Raiding Group* which had been formed from the original Airborne Brigade in November 1944. The *1st Raiding Group* consisted of two brigades of paratroops and one of glider borne troops. It included a small tank unit, support units and communication units. The *2nd Raiding Brigade* consisted of the *3rd Raiding Regiment (Parachute)* and *4th Raiding Regiment (Parachute),* each with a strength of about 700 men.

24. The *IJN Kishinami* was sunk in Luzon Strait at 13-12N, 116-37E.

25. The USS *Flasher* is officially credited with two Japanese destroyers in this fight, including the *IJN Iwanami* but this latter ship is not confirmed in Japanese records, which are known to be incomplete. *Flasher* went on to patrol off Indo-China where she sank another three large tankers.

26. The 38th Infantry Division was drawn from the National Guards of Indiana, Kentucky and West Virginia. It was inducted into Federal Service on January 17, 1941 and trained at Camp Shelby, Mississippi. After training and maneuvers it departed New Orleans and arrived in Hawaii on January 21, 1944. It arrived in New Guinea July 23, 1944 and on Leyte December 16, 1944, although elements such as the 149th Infantry arrived prior. It served in the New Guinea, Southern Philippines and Luzon Campaigns. Its commander at this time was Major General Henry L. C. Jones.

27. The 149th Infantry Regiment originated as the 2nd Kentucky Volunteers on May 23, 1846. It fought at the Battle of Buena Vista in the Mexican War before becoming the State Guard of Kentucky after the war. Elements of the Kentucky National Guard fought on both sides of the Civil War, including the 2nd Kentucky Volunteers which fought at Murfreesborough, Chickamauga, West Virginia and Mississippi. Between the wars the National Guard units underwent repeated reorganizations until mustered into Federal Service in 1917 when various units were consolidated into the 149th Infantry Regiment. It did not reach France until after hostilities had ceased. After the war assigned to the 38th Division. Federalized January 17, 1941. Fought in the New Guinea, Leyte and Luzon Campaigns of World War II.

28. The 152nd Infantry Regiment originated as the 3rd Regiment of Indiana Volunteers on June 24, 1846 and fought at Buena Vista during the Mexican War. Reorganized as the 6th and 8th Indiana Volunteers they were mustered into Federal Service April 1861 and fought in the Murfreesborough, Vicksburg, Chickamauga, Chattanooga, Atlanta, West Virginia, Alabama, Arkansas, Mississippi, Tennessee, Missouri, Louisiana, Virginia (1864) and Georgia (1864–65) Campaigns. Re-designated as the 152nd Infantry and assigned as the Indiana National Guard it was Federalized in 1917 but arrived in France as hostilities ceased. Assigned to the 38th Division the regiment was Federalized January 17, 1941 and fought in the New Guinea, Leyte and Luzon Campaigns of World War II.

CHAPTER 7: THE "OLD BASTARDS" LAND

1. Rear Admiral Arthur Dewey Struble was born in Portland, Oregon on June 28, 1894 and commissioned from Annapolis in 1915. He served in the office of the Chief of Naval Operations 1939–1940 and then commanded the cruiser USS *Trenton*, 1941–1942. Promoted Rear Admiral In October 1942 he was appointed Chief of Task Force 122 in the Twelfth Fleet. Commander Amphibious Group Two 1944–1945. Retired as Admiral July 1956.

2. The Curtiss P-40 fighter plane, known variously as the "Tomahawk," "Kittyhawk" or "Warhawk," was a single seat fighter plane armed with six .50 caliber machine guns. It could carry one 500 pound or two 100 pound bombs. Republic's P-47 "Thunderbolt" was also a single seat fighter plane armed with six .50 caliber machine guns and which could carry a load of bombs or rockets up to 2,500 pounds. The Vought F4U

"Corsair" was a gull winged single seat fighter plane used mostly by the Marine Corps, later the Navy and which was armed with six .50 caliber machine guns and capable of carrying up to 2,000 pounds of bombs or rockets.

3. The initial intake of this division included some men in their late forties and early fifties, including some who had served in the division during World War I and had remained active in the Army Reserve. They volunteered to remain with the division when it was activated for World War II.

4. As noted previously General Woodruff was now commanding the 24th Infantry Division on Leyte.

5. The 7th Infantry Division also trained in amphibious tactics.

6. The 306th Infantry Regiment originated August 5 1917 in the National Army and was assigned to the 77th Division. After the war it was made a part of the Organized Reserve from New York, New York. In was ordered into Federal Service March 25, 1942 and served in the Western Pacific (Guam), Leyte and Ryukyus Campaigns. It earned a Presidential Unit Citation for Ie Shima and another for Okinawa during the Ryuykus campaign.

7. The 307th Infantry Regiment originated August 5, 1917 in the National Army and was assigned to the 77th Division. After the war it was made a part of the Organized Reserve from New York, New York. It was ordered into Federal Service March 25, 1942 and served in the Western Pacific (Guam), Leyte and Ryukyus Campaigns. It earned a Presidential Unit Citation for Okinawa.

8. The 305th Infantry Regiment originated August 5, 1917 in the National Army and was assigned to the 77th Division. It fought in the Oise-Aisne, Meuse-Argonne, Lorraine and Champagne campaigns of World War I. After the war it was made a part of the Organized Reserve from New York, New York. It was ordered into Federal Service March 25, 1942 and served in the Western Pacific (Guam), Leyte and Ryukyus Campaigns of World War II. It earned two (1st Battalion and 3rd Battalion) Presidential Unit Citations for the Okinawa campaign.

9. The 226th Field Artillery Battalion originated in the New York National Guard as the 1st Battalion, Field Artillery February 23, 1908 with headquarters in Bronx County. Reconstituted and re-designated several times over the next few years it was re-designated as the 105th Field Artillery and assigned to the 27th Division October 1, 1917. It fought in the Meuse-Argonne and Lorraine Campaigns of World War I. After the war the 1st Battalion was reorganized as the 226th Field Artillery Battalion and relieved from assignment to the 27th Division effective September 1, 1942. It served in the Leyte and Ryukyu Campaigns as part of Corps Artillery, XXIV Corps.

10. Lt. General E. M. Flanagan, Jr. (Ret.). *The Angels. A History of the 11th Airborne Division.* op. cit. P. 146.

11. The Type 100 Heavy Bomber was known by the Allied code name "Helen." It was a twin engine mid-wing monoplane with a rear tail turret armed with four 7mm and one 79mm machine guns along with one 20mm cannon. It could carry a bomb load up to 2,300 pounds. It carried a crew of five to seven and had a service ceiling of 38,000 feet.

12. The Type 100 Transport was known by the Allied code name "Topsy." Also called

by the Japanese the Mc 20, it was a twin-engine low wing unarmed monoplane capable of carrying 2,360 pounds of freight or equivalent weight in paratroops. It carried a crew of four and had a service ceiling of 23,000 feet.

13. This flag was later captured by the 11th Airborne Division on Leyte.

14. This second echelon consisted of the *3rd* and *Heavy Weapons Companies* of the *3rd Raiding Regiment*. There was a third echelon planned, consisting of the remaining 80 men of the regiment, which never left the ground.

15. The standard U.S. Army infantry division of World War II at full strength numbered about 12,000 officers and men, and usually had attached units of battalion size or smaller which brought it closer to 15,000 men. In Europe the smallness of the airborne division brought about the attachment of another parachute regiment as more or less a permanent part of those divisions. Although the Southwest Pacific Theater did have another parachute regiment, the 503rd Airborne Infantry, it was never permanently attached to the 11th Airborne Division.

16. Brigadier General Albert Pierson was born in Brooklyn, New York on July 10, 1899 and attended Cornell University before being commissioned into the infantry in 1918. He returned to Cornell after World War I and then was an Assistant Professor of Military Science at the school 1922–1926. He graduated from the Command and General Staff School 1937 and the Army War College 1940. Then served on the War Department General Staff 1940–1942. Promoted Brigadier General February 1943 and assigned as Assistant Division Commander, 11th Airborne Division through October 1945.

17. This Japanese technique of trying to keep enemy forces awake at night began with the first "Washing Machine Charley" at Guadalcanal.

18. The 511th Parachute Infantry Regiment was constituted November 12, 1942 in the Army of the United States. Activated at Camp Toccoa, Georgia on January 5, 1943 it was assigned to the 11th Airborne Division on February 25, 1943. It fought in the New Guinea, Leyte and Luzon Campaigns of World War II and earned two Presidential Unit Citations, one for Manila and the other for Luzon.

19. The battalions had only three rifle companies, no heavy weapons companies. A small group of machine guns and mortars was carried by the battalion headquarters companies.

20. The 187th Glider Infantry Regiment was constituted November 12, 1942 in the Army of the United States. It was assigned to the 11th Airborne Division February 25, 1943 at Camp Mackall, North Carolina. It fought in the New Guinea, Leyte and Luzon Campaigns of World War II and again during the Korean War. It holds a Presidential Unit Citation for Tagaytay Ridge (Luzon) in World War II and several additional PUCs for Korea and Vietnam.

21. The 675th Airborne Field Artillery Battalion was constituted November 12, 1942 in the Army of the United States as the 675th Glider Field Artillery Battalion and assigned to the 11th Airborne Division. It fought in the New Guinea, Leyte and Luzon Campaigns of World War II and was awarded a Presidential Unit Citation for Nasugbu Point, Luzon.

22. The scout, known only as "Berg" made a successful landing in his new jump boots.

23. Flanagan, op. cit., P. 127.

24. The 503rd Parachute Infantry Regiment was constituted February 24, 1942 in the Army of The United States as the 503rd Parachute Infantry Battalion. Activated at Fort Benning, Georgia it was merged with the 504th Parachute Infantry Battalion and expanded to regimental size. The 2nd Battalion was separated and designated as the 2nd Battalion, 509th Parachute Infantry and sent to the Mediterranean Theater of Operations. The 503rd Parachute Infantry Regiment, less 2nd Battalion, went to Australia where a new Second Battalion was activated. The regiment remained as a separate regimental combat team and fought in New Guinea, Leyte, Luzon and Southern Philippines. It holds a Presidential Unit Citation for Corregidor and several others for the Vietnam War.

25. The 287th Field Artillery Observation Battalion was constituted February 25, 1942 in the Army of the United States. It was activated at Camp Bosie, Texas on May 20, 1943. It fought in the Leyte and Ryukyus Campaigns of World War II.

26. Second Battalion, 511th Infantry, 1st Battalion, 187th Glider Infantry, and 3rd Battalion, 306th Infantry.

27. The turncoat Filipino was later captured and turned over to the guerrillas, who executed him.

28. The battalion was severely under strength due to several detachments made before the crisis, including the entire Company C sent off into the mountains.

29. The 188th Glider Infantry Regiment was constituted in the Army of the United States on November 12, 1942 and assigned to the 11th Airborne Division. Activated at Camp Mackall, North Carolina, it was re-designated July 4, 1945 as the 188th Parachute Infantry Regiment. It fought in New Guinea, Leyte and Luzon and earned a Presidential Unit Citation for Luzon.

30. Flanagan, op. cit., P. 151.

31. Ibid, P.152–153. This incident is also related in other sources.

32. The 408th Quartermaster Company.

33. The 674th Glider Field Artillery Battalion was constituted November 12, 1942 in the Army of the United States and assigned to the 11th Airborne Division November 27, 1942 at Camp Mackall, North Carolina. It fought in the New Guinea, Leyte and Luzon Campaigns and earned a Presidential Unit Citation for Luzon.

34. The 149th Infantry Regiment was constituted as the 2nd Kentucky Volunteers on May 23, 1846 from volunteer militia of Kentucky. It served in the Mexican War at Buena Vista and in the Civil War at Shiloh, Murfreesborough, Chickamauga, West Virginia and Mississippi. Elements were also formed into Confederate Regiments and formed the basis of the Confederate "Orphan Brigade." Mustered into Federal service for the Mexican Punitive Expedition in 1916. Federalized for World War I and assigned to the 38th Division but did not enter combat prior to the end of the war. Reorganized as the 149th Infantry Regiment, Kentucky National Guard, July 1, 1921. Inducted into Federal Service January 17, 1941 and assigned to the 38th Infantry Division. Fought in New Guinea, Leyte and Luzon.

35. The 38th Infantry Division was formed with regiments of the Indiana, Kentucky and West Virginia National Guards. It was inducted into Federal service January 17,

1941 and fought in New Guinea, Southern Philippines and Luzon. This was the division which was later commanded by General Irving, formerly of the 24th Infantry Division on Leyte.

36. Flanagan, op. cit., P. 157. Also quoted in other sources.

37. Dencker, op. cit., P. 126.

38. A battalion each from the 11th Airborne, 38th Infantry and 96th Infantry Divisions.

39. War Department General Order Number 89, October 19, 1945.

40. Major General Ennis Clement Whitehead was born in Westphalia, Kansas on September 3, 1895 and attended the University of Kansas 1915–1917. He was commissioned into the Aviation Section of the Signal Corps in 1917. Resigned his commission and graduated from the University of Kansas with a B. E. in 1920. Commissioned in the Air Service same year. Graduated from the Command and General Staff School 1938. On the War Department General Staff 1938–1942. Brigadier General June 1942. Commanding General, Fifth U.S. Army Air Force 1942–1945. Major General March 1943. Lieutenant General June 1945.

41. The 902nd Field Artillery Battalion was constituted August 5, 1917 in the National Army as the 302nd Ammunition Train and assigned to the 77th Division. It fought in the Oise-Aisne, Meuse-Argonne, Champagne and Lorraine Campaigns of World War I. Re-designated as the 902nd Field Artillery Battalion on January 30, 1942 and allocated to the 77th Infantry Division. It fought in the Western Pacific, Leyte and Ryukyus Campaigns of World War II.

42. However, Morison, op. cit., P. 380 states that the enemy ships had already unloaded these same 4,000 troops and were empty when sunk. Naval records indicate that on this date only one Japanese "fast transport," the *Till*, was sunk five miles off Leyte (11-23N, 124-18E) by U.S. aircraft.

43. The USS *Mahan* was sunk at 1150 Hours, December 7th, 1944 at 10-50N, 124-30E.

44. The USS *Ward* was sunk at 1000 Hours, December 7th, 1944 at 10-51N, 124-33E.

45. Camp Downes had been a pre-war Philippine Army and Constabulary camp. It sat on a plateau which was situated east of the highway and commanded all approaches, most of which were open and without cover to conceal approaching forces.

46. The 305th Field Artillery was constituted on August 5, 1917 as the 305th Field Artillery and assigned to the 77th Division. Re-designated as the 305th Field Artillery Battalion on January 30, 1942. It fought in the Oise-Aisne, Meuse-Argonne, Champagne and Lorraine Campaigns of World War I and the Western Pacific, Leyte and Ryukyus Campaigns of World War II.

47. General Order Number 382, General Headquarters, United States Army Forces, Pacific. (7 December 1945)

48. General Order Number 299, General Headquarters, United States Army Forces, Pacific. 30 October 1945). There is some confusion about Sergeant Medina's surname. On the General Order issuing the citation for the DSC it is spelled Nedina, but other references to him cite him as Medina. The author was unable to reconcile the difference and used the more common spelling.

CHAPTER 8: THE LAST VALLEY

1. Commander, Destroyer Squadron 14.
2. The destroyers were the USS *Caldwell, Reid, Conyngham, Smith, Coughlan* and *Edwards.*
3. The Wright F4U/FG/F3A Corsair was a gull winged single seat fighter aircraft flown initially only by the U.S. Marine Corps. It had a speed of 425 mph and was armed with six fifty caliber guns. It was capable of carrying a bomb load of up to 2,000 pounds.
4. The USS *Reid* sank at 1700 Hours, December 11th, 1944 at 09-50N, 124-55E.
5. This may have been the *IJN Uzuki* but the ship was also claimed by PT-492 and 490 (Lieutenant (s.g.) Melvin W. Haines USNR) in a fight that same evening off Palompon. Records indicate that the *IJN Uzuki* was sunk 50 miles NE of Cebu at 11-03N, 124-23E by the two PT Boats. The *IJN Yuzuki* was sunk 65 miles NNW of Cebu at 11-20N, 124-10E by USMC Aircraft.
6. Commander, Destroyer Squadron 5.
7. The USS *Mugford* (Commander M. A. Shellabarger) and USS *LaVallette* (Commander W. Thompson).
8. The *Tasmania Maru.*
9. First Lieutenants Stanley Picak, Harry O'Hara and Richard E. Eacobacci.
10. Robert Sherrod. History of Marine Corps Aviation in World War II.(Baltimore, Maryland: Nautical & Aviation Publishing Co. of America, Inc., 1980). P. 280–281.
11. One plane had returned to base with operational difficulties.
12. Sherrod, op. cit., P. 283.
13. The full name of this Japanese Officer, whom the Japanese command regarded as highly successful in delaying the Americans at Ormoc, has been lost to history.
14. The rest of this battalion was assigned to beach defense.
15. According to the prisoner reports these were the latest Japanese amphibian tank, probably the Type 3 Ka-Chi. At 29 tons this was the largest such tank and carried a 37mm main gun and two machine guns in the hull. It was fitted with sponsons and waterproofing gear which were dropped when the vehicle came ashore. Water propulsion was provided by twin screws and steering by twin rudders. One intact tank was captured abandoned at Ormoc after this landing attempt.
16. War Department General Order Number 16, February
17. War Department General Order Number 16, 8 February 1946.
18. Sometimes spelled Majunag.
19. Flanagan, op. cit., pp. 166–167.
20. War Department General Order Number 35, 9 May 1945.
21. Flanagan, op. cit., p. 170.
22. Ibid, p. 171.
23. The hill was named after the Regimental Commander, Colonel Orin D. "Hard Rock" Haugen.
24. The 457th Parachute Field Artillery Battalion was constituted in the Army of the United States on 12 November 1942 and assigned to the 11th Airborne Division 27 November 1942. It fought in the New Guinea, Leyte and Luzon Campaigns.

25. Lieutenant General Tadasu (Kaoru) Kataoka was commissioned a 2nd Lieutenant of Cavalry in December 1915. He graduated from the War College November 1925, before serving on the Army General Staff. He instructed at the War College March 1931, before becoming a member of the Army General Staff. Promoted to Lieutenant Colonel August 1934. Promoted to Colonel March 1938. Commander of Imperial Guard Cavalry Regiment April 1939. Commander of Imperial Guard Reconnaissance Regiment December 1940. Promoted Major General and Commander of the 3rd Cavalry Brigade March 1941. Acting commander, 1st Infantry Division, China, August 1944. Promoted Lieutenant General November 1944.

26. Lauer, op. cit., p. 187.

27. War Department General Order Number 82, 27 September 1945.

28. War Department General Order Number 66, 1945.

29. War Department General Order Number 83, 2 October 1945.

30. Lauer, op. cit., p. 192.

31. Ibid.

32. War Department General Order Number 60, 26 June 1946.

33. General Order Number 55, General Headquarters, United States Army Forces, Pacific, 16 July 1945.

34. Ibid.

35. 77th Infantry Division History, op. cit., p. 173.

36. The 304th Field Artillery Battalion was constituted 5 August 1917, in the National Army as the 304th Field Artillery and assigned to the 77th Division. It served in the Oise-Aisne, Meuse-Argonne, Champagne and Lorraine Campaigns of World War I. Assigned to the Organized Reserves after the war it was re-designated as the 304th Light Field Artillery. Re-designated again on 30 January 1942, as the 304th Field Artillery Battalion it served in the Western Pacific, Leyte and Ryukyus Campaigns of World War II.

37. General Order Number 72, General Headquarters, United States Army Forces, Pacific, 27 July 1945.

38. General Order Number 89, General Headquarters, United States Army Forces, Pacific, 3 August 1945.

39. War Department General Order Number 24, 7 March 1946.

40. "Oscar" was the American code name for a single-engine, low-wing monoplane Japanese fighter plane armed with two machine guns.

41. The "Tony" was a single-engine fighter aircraft and a rarity among Japanese planes at this time in that it had armor protecting the pilot. It carried four machine guns and could carry a bomb load of 1000 pounds.

42. War Department General Order Number 25, 7 April 1945.

CHAPTER 9: THE JAPANESE RETREAT

1. War Department General Order Number 49, June 28, 1945.

2. Brigadier General Edwin Hubert Randle was born October 11, 1894 in Springfield, Illinois. He earned a B. A. from DePauw University I 1917. He was commissioned into the Infantry in 1917 and wounded in the Meuse-Argonne Offensive in World

War I. After the war he was an assistant Professor of Military Science and Tactics at Lafayette College, later full professor, 1927–1934. Served in Puerto Rico 1934–1936. He was then assistant Professor of Military Science and Tactics at Pennsylvania State College 1938–1940. He commanded a battalion of, and then the full, 47th Infantry Regiment, 9th Infantry Division July 1940–June 1943. Promoted Brigadier General June 1943 and appointed Assistant Division Commander, 77th Infantry Division 1943–1945. Retired June 1948.

3. Sergeant Lowery was awarded a Silver Star. See Wright, op. cit., P. 92.

4. Ibid., P. 93.

5. During the Second World War the American army emphasized what was termed "fire and movement" tactics during ground attacks. This involved a portion of the attacking force laying down a protective cover fire from rifles and machine guns while the other segment moved forward by leaps and bounds. Then the first group would move forward, covered in turn by the second group. This was repeated until the objective was attained.

6. Private First Class Castro, Master Sergeant Locke and Sergeant Denman were all awarded Silver Stars, Master Sergeant Locke posthumously.

7. General Orders Number 48, 1945, U.S. Army, Pacific.

8. The gun and equipment were later recovered when one ingenious engineer rigged up a diving mask from a gas mask and dove into the river to attach towing cables to the sunken equipment.

9. For those following the amphibious landings during the Leyte Campaign, this would make the seventh within two months. (Homonhan Island, Suluan Island, Dinagat Island, Panaon Strait, San Pedro Bay [Multiple], Ormoc Bay and now Palompon.)

10. Joint Assault Signal Company. These were special units which had come about with the development of the American amphibious assault technique. They consisted of Army and Navy personnel whose main function was to observe and control naval support gunfire, although they also often controlled air support and field artillery as well.

11. Other units within the Special Task Force included a detachment of the 306th Field Artillery Battalion and a detachment from Battery A, 531st Field Artillery Battalion. In addition, although not a part of the Special Task Force, Battery A, 531st Field Artillery Battalion (155mm Guns) was moved with great difficulty to San Jose from which its guns could reach Palompon.

12. This journey of 44 miles took ten hours to complete.

13. Two P-40s, two P-47s, one P-51 and one B-25 Bomber.

14. Actually this was not the complete battalion, consisting of only Company E and detachments from Companies F and H along with supporting attachments.

15. General Suzuki and his *35th Army* Headquarters were still on the island and still in intermittent communication with Luzon.

16. The 164th Infantry Regiment was constituted as the 1st Regiment, Dakota Territory on January 31, 1885 from new and existing militia companies. It was re-designated as the 1st Infantry, Dakota Militia and divided between North and South Dakota by Act of Congress February 22, 1889. Redesignated as the Dakota National Guard

March 6, 1891. Mustered into Federal Service May 20, 1898 and sent to serve in the Philippines. Called into Federal Service 1917 and assigned to the 41st Division but did not participate in World War I campaigns. Assigned to the 34th Division, May 16, 1923. Called into Federal Service February 10, 1941 and detached from the 34th Division. Attached to the Americal Division. Served in the War With Spain and three Philippine Insurrection campaigns. Served in the Guadalcanal, Northern Solomons, Leyte and Southern Philippines Campaigns of World War II. Awarded a Presidential Unit Citation for Guadalcanal.

17. The Americal Division was a unique organization in the U.S. Army during World War II. When the Army trimmed its infantry divisions from four to three regiments apiece several regiments were left without higher command units. Several of these were sent off to the frontiers to protect U.S. Territory until an offensive could be mounted. When it was, three of these "orphan" regiments were united under the banner of the newly created divisional headquarters known as the Americal—for Americans in New Caledonia—Division. It was the only division in World War II without a number or other specific designation despite the fact that it remained organized as the standard infantry division of the U.S. Army in World War II. The division was organized in New Caledonia on May 24, 1942 and fought in the Guadalcanal, Northern Solomons, Leyte and Southern Philippines Campaigns. It was awarded a Presidential Unit Citation for Guadalcanal.

18. The *35th Army*'s operational area was the southern Philippines, of which Leyte was the northernmost island.

19. Saburō Ienaga. *The Pacific War, 1931–1945.* (New York: Pantheon Books, 1978). P.147.

CHAPTER 10: THE BITTER END

1. Valtin, op. cit., P. 279.
2. Quoted in Falk, op. cit., P. 308.
3. Ibid.
4. Ibid.
5. Ibid, P. 313.
6. Lieutenant General Shinpei (also spelled Shempei, Shimpei, Simpei, Senehira) Fukei (also spelled Fukuyu and Fukue) had taken command of the *102nd Infantry Division* from his former post as Commander of Prisoner of War Camps in Singapore where he had executed several Allied Prisoners of War who had attempted to escape. He was appointed Commanding General of the division upon its activation in June of 1944. At the end of the war he was tried, convicted and executed as a war criminal for his actions in Singapore.
7. This report probably refers to the landing of the *68th Independent Mixed Brigade* which was one of the last reinforcements to land on Leyte before such operations ceased. At this time it was operating in the mountains of western Leyte as one of the last fully operational units left to the *35th Army*.
8. Ibid, P. 282.
9. Ibid.

10. These were the 1st Cavalry Division, 11th Airborne Division, 7th Infantry Division, 32nd Infantry Division, 77th Infantry Division, 81st Infantry Division, 96th Infantry Division and American Division.

11. Lieutenant General Robert L. Eichelberger. Our Jungle Road to Tokyo. (Nashville, Tennessee: Battery Press, 1989). P. 181.

12. Ibid, P. 183.

13. The 81st Infantry Division was activated at Camp Rucker, Alabama on June 15, 1942 and trained in various maneuvers within the United States until it departed San Francisco July 3, 1944. It fought at Angaur Island and Peleliu Island in the Palau Islands before recuperating in New Caledonia. Arrived on Leyte May 16, 1945 where it staged for the planned invasion of Japan.

14. General Order Number 99, General Headquarters, United States Army Forces, Pacific. (8 August 1945)

15. Major General William Howard Arnold was born in Dyersburg, Tennessee on January 18, 1901 and commissioned into the Infantry from West Point in 1924. He served in China 1934–1936 before graduating from the Command and General Staff School in 1938. Served as aide to Brigadier General Oscar W. Griswold 1940–1941, then deputy Chief of Staff of IV Corps before promotion to Brigadier General September 1943. Chief of Staff of XIV Corps 1943–1944 and promoted Major General November 1944. Commanding General, American Division November 1944–December 1945.

16. The 245th Field Artillery Battalion was constituted in the Army of the United States on July 17, 1942 and assigned to the American Division. It was formally activated August 15, 1942 in New Caledonia. It fought in the Guadalcanal, Northern Solomons, Leyte and Southern Philippines Campaigns of World War II and earned a Navy Presidential Unit Citation for the Guadalcanal Campaign.

17. The 182nd Infantry Regiment was constituted as the North Regiment on October 7, 1636 from existing militia companies around Charlestown, New Town, Watertown, Concord and Dedham in the colony of Massachusetts. It underwent scores of redesignations over the years until it was designated the 182nd Infantry after World War I and assigned to the 26th Infantry Division, Massachusetts National Guard. Inducted into Federal Service January 16, 1941 it was relieved from assignment to the 26th Infantry Division and assigned to Task Force 6814 which eventually developed into the American Division. It bears campaign streamers from the American Revolution, War of 1812, Civil War, World War I and Guadalcanal, Northern Solomons, Leyte and Southern Philippines in World War II. It earned a Navy Presidential Unit Citation for Guadalcanal.

18. General Order Number 67, General Headquarters, United States Army Forces, Pacific. (22 July 1945)

19. The 132nd Infantry was organized in Chicago May 4 1861 from separate companies and entered Federal Service as the 19th Illinois Volunteer Infantry. It underwent several consolidations and reorganizations after the Civil War until entered Federal Service July 19, 1917 as the 132nd Infantry, Illinois National Guard. Assigned to the 33rd Division it fought in the Picardy, Somme Offensive, Meuse-Argonne and Lorraine

Campaigns of World War I. It was again inducted into Federal Service March 5, 1941 at Chicago and relieved from the 33rd Division and assigned to Task Force 6814 which eventually developed into the American Division. It earned a Navy Presidential Unit Citation for Guadalcanal.

20. General Order Number 295, General Headquarters, U.S. Army Forces, Pacific. (2 October 1945)

21. Brigadier General Eugene Ware Ridings was born on January 9, 1899 in Grant County, Oklahoma and commissioned in the infantry from West Point in 1923. He served in China and then instructed at West Point 1933–1936. Graduated from the Command and General Staff School 1937 and the Army War College in 1940. Served on the War Department General Staff 1940–1942, then assistant Chief of Staff for Operations at VII Corps, then XIV Corps, 1942–1944. Brigadier General January 1945. Assistant Division commander, Americal Division, July 1944–December 1945.

22. American estimates state that there were still some 13,000 Japanese soldiers on Leyte when General Suzuki departed the island. This roughly agrees with the estimates of General Suzuki's Chief of Staff made after the war.

23. Paul John Mueller was born November 16, 1892 in Union, Missouri. He was commissioned into the infantry from West Point in 1915 and was a battalion commander in the 64th Infantry during World War I. He graduated from the Command and General Staff School in 1923 and the Army War College in 1928. He served with the War Plans Division of the General Staff 1931–1934 and instructed at the Command and General Staff School 1935–1940. He was Chief of Staff of the Second U.S. Army and a Brigadier General in October 1941. Promoted to Major General in September 1942, he was appointed commander of the 81st Infantry Division, a post he held throughout the war. Retired September 1954.

24. While the 81st Infantry Division was assigned to the Sixth U.S. Army for the coming invasion of Japan, in which it would play an assault role, during its mopping-up duties on Leyte it was also under the command of the Eighth U.S. Army. Both Generals Krueger and Eichelberger visited the division during its stay on Leyte. Despite the potential for confusion, no difficulties resulted from this dual command arrangement.

25. The 321st Infantry Regiment was organized in the National Army August 5, 1917 and assigned to the 81st Division. It fought in the Meuse-Argonne and Lorraine 1918 Campaigns of World War I before being demobilized on June 28, 1919. It was reconstituted June 24, 1921 as a part of the Organized Reserves. It was ordered into Federal Service June 15, 1942 at Camp Rucker, Alabama and served with the 81st Infantry Division in the Western Pacific (Palau) Campaigns and Leyte.

26. See appendix for chart detailing American casualties during the Leyte Campaign.

27. I Corps, IX Corps, XI Corps and V Marine Amphibious Corps.

28. Quoted in Kevin C. Holzimmer, *General Walter Krueger, Unsung Hero of the Pacific War*. (Manhattan, Kansas: University Press of Kansas, 2007). P. 244.

29. Something General Eichelberger never received and about which he remained bitter the rest of his life.

30. Lieutenant General Tolson, quoted in William M. Leary, Ed., *We Shall Return!*

MacArthur's Commanders and the Defeat of Japan. (Lexington, Kentuckt: University Press of Kentucky, 1988). P. 86.

31. Ibid.

32. Gen. George P. Hays commanded the 10th Mountain Division during the Italian Campaign, 1944–1945. Gen. Mark W. Clark commanded the 5th U.S. Army and later the 15th Army Group in the Italian Campaign. Later, after commanding Sixth U.S. Army, he would assume command of United Nations forces in Korea.

APPENDIX 1: UNITED STATES FORCES ORDER OF BATTLE

1. Less Company C which was assigned to the Morotai Invasion Force.

APPENDIX 2: JAPANESE ORDER OF BATTLE

1. This unit was a "Type 'A' Strengthened (Modified) Division." As such it was equipped with 10, 000 rifles, 410 light machine guns, 450 grenade dischargers, 114 heavy machine guns, 18 47mm antitank guns 36 70mm battalion guns and 7 armored cars or "tankettes." This unit was first activated in 1870 and reorganized several times over the years. It participated in the Sino-Japanese War of 1894–95 and the Russo-Japanese War of 1904–05. It spent the early part of World War II in China and Manchuria before landing at Ormoc, Leyte in October 1944.

2. This unit was equipped with 9 75mm field guns, 18 105mm howitzers and 9 150mm howitzers.

3. This unit was a "Type 'B' Standard Division" 1944 organization. As such it was equipped with 6,867 rifles, 273 light machine guns, 254 grenade dischargers, 78 heavy machine guns, 14 37mm or 47mm antitank guns, 18 70mm battalion guns, 12 75mm regimental guns, 16 armored cars or "tankettes", 3,466 horses and a total strength of between 15,000 and 16,000. Activated at Kyoto, Japan in 1905 it had assaulted the Philippines in December 1941 and remained on Luzon until transferred to Leyte in April, 1944.

4. This unit was equipped with 12 75mm field guns and 24 105mm howitzers.

5. For organization and equipment see note 3 above. This unit was supported by the Nagoya Depot, Japan and served in North China before being deployed to the Philippines in August 1944.

6. This unit was equipped with 16 75mm field guns, 4 75mm mountain guns and 4 150mm howitzers.

7. For organization and equipment see note 3 above. The division was activated in China in June 1943 from cadres provided by the *5th, 19th* and *20th Divisions* and moved to Korea. It was later forwarded to the Philippines.

8. This was actually the second *41st Infantry Regiment,* replacing an earlier unit which was destroyed in New Guinea.

9. This unit was equipped with 12 75mm field guns and 12 105mm howitzers.

10. This unit was a "Type 'C' or 'Brigaded' Division" and contained between 10,000–12,000 men. It was armed with 5,940 rifles, 371 grenade dischargers, 336 light machine guns, 64 heavy machine guns, 32 75mm infantry Guns, and 40 trucks. Supported by the Kumamoto Depot, Japan, it was activated in the summer of 1944

from the *31st Independent Mixed Brigade* and deployed to the Philippines.

11. The equipment of this unit is unknown but the standard for this type of division was 32 75mm infantry guns.

12. These formations had a total strength of about 4,650 officers and men and contained from three to six infantry battalions. They were armed with 510 rifles, 37 grenade dischargers, 36 light machine guns, 8 heavy machine guns, 4 20mm antitank rifles and 4 70mm infantry guns per battalion. The artillery unit was armed with 8 75mm field or mountain guns or howitzers. On occasion, these were substituted with 90mm mortars. This unit was organized at the Utsunomiya Depot, Japan, from the *57th Line of Communication Sector Unit* and deployed in May 1944.

13. This unit was organized at the Hirosaki Depot, Japan and deployed to the Philippines in July, 1944.

14. Despite its prominent role in the battle, I have been unable to determine the composition of this unit. In organization and equipment, it would have similar characteristics to the other Independent Mixed Brigades described above.

BIBLIOGRAPHICAL NOTE

Any historian, particularly one who specializes in the Second World War as it impacted the United States military, is indebted deeply to the National Archives and Records Service. The World War II records are primarily stored at Archives II, located in College Park, Maryland. In addition to the vast array of records available there, the dedication and determination of the Archives staff, at all levels, is above and beyond the normal expectations of researchers. They have been called upon at little, or no, notice to provide access to records, many of which have never been reviewed before, and have not only managed to find documents swiftly and accurately, but have added their own suggestions for additional research, which invariably lead to even greater finds. The staff of the still photograph division, on the fifth floor, is equally dedicated and helpful, taking the novice, as well as experienced, researcher into additional areas to seek the ideal illustrations to highlight each particular work. No study of the history of the American military's involvement in World War II can be completed without them.

The study of the Leyte Campaign should start with the United States Army's own historical series, *United States Army in World War II*, sometimes referred to as "The Green Books," from their covers, and in particular the segment *The War in the Pacific*. Published by the Center of Military History over the past several decades, these books discuss the U.S. Army operations in specific theaters and campaigns throughout the conflict. For this work the key volume was *Leyte: The Return to the Philippines*, by M. Hamlin Cannon (Washington, DC, 1987). This was especially valuable in directing the researcher to studies prepared during and immediately after the war by historians on various aspects of the campaign, including views from the other side. Most of these are available at the Office of the Chief of Military History. To put the Leyte campaign in full context, *The Approach to the Philippines* (Robert Ross Smith: Washington, DC, 1984) and *Tri-*

umph in the Philippines (Robert Ross Smith; Washington, DC, 1984) are recommended. Similarly, Army Air Force records are summarized within Wesley Frank Craven and James Lea Cate, eds., *The Army Air Forces in World War II: Vol. V, The Pacific: Matterhorn to Nagasaki* (Chicago: University of Chicago Press, 1953).

The records of the units which took part in the Leyte Campaign are, as to be expected, uneven in quality. The Sixth United States Army Records are quite complete and in good condition. The operations, intelligence and other staff reports are good to excellent and contain the daily messages, reports and memoranda exchanged before, during and after the campaign. The usual administrative orders are present as well as intelligence estimates of the enemy. It should be noted that after 26 December 1944, the researcher must look to the Eighth U.S. Army for the continuation of the Leyte Campaign reports, as this is the date when the Sixth Army turned the campaign officially over to the Eighth Army.

The reports of the two field corps that participated in the main battles for the island are less well prepared. The X Corps has brief reports, but its journals make up somewhat for the other missing pieces. The XXIV Corps has even less satisfactory records, most of them brief and with little detail. Some short histories were prepared by XXIV Corps to make up the difference, but these consist mainly of photographs of individuals and personnel turbulence. The same holds true generally for the Sixth Army Service Command.

The records of the 1st Cavalry Division are generally good, although the two cavalry brigades are less than satisfactory. The division itself and its regiments made up for this lack of detail and for additional information, particularly on the experience of the individual cavalryman on Leyte and Samar, the researcher is referred to Bertram C. Wright's *The First Cavalry Division in World War II* (Tokyo: Toppan Printing Co., 1947).

The appendices of the 7th Infantry Division's operations report are more detailed than the report itself. The operations reports and the journals are useful, but limited. The infantry regiments are better, in particular those of the 32nd Infantry Regiment, which are excellent. For a general overview and a view from the infantrymen's perspective, the division's history, *The Hourglass: A History of the 7th Infantry Division in World War II* (Edmund G. Love. Washington, DC: Infantry Journal Press, 1950) is recommended, although details of the larger battle are lacking.

A similar situation exists with regard to the 11th Airborne Division. The records are poor, often incomplete, and inadequate. Here again, to get a better view of the paratrooper and gliderborne infantryman's war in the Southwest Pacific, the reader is referred to two books by a veteran of the division, Lieutenant General Edward M. Flangan, USA (Ret.). *The Angels: A History of the 11th Airborne Division* (Novato, California: Presidio Press, 1989) is a revised and enlarged version of the earlier work (Washington, DC: Infantry Journal Press, 1948) by the same name. A completely new work by General Flanagan, entitled *The Rakkasans; The Combat History of the 187th Airborne Infantry* (Novato, California: Presidio Press, 1997), is a history of one of the regiments of the division in World War II and Korea.

The 24th Infantry Division's records are generally quite good, with a very readable operations journal and report. The same records at the regimental level are just the opposite, few and far between. Many simply cannot be found, if they exist. Ironically for a unit with good reports at the divisional level, few written works have been published about this workhorse division during the Southwest Pacific Campaign. Perhaps because its units were often detached for assignments under other commands, its own history has yet to be written. Just about the only available published volume, albeit disguised, is *Children of Yesterday* by Jan Valtin (pseudonym for Richard J. H. Krebs, a veteran of the division) which was published soon after the war ((New York: The Reader's Press, 1946).

Sadly, the records of one of the most distinguished units of the Pacific War, the 32nd Infantry Division, are poor, if not lacking. This division, which fought in every major battle from Buna in 1942 to Luzon in 1945, has limited historical records available. The historian is forced to rely on Harold W. Blakely's *32nd Infantry Division in World War II* (Madison, Wisconsin, 1957) which while good, is lacking in many details. Another work by John M. Carlisle deals only with the exploits of the division on Luzon, with no details concerning the earlier campaign on Leyte.

The 77th Infantry Division, thrust unexpectedly and quickly into the Leyte Campaign, maintained good operations reports, but thin journals. Here again they are redeemed, if such is the case, by an excellent published history, *Ours to Hold It High: The History of the 77th Infantry Division in World War II* (Max Meyers, ed. Washington, DC: Infantry Journal Press, 1947). Far more detail is available regarding the experiences of the individual rifleman, including the destruction of the general's personal latrine, than is found in the journals. Finally, the reports of both the 96th Infantry Division and the American Division are good and quite usable for the historian's purposes. To add details, the 96th Infantry Division produced their own history, *The Deadeyes: The Story of the 96th Infantry Division* (Orlando R. J. Davidson, Carl Williams and Joseph A. Kahl; Washington, DC: Infantry Journal Press, 1947). So too, did the American Division with *Under the Southern Cross: The Saga of the American Division* (Francis D. Cronin, Boston, Massachusetts: American Division Veterans Association, 1978). This work compensates, in part at least, for its mediocre record-keeping during the war.

Recent studies of the independent small units which participated in the campaign have appeared to round out the story of the Leyte Campaign. Two books, for example, now deal with the histories of the individual tank battalions which supported the infantry throughout the battle. Gene Eric Salecker's *Rolling Thun-*

der Against the Rising Sun: The Combat History of the U.S. Army Tank Battalions in the Pacific in World War II (Mechanicsburg, Pennsylvania: Stackpole Books, 2008) and Harry Yeide's *The Infantry's Armor: The U.S. Army's Separate Tank Battalions In World War II* (Mechanicsburg, Pennsylvania: Stackpole Books. 2010) are two examples. Some others include Robert W. Black's *Rangers in World War II* (New York: Ivy Books, 1992) and Commander Francis Douglas Fane, USNR (Ret.) and Don Moore's *The Naked Warriors: The Story of the U.S. Navy's Frogmen* (Annapolis, Maryland: Naval Institute Press, 1956 [reprint 1995]). Recently some books have appeared dealing directly with the Southwest Pacific Theater's combat actions. Two of these are, for example, Larry Alexander's *Shadows In the Jungle: The Alamo Scouts behind Japanese Lines in World War II* (New York: Caliber, 2009) and Lance Q. Zedric's *Silent Warriors of World War II: The Alamo Scouts Behind Japanese Lines* (Ventura, California: Pathfinder Publishing, 1995).

Understanding the intelligence gathering operations of the Southwest Pacific campaigns requires reading Edward J. Drea's *MacArthur's Ultra: Codebreaking and the War Against Japan, 1942–1945* (Lawrence, Kansas: University Press of Kansas, 1992). More recently Ken Kotani's *Japanese Intelligence in World War II* (Oxford, UK: Osprey Publishing, 2009) gives a view from the other side of the hill, often ignored in earlier histories. A review of the guerrilla fighting and its American support can be found in William B. Breuer's *MacArthur's Undercover War* (New York: John Wiley & Sons, Inc., 1995).

For the leadership of these and other campaigns in the theater there are several good studies. Included among them are Clay Blair's *MacArthur* (Garden City, NY: Doubleday, 1977), and D. Clayton James' *The Years of MacArthur* (New York: Houghton Mifflin, 1972), among several others. Certainly one of the least known, but most important leaders of these campaigns was Lieutenant General Walter Krueger, who led the U.S. Sixth Army in countless invasions and island conquests. He remains one of the least known but truly most successful American army commanders of the Second World War. Recently, Kevin C. Holzimmer's *General Walter Krueger: Unsung Hero of the Pacific War* (Lawrence, Kansas: University Press of Kansas, 2007) has begun to lift the veil first disturbed by William M. Leary's essay "Walter Krueger: MacArthur's Fighting General" in his own *We Shall Return! MacArthur's Commanders and the Defeat of Japan, 1942–1945* (Lexington, Kentucky: University Press of Kentucky, 1988). Of course, General Krueger himself wrote a history, but it was more of a history of his men than himself, although *From Down Under to Nippon: The Story of the Sixth Army In World War II* (Nashville, Tennessee: Battery Press, 1989 [reprint]) does reveal some of the general's problems and concerns during the various campaigns.

Eighth Army's General Eichelberger wrote his own history as well. In addition to *Our Jungle Road to Tokyo* (New York: Viking Press, 1950) there are several books dealing with General Eichelberger's war. Included among these are Paul

Chwialkowski's *In Caesar's Shadow: The Life of General Robert Eichelberger* (Westport, Connecticut: Greenwood Press, 1993), John Francis Shortal's *Forged By Fire: Robert L. Eichelberger and the Pacific War* (Columbia, SC: University Press of South Carolina, 1987) and the essay by Jay Luvaas and John F. Shortal entitled "Robert L. Eichelberger: MacArthur's Fireman" included in William Leary's *We Shall Return* (op. cit.). The senior air commander of the campaign, Lieutenant General George C. Kenney, wrote his own story of the campaign within his *General Kenney Reports* (New York: Duell, Sloan and Pearce, 1949). The senior naval commander, Admiral Thomas C. Kinkaid, is well documented in Gerald E. Wheeler's *Kinkaid of the Seventh Fleet: A Biography of Admiral Thomas C., Kinkaid, U.S. Navy* (Annapolis, Maryland: Naval Institute Press, 1996).

Almost nothing has been written about the corps and division commanders who carried the fight to the enemy, often from front-line positions, and who led the American army to victory in the Pacific between 1941 and 1945. The only example available is that of the commander of the 32nd Infantry Division at Leyte and throughout the Southwest Pacific, Major General William H. Gill. His writing, assisted by Edward Jaquelin Smith, is titled *Always A Commander: The Reminiscences of Major General William H. Gill* (Colorado Springs, CO: The Colorado College, 1974) and is a rarity among histories in that it deals with the daily concerns of a division commander at war.

As "The Greatest Generation" thins over the years, more and more personal stories are becoming available for historians and students of military history to study, but they are far from sufficient. With regard to the Leyte Campaign there are few. Among them are mortar man Donald O. Dencker's *Love Company: Infantry Combat against the Japanese in World War II, Leyte and Okinawa* (Manhattan, Kansas: Sunflower University Press, 2002). Many more are needed to fully interpret the Leyte Campaign. Gerald Astor's anthology *Crisis in the Pacific: The Battles for the Philippine Islands by the Men Who Fought Them* (New York: Donald I. Fine Books, 1996) fills in several gaps, but by no means completely.

Indeed, the documentation of the U.S. Sixth Army's ground campaign for the island of Leyte in 1944–1945, is rather barren when compared to the vast and growing literature of the naval Battle of Leyte Gulf. Given the fact that far more men—American, Philippine and Japanese—participated in the ground campaign for a much longer period of time, and that the Japanese considered it the decisive battle for the Philippines, and by extension for their cherished goal of a negotiated peace in the Pacific, it is a strange oversight. Moreover, despite the fact that it was a bitter, frustrating and difficult campaign, the Leyte struggle paid large strategic dividends for the Allies, and of course especially for the Americans. It destroyed the cream of the Imperial Japanese Army defenders of the Philippines; it firmly established the Americans and their allies in the Philippines, thereby giving them advance bases for the continued advance against Japan; it cut critical Japanese supply lines by providing air and naval bases from which Allied Naval and Air Forces could seek out and destroy those Japanese lines of communications. It prompted the decisive naval engagement of Leyte Gulf, which destroyed the remaining might of the Imperial Japanese Navy and shredded what was left of the air forces of both services, leaving only the deadly Kamikaze as Japan's air defenders. With these results it became perfectly clear, even to the Japanese, that Imperial Japan could only remain on the defensive, and that such a defense was doomed to failure over time and space. For a battle which contributed results not unlike Guadalcanal or Saipan, Leyte is insufficiently recognized.

INDEX